DATE DUE

LESBIAN ETHICS

FIRST EDITION

First printing, December, 1988
Second printing, April, 1989
Third printing, April, 1990

Cover design and chapter illustrations: Nett Hart
Manuscript editor: Harriet Ellenberger
Typesetting: Annie Graham Publishing Services
Book design and production: Nett Hart, Jensen-Hart Design
Indexing: Mary O'Leary
Printing: Bolger Creative Printing

This book is set in Plantin and Plantin Italic.

Library of Congress Cataloging-in-Publication Data

Hoagland, Sarah, 1945–
    Lesbian ethics.

    Includes Bibliography: p.
    Includes Index.
    1. Lesbianism – United States – Moral and ethical aspects. 2. Sexual ethics – United States. 3. Political ethics – United States. 4. Ethics, Modern – 20th century.

    I. Title.

HQ75.6.U5H63   1988   306.7′663   88-81498
ISBN 0-934903-03-4

        3   4   5   6   7   8   9

LESBIAN ETHICS

Toward New Value

Sarah Lucia Hoagland

INSTITUTE OF LESBIAN STUDIES
Palo Alto, California

Credits

I wish to acknowledge and thank the following authors and publishers and copyright holders for permission to reprint material in this volume:

From "Womanslaughter" by Pat Parker, in *Womanslaughter,* published by Diana Press and in *Movement in Black,* published by Diana Press and The Crossing Press, copyright 1978, reprinted by permission of Pat Parker; "(*The Floating Poem, Unnumbered*)" reprinted from *The Dream of a Common Language, Poems 1974-1977* by Adrienne Rich, by permission of the author and W.W. Norton & Company, Inc., copyright (c) 1978 by W.W. Norton & Company, Inc.; from *Women and Nature: The Roaring Inside Her* by Susan Griffin, copyright 1978 by Susan Griffin, reprinted by permission of the author and Harper & Row, Publishers, Inc.; from "Clowns" by Anne Cameron in *Daughters of Copper Woman,* published by Press Gang Publishers, copyright 1981, used by permission of Anne Cameron; from "Some Like Indians Endure" by Paula Gunn Allen, published by *Common Lives/Lesbian Lives: A Lesbian Feminist Quarterly,* copyright 1982, reprinted by permission of Paula Gunn Allen; from *Zami: A New Spelling of My Name* by Audre Lorde, Persephone Press and then The Crossing Press, copyright 1982, and from *Sister Outsider* by Audre Lorde, The Crossing Press, copyright 1984, used by permission of Audre Lorde; from "Pleasures" by diane hugs, reprinted from *My Story's On! Ordinary Women, Extraordinary Lives* published by Common Differences Press and from *With the Power of Each Breath: A Disabled Women's Anthology,* published by Cleis Press, copyright 1985, reprinted by permission of Common Differences Press, Cleis Press, and diane hugs; from *Are We There Yet? A Continuing History of 'Lavender Woman': A Chicago Lesbian Newspaper, 1971-1976* by Michal Brody, published by Aunt Lute Book Company, now Spinsters/Aunt Lute, copyright 1985, used by permission of Michal Brody; from "Non? Monogamy?: A Readers' Forum" by Kate Moran, published by *Lesbian Ethics,* copyright 1985, reprinted by permission of Kate Moran; from "Celebration," by Deidre D. McCalla, copyright 1986 Chetwood Arts Music, and from "Long Lonely Road" by Deidre D. McCalla, copyright 1986 Chetwood Arts Music, used by permission of Deidre D. McCalla; from "The View from Over the Hill: Notes on Ageism Between Lesbians" by Baba Copper, published by *Trivia,* also in *Over the Hill: Reflections on Ageism Between Women,* published by The Crossing Press, copyright 1986 and 1988, used by permission of Baba Copper; from "Therapy: The Evil Within" by Anna Lee, published by *Lesbian Ethics,* copyright 1986, used by permission of Anna Lee; from "Playfulness, 'World'-Travelling, and Loving Perception" by María Lugones, copyright 1987, used by permission of the author and *Hypatia;* and from "New Ground" by Alix Dobkin, copyright 1988, used by permission of Alix Dobkin.

To:
Deidre, for the water
Julia, for the air
Mary, for the fire
Anne, for the earth

And to Smaug, Samantha, Scathach, Alaka, and Elfyn, who wait patiently for lesbian transformation even if it means they have to deal with dogs.

Annotated Table of Contents

Chapter 1
Separating from Heterosexualism

Chapter 2
The Feminine Virtues and Female Agency 69

Chapter 3
Power, Paternalism, and Attending 114

Chapter 4
Integrating Reasoning and Emotions 157

Chapter 5
Moral Agency and Interacting 198

Preface

This is not a book to be read in an afternoon. It is complex, and I intend it, or parts of it, not to be skimmed casually, but to be mulled over, discussed, and argued about. I wrote this book in the hope that it will provoke discussion which will take us beyond where we are in our understanding and actions. I will consider the book successful if it inspires lesbians to get together in something like consciousness-raising groups to discuss the suggestions here: how they might work, whether they apply in different situations, whether they are capable of helping us avoid some of the pitfalls we have faced up to now, whether ultimately lesbians prefer this way of approaching things, and if so, what new value we can go on to create.

I also wrote this book to express my perceptions about the importance of lesbian focus and lesbian community to our existence as lesbians. This material is located in u.s. lesbian communities; what I have developed comes from my experience and observations in diverse u.s. lesbian communities – particularly but not exclusively, midwest communities. Nevertheless I believe that the theory has relevance to any lesbians affected by anglo-european culture.

A word about traditional philosophy. In embarking on this work, I did not begin with traditional ethics even though the chapters are set up in a way that would suggest I had. I felt that if I started there, I would never get out of its framework. Instead, in exploring Lesbian Ethics, I focused on actual proceedings in actual lesbian communities through participation, interviews, gossip, discussions, through lesbian and feminist writings, and through reading the heated exchanges in our journals. As I wrote the drafts of the manuscript, it would become clear why an idea from the tradition was inadequate for what I am attempting. I have included some discussion of traditional material, in particular those aspects of the tradition with which I find lesbians caught up; I think it important to know from where these ideas come and how the tradition functions among us.

I realize, however, that not all readers will want to go through the analysis of traditional philosophy. For that reason, I have created an annotated table of contents and include the section titles in the margins of the text. If you find yourself bogged down in one section of a chapter, go to the next section that seems interesting.

Finally, a note on style. In the text I capitalize the phrase 'Lesbian Ethics', names of books and journals, names of people, the word 'I,' and the first words of sentences only. I follow Marilyn Frye in using single quotation marks when referring to words or concepts. And I use double quotation marks around words or phrases I wish to stress as remarkable in one way or another, which remarkableness should be clear from the context.

Acknowledgments

Many lesbians have contributed significantly to this project. A number read portions of the manuscript; some even braved comments and criticisms on two very rough versions: Marilyn Frye, Claudia Card, Juana María Paz, Bev Jo, Jeanette Silveira, Lise Weil, Julien S. Murphy, Jacquelyn N. Zita, Jeffner Allen, and Bett Farber.

In addition, a number of lesbians have come into my life at various points and believed in and contributed significantly to what I have been doing, some by reading and having long discussions with me about the manuscript, some in other important ways: Deidre D. McCalla, Julia Penelope [Stanley], Kathy Munzer, Elaine Stocker, Claudia Christensen, Ariane Brunet, Nancy Loving, Billie Potts, Florencia Carolina, Anna Lee, Ellen Meredith, Anne Throop Leighton, Rosemary Schachte, Bette S. Tallen, Nett Hart, Alice Molloy, Diane Bernardi, Lorraine Ironplow, and Barbara Grier.

Other lesbians have supported this work in a number of vital ways: Sid Spinster, Vernita Gray, Kay Miles, María Lugones, Marthe Rosenfeld, Ginny Zipperer, Lee Lanning, Ann Scales, Kay Hagan, Kate Moran, Shelley Morrison, M. J. François, Tara Adlin, Selma Mirian, Sally Neely, Susan Ritter, Janice Anderson, Dorothe Rigby, Tracy Baim, Annie Cheatham, Mary Clare Powell, Jacquie Harper, Sally Tatnall, Maril Gould, Joan Nestle, Theresa McCraw, and Jan Raymond. In addition, the workers at women and children first bookstore in chicago helped me obtain many crucial bits of information.

Finally, Harriet Ellenberger edited this manuscript, taking what was essentially dense material and crystallizing it with her gift of language. I turned to her because she, along with Catherine Nicholson, encouraged radical lesbian voices with a magazine called *Sinister Wisdom,* and believed in the cobwebs of my mind. And Jorjet Harper did a final edit, enabling me to stop after I finally admitted I would never finish.

I was awarded a sabbatical leave from northeastern illinois university to write the first draft of this manuscript and a uni foundation fellowship to complete the second draft.

Introduction

IT IS POSSIBLE for us to engage in moral revolution and change the value we affirm by the choices we make. It is possible for lesbians to spin a revolution, for us to weave a transformation of consciousness.

Indeed, during the emergence of the u.s. women's liberation and gay liberation movements we began to do just that. In our moral outrage we turned our backs on the fathers' categories and began to focus on each other. We began to follow our own agendas, to listen to, argue with, criticize, befriend, celebrate, in short, to *acknowledge,* each other. And in the process we began to enact new values. We worked to develop nonoppressive structures, and we created conceptual frameworks outside the values of the fathers. In that brief burst, hundreds of lesbian projects began: collectives, newspapers, record companies, bookstores, presses, film companies, schools, lesbian community centers, libraries and archives, credit unions, magazines, healing centers, restaurants, radio stations, food co-ops, alcoholism detox centers, rape crisis centers, bands, womyn's land, music festivals, more bars, and on and on.

During the latter part of that time, I observed many of our organizations grow and then fall apart. This collapse occurred for a number of reasons. In direct response to our efforts to challenge the oppressive values we lived under and to create alternatives, we faced outright violence, severe economic limits, legal threats, f.b.i. penetration and disruption, and all manner of other male sabotage, such as feminist men filing discrimination suits so they could enter our events or transsexual men claiming a right to lesbian space. In addition, we carried deep within us the values of the fathers, including classism, racism, ageism, antisemitism, sizeism, ablebodyism, and imperialism, as well as sexism and heterosexism – all of which informed our perceptions and none of which we immediately, nor have we yet, divested ourselves of. And of course we made significant mistakes as we traveled this new path, such as believing that because we were all women or all lesbians we could automatically trust each other.

The demise of lesbian projects   But aside from these formidable obstacles there seemed to be yet two other factors. I found it significant that despite our best intentions, our interactions with each other failed much more often than not, we attacked each other far more vehemently than we ever dared attack men, and generally we were doing each other in. Much of this was owing to class and race differences, and much of it was not. But in all cases it seemed to me that our survival skills were going awry. In *Women and Honor: Some Notes on Lying* Adrienne Rich wrote provocatively of ways we use lying against each other.[1] And that pamphlet was an inspiration for this work.

We had most of us learned well how to survive in the patriarchy, though often our skills varied according to race and class. We'd learned how to survive on the street, on the job or through the welfare office, in the bedroom – and we were using those survival skills against each other. It seemed to me that the destructiveness of our interactions resulted partly from our lack of awareness of how we use survival skills and partly from our reliance on traditional anglo-european ethical values to structure our judgments about how to act with each other. And I found both our survival skills and our ethical judgments undermining rather than promoting lesbian connection[2] and community.

It became clear to me that we were losing every gain the fathers bestowed – and that was no real surprise. However, we were also losing what I consider our most precious achievement, our connection among ourselves across many barriers. Our efforts to create lesbian community were in serious jeopardy both from without and from within. And so I began to analyze concepts which structure our interactions and our practical efforts, concepts which I found encouraged attacks and manipulation rather than centeredness and directness.

Generally, we have not been able to hold our connections with each other and become a force capable of resisting and ultimately undermining oppression. We have not created a viable lesbian community. My thesis is that the norms we've absorbed from anglo-european ethical theory promote dominance and subordination through social control (what I call heterosexualism). As a result they thwart rather than promote the successful weaving of lesbian community. This book is my attempt, with much stimulation and input from a number of lesbian communities, to describe at least one way we might continue to move toward lesbian connection and create a means by which we spin out of oppression. I call this attempt Lesbian Ethics.

Lesbian

I AM A lesbian. While there was a period in my life when I was not a lesbian, I found that coming out was, for me, coming home. I experienced the sensation of landing and centering. It is lesbians who inspire me, lesbian energy which enlivens me, and lesbian community to which I refer. I will be purposefully vague about the term 'community', but I have in mind the loose network—both imagined and existing now—of those who identify basically as lesbians. What I am calling 'lesbian community' is not a specific entity; it is a ground of our be-ing; and it exists because we are here and move on it now.

I write as well within a context of oppression. Lesbians have been and are oppressed, to my knowledge, in all societies under the rule of the fathers. We also are agents of oppression, for the values we most often appeal to, affirm, and are limited by are the same values which affirm and are limited by oppression. These values have been forced on us, but we have adapted them to our survival.

Before we will be capable of resisting and undermining oppression, we must be able to work together in ways that do not nourish thinking which makes oppression credible. This is not a "personal," "private" matter. I believe that without certain changes in the values we affirm through our interactions, there can be no social change which will undermine oppression. Male-led revolutions—economic and military and intellectual—have not changed the essential dominance/subordination relationship at the heart of oppression.

I do not believe oppression is going to be lifted from us. And even if it were—whatever that might mean—I think our perceptions and judgments would continue to affirm the values of the fathers. If oppression is going to end, we must move out of it. And in part that means becoming beings who are no longer in the habit of enacting oppressive values (values which contribute either to the oppression of ourselves or others).

Our energy is vibrant; our abilities, myriad; our accomplishments—the organizing, the healing, the creating, the dreaming—phenomenal. From where we come, we bring many gifts: experience, skills, understanding, perceptions, humor, imagination, intuition. And what we accomplish does not and cannot emerge from individual lesbians in isolation. These possibilities flower among friends in community where we move. For here we love and hurt and get it wrong and laugh and risk and plot, resist and change. Here we focus on ourselves and so create lesbian possibility. When we are centrally lesbian, we spin magic.

Lesbians have, I believe, a particular relationship to oppression. Lesbians are beaten up, denied jobs, denied housing, denied custody of children; we are expelled from universities, put in mental hospitals, experimented on, murdered, and face every brutality which anyone faces under any form of oppression. Nevertheless, though its effects are similar, I think the form of lesbian oppression distinct from other forms of oppression.

Lesbian oppression is not a relationship

In my estimation, lesbians as a group are not primarily targeted as scapegoats, as, for example, the oppression of jews has been constructed. Lesbians as a group are not primarily characterized as inferior and culturally backward in ways that justify enslavement or economic exploitation, as the oppression in the u.s. of blacks, japanese, and chinese, among others, has been constructed. Lesbians have not had lands stolen and then been rounded up and placed on reservations as the oppression of native americans in the u.s. has been constructed. And lesbians are not primarily characterized in relation to others in ways that depict our identities as completed and our nature fulfilled through subordinating our lives to those of dominant members of society, as the oppression of women has been constructed. The *form* of lesbian oppression is not primarily a relationship.

Lesbian existence is formally denied

The society of the fathers, rather, formally denies lesbian existence: A lesbian is said to be a (heterosexual) woman who hates men (a manhater); lesbianism is said to be a phase in some (heterosexual) women's lives; a lesbian is said to be a (heterosexual) woman who cannot get a man; a lesbian is said to be a man in a (heterosexual) woman's body. The perception of a lesbian as a man in a (heterosexual) woman's body, for example, emerges from sex-role stereotypes – the judgment that certain qualities are male (masculine) while others are female (feminine). Thus a female whose behavior is perceived to conform to the masculine stereotype – for example, a dyke – is actually considered a man in a woman's body. Further, given sex-role stereotypes, we have the idea that for completion a female needs maleness (rationality, or the ability to construct nuclear weapons; aggressiveness, or the ability to maim and destroy, etc.). And the idea of women loving women is impossible, inconceivable.

The equation of 'lesbian' with 'manhater' is also interesting. Certainly many lesbians hate men, and there is reason to believe that manhating is important to moving out of oppression.[3] But many, many heterosexual women also hate men. This is clear in their art, their writing, their gossip. For example, antifeminists make clear their sentiments as they exhort a woman to stand by her man no matter what stupid thing he might try.[4] Many heterosexual radical feminists make manhating statements more often and more virulently than most lesbians. And many "apolitical" housewives are quite clear about their disgust with men. This is significant, considering that blatant admission of manhating is taboo while blatant womanhating is pervasive. But it is also significant that 'lesbian' is *equated* with 'manhating' while 'woman' is not.

Lesbians love lesbians, so some lesbian energy and focus is not accessible to men. But how is this manhating? After all, heterosexual men are not considered manhaters nor heterosexual women, womenhaters. So why are lesbians as a group perceived as manhaters? To hate someone is to direct energy toward them, albeit negative energy, to maintain an aggressive connection. So how is lesbian denial of energy to men such an aggression? When is a withdrawal an attack?

A withdrawal of something is an attack on someone only if that which is withdrawn is considered essential to that person's health, well-being, or survival. Thus if I gathered men in a room and withdrew air from that room, my withdrawal could be considered an attack. Or again, if I withheld food from men, my actions would be an attack. The lesbian withdrawal of energy from men must, therefore, be considered an attack because the fathers regard female energy as vital to men's health, well-being, survival. And such energy is apparently so vital to men that women are not to be allowed to realize there are other than heterosexual ways of being in the world. When actual lesbians insist on being perceived, when we can no longer be ignored, we are used to scare women into line,[5] lest they become monsters like us.[a]

This female energy which men, and the fathers' society as a whole, apparently consider so vital is more than the love of women for women. Historical and material conditions surrounding lesbian lives in europe and the u.s. have changed recently to expose/create a lesbian challenge to masculine-defined female agency. According to Lillian Faderman:

> the major difference [between nineteenth-century romantic friendships, which were not stigmatized, and twentieth-century lesbian-feminist relationships, which are stigmatized] had much less to do with overt sexual expression than with women's greater independence in the twentieth century: Now a woman can hope to carry on a love relationship with another woman for life. It can become her primary relationship, as it seldom could have with romantic friends of the past for economic reasons if for no other.[7]

The current social concern with lesbian withdrawal has to do with our

---

a Hence Sue Fink and Joelyn Grippo's song "Leaping Lesbians."[6]

usurping men's access to women; it involves the very structure of society. In discussing the terror both men and women exhibit at the prospect of feminist separatism Marilyn Frye notes:

> Male parasitism means that males *must have access* to women; it is the Patriarchal Imperative. But feminist no-saying is more than a substantial removal (redirection, reallocation) of goods and services because Access is one of the faces of Power. Female denial of male access to females substantially cuts off a flow of benefits, but it has also the form and full portent of assumption of power.[8]

If lesbians were truly perceptible in society, then the idea that women can survive without men, do not need to put up with men, might work its way into social reality. And it is to avoid this and maintain primary access to females that male-dominated society attempts to render lesbianism nonexistent.

Lesbian ability to resist and refocus

This erasure of our real, material lives suggests that lesbian existence is connected logically or formally in certain ways with female agency. That is, at this point in time lesbian existence holds a certain possibility which can effect a transformation of consciousness: the conceptual/material possibility of female agency not defined in terms of an other. And this possibility is key to the focus of my work.

Besides a conceptual/material—i.e., a logical—possibility, I find a more concrete possibility emerging from lesbian existence.[9] As Alix Dobkin sings, "There's something about a Lesbian."[10] In introducing her lesbian herbal, *Witches Heal*, Billie Potts writes:

> For me, the keystone of the lesbian outlook is womon-identification, trusting and giving primary allegiance to womon-energy. For this reason, I believe, lesbians today are more willing to take risks treating ourselves with womon-recommended remedies. It ties in with the politics of questioning authority and our deep, lifelong struggle to resist male authority.[11]

There is something in each lesbian which encourages us to affirm a connection with lesbians. There is something in each lesbian that questions the norm at some level and starts us on our own path. That is, there is something within each lesbian of the spirit I consider crucial to the sort of ethical concepts I'm interested in working on. It is a certain ability to resist and refocus, and it is this ability in all lesbians which draws me.

We are located in a reality which excludes us; yet we realize we exist if we realize nothing else. Thus in merely affirming our lesbianism, we have questioned social knowledge at some level. Our existence is itself a break past some of the limits of fatherly knowledge and perception, and it can thereby provide a basis for challenging that world view out of which the denial of our existence arises. By our very existence lesbians challenge the social construction of reality.

This is not to say that as lesbians we are less likely to have absorbed the values of the fathers. Members of oppressed groups will absorb significant aspects of the dominant culture; for while survival requires maintaining a separate status in certain respects, in other respects it requires assimilating into the dominant culture. As lesbians we have also participated in oppression – our efforts to date have been fraught with the agendas of the fathers. I do not find it surprising that we carry with us the tools of the fathers, including a most pronounced internalized heterosexism. What I find significant is that, despite the conceptual coercion of the fathers' framework, many lesbians have begun to break from it.

In spite of our varied assimilation, through lesbian existence comes a certain ability to resist and to refocus, an ability which is crucial to the sort of moral change I think can occur. And because of this, my focus is lesbian.

I did not appreciate all this at first. As I was coming to lesbian-feminist consciousness out of my earlier political consciousness, like many I came to believe that feminism was the theory and lesbianism the practice.[12] But over time I slowly became dissatisfied; I had stopped dreaming, stopped being inspired and inspiring. Then, as a result of prodding from Ariane Brunet of *amazones d'hier, lesbiennes d'aujourd'hui* of québec, I began to realize I was focusing on lesbians both in and outside feminism. In response to my panic that if I did not talk of lesbian-*feminism*, I would have no political base, she merely replied, "Then you don't perceive lesbianism as political?" And at some incomprehensible level, I began again to dream: I dreamed lesbianism the theory, my theory.

And I began to question the focus of u.s. feminism. Thinking about analyses developed by radical lesbians in québec and france, I have become convinced that the concept 'woman' is a created category, like the concept 'feminine', and is bankrupt. 'Woman' exists only in relation to 'man' (someone who dominates), and as long as this identity holds, male domination of women will appear socially desirable and, even, natural.

As a result, I mean to contrast lesbianism and heterosexualism. What I am talking about when I talk about heterosexualism is not simply a matter of men having procreative sex with women. I am talking about an entire way of life promoted and enforced by every formal and informal institution of the fathers' society, from religion to pornography to unpaid housework to medicine. Heterosexualism is a way of living that normalizes the dominance of one person and the subordination of another.

Heterosexualism

The relationship between women and men is considered in anglo-european thought to be the foundation of civilization. I agree. And it normalizes that which is integral to anglo-european civilization to such an extent that we cease to perceive dominance and subordination in any of their benevolent capacities as wrong or harmful: the "loving" relationship between men and women, the "protective" relationship between imperialists and the colonized, the "peace-keeping" relationship between democracy (u.s. capitalism) and threats to democracy. I believe that unless heterosexualism as a way of relating is undermined, there will always remain in social conscience concepts which validate oppression.

Thus, I focus on 'lesbian' because I am interested in exploring lesbianism as a challenge to heterosexualism, where heterosexualism is a matter of men (or the masculine) dominating women (or the feminine), whether that be as protectors or predators, whether that domination be benevolent or malevolent. And I am interested in exploring ways to work the dominance and subordination of heterosexualism out of lesbian choices.

In general, aside from the fact that the situations I write about are located in lesbian community, I dream lesbianism mostly because of certain possibilities embedded in it. More importantly, lesbian connection and creation to date move me as a lesbian – and make these possibilities I write of more than idle speculation.

Some will wonder whether others besides lesbians fit in what I am calling Lesbian Ethics. My answer is that, of course, others can fit in what I am saying. Heterosexual women can fit in this schema, for example. However, they fit in exactly the way lesbians fit in heterosexual society. We fit there, but not as lesbians. Heterosexual women can fit here, though not as heterosexual women – that is, not as members of the category 'woman'.

In naming this work 'lesbian', I invoke a lesbian context. And for this *Lesbian context* reason I choose not to define the term. To define 'lesbian' is, in my opinion, to succumb to a context of heterosexualism. No one ever feels compelled to explain or define what they perceive as the norm. If we define 'lesbianism', we invoke a context in which it is not the norm.

Further, when we try to focus on ourselves, often we feel compelled to define what it means to be a lesbian. And immediately the question arises of who gets to count. We feel we must define what a lesbian is so we can determine who is a lesbian and thereby defend our borders from invasion. We feel threatened from the outside, and we want to determine whom we can trust.

Yet we've found we cannot trust someone simply because she's female or because she's lesbian. Even if we had a firm and theoretically coherent definition which articulated the borders of lesbian community, it would not serve us in the way we have imagined. So I let go of the urge to define. And I begin to think of lesbian community in a different way.

I think of contexts. I think of lesbian context, and I do not think of defining its borders. I do not use the metaphor of a fortress which requires defending from invasion. I think of lesbian community as a ground of lesbian be-ing, a ground of possibility, a context in which we perceive each other essentially as lesbians, a context in which we create lesbian meaning. This context exists, not because it has walls, but because we focus on each other as lesbians.

In stressing a centered focus rather than one riveted outward, I do not encourage a uniform perception of each other. I mean to suggest that we perceive each other in all our aspects, from our varied backgrounds to our political differences. But I also mean to suggest that we move among each other as 'lesbians', not as 'women'.

One of the devastating effects of heterosexualism on lesbians is an erasure of lesbian meaning. When we interact as lesbians, out of that interaction comes the meaning of our lesbian lives. When we do not interact as lesbians, there can be no lesbian value.

Once it was enough to just come out as a lesbian. Now we know better. We understand that being lesbian at most creates the possibility of a certain kind of female agency. I want to get on with the project of realizing this agency. And that involves the area of ethics.

Ethics

SINCE 1977 I have been developing this material I now call Lesbian Ethics. At first I refused to address the area of ethics. As a philosopher I had been drawn to epistemology (the study of knowledge), and before that, existentialism; and women finding jobs in philosophy who wanted to address feminist issues were assumed to be concerned with ethics. I did not agree that feminism was simply a part of ethics; I also resented being relegated to what many clearly considered "women's place" in philosophy. I proceeded to explore feminism as having the ability to give meaning to questions of metaphysics and epistemology – what counts as reality, and how we know it.

Then from minnesota, Toni McNaron invited me to do a weekend workshop on lesbian ethics at maidenrock women's learning institute, and I happily settled down to play with ideas I found central in lesbian lives. I prepared a program for maidenrock which involved four parts: power, sabotage, survival, and support. During this time I began to feel that ethics was an important area of feminist thought and not simply a matter of the boring old male question of whether women should have equal rights, which I simply refused to discuss. And I began to feel that examining the area of ethics is crucial to understanding much of what goes on among us.

As we worked with each other on various projects, over time we found *Uses of ethics* we were less than ideal lesbians. So we began to concern ourselves with ethical behavior in addition to political activism. However, our choices mostly resulted in undermining lesbian connection rather than promoting it. Part of the reason for this has involved our perception of ethics.

Typically, when we reach for ethics, we want rules or standards or principles. We want to know what is the "right" thing to do in a given situation; that is, we want to get through a situation safely and without making mistakes. Alternatively, we appeal to ethics because we want a tool we can use to make others behave; that is, we want to get them to do what we think they should do. These are traditional uses of ethics, and I think they are both a mistake.

Professional philosophers will argue that if there are no general principles to which we can appeal as the foundation of moral choice—to determine right and wrong—then ethics is impossible.[13] And lesbian desire for principles is equally strong. We tend to feel that if we have no ultimate principles with which to judge ourselves and each other right or wrong, then ethics has no meaning.

But there are several problems with appeals to rules or principles. Prin-*Principles* ciples cannot guarantee good behavior; they are of no use if individuals are not already acting with integrity. At most they serve as guides for those who already can act with integrity. Thus, for example, we have fairly intricate strategies for fair fighting or conflict resolution, and yet we can use them to sabotage mediation and to undermine integrity.[14]

Secondly, rules or principles don't tell us how to apply them. When making a moral decision, we must first decide which principles apply in a given situation and how. For example, suppose that we agree we should always be honest with each other. What counts as being honest, especially if, as Adrienne Rich has pointed out, silences can be lies too?[15] Should I interrupt absolutely anything you are doing to tell you how I feel? If I don't, am I being dishonest by withholding information? While the questions may sound silly, we have done the former and accused each other of the latter. Or, if you don't want to address something and always change the subject when I bring it up, perhaps breaking down in tears, am I lying to you if I do not force the issue? It is not always clear what counts as being honest.

Thirdly, when two lesbians seriously disagree, often we will also disagree about which principles we think apply. Alternatively, lesbians will be focused on different principles—"she's being racist" versus "she's applying double standards"—each riveted on the fact that the other is not adhering to the principle she's concerned with. Ironically, principles only work when they really aren't needed.

Our own attraction to rules and principles comes in part from a desire to be certain and secure. If someone will only tell us a rule we can follow, we won't have to be in doubt about what we are choosing – we won't have to worry about being mistaken. Or if someone will only set down the rules, then everyone will have to conform. (This, of course, is simply false. Refusal to conform is part of what makes us lesbians.)

Our desire for certainty also involves a desire to make judgments regardless of particular circumstances and regardless of individual intentions. If we have a principle or rule, then we can hold another accountable for her actions without having to investigate the particulars involved in her choice. We set up principles and codes, and we begin to cease considering the transformations we go through in our lives as a result of our choices; we ignore a great deal. Acting from principle interferes with rather than enhances our ability to make judgments.

I am not suggesting that we never articulate or use principles or that we abandon strategies and rules of thumb, such as fair fighting, being honest, or antiracism. We have begun developing fairly intricate strategies for interacting.[16] I am merely suggesting that what *counts* as an application of a given principle depends on the circumstances of our lives. And when appeal to principles works, it is because we are already acting with integrity.[b]

To apply principles, we must have an ability to make judgments, and we must be able to gain and assess information about a given situation; we must be adept at making judgments. With that ability and that information, acting from principle becomes superfluous. Principles are not something we can appeal to when all else fails.[18]

And yet this is exactly the illusion traditional ethics fosters. So I find myself drawn to examining the *function* of moral rules and principles designed to help us judge what we ought or ought not do in order to be good. For much of what is called ethics in our culture involves, not the integrity and moral capability of an individual, but rather the extent to which she participates in the structural hierarchy of a social group or organization by adhering to its rules. The ethical virtues as we know them are master/slave virtues. Even in its most subtle form, traditional, normative (everyday) ethics involves principles or rules of obligation to those

Traditional ethics

---

b   For example, as Denslow Brown points out, in conflict resolution the least honest lesbian will set the tone and pace of the proceedings. Conflict resolution will work only if, beyond their anger and pain, those involved want it to work.[17]

higher in the hierarchy (including gods) and principles or rules of responsibility for those lower in the hierarchy, often "for their own good." (Current discussions in medical ethics are illustrative.) I find that the function
of traditional ethics involves promoting social organization and control at
the expense of individual integrity and agency.

And this leads me to consider the basic value of traditional ethics. I am
concerned with value, though not so much in the usual sense of determining which acts are right or wrong, nor in the more philosophical sense of
considering theoretical principles we can appeal to in order to justify particular moral principles or rules. My concern lies with value inherent in
our perceptions of reality, value presupposed by the way we address the
world. What I am talking about is not value we deliberate about or think
we ought to choose, but a deeper value, the value we give life to by virtue
of our choices. And the value I find at the heart of traditional ethics is
dominance and subordination.

My thesis about traditional ethics is this: (1) The focus and direction
of traditional ethics, indeed its function, has not been individual integrity
and agency (ability to make choices and act) but rather social organization
and social control. (2) The values around which traditional ethics re-
volve are antagonistic, the values of dominance and subordination. As a
result, (3) traditional ethics undermines rather than promotes individual
moral ability and agency. And (4) these aspects of traditional ethics combine to legitimize oppression by redefining it as social organization. Appeal to rules and principles is at the heart of this endeavor.

When I think about ethics, I think about individuals making choices,
that is, making judgments and acting. I think about our ability to interact,
to connect, to be intimate, to respond. I think about our ability to perceive and judge, our ability to gain and attend information. I think about
constraints on our choices, limits on our options. I think about transformations we undergo as a result of our choices—how we grow and
change. I think about our ability to create lesbian meaning. When I think
about ethics, I think about choice under oppression, and I think about lesbian moral agency.

*Moral agency under
oppression*

What I am calling Lesbian Ethics focuses on enabling and developing
individual integrity and agency in relation to others. I mean to invoke a
self who is both separate and related, a self which is neither autonomous
nor dissolved: a self in community who is one among many, what I call
autokoenony (ô´ to kēn o´ nē).

In stressing a focus on choice and moral agency, I do not mean to deny
that factors affect us which we do not control. Rather I mean to defy a
masculine myth that says we must be in control of a situation to make
choices. A moral or political theory useful to anyone under oppression

must not convince the oppressed that we are total victims. While we don't control situations, we do affect them. In focusing on choice and moral agency, I mean to invoke lesbian ability to engage, to act in situations – that we move here now makes a difference. And I mean to suggest that whatever limits we face, our power – ability and agency – lies in choice.

What I need and what I hope to have developed in this book, among other things, is a notion of moral agency under oppression. This includes developing ability within a situation without claiming responsibility for the situation. It involves resisting de-moralization under oppression. And it involves resisting the belief that if we can't control a situation, our actions make no difference and we are powerless. Moral agency involves the ability to go on under oppression: to continue to make choices, to act within the oppressive structure of our society and challenge oppression, to create meaning through our living.

Thus, what I am calling Lesbian Ethics is not a set of rules of right behavior, a list of do's and don't's aimed at guaranteeing happiness and success or freedom from pain or mistakes. I am interested, not in principles to guide and direct our behavior, but rather in the function of our ethical judgments, the central value of ethical judgments, and our lesbian moral agency.

What I will discuss involves ways of perceiving (that is, judging) situations, ways we affirm values (often unwittingly) by our choices in situations, and ways of developing our moral agency in community. Ethics starts with our interactions and with the values we spin and weave through those interactions. I am interested in weaving new values through our choices: values which develop lesbian agency and be-ing, preserve our integrity, and make us less susceptible to oppressive values. This is what concerns me when I think about ethics.

Language

I WORK WITH language and concepts because I am a philosopher. While I am formally trained in the profession, since childhood I have pondered philosophical questions (including some designated as philosophical by professors of the discipline). I am prone to mulling things over; figuring things out and articulating them make me feel alive. Sometimes when I put pen to paper, I reach an altered state of consciousness.

More importantly, I work with language and concepts because language is involved in any transformation of consciousness as well as in resistance to such transformation. Yet many lesbians feel that attending to language is a waste of time. Indeed, some have argued that to focus on language is classist.

Language, of course, is not the only source of oppression nor the only tool of domination. But the use of language in structuring reality and trapping us in oppression is not separate and distinct from the manipulation of the material conditions of our existence to structure reality and trap us in oppression.[19] For example, the process of colonization includes sending in christian missionaries to write down and categorize the language of colonized peoples. The missionaries set up schools where the children are forced to learn their "native" language through christian and colonial categories (for example, deities assume a masculine gender; 'ownership' replaces 'sharing') and then produce for the sake of those categories.

Language as a tool of oppression

Language is a tool of oppression, for we remain trapped in oppression when we perceive only what the oppressors perceive, when we are restricted to their values and categories. Language interests me because of its insidiousness as a means of maintaining a political perspective, and because of its susceptibility to change. However, language use has a contradictory dynamic for those under oppression—it is a matter both of agreement and of coercion: in using language we participate in a consensus, often unwittingly; but our participation is also coerced.[20]

Language as consensus

In the first place, the values embedded in language are a matter of agreement, of consensus. That is, no matter what laws (rules) are passed, the values embedded in our use of language persist or change because of a general consensus in our usage and in our perceptual judgment. I do not mean that we get together and reach agreement about these matters; I mean that we don't disagree, we don't argue about them. We *agree* in that we continue to use certain concepts without question.[21] 'Femininity' (in dualistic opposition to masculinity) is such a conceptual value: no matter what kind of research scientists do in connection with so-called feminine behavior, and no matter what kind of qualifications feminists and lesbians include when appealing to the feminine, through these activities we all participate in the consensus that femininity is a fundamental category of understanding.

Language and perceptual judgment are a matter of consensus in that certain judgments go unquestioned, held in place by all that surrounds them, from research to gossip. This core has no justification, and it does not justify. Rather, our knowledge holds in place what is central to it.

This is not our understanding of the foundation of knowledge from philosophy and science. Traditionally, the foundation of knowledge has been conceived of as a bedrock—holding up, supporting, justifying everything else.[22] Ludwig Wittgenstein suggests a different metaphor: a foundation is like an axis, held in place by what revolves or spins around it.[23] In this respect, a "foundation" does not justify our everyday or scientific judgments, nor is it justified by anything else; rather, the "foundation" determines the limits of what we recognize as justification. It is what goes unquestioned—held in place by what surrounds it. Should someone bring this core into question and challenge it or even try to justify it, its status as a "foundation" would be threatened.[24]

For example, the concept of 'woman' is not based on a bedrock of female behavior. Rather, the concept of 'woman' determines what counts as normal female behavior. And the concept is held in place by, for example, the kind of research scientists do, advertisements directed at women and also at men, the sorts of things news media report and the details reported, the ways females are portrayed for men's sexual entertainment or religious edification or medical experimentation or military inspiration. The category 'woman' is not a reflection of fact but instead tells us how to determine fact. And it is a matter of agreement in that those engaged in such social activities do not disagree about how they perceive women.[c]

Thus, while the core of our knowledge is held in place by what revolves around it, it also limits and focuses our perception and judgment: Although the concept of 'woman' appears to be a descriptive category, it determines for the unquestioning perceiver what would count as a woman. It determines our perception of normal female behavior. A particularly tidy illustration of this comes in the form of a well-known riddle: A father and his son were driving when they had a bad accident. They were rushed to the nearest hospital, and the surgeon on duty was called. The surgeon entered the son's room and exclaimed, "Oh my god, that's my son." How can this be?

Language focuses perception

The solution to the riddle, of course, is that the surgeon is the son's mother. However, those lodged in masculinist thought will miss it; and while they will come up with creative answers— the surgeon was a priest, he was a grandfather, he was the stepfather—their imagination will be limited to male categories. Through her linguistic research, Julia Penelope [Stanley] has found that words in english denoting powerful and prestigious positions like 'surgeon' carry with them a value marking of 'male' and 'white': we presume surgeons to be male and white unless told otherwise.[25] Our judgment, our perception, is directed by the values embedded in the language we use, setting limits to what we might imagine. If language did not focus and limit thought this way, the surgeon riddle would not be a riddle.

And this brings me to the way language, while a consensus, can also in-

---

c   In this respect one can understand how lesbians threaten the foundation of heterosexualism.

volve coercion. For the language we speak is the language of the fathers. I do not mean to challenge the idea of focus and limits in language. After all, it is limits and focus which help us give form to what we're doing. My concern is with the type of limits patriarchal language sets and the means by which the fathers set them.

The consensus is coerced in that men have stolen the power of naming from us, as Mary Daly explores in depth.[26] 'Femininity' is a name for females, which men have developed, that normalizes female subordination. What does not serve men's needs is called "unnatural." We have not named ourselves 'women' for ourselves.

This is most obvious in the academies – religious, educational, scientific, political, legal, and military: men excluded women and then proceeded to name them. Aside from such overt activities, masculinist values have been embedded in language, in this case english, both through semantics ("meaning") and syntax ("grammar"). Since in masculinist culture women are primarily listeners and readers rather than speakers and writers, women's perceptions do not inform the language.

In the area of semantics several feminist linguists have written of the systematic derogation of women. For example, Muriel Schultz has explored a number of different categories of terms for women (in contrast to terms for men) and found that over time, terms for women having positive connotations will eventually acquire negative ones *and* come to mean those who relate sexually to men.[27] Julia Penelope [Stanley] has analyzed a list of 220 terms for heterosexual women (women who relate sexually to men) and found that the words can be mapped on a grid whose parameters are the length of contact with a man and the amount of cost to a man – that is, the meaning of these words fall in this domain. The paradigm of woman as prostitute shapes social perception and creates stereotypes of women with which we have to live.[28]

Drawing on the work of Muriel Schultz and Julia Penelope [Stanley], Dale Spender articulates two semantic rules governing english usage. First, *"any* symbol which is associated with the female must assume negative (and frequently sexual – which is also significant) connotations" over time.[29] Secondly, "there are two fundamental categories, *male* and *minus male*. To be linked with male is to be linked to a range of meanings which are positive and good; to be linked to minus male is to be linked to the *absence* of those qualities."[30] This is significant, for insofar as we accept english uncritically, by virtue of the very language we use, we will be expressing values we never agreed to, certainly that we never fully evaluated (for example, using 'son of a bitch' as a pejorative about a man).

In addition to sexist and heterosexist values, english is laden with racist values – the most notable example being terms for 'light' and 'dark', which carry positive and negative connotations respectively. Also permeating the language are ablebodyist values (for example, words which equate sight, not just with one form of knowing, but with knowledge itself such as "I see what you mean," or terms which equate blindness with a lack of understanding such as "She remained blind to her own oppression"[31]) as well as sizeist values ("cutting the fat out of the budget,"[32] "this sign belittles women").

Aside from the area of semantics, values become embedded in language through syntax. Perhaps the most a-mazing work in this area has been done by cunning linguists.[33] Drawing on her own work as well as work done in conjunction with Susan J. Wolfe, Julia Penelope [Stanley] shows us how — through mere stylistic choices — something someone *does* to a woman becomes something that *happens* to her. Then what *happens* to her can develop into a temporary or accidental *characteristic* of that woman and, from there, become an *essential* part of her state or character.[34] When it occurs, this is a process whereby speakers and writers embed values. And since this process occurs in stylistic choices in language use — rather than through discussion, argument, and justification — readers and listeners don't always have a chance to examine, and either challenge or accept, the valuation unless they are extremely sensitive to language and are looking for such valuation.

Consider the sentence Julia Penelope [Stanley] offers:

John beat Mary.

Here we have an agent, John, an action, beating, and a recipient or object of that agent's action, Mary. John is the main topic of the sentence. Generally, if we were to ask questions, we would want information about the situation: but our focus would be on John, for the speaker has directed our attention to him by placing 'John' first in the sentence.

On the other hand, consider the passive construction of the same situation:

Mary was beaten by John.

In this case, the speaker directs our attention to Mary; and if we were to ask questions about the situation, our focus, unless we redirected it to John, would be on Mary.

Further, the passive construction makes sense without an agent:

Mary was beaten.

In this case, the speaker has focused our attention even more directly on Mary, and it becomes difficult to ask questions about John. Losing awareness of John is significant, for we cease thinking of how he was related to

Mary; indeed, we lose awareness of the idea of a relationship altogether. Instead, we are led to ask of Mary: How? When? Where? Why? Is she all right? We likely will also ask, assuming we would want to hear anything (more) about it: Who did it? But our focus is still on Mary and why and how this happened rather than on John and why he did it.

Finally, once we have enough Marys, we have a number of:

women beaten.

Then, as Julia Penelope [Stanley] explains, through the stylistic choice of treating the action (beating) as a modifier ('beaten') and moving the verb-turned-modifier in front of the noun (thereby changing the truncated passive to a passive adjective), we get:

beaten women

or

battered women.

Now something *men do to women* has become instead something that is a part of *women's nature*. And we lose consideration of John entirely. He didn't really do anything, he is incidental to the event. Mary got herself beaten because of something in her nature. Thus, statements like the following abound: "According to f.b.i. statistics, one-half to two-thirds of women who live with a man will be beaten." We never come across statements such as: "According to f.b.i. statistics, one-half to two-thirds of all men who live with a woman will beat her."[d]

The consensus is coerced through men's overt exclusion and naming of women and through less obvious masculinist semantic and syntactic con-

---

d Indeed, research funded almost always delves into the nature and character of women whom men batter, how women whom men beat are different from other women, why battering is peculiar to them, why some return to men. And almost no questions are asked which focus on men, such as: (1) whether living with women has something to do with why men batter; (2) why men won't let the women go who try to leave them;[35] (3) why some men hold men who batter in contempt;[36] (4) why funding is being withdrawn from shelters for women whom men beat; (5) why so many men beat the woman they live with; or (6) what kind of tactics men use to lure and coerce women and girls into female sexual slavery.[37]

I do not mean to suggest that no attention should be given to a woman who has been beaten. Rather, I mean to suggest that we understand the nature of the problem and act accordingly. Suppose that men are like cars and that, regardless of the design, two-thirds of the time when a woman gets into a car she is hurt. It is important to treat her injuries. But our attention would focus on a solution – recalling the cars and finding another means of transportation.[38]

ventions. The consensus of language is further coerced through men's resistance to feminist challenges—for example, ridicule. When feminists
agreed upon 'ms.' to replace 'mrs.' or 'miss', thereby challenging mandatory public announcement of the sexual availability of women to men, we
met with heavy ridicule and disdain. Editorial complaints regularly appear about how women and other oppressed groups "bastardize" the language. And the media named movement activists 'women's libbers'—a
discrediting experienced by no other liberation movement.

Further, those who challenge the consensus are not likely to gain positions within institutions from which the naming emanates. And if they
do, they will be isolated and dismissed, judged politically biased (unlike
their colleagues), hence unscholarly, and thus ignored. While the acad-
emy espouses "freedom of speech," there are many things one cannot
communicate there.

Finally, those individuals who have perceptions undermining the consensus are discounted and rendered imperceptible, even labeled "mentally ill." That is, if someone rejects the presuppositions of consensus
reality, she may at first be treated as if she is mistaken; those in power may
marshal "evidence," "fact," to prove her "error." However, because her
questioning challenges the core of knowledge, the "facts" are irrelevant.
If she continues to resist "correction," she is neutralized—fired, married,
locked up.

Now, given these ideas of a consensus that is also coerced and a foundation held in place by what surrounds it, there remains the question of how   *Change*
change can occur. Certainly change is not simply a matter of providing
new information which people then note and accept. In discussing scientific revolution, Thomas Kuhn suggests that science proceeds by leaps
and bounds from one paradigm or model to another. He argues that
within a given paradigm or conceptual framework, science is puzzle solving: normal science is a matter of "strenuous and devoted attempts to
force nature into the conceptual boxes supplied by professional educators."[39] In other words, within one conceptual framework scientists
create names (boxes),[e] test their hypotheses, and develop knowledge until
the limits of that framework yield too many contradictions. At this point,
a revolution in thought will occur, and knowledge and understanding
will leap to a new framework. The copernican revolution was one such
leap in masculinist thinking.

---

e   Using Kuhn's analysis, Vivian F. Mayer offers a provocative analysis of how doctors in
"obesity science" interpret data concerning the effects of being fat to fit the existing antifat
conceptual framework.[40]

Sonia Johnson addresses the question of change by making reference to other theories.[41] Perhaps most interesting is the theory of morphogenesis, or the hypothesis that, at least among sentient beings, there are no laws of nature, only habits. Thus change can be a matter of breaking habits, and when a few individuals begin to break those habits, at a certain point a critical mass will be reached and a new morphogenetic field, paradigm perhaps, is created, bringing new habits. The great puzzle, of course, is what makes what Tremor calls "the hundredth lezzie."[42]

Given that lesbians are involved in a transformation of value, how such transformation can take place is an important question. Part, at least, of that transformation involves language. In this respect, following Mary Daly,[43] I want to suggest that our strategy need not be one of trying to prove oppressive values false, thereby working within the existing paradigm, since that merely affirms those values and habits. Rather our strategy can be one of transforming perception so that existing values cease to make sense. This is not an individual project, but it begins with individuals. And that, of course, is where ethics begins.

During the emergence of the women's liberation movement, such a transformation of consciousness began. The movement began, for a few years, to challenge the consensus about 'women', to give rise to a new concept, 'womyn', which had not been present in masculinist thought. This conception did not result from laws passed or from men's benevolence but from something many lesbians and women were doing, from a breach in the masculinist consensus of women's place. We stopped focusing on the social conception of what it meant to be a woman – namely, someone who is by nature helpmate to a man – and simply acted. There were bursts of anger and outrage, bursts during which we interrupted (that is, stopped responding to) the fathers' categories. These categories held in place the patriarchal foundation of male domination and female subordination. They embedded the implication in general, liberal, humanist perception that it is reasonable and rational to discuss whether women should have equal rights, even though the value men embrace as they strut with their nuclear toys threatens to destroy the planet. In outrage we disdained the debates, refused to honor the consensus, stopped trying to justify our rights, and simply claimed our due. As a result, women's liberation, not women's subordination, was the value held in place by our actions, the value around which we spun our choices. We were focusing on ourselves in a way not present in mass media portrayals of women, acting for ourselves in our own names and independent of male approval or sanction.

For a number of reasons this focus began to ebb. But for awhile the focus was there, and it was powerful (that is, enabling), giving rise to a different reality, which then allowed women to develop in new directions. This focus of our attention was a matter of value, a matter of judgment at the level of perception. And it was a breach in the previous agreement, a challenge to the consensus and the coercion. We ceased participating in the consensus that held male domination to be natural and acceptable – indeed necessary – to the preservation of "civilization." When the women's liberation movement called the concept 'woman' into question, part of the foundation of knowledge was called into question and be-began to lose its status as a foundation.

I want us to continue moving, to continue challenging oppressive value and creating new value. I start with language because I am not interested in improving the way we act on existing values. Nor am I interested in directly confronting the existing values and proving them false. No, my desire is for us to pursue our transformation of consciousness, continuing to create a new conceptual framework, so that existing values – values which make oppression credible and acceptable – cease to make sense. It is possible for us to spin a revolution. And I begin with the values we weave in our actions with each other.

Directions

IN MY OPINION dominance and subordination lie at the heart of social interactions in the form of the institution of heterosexuality, and so long as that axis remains intact, oppression will be a reality – all forms of oppression, not just male domination of women. There are those who argue *for* oppression – Hitler was one – and the justification is fairly complete. Under fascist ideology, subordination to a higher order is essential for humans to become moral agents: obedience and the cessation of individual judgment are the essence of what it means to be moral and achieve meaning. Within that framework, what I am discussing as moral agency is unintelligible, makes no sense.

What I am after is a dismembering of the existing conceptual schema by calling into question its foundation and participating in the weaving of a new conceptual schema. In so doing, I will not be proving that one is right and the other is wrong, though of course I do choose one rather than the other. To say that the foundational values of dominance and subordination are morally wrong is no different from saying that dominance and subordination are oppressive. And that is really no different from saying dominance and subordination are dominance and subordination.

Thus, rather than prove false a patriarchal framework which revolves around dominance and subordination, I want to clarify its boundaries, show that some of what is claimed in this framework is a contradiction, and dislodge its foundation. I want to suggest how dominance figures our perceptions in ways and areas we might not have suspected. And I want to make some suggestions about how our perceptions and judgments can be different.

At this book's heart is a certain judgment: namely, that the relationship of dominance and subordination undermines moral agency. This is not a judgment which can be defended so much as a judgment that can be held in place by what surrounds it, by the daily choices we lesbians make. It may well be that many simply reject the axis of value I am suggesting. And if that is so, then their ethical needs can be more than adequately met by traditional anglo-european ethics.

But my idea is that without tacit agreement, consensus, concerning the value of our integrity, there will be no moral agency for us outside the master/slave virtues of the fathers. And even with such agreement, our efforts can seriously go awry, owing, at least in part, to the ideology we've adopted from dominant anglo-european ethical systems.

Further, what I am outlining here is not a program for guaranteeing behavior; it is not a program for getting lesbians to act ethically. It is a program for lesbians who already want to be ethical, want to act with integrity. That is, we make many mistakes, and sometimes we stay in patterns for a long time as we try understand them. But when we finally understand how a given pattern functions destructively, we act to change. This is not a book for those who have no desire to make changes.

I want to add that what I have in mind concerning the shifts in perception which I am calling Lesbian Ethics are meant to be used in lesbian community, among ourselves, as we weave new value, as we try to work out of the habit of dominance and subordination, thereby becoming beings who are not used to it. Whether these values can be developed from a different angle as part of a political strategy to confront patriarchy is an open question. On the one hand, it seems that giving up our survival skills in a framework of dominance and subordination is a mistake. On the other, I am finding that more and more, for myself, the values I am trying to articulate here are a source of empowerment in patriarchy in a way that our survival skills are not. I once felt that these values were meaningless in patriarchy. I am no longer sure.

Nevertheless, my focus is lesbian community, for it is within this context that these values make sense and have a chance of developing. There is new value emerging in lesbian community—for I have not woven this work in a vacuum; and what I hope for in the transformation possible in lesbian living involves a conceptual framework, a new paradigm, in which oppression is not automatic—where rape, pogroms, slavery, lynchings, and colonialism are not even *conceivable*.[44] My purpose here is to suggest a direction to move in which might yield a shift to new value. Such a shift must be accompanied by a shift in material conditions. I consider what follows part preparation for such shifts.

Finally, in attempting to develop a different conceptual schema, I in no way mean to suggest that if it works, there will be no problems, no pain, no error, no misunderstanding. But if the values of oppression are no longer normalized—are no longer fully integrated into our lives—our interactions will less readily result in destruction. If we can interact in ways that weave a different locus of value, then our habits and instincts and reactions will less likely lead us back to the fathers. And then we may become an energy field capable of resisting oppression.

1
Separating from Heterosexualism

IN WRITING A book on Lesbian Ethics, I am concerned with moral

Moral reform versus moral revolution change. And given that lesbians are oppressed within the existing social framework, I am concerned with questioning the values of such a framework as well as with considering different values around which we can weave a new framework. In other words, I am interested in moral revolution. Significantly, however, within traditional ethics the only type of moral change we tend to acknowledge is moral reform. Thus in this chapter I want to explore the existing social framework and raise the issue of separating from it.

Moral reform is the attempt to bring human action into greater conformity with existing ethical principles and thereby alleviate any injustice which results from the breach of those principles. In addressing the question of moral change, Kathryn Pyne Addelson argues:

> The main body of tradition in ethics has occupied itself with the notions of obligation, moral principle, justification of acts under principle, justification of principle by argument. When moral change was considered at all, it was seen as change to bring our activities into conformity with our principles, as change to dispel injustice, as change to alleviate suffering.[1]

She goes on to suggest:

> But moral reform is not the only type of moral change. There is also moral revolution. Moral revolution has not to do with making our principles con-

sistent, not to do with greater application of what we *now* conceive as justice. That is the task of moral reform, because its aim is the preservation of
values. But the aim of moral revolution is the creation of values.[2]

In recognizing only moral reform, traditional ethics discourages us
from radically examining the values around which existing principles re-
volve, or the context in which we are to act on those principles (such as
oppression), or the structure which gives life to just those values. Traditional ethics concerns itself almost exclusively with questions of obligation, justification, and principle, and does not leave room for us to examine underlying value or create new value. As a result, Kathryn Pyne
Addelson argues, "the narrow focus of traditional ethics makes it impossible to account for the behavior of the moral revolutionary *as* moral behavior."[3]

For example, someone engaged in moral reform might question the use
of the concept of 'evil': she might question the concept of 'woman' as evil
(the myth of eve) or the concept of 'jew' as evil (the jewish blood libel[a]), or
she might question the concepts of 'black' and 'darkness' as sinister and
evil, suggesting that these are all inappropriate applications of 'evil'.
Nevertheless, she would not question the concept of 'evil' itself; her concern would be with its application.

On the other hand, someone engaged in moral revolution might question the concept of 'evil', arguing that 'evil' is a necessary foil for 'good' —
that there must be something designated as evil to function as a scapegoat
for the shortcomings or failures of that which is designated as good. She
might point out that 'good' requires 'evil' and therefore that evil can never
be eradicated if good is to prevail. She might suggest that we could create
a moral value in which we had no need of the concepts of 'good' or 'evil'.

I want a moral revolution. I don't want greater or better conformity to
existing values. I want change in value. Our attempts to reform existing
institutions merely result in reinforcing the existing social order.

For example, a woman may elect to teach a women's studies course using writings on women's rights. She may present classic arguments in
favor of women's rights: exposing the contradiction of denying women's
rights while affirming democratic ideals, or exposing the hypocrisy in re-
cruiting women during times of need and yet espousing an ideology

---

a This is the myth that jews slaughter christian children on easter and use their blood
during passover, for example, in baking matzoh. It is the myth which justified the christian
slaughter of jews during easter which dates back to the middle ages. Similar muslim perse-
cutions of jews date back to the fifteenth century, and there are references to use of the libel
by muslims as late as the nineteenth century.[4]

which negates women's competence. And she could include absurd anti-feminist documents, such as material by a woman doctor denying that women should be professional, or a piece which argues that a woman should stand by her man – no matter what – for the "good" of "society." To give the illusion of objectivity, she might even invite speakers to present arguments against equal rights for women, thereby airing "both sides" of the issue.

However, in addressing and defending women's rights, she is implicitly acknowledging that women's rights are debatable. She is, by that very act, affirming that there is a legitimate question concerning women's rights, even if she is quite clear about the answer she espouses. And she is agreeing that society has a "right" to determine women's place.

Significantly, however, she cannot broach or even formulate a question about men's rights or men's competence without appearing radical beyond reason. That is, men's rights are not debatable.[b] Thus, in agreeing to defend women's rights, she is solidifying status quo values which make women's but not men's rights debatable in a democracy.

A feminist challenging sexist values by defending women's rights is actually coerced into agreeing with the sexist structure of society at a more basic level. And insofar as her challenge appeals to ethical questions of justice, it is subject to consideration of whether such rights are consistent with the existing social order.

I want a moral revolution.

Heterosexualism

IN HER 1949 ground-breaking work *The Second Sex*, Simone de Beauvoir asked, "Why is it that women do not dispute male sovereignty?"[5] Her question presupposes a particular philosophical theory about human nature and interaction developed by Hegel. This theory is that each consciousness (person) holds a fundamental hostility toward every other consciousness and that each subject (person) sets himself up as essential by opposing himself to all others. That is, human relations are fundamentally antagonistic, and the hostility is reciprocal. One who does not succeed in opposing another finds himself having to accept the other's values and so becomes submissive to him.[6] Now, in asking why women do not dispute male sovereignty, Simone de Beauvoir is asking why women have not antagonistically opposed men as men have opposed women and each other. In asking this question, she is suggesting (1) that

---

b   Of course, men do engage in questions about other men's rights. But there is no general idea that perhaps men as a group ought to be written out of the u.s. constitution.

women have never opposed men and so are submissive, not from having lost to men, but from having accepted a position of subordination, and (2) that to achieve the status of subject, to resist male domination, among other things, women must oppose men as men have opposed women and other men.[c]

In discussing women's subordination, Simone de Beauvoir argues that "the couple is a fundamental unity with its two halves riveted together." The basic trait of woman is to be fundamentally the other. Thus, women have gained only what men have been willing to grant, and have taken nothing.[9]

Simone de Beauvoir suggests several reasons for this: women lack the concrete means of organizing; women have no past or history of their own; women have lived dispersed among men; and women feel solidarity with the men of their class and race. She points out, for example, that white women hold allegiance to white men, not to black women.[10] She adds that to renounce the status of other is to renounce the privileges conferred through alliance with a superior caste.[11] She concludes:

> Thus woman may fail to lay claim to the status of subject because she lacks definite resources, she feels the necessary bond that ties her to man regardless of reciprocity, and because she is often very well pleased with her role as *Other*.[12]

In other words, according to Simone de Beauvoir, yet another reason women have not disputed male sovereignty and laid claim to their own existence is that women are not fully displeased with being defined as other.

Simone de Beauvoir then discusses how all this came to be, because, as she announces:

> One is not born, but rather becomes a woman.[13]

One is not born a woman because 'woman' is a constructed category. And it is intimately connected to the category 'man'.

While I disagree that women always have been under men and also I disagree that to resist male sovereignty women must become like men, nevertheless a basic relationship of dominance and subordination ap-

---

c Indeed, Simone de Beauvoir argues that in giving life, women are merely ensuring repetition and are no different than other animals. However man, in risking his life (by becoming a warrior and attempting to take life), is transcending it and is thereby creating value.[7] As Nancy Hartsock notes, "Thus, it is woman's failure to engage in combat that defines her static and repetitive existence, her maternity that condemns her to give life without risking her life."[8]

pears to exist between men and women, and it is not clear, with a few notable exceptions since the onset of patriarchy, that women have resisted that relationship.[d] In my opinion, to fully evaluate the relationship of dominance and subordination we need concern ourselves not only with addressing sexism, or even homophobia or heterosexism, but more substantially, with the actual relationship of heterosexualism.

Understanding sexism involves analyzing how institutional power is in the hands of men, how men discriminate against women, how society classifies men as the norm and women as passive and inferior, how male institutions objectify women, how society excludes women from participation as full human beings, and how what has been perceived as normal male behavior is also violence against women. In other words, to analyze sexism is to understand primarily how women are victims of institutional and ordinary male behavior.

Understanding heterosexism, as well as homophobia,[e] involves analyzing, not just women's victimization, but also how women are defined in terms of men or not at all, how lesbians and gay men are treated – indeed scapegoated – as deviants, how choices of intimate partners for both women and men are restricted or denied through taboos to maintain a certain social order. (For example, if sexual relations between men were openly allowed, then men could do to men what men do to women[16] and, further, (some) men could become what women are. This is verboten. In addition, if love between women were openly explored, women might simply walk away from men, becoming 'not-women'. This, too, is verboten.) Focusing on heterosexism challenges heterosexuality as an institution, but it can also lead lesbians to regard as a political goal our acceptance, even assimilation, into heterosexual society: we try to assure heterosexuals we are normal people (that is, just like them),that they are being unjust in stigmatizing us, that ours is a mere sexual preference.

In her ground-breaking work on compulsory heterosexuality, Adrienne Rich challenges us to address heterosexuality as a political institution which ensures male right of physical, economical, and emotional access

Heterosexualism involves a relationship

---

d   Two notable recent exceptions are the european beguines and the chinese marriage re-sisters.[14]

e   Celia Kitzinger suggests we stop using 'homophobia' altogether. She argues that the term did not emerge from within the women's liberation movement but rather from the academic discipline of psychology. She questions characterizing heteropatriarchal fear of lesbians as irrational, she challenges the psychological (rather than political) orientation of 'phobia', and she notes that within psychology, the only alternative to 'homophobia' is liberal humanism.[15]

to women.[17] Jan Raymond develops a theory of hetero-reality and argues: "While I agree that we are living in a heterosexist society, I think the wider problem is that we live in a hetero-relational society where most of women's personal, social, political, professional, and economic relations are defined by the ideology that woman is for man."[18] I go a bit further.

Understanding heterosexualism involves analyzing the relationship between men and women in which both men and women have a part. Heterosexualism is men dominating and de-skilling women in any of a number of forms, from outright attack to paternalistic care, and women devaluing (of necessity) female bonding as well as finding inherent conflicts between commitment and autonomy and consequently valuing an ethics of dependence. Heterosexualism is a way of living (which actual practitioners exhibit to a greater or lesser degree) that normalizes the dominance of one person in a relationship and the subordination of another. As a result, it undermines female agency.

What I am calling 'heterosexualism' is not simply a matter of males having procreative sex with females.[19] It is an entire way of living which involves a delicate, though at times indelicate, balance between masculine predation upon and masculine protection of a feminine object of masculine attention.[f] Heterosexualism is a particular economic, political, and emotional relationship between men and women: men must dominate women and women must subordinate themselves to men in any of a number of ways.[g] As a result, men presume access to women while women remain riveted on men and are unable to sustain a community of women.

In the u.s., women cannot appear publicly without some men advancing on them, presuming access to them. In fact, many women will think something is wrong if this doesn't happen. A woman simply is someone toward whom such behavior is appropriate. When a woman is accompanied by a man, however, she is usually no longer considered fair game.

Protection and predation

---

f   I think the main model for personal interaction for women and lesbians has been heterosexual. However, for men in the anglo-european tradition there has also been a model of male homosexual interaction – a form of male bonding, even though sex between men has come to be persecuted. And while it is not my intention here to analyze the model, I will suggest that it revolves around an axis of dominance and submission, and that heterosexualism is basically a refined male homosexual model.[20]

g   Julien S. Murphy writes: "Heterosexuality is better termed heteroeconomics, for it pertains to the language of barter, exchange, bargain, auction, buy and sell. . . . Heterosexuality is the economics of exchange in which a gender-based power structure continually reinstates itself through the appropriation of the devalued party in a duo-gendered system. Such reinstatement happens through each instance of 'striking a deal' in the market of sex."[21]

As a result, men close to individual women—fathers, boyfriends, husbands, brothers, escorts, colleagues—become protectors (theoretically), staving off advances from other men.

The value of special protection for women is prevalent in this society. Protectors interact with women in ways that promote the image of women as helpless: men open doors, pull out chairs, expect women to dress in ways that interfere with their own self-protection.[22] And women accept this as attentive, complimentary behavior and perceive themselves as persons who need special attention and protection.[h]

What a woman faces in a man is either a protector or a predator, and men gain identity through one or another of these roles.[23] This has at least five consequences. First, there can be no protectors unless there is a danger. A man cannot identify himself in the role of protector unless there is something which needs protection. So it is in the interest of protectors that there be predators. Secondly, to be protected, women must be in danger. In portraying women as helpless and defenseless, men portray women as victims . . . and therefore as targets.

Thirdly, a woman (or girl) is viewed as the object of male passion and thereby its cause. This is most obvious in the case of rape: she must have done something to tempt him—helpless hormonal bundle that he is. Thus if women are beings who by nature are endangered, then, obviously, they are thereby beings who by nature are seductive—they actively attract predators. Fourthly, to be protected, women must agree to act as men say women should: to appear feminine, prove they are not threatening, stay at home, remain only with the protector, devalue their connections with other women, and so on.

Finally, when women step out of the feminine role, thereby becoming active and "guilty,"[i] it is a mere matter of logic that men will depict

---

h   In questioning the value of special protection for women, I am not saying that women should never ask for help. That's just foolish. I am talking about the ideal of women as needing sheltering. The concept of children needing special protection is prevalent and I challenge that concept when it is used to abrogate their integrity "for their own good." But at least protection for children theoretically involves ensuring that (male) children can grow up and learn to take care of themselves. That is, (male) children are protected until they have grown and developed skills and abilities they need to get on in this world. No such expectation is included in the ideal of special protection for women: the ideal of special protection of women does not include the expectation that women will ever be in a position to take care of themselves (grow up).

i   In her analysis of fairy tales, Andrea Dworkin points out that an active woman is portrayed as evil (the stepmother) and a good woman is generally asleep or dead (snow white, sleeping beauty).[24]

women as evil and step up overt physical violence against them in order to reaffirm women's victim status. For example, as the demand for women's rights in the u.s. became publicly perceptible, the depiction of lone women as "sluts" inviting attack also became prevalent. A lone female hitchhiker was perceived, not as someone to protect, but as someone who had given up her right to protection and thus as someone who was a target for attack. The rampant increase in pornography — entertainment by and for men about women — is men's general response to the u.s. women's liberation movement's demand of integrity, autonomy, and dignity for women.

What radical feminists have exposed through all the work on incest (daughter rape) and wife-beating is that protectors are also predators. Of course, not all men are wife- or girlfriend-beaters, but over half who live with women are. And a significant number of u.s. family homes shelter an "incestuous" male.[25]

Although men may exhibit concern over womanabuse, they have a different relationship to it than women; their concerns are not women's concerns. For example, very often men become irate at the fact that a woman has been raped or beaten by another man. But this is either a man warming to his role of protector — it rarely, if ever, occurs to him to teach her self-defense — or a man deeply affected by damage done to his "property" by another man. And while some men feel contempt for men who batter or rape, Marilyn Frye suggests it is quite possible their contempt arises, not from the fact that womanabuse is happening, but from the fact that the batterer or rapist must accomplish by force what they themselves can accomplish more subtly by arrogance.[26]

The current willingness of men in power to pass laws restricting pornography is a matter of men trying to reestablish the asexual, virginal image of (some) women whom they can then protect in their homes. And they are using as their excuse right-wing women as well as feminists who appear to be asking for protection, like proper women, rather than demanding liberation. Men use violence when women don't pay attention to them. Then, when women ask for protection, men can find meaning by turning on the predators — particularly ones of a different race or class.

In other words, the logic of protection is essentially the same as the logic of predation. Through predation, men do things to women and against women all of which violate women and undermine women's integrity. Yet protection objectifies just as much as predation. To protect women, men do things to women and against women; acting "for a woman's own good," they violate her integrity and undermine her agency.

Protection and predation emerge from the same ideology of male dominance, and it is a matter of indifference to the successful maintenance of male domination which of the two conditions women accept. Thus Sonia Johnson writes:

> Our conviction that if we stop studying and monitoring men and their latest craziness, that if we abandon our terrified clawing and kicking interspersed with sniveling and clutching — our whole sick sadomasochistic relationship with the masters — they will go berserk and kill us, is the purest superstition. With our eyes fully upon them they kill us daily; with our eyes riveted upon them they have gone berserk.[27]

Colonization   Early radical feminists claimed that women are colonized.[28] It is worth reconsidering this claim. Those who wish to dominate a group, and who are successful, gain control through violence. This show of force, however, requires tremendous effort and resources; so colonizers introduce values portraying the relationship of dominant colonizer to subordinate colonized as natural and normal.

One of the first acts of colonizers after conquest is to control the language, work often accomplished by christian missionaries. Their mission is to give the language written form and then set up schools where it is taught to those native to the land. Here new values are introduced: for example, concepts of 'light' and 'dark' as connoting good and evil respectively. Words for superiors and deities then begin to carry a 'light' connotation as well as appear in the masculine gender. Further, values are embedded which support colonial appropriation of natural resources, and which disavow the colonized's ancestral ways and economic independence. As the colonized are forced to use the colonizers' language and conceptual schema, they can begin to internalize these values. This is "salvation," and colonizers pursue what they have called manifest destiny or "the white man's burden."

The theory of manifest destiny implies that colonizers are bringing civilization (the secular version of salvation) to "barbarians" ("heathens"). Colonizers depict the colonized as passive, as wanting and needing protection (domination), as being taken care of "for their own good." Anyone who resists domination will be sorted out as abnormal and attacked as a danger to society ("civilization") or called insane and put away in the name of protection (their own or society's).

Thus colonizers move from predation — attack and conquest — to benevolent protection. Those who have been colonized are portrayed as helpless, childlike, passive, and feminine; and the colonizers become benevolent rulers, accepting the burden of the civilized management of resources (exploitation).

After the social order has been established, should the colonized begin to resist protection and benevolence, insisting that they would rather do it themselves regardless of immediate consequences, the colonizers will once again turn predators, stepping up violence to convince the colonized that they need protection and that they cannot survive without the colonizers. One of the lines attributed to Mahatma Gandhi in the movie *Gandhi* is significant to this point: "To maintain the benevolence and dominate us, you must humiliate us." When all else fails, men will engage in war to affirm their "manhood": their "right" to conquer and protect women and other "feminine" beings (i.e., anyone else they can dominate).

The purpose of colonization is to appropriate foreign resources. It functions by de-skilling a people and rendering them economically de- *De-skilling* pendent. In his book on colonialism, *How Europe Underdeveloped Africa*, Walter Rodney argues that african societies would not have become capitalist without white colonialism.[29] His thesis is that africa was proceeding economically in a manner distinct from precapitalist development until europeans arrived to colonize africa and underdevelop it. Aborting the african economy and making it over to meet their own needs, europeans robbed africans of their land and resources. Further, europeans robbed africans of their autonomous economic skills, primarily by means of transforming the education system and teaching african peoples to disavow the knowledge of their ancestors. This de-skilling of conquered peoples is crucial to domination because it means that the colonized become dependent on the colonizers for survival. Actually, however, it is the colonizers who cannot survive—as colonizers—without the colonized.

Bette S. Tallen suggests that, in like fashion, women have been deskilled under heterosexualism, becoming economically dependent on men, while men appropriate women's resources.[30] As Sonia Johnson notes:

> According to United Nations statistics, though women do two-thirds of the world's work, we make only one-tenth of the world's money and own only one-hundredth of the world's property.[31]

The de-skilling of women differs depending on specific historical and material conditions. For example, in her analysis of pre-industrial, seventeenth-century britain, Ann Oakley notes that women engaged in many trades separate from their husbands, or as widows. The industrial revolution changed all that and deprived many women of their skills.[32] Prior to this, during the burning times, european men appropriated women's healing skills, birthing skills, and teaching skills, and attempted to destroy women's psychic skills.[j] As Alice Molloy writes, "the so-called history of witchcraft is simply the process by which women were separated from each other and from their potential to synthesize information."[34] In general, many women no longer have their own programs, they've lost access to their own tools. As a result, they are coerced into embracing an ideology of dependence on men.

Heterosexualism has certain similarities to colonialism, particularly in its maintenance through force when paternalism is rejected (that is, the stepping up of male predation when women reject male protection) and in its portrayal of domination as natural (men are to dominate women as naturally as colonizers are to dominate the colonized, and without any sense of themselves as oppressing those they dominate except during times of overt aggression) and in the de-skilling of women. And just as it is colonizers who cannot survive as colonizers without the colonized, so it is men who cannot survive as men (protectors or predators) without women.

Complementing the protector/predator function of men is the concept *What 'woman'* of 'woman', particularly as it functions in mainstream u.s. society. Con-*excludes* sider what the concept lacks. It lacks (1) a sense of female power, (2) any hint that women as a group have been the targets of male violence, (3) any hint either of collective or individual female resistance to male domination and control, and (4) any sense of lesbian connection.

The concept of 'woman' includes no real sense of female power. Certainly, it includes no sense of women as conquering and dominating forces. More significantly, it includes no sense of strength and competence. I am not denying that there are many strong women. And where women encourage each other in defiance of the dominant valuation, significant images appear. But over time, under heterosexualism, these images tend to be modified by appeals to femininity or are used against women. Without sufficient deference to men, women will find 'castrating bitch' or 'dyke' or comparable concepts used to keep them in line.

Men of a given group will partially modify 'femininity' in order to emphasize female competence and skill when they absolutely need extra help: during wars – Rosie the riveter, for example – or on small nebraska farms or in revolutionary movements or in kibbutzim when the state is unstable or in a community deeply split under oppression. But once their domain is more firmly established, men drag up the feminine stereotype (while nevertheless expecting women to do most of the work with none of the benefits).

In her essay for black women in the cities, Pat Robinson connects the

---

j Currently, men are attempting to control woman's procreative abilities altogether by controlling female generative organs and processes.[33]

loss of a people's self-awareness and power with the loss of their deities. She states, "When a group must be controlled, you always take away from them their gods, their very reflections of themselves and their inner being."[35] Where we find reference to goddesses of any culture in dominant anglo-european scholarship, they are being kidnapped or raped, and/or they are mothers.[k] Significantly, the one female figure present in anglo-european thought is the virgin Mary, remnant of an ancient goddess transformed into a model rape victim, reputed to have said to a god, "Do unto me as thou willest."

Pat Robinson goes on to note that to control a people, while one must take from them their very reflections of themselves, one must first use force.[38] (This, of course, is the initial process of colonization.) A second notable lack in the concept of 'woman' is a sense that force is ever used against women as a group. Feminist literature has appeared about the massacre of european witches. But the vast majority of u.s. women today remain unaware of the witch burnings. One might wonder how mass destruction could be eradicated from consciousness. Perhaps it was simply suppressed. But when a social order requires the extermination of a particular group and that extermination virtually succeeds, subsequent memory of the process can be eradicated by renaming. The massacre of witches in europe over a three-hundred-fifty-year period has endured just such a renaming. The caricature of witches assaults us annually in the form of a u.s. mass-media event: halloween.

The use of force or violence against women as a group has not been limited to europe. Mary Daly among others has attempted to bring into u.s. feminist consciousness the fact that such force has been and continues to be used against women in every part of the world.[39] And while the practice of indian dowry murders has been acknowledged as a problem, it is only because men in power have recently named it a problem. Further, while in china the fathers deemed footbinding uneconomical and therefore immoral, our memory and awareness of what led to it and why it was perpetuated for so long is fading. And female infanticide has taken its place as an expression of misogyny.

Because there is no sense that violence has ever been directed at women

---

k   There were many more goddesses than fertility and mother goddesses. There were goddesses of the hunt, of weaving, of wisdom, of change, of winter, of the forest, of the land, of the dead, of justice, of love, of food, of the sun, of fire, of writing, of the dawn, of revenge, of menarche, of the moon, of the sea, of volcanoes, and of witches and magic – to name but a few.[36] Further, there is reason to believe that fat goddesses, such as the venus of willendorf, represented not mothering but power: the rolls of fat were rolls of power.[37]

as a group, it is difficult to gain a perspective on the magnitude of the force used against women now. While u.s. women may be horrified at the specter of african genital mutilation and indian dowry deaths, african (particularly nigerian) and indian students in my classes are no less horrified at the incidence of rape and the amount of pornography which form a daily part of u.s. women's lives. Except for radical feminists, no one in the united states perceives the phenomenal rate of incest (daughter rape), wife beating, rape, forced prostitution, and the ideology of pornography—depicted not only in men's magazines but on television, billboards, in grocery stores, in schools, and in general in every public and private sector a woman goes—as any kind of concerted assault on women. There is no general sense that, as Sonia Johnson points out, men have declared war on women;[40] rather this assault—because men are paying attention to women—is called "attraction," even "admiration."

Thirdly, the concept of 'woman' includes no sense of female resistance—either collective or individual—to male domination. While there is evidence that amazons once lived in north africa, in china, in anatolia (turkey), and between the black and the caspian seas,[m] amazons are repeatedly treated as a joke or buried. Yet as Helen Diner writes:

> At the celebrations in honor of the dead, Demosthenes, Lysias, Himerios, Isocartes, and Aristeides praise the victory over the Amazons as more important than that over the Persians or any other deed in history. . . . The wars between the Greeks and Persians were wars between two male-dominated societies. In the Amazon war, the issue was which of the two forms of life was to shape European civilization in its image.[42]

Significantly, even feminists and lesbian-feminists shun amazons, apparently for fear of appearing out of touch with reality (with the consensus). With a few notable exceptions, we are not responding to Maxine Feldman's call, "Amazon women rise."[43] There is little celebration of amazons (even though we are beginning to hear again of goddesses and witches). We do not acknowledge the amazons even as symbolic defenders of womanhood—and this at a time when male violence against women is blatant. Instead, even radical feminists push for greater police and state protection. The amazons—as well as female warriors such as those of the dahomey or the nootka societies—simply do not fit within the

---

m   In 1979, the *Chicago Sun-Times*, for example, reported the finding of the remains of an amazon tribe that lived twenty-five hundred years ago in the soviet republic of moldavia. Soviet archaeologists found a "woman warrior, her war-horse, a spear, gold earrings and other adornments" in a burial site near the village of balabany in the southwestern soviet union.[41]

concept of 'woman' of mainstream u.s. society.[44]

Because there is no mythological, much less historical, memory of female resistance to male domination, isolated and individual acts of female resistance are also rendered imperceptible as resistance, particularly, as I argue below, through the concept of 'femininity'. A 'woman' is one whose identity comes through her alliance with a man to such an extent that any woman who resists male violence, male advances, and male access is not a real woman.

The value of 'woman', thus, excludes a sense of female presence, skill, and power, an awareness that violence has been and is perpetrated against women as a group, and a sense of female resistance to male domination. It also excludes a sense of lesbian connection. Adrienne Rich took on the task of addressing (1) the bias "through which lesbian experience is perceived on a scale ranging from deviant to abhorrent, or simply rendered invisible;" (2) "how and why women's choice of women as passionate comrades, life partners, co-workers, lovers, tribe, has been crushed, invalidated, forced into hiding and disguise;" and (3) "the virtual or total neglect of lesbian existence in a wide range of writings, including feminist scholarhip."[45] As Harriet Ellenberger writes:

> A central taboo in patriarchy is the taboo against women consorting with women – and yet that tabooed consorting, allying, connecting has gone on and goes on in front of their noses, and men and most women don't think it's real.[46]

What the concept of 'woman' includes is equally significant. Given the masculinist naming of women, a 'woman' is (1) male-identified, someone whose identity emerges through her relationship to a man, (2) someone who makes herself attractive to men, (3) an object to be conquered by men, and (4) a breeder (of boys). *What 'woman' includes*

A woman's identity is incorporated in her relationship with a man: she is first and foremost some man's but not some woman's mother, wife, mistress, or daughter. As the radicalesbians argued in 1970:

> We are authentic, legitimate, real to the extent that we are the property of some man whose name we bear. To be a woman who belongs to no man is to be invisible, pathetic, inauthentic, unreal.[47]

A woman belonging to no man either doesn't exist or is trying to be a man. Further, a 'woman' is responsible for the sexual servicing of men.[48] Her goodness or badness, her ethical status, is based on her sexual availability, cost, and fidelity to men.[49] Ultimately, a 'woman' is a virgin or a whore – that is, related through sex to a man.

Secondly, a 'woman' is someone who is attractive to men. If she does not try to make herself attractive to men, she is considered to have a serious problem. In mainstream u.s. society, attractiveness means she is white anglo, upper middle class, virtually anorexic (that is, unhealthy), and young enough to have no character lines on her face, though occasionally she may be dark and "exotic." Those women who fall outside these categories, while not entirely discounted as women, are nevertheless made to feel poor substitutes for a woman.[n] Further, a 'woman' is one who must be protected from what is evil (that is, dark) unless she is dark (that is, evil) herself—in which case, other women must be protected from her. The whiter she is, the purer she is. The darker she is, the more dangerously sexual she is. Again, she is a virgin or a whore—that is, white or black.

Thirdly, a 'woman' is someone who must be conquered by a man. The ideology of pornography, from soft porn to snuff, portrays a woman as an object (someone to be acted upon—in this case, attacked and overcome), someone who exists to be dominated. She is characterized by her sexual desire, and she is to be dominated through violation—which violation she will ultimately crave. The ideology of romanticism (popularly portrayed in the harlequin romances) is the same: A woman is an object (someone to be acted upon—in this case, protected and seduced), someone who exists to be conquered. She is characterized by her lack of sexual desire—she is to reject (male) sexual advances in order to display her modesty; and hence men know that when she says "no," she really means "yes." Thus she, too, is to be dominated through violation—violation of her integrity—which violation she suddenly starts to crave. Both pornography and romanticism tell us that a woman is to be conquered and dominated by the force of masculine will.

Finally, a 'woman' is a breeder. A woman is fulfilled through breeding, her basic ethical possibility is selfless giving and nurturing, and anything which interferes with this process is suspect. Further, whenever a people are in jeopardy because men play war, men stress breeding to the exclusion of all else, and carefully supervise it. In anglo-european, eurasian, and all mainstream american societies (central, south, and north), this function cannot be entrusted to her. Her body is not hers to determine. For example, the issue of abortion, as it is being played out in the u.s., is not a woman's issue. For the question concerns, simply, which men will

---

n   In other areas of the world different standards apply. In some places being catholic is essential to womanhood, or being fat or being dark, not pale. The model of 'woman' in terms of physical manifestation tends to adhere to the values of the men in power in a given location.

control women's abortions – the state or individual men.[50] And doctors exercising their paternalistic concern for social order sterilize women they deem inappropriate mothers, such as poor black and poor puerto rican women.[51] A 'woman' is a breeder, and breeders need caretakers who make breeding decisions, including genetic reconstruction. Further, of course, when a woman breeds successfully, what she breeds is male – that is, someone who carries on her husband's line.

A 'woman', thus, is a sex object essentially submissive to and dependent on men, one whose function is to perpetuate the race (while protectors and predators engage in their project of destroying it). No, one is not born a woman.[p]

I want a moral revolution.

The primary concept used to interpret and evaluate individual women's choices and actions is 'femininity'. 'Femininity' normalizes male domination and paints a portrait of women as subordinate and naively content with being controlled. Thus patrihistorians claim that women have remained content with their lot, accepting male domination throughout time, with the exception of a few suffragists and now a few aberrant feminists.

'Femininity' obscures resistance

p   It is no accident that just as the feminist demand for rights again achieved public recognition, those in power diverted ethical attention to biology – this time, sociobiology. Here, amid allegedly objective descriptions of animal behavior, E. O. Wilson claims that it is a "near-universal phenomenon that males are dominant over females among animals."[52] Nowhere does Wilson defend this claim; rather, it appears to be substantiated as he merely describes the facts. For example, he uses the word 'harem' to describe a hamadryas baboon society in which females are terrorized into submission and loyalty by a threatening male. However, he also uses it to describe female-centered societies such as the mountain sheep.[53] The mountain sheep herd is female-centered,[54] females "inherit" home ranges from other females,[55] and the females allow only a few males to "associate" with them – and then only during the mating season.[56] Yet by Wilson's use of the word 'harem', the reader is left with the impression that males dominate females in that society.

Significantly, Wilson regards the hamadryas baboon society a model of ultimate development (of heterosexualism) in higher vertebrates.[57] He describes threatened and attacked females as "consorts" who have been "recruited"; and if they escape, according to him they have "strayed." Elsewhere in the book Wilson labels the initial stages of this threatening male behavior "mothering."[58]

Perhaps Wilson's most revealing judgment emerges as he interchanges the phrase "female *receptive* posture" with the phrase "female *submissive* posture."[59] Through this equation, he implies that by merely engaging in heterosex, females are dominated by males. Wilson describes females who do not engage in heterosex as "maiden aunts," or as "antisocial" if they try to escape (as did the anubis female baboons which, in an experiment, scientists put into a hamadryas society). Since females having sex with males is "natural," it logically follows that male domination is "natural." In short, under the existing conceptual framework, male penetration equals male domination.[60]

Yet if we stop to reflect, it becomes clear that within the confines of the feminine stereotype no behavior *counts* as resistance to male domination. And if nothing we can point to or even imagine counts as proof against the claim that all (normal) women are feminine and accept male domination, then we are working within a closed, coercive conceptual system.

For example, some acts which men claim support the feminine stereotype of white middle-class women indicate, instead, resistance. Alix Kates Shulman in *Memoirs of an Ex-Prom Queen* portrays a "fluffy-headed" housewife who regularly burns the dinner when her husband brings his boss home unexpectedly, and who periodically packs raw eggs in his lunch box.[61] Such acts are used by those in power as proof that women have lesser rational ability, but actually they indicate resistance—sabotage. Such acts may or may not be openly called sabotage by the saboteurs, but women engage in them as an affirmation of existence in a society which denies a woman recognition independently of a man.

Donna Deitch's documentary *Woman to Woman* offers a classic example of what I am calling sabotage.[62] Four females—two housewives, a daughter, and the interviewer—sit around a kitchen table. One housewife protests that she is not a housewife, she is not married to the house. The interviewer asks her to describe what she does all day. The woman relates something like the following: she gets up, feeds her husband, feeds her children, drives them to the school bus, drives her husband to work, returns to do the dishes, makes the beds, goes out to do the shopping, returns to do a wash. The woman continues listing her activities, then stops, shocked, and says: "Wait a minute, I *am* married to the house." She complains of difficulty in getting her husband to give her enough money for the household, of frustration because he nevertheless holds her responsible for running the house, and of degradation because she must go to him, apologetically, at the end of each budget period to ask for extra money to cover expenses when he could have provided her with sufficient funds from the beginning.

Suddenly she gets a gleam in her eye, lowers her voice, and leans forward, saying: "Have you ever bought something you don't need?" She explains that she buys cans of beans and hoards them. Then she says: "You have to know you're alive; you have to make sure you exist."[63] She has separated herself from her husband's perceptions of her: she is not simply an extension of his will, she is reclaiming (some) agency—sabotage. Yet under the feminine stereotype, we are unable to perceive her as in any way resisting her husband's domination.[q]

---

q   There have been many unacknowledged forms of resistance to male domination, for ex-

Significantly, 'femininity' is a concept used to characterize any group which men in power wish to portray as requiring domination. Kate Millett points out that 'femininity' characterizes traits those in power cherish in subordinates.[66] And Naomi Weisstein notes that feminine characteristics add up to characteristics stereotypically attributed to minority groups.[67] The literature indicates that nazis characterized jews as feminine, using the ideology in justification of their massacre. Men accused at the salem witch trials were characterized as feminine.[68] Mary Daly notes that the iroquois were "cast into a feminine role by the jesuits."[69] An investigation of anthropological literature from the first part of this century reveals that white british anthropologists described the physiological characteristics of black africans—men and women—in a bestially feminine manner. And as Kate Millett points out, Jean Genet's definition of 'femininity' in male homosexuality is "submission to the imperious male."[70]

The concept of 'femininity' provides a basic model for oppression in anglo-european thinking.[r] A feminine being is by nature passive and de-

---

ample, the use of purity to control male sexual aggression[64] as well as the use of piety to challenge a husband's authority. Further, many women entered convents to avoid marriage.[65] Typically, patrihistorians describe such strategies in ways that make it impossible to perceive them as resistance.

r   In pointing out how the concept of 'femininity' applies to various oppressed peoples, I do not mean to suggest that the *experience* of oppression is the same. The experience of black men or the experience of jewish men has not been the same as that of poor white gentile women or black women or jewish women or wives of southern plantation owners. Black male slaves were depicted as strong, virile beasts. If wives of southern plantation owners were also perceived as animals (pets), still there were crucial differences. And black slave women were treated as the opposite of the white southern belle. As Angela Davis points out, black women slaves were treated essentially as beasts of burden. Most worked in the fields, and some worked as coalminers or lumberjacks or ditchdiggers. And while white masters raped them in a show of economic and sexual mastery, black women were compelled to work while pregnant and nursing, and their children were treated like the offspring of animals—to be sold off.[71] Or again, poor white southern women and wives of plantation owners had significantly different experiences. My point is that the concept of 'femininity' operates to depict those who are dominated as dependent, incapable of caring for themselves—whether virile or otherwise—and as virtuous when subservient.

Bell Hooks challenges the theory that black men were emasculated by slavery on the grounds (1) that the black man's masculinity was almost reified, (2) that such a theory presupposes a classist assumption about black men getting their identities as breadwinners, and (3) that if emasculinization was an effect of slavery, then it would follow that black women were not affected—such a characterization renders women imperceptible. For example, if 'emasculinization' means 'dehumanization', then it implies that women are not human. Further, if the effect of slavery on black men was emasculinization, then the obvious solution is for black men to reclaim their masculinity, which means, among other things, an ability to dominate women.[72]

pendent. It follows that those to whom the label is applied must by their very nature seek protection (domination) and should be subjected to authority "for their own good." 'Femininity' portrays those not in power as needing and wanting to be controlled. It is a matter of logic, then, that those who refuse to be controlled are abnormal.

Consider the fact that white history depicts black slaves (though not white indentured servants) as lazy, docile, and clumsy on grounds such as that slaves frequently broke tools. Yet a rational woman under slavery, comprehending that her situation is less than human, that she functions as an extension of the will of the master, will not run to pick up tools. She acts instead to differentiate herself from the will of her master: she breaks tools, carries on subversive activities – sabotage. Her master, in turn, perceiving her as subhuman and subrational, names her "clumsy," "childlike," "foolish" perhaps, but not a saboteur. Some sabotage was detected and punished, for example, when slave women poisoned masters or committed arson. However records of such events were often buried,[73] and the stereotype of slaves as incompetent persists. Perhaps most powerful was the use of spirituals to keep present the idea of escape, songs such as "Swing Low, Sweet Chariot" or songs about Moses and the promised land. They also announced particular escape plans such as the departure of Harriet Tubman on yet another trip to the north. Whites perceived the happy song of simple-minded folk.[74]

If officially slaves are subhuman and content with their lot and masters are acting in slaves' best interests, then it follows that any resistance to the system is an abnormality or an indication of madness. Indeed, in recollecting the stories of her grandmother's slave days, Annie Mae Hunt tells us that "if you run off, you was considered sick."[75] That is to say, slaves existed in a conceptual framework where running away from slavery was generally perceived by masters and even at times by slaves as an indication, not of (healthy) resistance, but of mental imbalance.

Such was the extent of the coercion of the masters' framework. However, creating a different value framework, we can understand the be-

---

However, while the physical prowess of black slave men was played up, still, black slave men were dominated, which to men means being made like females. In heterosexual terms, to dominate is to feminize. That is why the concept of 'femininity' is bankrupt. Thus while I agree with Bell Hooks's analysis, I would still argue that the concept of the 'feminine' applies to black male slaves. Whites treated black men as beast-like, hence as something to be tamed or conquered, and hence as a feminine object. This is the contradiction in the stereotype of the black male slave. And those who stood up and resisted, both men and women, challenged the feminine stereotype. Unfortunately, some black and some jewish men and some chinese and native american men are currently emerging from under the domination of 'femininity' by laying claim to 'masculinity'.

haviors of slaves, out of which the masters constructed and fed the slave stereotypes, as providing ample evidence of resistance and sabotage.[76]

During the holocaust and, more significantly, after it, in the telling of the stories, patrihistorians have depicted jews under nazi domination as cooperative and willing (feminine) victims. This stereotype – as is true of the slave stereotype – is still alive today. Yet again, we can ask: What would *count* as resistance? For example, jews at auschwitz who committed suicide by hurling themselves against an electric fence have been depicted as willing victims. But the nazis did not leave their bodies for all to see, they quickly took them away. In determining the time of their own deaths, those who committed suicide were resisting nazi domination by exercising choice, interrupting the plans of the masters, and thus differentiating their selves from the will of their masters.

Many, many types of resistance occurred. From Simone Wallace, Ellen Ledley, and Paula Tobin:

> Each act of staying alive when the enemy has decided you must die is an act of resistance. The fight against a helplessness and apathy which aids the enemy is resistance. [Other acts include]: sabotage in the factories, encouraging others to live who are ready to give in and die, smuggling food and messages, breaking prison rules whenever possible, simply keeping themselves alive. Other forms of resistance, even more readily recognizable as such, took place from the killing of guards, bombing of factories, stealing guns, Warsaw uprisings, etc.[77]

Literature about the holocaust is full of jewish resistance, of sabotage; yet for the most part, short of armed uprisings such as happened in the warsaw ghetto, that resistance is not recognized or not acknowledged, and the stereotype of the willing (feminine) victim persists.

If we operate in a conceptual framework which depicts humans as inherently dominant or subordinate, then we will not perceive resistance or include it in our descriptions of the world unless those who resist overthrow those who dominate and begin to dominate them (i.e., when there is essentially no revolution in value). For example, the strategies of the women at greenham common, in resisting the deployment of u.s. cruise missiles, involve innovative means of thwarting the dominant/subordinate relationship – the women simply don't play by the rules and instead do the unexpected. Their strategies are characterized by spontaneity, flexibility, decentralization, and they work creatively with the situations that present themselves.[78] When we recognize as resistance only those acts which overthrow the dominators, we miss a great deal of information.

Consider the white upper-class victorian lady. In *The Yellow Wall-*

paper, Charlotte Perkins Gilman portrays conditions faced by such women in the 1880s.[79] These conditions included a prescription of total female passivity by mind gynecologists such as S. Weir Mitchell,[80] prescriptions resulting from male scientists' sudden interest in women as the first wave of feminism attracted their attention, prescriptions enforced by those in control. The heroine is taken by her husband to a summer home for rest. He locks her in a nursery with bars on the windows, a bed bolted to the floor, and hideous wallpaper, shredded in spots. He rebuts her despair with the rhetoric of protection, refusing to indulge her "whims" when she protests the room's atrocity. He also stifles all her attempts at creativity, flying into a rage when he discovers that she has been writing in her diary. In the end she manages to crawl behind the wallpaper, escaping into "madness." Charlotte Perkins Gilman shows us a woman with every avenue of creativity and integrity patronizingly and paternalistically cut off "for her own good"; and we watch her slowly construct her resistance. Not surprisingly, male scientists and doctors of the day perceived nothing more in the story than a testament of feminine insanity.[81]

Resistance, in other words, may even take the form of insanity when someone is isolated within the confines of domination and all means of maintaining integrity have been systematically cut off. Mary's journey into oblivion with morphine in *Long Day's Journey into Night* is another example of resistance to domination, to the fatuous demands of loved ones, of husband and adult male children.[82] But the framework of 'femininity' dictates that such behavior be perceived as part of the "mysterious" nature of woman rather than recognized as resistance.

Significantly, one and the same word names 'insanity' and 'anger': 'mad'. As Phyllis Chesler documents, mind gynecologists call women "mad" whose behavior they can no longer understand as functioning in relation to men.[83] On the other hand, 'madness' in relation to 'anger' is defined as "ungovernable rage or fury."[84] We can ask, ungovernable by whom? Madness in anger and madness in insanity indicate that men have lost control.[s] When women are labeled "mad," they have become useless to men, a threat to male supremacy.

Thus, to maintain the feminine stereotype, men will characterize

---

s   When reading between the lines and reclaiming women from the past, we can examine the alternatives available to them and in that context understand their behavior. Thus, insanity itself can be a form of resistance, as can suicide. On the other hand, behavior that is not insanity may nevertheless be depicted as insane. As a result, there is a fine line, which can fade at times, between insanity as resistance and the behavior of the resistor who has not gone insane—who has maintained the confidence of her perceptions.

overt, clear-cut, obvious forms of resistance as insanity when women engage in them.[t] Just as slaves who ran away from masters were perceived as insane, so are women who fight back against battering husbands. Women who kill long-term battering husbands are, for the most part, forced to use the plea of insanity rather than the plea of self-defense: lawyers advise clients to plead insanity, and juries convict those who instead plead self-defense. As a result, the judicial system promotes the idea that the woman who effectively resists aggressive acts of male domination is insane. Insanity, thus, becomes part of women's nature, and resistance to domination becomes institutionally nonexistent.

However, institutionally characterizing women who fight back as insane is still not enough for men in power. Perceiving the plea of insanity as a license to kill, even though it means incarceration for an unspecified amount of time, media men began a campaign against women who fought back against husbands and boyfriends who beat them—depicting these women as "getting away with" murder.[86] Our governing fathers have reduced or, in some places, completely withdrawn funding of shelters for women, especially if there is lesbian presence, on the grounds that these shelters break up the family. And agencies on "domestic violence" work to keep the family intact, burying the conditions of oppression women face within the nuclear and extended family by obliterating the distinction between aggressor and victim.[87] The concept of 'femininity' not only blocks social perception of female resistance. When female resistance threatens to break through the stereotype and become socially perceptible, the conceptual framework comes full circle: authorities deny that the "problem" is the result of male domination.

Finally, many social scientists regard female competence itself in women as threatening to men, as subversive to the nuclear or extended family, and as going against the grain of civilization, hence as socially undesirable. For example, the moynihan report yielded a resurgence of white as well as black men espousing the theory of the black matriarch who "castrates" black men—implying that for black men to claim their manhood, or masculinity, black women must step behind and become subordinate to them.[88]

---

t   In 1916, a play by Susan Glaspell was first performed about a nebraska woman who strangled her husband in his sleep. The (male) authorities arrive on the scene all officious and yet cannot discover the motive—without which they cannot convict her. Their wives, having come along to get some clothes for the woman in jail, discover a number of things, including the body of a canary whose neck had been wrung. Joking about women's work, the men ignore the women, thinking them dealing with "trifles." Comprehending what had happened, the women hide the evidence; the woman who killed her husband is found innocent by a "jury of her peers."[85]

'Femininity' functions as a standard of heterosexualism. Standards or measures determine fact and are used to create (and later discover) fact; they themselves, however, are not discovered. An inch, for example, was not discovered. It was created and is used to determine boundaries. No amount of investigation into surfaces will ever confirm or disprove that inches exist or that inches accurately reflect the world. A standard is a way of measuring the world, of categorizing it, of determining its boundaries so men can act upon it. 'Femininity' is such a standard: it is a way of categorizing the world so that men can act upon it, and women can respond.

'Femininity' is a label whereby one group of people are defined in relation to another in such a way that the values of dominance and subordination are embedded in perceptual judgment of reality as if they were the essence of those involved. Under the feminine characterization, women appear naively content with being controlled to such an extent that resistance to domination ceases to exist—that is, goes undetected. Female resistance is rendered imperceptible or perceived as abnormal, mad, or of no significance by both women and men.

Sabotage as self-defeating

Now, some might object that (some of) the choices I've described as resistance or sabotage are self-defeating. For example, the housewife who spends money on items she does not need is limiting her ability to obtain things she does need. Thus, through this act of defiance she is really hurting herself. Or, the woman who burns dinners when her husband brings his boss home unexpectedly is still dependent on her husband having a job and would benefit from any promotion he might receive. If she fails to present herself as a competent hostess, the boss may decide against promoting her husband, noting that her husband does not have the trappings necessary for the social atmosphere within which business deals are made—namely, a charming wife and competent hostess. Thus, in sabotaging her husband's plans when he is inconsiderate, she appears to be acting against her own best interests.

Or, again, the slave who breaks her master's tools could find herself in even more dire circumstances. Although she is slowing the master's work, she will likely be punished for it. And should she appear too incompetent (unruly), she could be sold to someone perhaps more physically brutal, separated from those who know and care about her. Her sabotage seems to do more damage to herself than to anyone else. Someone might object that a woman making these choices may be resisting, but ultimately she is "cutting off her nose to spite her face." The woman who becomes an addict or an alcoholic or the woman who chooses suicide . . . surely their acts are self-defeating, for the women lose themselves.

In a certain respect such acts of sabotage are self-defeating, but in other respects this is inaccurate. I have suggested that in situations in which a woman makes such choices, often she acts to differentiate herself from the will of the one who dominates. The one who dominates may be able to severely restrict the range of her choices, he may physically threaten her, he may have legal power of life and death over her. But it is yet another matter for him to totally control her, to make her believe she is nothing but an extension of his will.

My thesis is that when someone is in danger of losing any sense that she has a self about whom she can make decisions, she will in some way resist. When a man regards a woman as a being whose will should effectively be merged with his such that she is a mere extension of it, she will act in basic ways to block that merger and separate herself from his will. In such circumstances sabotage cannot logically be self-defeating because, simply, the situation allows for no self to begin with.

Acts of sabotage can function to establish that self, to affirm a woman's separateness in her own mind. It may be more important to the woman who burns dinners to remind her self (and maybe her husband) that he cannot take her for granted than it is for her to rise socially and economically if that means that in doing so she will be taken for granted to an even greater extent. And it may be more important to the slave that she affirm her existence by thwarting the master's plan in some way than it is to try to secure safety in a situation in which believing she is safe is dangerously foolish. Even when a woman withdraws herself through alcohol or takes herself out still further through suicide, she may be establishing, rather than defeating, the self as a separate and distinct entity.[u] If a woman establishes her self as separate (at least in her own awareness) from the will of him who dominates by making certain decisions and carrying them out, then those choices are not self-defeating, since without them there would be no self to defeat.

In other respects, however, such actions *are* self-defeating. In the first place, to be successful, acts of sabotage cannot be detected as sabotage in a system where there is no hope of redress. While they may function to differentiate one's self from those who dominate, they do not challenge the feminine stereotype, rather they presuppose it. Even when engaged in by a majority of women, isolated and individual acts of sabotage do not change the conceptual or material conditions which lead a woman to engage in such acts. Instead, those in power will use such actions to bolster the idea that dominated beings require domination (protection) "for their

---

u   Thus alcoholism among lesbians has been a way of pursuing lesbian choices while rejecting the coercion of heterosexualism and the concept of 'woman'.

own good." In this respect, then, acts of sabotage could be said to be self-defeating. But then the same could be said of any act a woman engages in. This is the trap of oppression,[89] the double bind of heterosexualism.

More significantly, acts of sabotage become self-defeating if the one who engages in them begins to internalize the feminine stereotype. For example, the woman who hoards beans may be resisting her husband's tyranny over the family budget, resisting his perception of her as merely existing to carry out his plans. But if he regards control of her budget as part of his god-given right – no, duty – as a man, then any resistance from her will have to be nipped in the bud, and if it recurs, severely dealt with. Now, in wasting household money, she may be affirming her self while not wishing to openly challenge his perceptions and bring his wrath upon her. But if she must attend too closely to his perceptions and encourage them, she may cross over and come to believe she is incompetent. And at this point her acts become self-defeating.

Or, the woman who "accidentally" burns dinners when her husband's boss comes in unexpectedly may be resisting her husband's vacuous perception of her. If his taking her for granted is a result of his sense of order in the universe such that she is simply not the sort of being who could have any say in things, then trying to prove otherwise may be fruitless. Instead, her goal may be to resist his psychological coercion by playing with his mind, acting the fluffy-headed housewife in order to thwart his expectations of her.

In this case the woman is using the traditional feminine stereotype to her (momentary) advantage. But in so doing, she may undermine her sense of self (unless she has an extremely strong capacity to maintain the sense of what she is doing in direct opposition to the entire set of values within which she must function). The stakes involved here are high – just as when a woman uses stereotypic feminine behaviors to get what she wants and make herself feel superior to the men she manipulates. She is in serious danger of internalizing the social perception of her self as 'feminine'. And should she internalize that value, her acts do become self-defeating.

A woman acting in isolation to maintain a sense of self under heterosexualism faces significant obstacles, for her choices have repercussions beyond an individual level. Again, while such acts of sabotage may be resistance, they don't effect change. For resistance to effect change, there must be a movement afoot, a conspiracy, a breathing together. And this brings up a third way acts of sabotage can be self-defeating. Since successful acts of sabotage cannot be detected as sabotage by those who dominate, then when there is a movement afoot, the choice to commit acts of sabotage becomes no different than the choice to participate in the dominance/subordination relationship of heterosexualism by embracing and developing feminine wiles.

That is, during times when a movement is afoot, when there is a conspiracy of voices, those women who choose to remain isolated from other women and yet engage in acts of sabotage when necessary may well be engaging in truly self-defeating behavior. They are bypassing a chance for more effective resistance and are in even greater danger of internalizing the values of heterosexualism. In this way, isolated acts of resistance can be self-defeating.

'Femininity' is a concept which goes a long way in the social construction of heterosexual reality. A movement of women could withdraw from *A movement of* that framework and begin to revalue that reality and women's choices *women* within it. A movement of women can challenge the feminine stereotype, dis-cover women's resistance, and provide a base for more effective resistance. A movement of women can challenge the consensus that made the individual act of sabotage plausible.

Yet if that movement does not challenge the concept of 'femininity', ultimately it will not challenge the consensus, it will not challenge the dominance and subordination of heterosexualism. For example, radical feminists and revolutionary feminists in england criticize the women's work at greenham common for appealing too much to traditional feminine stereotypes, including woman as nurturer and peacemaker as well as sacrificer for her children. As a result, they argue, the peace movement coopts feminism.[90]

Further, feminism itself is in danger of perpetuating the value of 'femininity' in interpreting and evaluating individual women's choices. Feminists continue to note how women are victims of institutional and ordinary behavior, but many have ceased to challenge the concept of 'woman' and the role men and male institutions play as "protectors" of women. And feminism is susceptible to what Kathleen Barry calls 'victimism', which in effect portrays women as helpless and in need of protection.[91]

So much of our moral and political judgment involves either blaming the victim[92] or victimism. Victimism is the perception of victims of ack- *Blaming the victim* nowledged social injustice, not as real persons making choices, but in- *and victimism* stead as passive objects of injustice. Kathleen Barry explains that in order to call attention to male violence and to prove that women are harmed by rape, feminists have portrayed women who have been raped by men as victims pure and simple — an understandable development. The problem is that

the status of "victim" creates a mind set eliciting pity and sorrow. Victimism denies the woman the integrity of her humanity through the whole experience, and it creates a framework for others to know her not as a person but as a victim, someone to whom violence was done. . . . Victimism is an objectification which establishes new standards for defining experience; those standards dismiss any question of will, and deny that the woman even while enduring sexual violence is a living, changing, growing, interactive person.[93]

For my purposes, blaming the victim involves holding a person accountable not only for her choice in a situation but for the situation itself, as if she agreed to it. Thus in masculinist thought, a woman will be judged responsible for her own rape. Victimism, on the other hand, completely ignores a woman's choices. In other words, victimism denies a woman's moral agency. Under victimism, women are still passive, helpless, and in need of special protection – still feminine.

A movement which challenges the dominant valuation of women will focus on women as agents in a relationship rather than as a type. A woman is not a passive being to whom things unfortunately or intentionally happen. She is a breathing, judging being, acting in coerced and oppressive circumstances. Her judgments and choices may be ineffective on any given occasion, or wrong, but they are decisions nevertheless. She is an agent and she is making choices. More than a victim, Kathleen Barry suggests, a woman caught in female sexual slavery is a survivor, making crucial decisions about what to do in order to survive. She is a moral agent who makes judgments within a context of oppression in consideration of her own needs and abilities.

Survival choices   By perceiving women's behavior, not through the value of 'femininity', but rather as actions of moral agents making judgments about their own needs and abilities in coerced and oppressive circumstances, we can begin to conceive of ourselves and each other as agents of our actions (though not creators of the circumstances we face under oppression). And this is a step toward realizing an ethical existence under oppression, one not caught up with the values of dominance and subordination.

Further, we can also begin to understand women's choices which actually embrace the feminine stereotype. Some women embrace 'femininity' outright, man-made though it is, or embrace particular aspects of it which involve some form of ritual or actual subordination to men, in the pursuit of what these women judge to be their own best interests. Some women embrace 'femininity' in a desperate attempt to find safety and to give some meaning to their existence.

In the first chapter of *Right-Wing Women,* Andrea Dworkin analyzes the choices of some white christian women, arguing that "from father's house to husband's house to a grave that still might not be her own, a woman acquiesces to male authority in order to gain some protection from male violence."[94] She argues that such acquiescence results from the treatment girls and women receive as part of their socialization:

> Rebellion can rarely survive the aversion therapy that passes for being brought up female. Male violence acts directly on the girl through her father or brother or uncle or any number of male professionals or strangers, as it did and does on her mother, and she too is forced to learn to conform in order to survive. A girl may, as she enters adulthood, repudiate the particular set of males with whom her mother is allied, run with a different pack as it were, but she will replicate her mother's patterns in acquiescing to male authority within her own chosen set. Using both force and threat, men in all camps demand that women accept abuse in silence and shame, tie themselves to hearth and home with rope made of self-blame, unspoken rage, grief, and resentment.[95]

Andrea Dworkin also argues that some women continue to submit to male authority because they finally believe it is the only way they can make sense of and give meaning to their otherwise apparently meaningless existence as women.[96] They find meaning through being bound to their protectors and having a common enemy. Their anger is thus given form and a safety valve, and is thereby deflected from its logical target. They become antisemites, queer-haters, and racists, and so create purpose in their existence.

Andrea Dworkin's analysis highlights two points of interest here. First, these women have the same information that radical feminists have (they know what men do), yet they are making different choices. Secondly, their choices stem from judgments they make about their own best interests. That is, they are choosing what they consider their best option from among those available. These are survival choices made in circumstances with restricted options.

Another group of women embrace 'femininity' from a different direction. In discussing why more black women are not involved in activist women's groups, instead considering themselves "Black first, female second" and embracing a version of the feminine ideal, Brunetta R. Wolfman presents a number of factors. She points to the traditionally greater independence black women enjoy from black men in the united states, since the legal end of slavery, than white women have enjoyed from white men. And she points to the commitment of women to the black church, in terms of time and loyalty, whereby a "scrub woman or maid could aspire to be the head of the usher board and a valuable, respected member of the congregation."[97]

However, she notes that the pattern in the black church here as well as in civil rights groups such as the n.a.a.c.p. or the urban league, has been one of women assuming secondary roles in deference to male leadership.

She also points to the romantic sense of nobility, purity, and race pride personified in the stereotype of 'the black woman' and promulgated by nationalistic ideologies such as that of Marcus Garvey or the black muslims:

> The Muslims have taken the idealized Euro-American image of the middle-class wife and mother and made it the norm for the sect so that the women members must reject the traditional independence of black women, adopting another style in the name of a separatist religious ideology. In return, Muslim men must respect and protect their women, a necessary complement to demands placed on females.[98]

This point is reiterated by Jacquelyn Grant as she argues:

> It is often said that women are the "backbone" of the church. . . . It has become apparent to me that most of the ministers who use this term are referring to location rather than function. What they really mean is that women are in the background and should be kept there: they are merely support workers.[99]

Brunetta R. Wolfman goes on to discuss demands placed on black women by the black community as well as community expectation of a subordinate position for women. For example, she points out that women in the movement '60s were expected to keep black men from involving themselves with white women. She argues that this "duty is in keeping with a traditional feminine role, that of modifying or being responsible for the behavior of the group in general and the males in particular."[100] Further, she points out how feminist values such as control of one's own body were undermined as black (and white) men told black women there was no choice but to bear children in order to counterattack the white racist plan of black genocide being carried out through birth control programs.

While noting that the women's liberation movement included many demands that would help the social and economic position of black women, Brunetta R. Wolfman suggests that (many) black women have not responded to it, instead becoming a conservative force in the black community, partly because they have a strong sense of self as contributor to the survival of the black community and partly because they have been identified by american society as the polar opposite of the feminine ideal.[101] That is, since they have been excluded from the feminine ideal, they now embrace it.[v]

---

v   Other women have not involved themselves in the women's movement or have withdrawn from it because of racism among white women. My focus here is on women who embrace an ideal of feminine behavior in lieu of resistance to male domination.

The jeopardy of racial genocide stemming from an external enemy and used to justify the ideology of male domination is real for u.s. black and other women of color in a way that it is not for u.s. right-wing christian white women. Nevertheless, the choice of embracing 'femininity' and male authority is similar in both cases, as is the threat members of each group face from men.

Further, such choices are not qualitatively different from choices made by feminists to defer to men and men's agendas and to soothe male egos in the pursuit of women's rights. (And such choices do not preclude acts of sabotage of the sort I've discussed when male domination encroaches too far upon a woman's sense of self.) They are survival choices. And what we can consider from outside the feminine valuation is whether such choices in the long run are self-enhancing or self-defeating.

The answers are varied and complex. But insofar as they lean toward the idea that embracing 'femininity' is not self-defeating, they also per-petuate what it means to be a 'woman': to be a 'woman' is to be subject to male domination and hence to be someone who enacts her agency through manipulation—exercising (some modicum of) control from a position of subordination. Should she act in any other way, she is, under hetero-sexualism, not only unnatural but also unethical.

Thus, while promoting an ethic for females, heterosexualism is a set of values which undermines female agency outside the master/slave values. Women hang on to those values out of fear, out of a choice to focus on men while taking women for granted, and out of a lack of perception of any other choices. As a result, although many women individually have resisted male domination—in particular, men's attempts to make women mere extensions of men's will—it is less clear that (with a few notable ex-ceptions), as Simone de Beauvoir suggested, women as a group dispute male sovereignty. However, in claiming this, I am not suggesting that disputing male sovereignty means attempting to oppose men as men have opposed women.ʷ Rather, I am suggesting that it seems, for the most

---

w   Even what the amazons from between the black and caspian seas are reputed to have done was not a matter of opposing men as men have opposed women. At various times, some worry that women or lesbians or separatists want to do to men what men have done to women. Yet nowhere have I found any indication of women or lesbians wanting to subject men the way men have subjected women: have men de-skilled and dependent on women, have men find their identity through their relationships with women, have men isolated in women's houses waiting to care-take women, and so on. Mostly, I suspect, women and les-bians don't want the burden. Women's resistance to male domination has taken many forms. But in my understanding, it has never, even in fantasy, been a reversal of men's efforts.

part, that women, whether as saboteurs or acceptors of male domination, have not disputed the entire dominance/subordination game of heterosexualism.

I want a moral revolution.

Separation

SIGNIFICANTLY, JUST AS traditional ethics does not recognize moral revolution, so it does not acknowledge separation as an option for moral agents. Withdrawal or separation is not perceived as an option when the game played appears to be the only game in town and so is taken for reality. In a sense the game is reality, but its continued existence is not a matter of fact so much as a matter of agreement. The game is an agreement in value which players breathe life into. And this suggests that participation in the system at some level – support, reform, rebellion – must be an unquestioned norm and hence not itself perceived as a choice.[x]

Consider, again, that shelters for women who have been beaten by their husbands lose funding if shelter workers are suspected of encouraging those seeking refuge to withdraw or separate from the particular batterer or from marriage or from heterosexuality in general. Ethical considerations forced on most women whom men beat involve how to maintain the family unit, how to work with their husband's problems, how to restore his "dignity," how to help the children adjust – in short, how to go on as a (heterosexual) woman. Such judgments hold in place the feminine, in this case feminine virtue, and the function of such judgments is not to encourage the integrity of the individual in her choices. It is rather to maintain the social order and specific relationships and avenues of hierarchy within it.

I want to suggest that it is crucial to acknowledge withdrawal, separatism, as an option if we are to engage in moral revolution. Separation is a central option both as a political strategy and as a consideration in individual relationships. We may withdraw from a particular situation when it threatens to dissolve into a relationship of dominance and sub-

---

x   I do not mean to suggest that governments have not forced people into other options, for example, emigration from oppressive conditions or exile. But this has occurred precisely because such people have been considered not part of the moral community. Nor do I mean to suggest there have been no separatists. There have been many, many different groups of separatists. What I am suggesting in this section is that the tradition tends not to recognize separation as a choice among those considered moral agents because it cannot afford to acknowledge that participation is a choice.

ordination. And we may withdraw from a system of dominance and subordination in order to engage in moral revolution.

To withdraw from a system, a conceptual framework, or a particular situation is to refuse to act according to its rules. A system can only function if there are participants. A king can direct his domain only if most everyone else acknowledges him as king, if the couriers carry his messages.[102] If the messengers dump their messages and go on to something else, not only is the king's communication interrupted, so is his status, for the couriers are no longer focused on him and are therefore declaring themselves no longer couriers. If enough couriers lay down their messages, the king will not be able to amass sufficient power to force those messengers to again focus on him. *Refusing to play by the rules*

When we separate, when we withdraw from someone's game plan, the game becomes meaningless, at least to some extent, ceasing to exist for lack of acknowledgment. Of course if a tree falls in the forest, there are sound waves, whether or not there are human or other animal ears, or whether there are any other sorts of mechanisms in addition to the king's own ears to detect them. But if the listeners, the messengers, have withdrawn, then the sound waves can't be translated or even acknowledged. Thus the messages of the king in a certain respect make no sense, and in a certain respect have ceased to exist. So has the king . . . as a king.

Separation is a legitimate moral and political choice. (I mean by saying it is legitimate that it has a political and moral function.) That is, to engage in a situation or a system in order to try to change it is one choice. To withdraw from it, particularly in order to render it meaningless, is another choice. Within a given situation or at a given moment there are often good reasons for either choice. Further, both choices involve considerable risk; neither one comes with guarantees: while directly challenging something can validate it, withdrawing may allow it to continue essentially unhampered.

What is significant to me is that the choice to separate is not *acknowledged* as a legitimate ethical choice. There are considerable prohibitions in all quarters against withdrawal. Depending on various factors, including the location within the power hierarchy of the perceiver, the choice to withdraw is judged to be (a) functionally equivalent to collaborating with the enemy, (b) cowardly hiding from the situation and foolishly hoping it will go away, (c) an indication of dull-wittedness or an admission of defeat, (d) a refusal to be politically responsible, or (e) a denial of reality, indicating insanity. *Separation is not acknowledged*

For example, during a war—that is, a struggle over who will dominate—those in power regard draft dodgers and even conscientious objectors not as moral challengers but as immoral quitters, not significantly different from those who collaborate with the enemy. In time of war this moral equation is drawn because, to be successful, those who wage war must have grand-scale cooperation in order to defeat the enemy. And when social organization must be very tight, those who dissent and withdraw are perceived as no different from those who attack. (To some degree, this is an accurate perception.)

Those who withdraw may be perceived by their peers as cowardly hiding from the situation and hoping it will go away or as foolishly ignoring reality. For example, one who withdraws from a fight will often be considered a coward. Such labeling, of course, is an attempt to coerce participation. Alternatively, some who have opposed united states draft dodgers and conscientious objectors charge them with failing to recognize that if the enemy won, they would no longer have the right to dissent. And because of our (at least partial) withdrawal from the institution of heterosexuality, lesbians are accused of foolishly ignoring half the human race and hence of denying reality.

Certainly, there are those who believe problems will just go away. But I am concerned with the choice to withdraw as a political strategy. For example, the danes refused to cooperate with the nazi policy of identifying jews. This was a refusal to participate in the debate over who should be saved, and as a result it rendered the nazi effort at "purification" meaningless. Pacifism, too, is a withdrawal. And during world war ii, pacifists were perceived as cowards. In fact, the label 'passive resistance', itself a contradiction of terms, is an attempt to discredit the actions of those who refuse to play the games of dominance and subordination – Gandhi's strategy was hardly passive.

Political activists will often perceive withdrawing or separating as simply being politically irresponsible. For example, many will show overt hostility toward those who refuse to participate in the u.s. election process, even though they themselves are horrified by what passes for candidates, campaigning, and voting in this country. Those who refuse to vote, on the other hand, refuse to participate in the illusion. As one female nonvoter stated, "Oh, I never vote, it encourages them so."[103]

Lesbian separatists, too, are perceived as not caring about or wanting to end injustice. Separatists are often judged by liberals, socialists, and coalitionists as almost more morally reprehensible than those who control the system.[y] As a result, lesbian separatists are scapegoated.

---

y For example, it is argued in the community that separatism is racist.[104] In my opinion, that accusation has functioned to bury a form of what might be called a socialist/anarchist debate.[105]

In certain respects, to engage, to participate, in a situation or in a system is to affirm its central values. This is true whether we actively uphold   *Feminist reform* the system, attempt to change it through designated avenues of reform, or rebel against it through designated avenues of rebellion (act in ways named evil or bad within the system). For in acting in any of these capacities, we are operating within the system's parameters and are thus giving the system meaning by helping to hold its axis (what goes unquestioned) in place.

While a great deal is accomplished through reform, the change that occurs must fit within the (usually unacknowledged) parameters of the system. Thus "votes for women" was achieved only when women's suffrage was generally perceived as not altering the structure and value of patriarchal, heterosexual society. As Kate Millett points out in *Sexual Politics,* the first wave of the feminist movement failed to challenge the institution of the family, thereby ending in reform rather than revolution. She argues that without radical change in value, that which reformers found most offensive – "the economic disabilities of women, the double standard, prostitution, venereal disease, coercive marital unions and involuntary parenthood" – could not be eradicated.[106] Reform perpetuates existing value.

In the first place, feminist reform forces women to focus on men and address men's conceptions of women rather than creating and developing women's values about themselves. It forces women to focus on men's reactions and mass media stereotypes of women; it forces women to respond by means of apology to masculinist depictions of witches, manhaters, lesbians, and amazons. It forces women to prove that men's fears are unfounded – to prove that women, or "real" women, are not lesbians or manhaters. It forces women to appear feminine and prove they are not threatening. Feminist reform forces women to attend male fantasies and validate masculinist value. As a result men are invited to act out and are given even greater license to project their insecurities on women, while women must soothe and tend male egos. In other words, reform keeps women focused on finding ways of seducing men. I want a moral revolution.

Secondly, feminist reform makes the actual success of women's efforts depend on the intelligence, willingness, and benevolence of the men they're seeking to convince to enact reform. Efforts in this regard may at times gain relief for women, relief which is badly needed even if selective. But it is a relief of symptoms, not a removal of causes.[107] In this respect reform forces the reformer to restrict her imagination and efforts to the limits of those she's trying to convince. A feminist striving for change by working for reform within the dominant/subordinate framework is like a starving person seeking nourishment in junk food.

Finally, feminist reform sets up women to value change in men more highly than change in women.[z] It makes any failure a failure of effort on women's part, not a refusal on men's part. And it sets up women to fear risking any small gain they might have gotten. As a result, to avoid offending men, they promote lesbian erasure, thereby reinforcing heterosexualism.[a] This is one of the reasons some french-speaking radical lesbians insist that feminism is the last stronghold of patriarchy.[109]

Rebellion Aside from reform, there are also serious problems with rebellion, particularly when that rebellion fits the parameters of what counts as rebellion from the dominant perspective. For example, a young woman might rebel against her family by getting pregnant, or a high school student might rebel by becoming addicted to heroin. These actions, while not in conformity with what is called good in society, nevertheless support and uphold it; though they are designated as evil within the system, they are not real threats to it. Further, as I have suggested above, there are serious dangers involved in sabotage when a movement is afoot, when a group is interacting in ways which begin to challenge the consensus which made the individual act of sabotage plausible for the saboteurs.

Another form of rebellion—the male pornographic rebellion against the establishment—has been challenged by Mary Daly, Susan Griffin, Catharine A. MacKinnon, and Andrea Dworkin, each in her own way. For while pornographic sons rebel against church fathers, they nevertheless operate out of the same conceptual framework—a framework which gives rise to necrophilic hatred of the body.[110] Far from undermining the system, they infuse it with meaning. And when things get too far out of hand, protectors can target pornographers, launching a crusade to clean

---

z For example, many women's studies faculty value a male entering a women's studies class more highly than a female, take female students' presence for granted, and try to figure out how to increase male participation rather than focusing on how to get more women to investigate feminism—and more heterosexual women of color and lesbians of all colors to enroll.

a It is heterosexualism which keeps women believing that, for one reason or another, the agreement of men is necessary to women's efforts to change society. Yet whenever men are included, the goals and focus of women's projects transform into men's goals and focus. For example, once men entered Josephine Butler's campaign against the contagious diseases acts, male perceptions and values undermined the women's goals.[108] Further, I would argue that the most effective changes in black/white relations emerged from the black power movement when blacks ceased focusing on whites. While whites ultimately played a part in the change that occurred, the change did not occur as a result of blacks catering to or waiting on whites' agreement.

up our minds, all the while polluting our minds with church imagery which gives rise to pornography.

Significantly, the so-called sexual "revolution" is hardly a revolution of values but simply a reversal of certain polarities within the same value system. Thus, rather than being a "proper lady," a woman is now a "hot mama." Either way her sexual subordination to men remains unchallenged. The "sexual revolution" has displaced the women's movement in the media.

Advocates of sadomasochism also claim to be rebelling against the system, yet they are neither resisting it nor striving for change. In emulating nazi/jew or master/slave scenes, for example, sadomasochists contribute to the context which allows such institutions to flourish, thereby validating them. And rather than shock us into political awareness, as can a parody, such practices lull us into acceptance and resignation.[111]

In general, the system of the fathers designates as evil what it can tolerate and uses it as a safety valve. When things threaten to get out of hand, those in power can then scapegoat that which they designate as evil to explain why that which they designate as good — marriage, business, education, religion, medicine, for example — isn't working. And this suggests that withdrawal from and change in central values, rather than evil, are the real threats to the traditional framework of ethics and politics.

Upon examining the system, we may find we actually agree with the underlying value and structure. Alternatively, we may find we disagree significantly with it but judge that it is the best structure around or that the existing structure is better than no structure or better than the risk involved in creating a new one. We might even feel that a new structure would be preferable but that the current situation is a crisis which needs immediate relief, even though this results in incomplete solution and co-optation. After all, working to create a new value system hardly solves an immediate problem of starvation.

But what is missing from the focus of traditional ethics as well as from lesbian community ethics is acknowledgment that these choices involve agreement with the system in certain key ways, acknowledgment that such agreement is a choice, and acknowledgment that there is another choice. What is missing from traditional ethics is acknowledgment that there are ethical choices at this level, that participation is one of those choices, and that separation — at the very least from the belief system — is another.

Now beyond noting that withdrawal or separation is a crucial moral option, I want to suggest that such a choice is central to lesbian moral agency. What I am calling separation or withdrawal is not a set of rules we live up to, particularly in an attempt to be purists. It is rather a general ap-

Lesbians and separatism

proach to the world which involves various choices in various circumstances, choices which depend on various factors but which are choices from a lesbian center.

In her history and analysis of *Lavender Woman,* a chicago lesbian newspaper published between 1971 and 1976, Michal Brody offers a basic definition of separatism which, while apparently clear-cut, invited "universes of interpretation":

> The fundamental core of separation was separation of women from men. This was desirable for two basic reasons: 1) there was too much frustration and aggravation involved in trying to work or deal with men. Sexism, once perceived, became intolerable, and 2) it became urgent to understand the meaning and essence of womanhood as only we could define it for ourselves.[112]

I named myself separatist in 1976 in lincoln, nebraska, a little over a year after I came out and while teaching at the university of nebraska, as the result of a very simple statement from Julia Penelope [Stanley]. I had just returned from the second national women's music festival, where I observed Meg Christian and Holly Near defend women-only concerts and Holly Near participate in a group discussion on the issue. I was confused. They were all talking about separating from men, yet all they seemed to talk about was men. I, too, knew about men, but I didn't comprehend what the big issue was. Standing at her kitchen sink peeling potatoes, Julia said, quite simply, "Power." This made sense to me. Since that time, how and why I conceive and enact separatism has developed. What follows are those aspects of separatism I consider central to the continuing creation of lesbian community and meaning.

Separatism is, first, a way of pulling back from the existing conceptual framework, noting its patterns, and understanding their function regardless of the mythology espoused within the framework. For example, within the framework it is said that women don't resist male domination. However, by stepping out of the framework, we can detect quite another story. Separatism is a matter of deconstructing and revaluing existing perceptions and judgments.

In this way, withdrawing or separating is not the opposite of participating; rather, it is a form of engagement. While it is important for survival to stay in touch with what is going on, by becoming detached from belief in heterosexual values, we can move through the system in very different ways, noting very different things.[113]

Secondly, separatism is a way of undermining heterosexual patterns. As Marilyn Frye argues, feminist separation is

separation of various sorts or modes from men and from institutions, roles
and activities which are male-defined, male-dominated and operating for
the benefit of males and the maintenance of male privilege – this separation
being initiated or maintained, at will, *by women.*

The point of this is to undermine male parasitism:

> that it is, generally speaking, the strength, energy, inspiration and nurtur-
> ance of women that keeps men going, and not the strength, aggression,
> spirituality and hunting of men that keeps women going.[114]

Marilyn Frye goes on to argue that male parasitism means males must
have access to females, that total power is unconditional access, that the
first act of challenging this must be denying access in order to create a
power shift, and that such a denial of access is also to claim the power of
naming for oneself: "The slave who excludes the master from her hut
thereby declares herself *not a slave."*[115]

Thirdly, separatism is "paring away the layers of false selves from the
Self," as Mary Daly suggests.[116] What draws us to each other, I believe, is
a sense of female agency, a sense of inner strength. Separatism allows us
to expand our imaginations and hence our risks beyond the boundaries of
heterosexualism. It allows us an ethical option to the de-moralization that
results when we resign ourselves to the categories of the fathers and lose
each other.[117] Thus, it allows us the possibility of developing female
agency outside the master/slave virtues of heterosexualism.

Consequently, fourthly, lesbian separatism is a withdrawal from heterosexualism. Following Simone de Beauvoir's perception that we are
not born women, Monique Wittig announces that lesbians are not
women.[118] She argues:

> The refusal to become (or to remain) heterosexual always meant to refuse to
> become a man or a woman, consciously or not. For a lesbian this goes fur-
> ther than the refusal of the *role* "woman." It is the refusal of the economic,
> ideological, and political power of a man.[119]

And she concludes:

> Lesbianism is the only concept I know of which is beyond the categories of
> sex (woman and man), because the designated subject (lesbian) is *not* a
> woman, either economically, or politically, or ideologically. For what
> makes a woman is a specific social relation to a man, a relation that we have
> previously called servitude . . . a relation which implies personal and physi-
> cal obligation as well as economic obligation ("forced residence,"[120] domes-
> tic corvée, conjugal duties, unlimited production of children, etc.), a rela-
> tion which lesbians escape by refusing to become or stay heterosexual.[121]

Withdrawal or separatism is a refusal to participate in the heterosexual social construction of reality; to practice separatism is to deconstruct the dominant/subordinate relationship of men and women.

Monique Wittig goes on to argue that our task is to define oppression in materialist terms:

> to make it evident that women are a class, which is to say that the category "woman" as well as the category "man" are political and economic categories not eternal ones.[122]

She suggests that our strategy must be to

> suppress men as a class, not through a genocidal, but a political struggle. Once the class "men" disappears, "women" as a class will disappear as well, for there are no slaves without masters.[123]

Thus she does not advocate resisting male domination by trying to oppose men as men have opposed women, as Simone de Beauvoir seems to imply women must do if women are to resist male sovereignty. However, neither is her strategy a separatist one. She anticipates a struggle between men and women similar to a class struggle, a struggle in which gender categories will finally disappear, thereby ending the economic, political, and ideological order which perpetuates the dominance and subordination of heterosexualism:

> The class struggle is precisely that which resolves the contradictions between two opposed classes by abolishing them at the same time it constitutes them as classes. The class struggle between women and men, which should be undertaken by all women, is that which resolves the contradictions between the sexes, abolishing them at the same time as it makes them understood.[124]

Once this struggle breaks out, the violence of the categories (dominant/suppressed, male/female) becomes apparent, and what was considered natural differences now can be understood as material opposition.

While I agree that heterosexualism is a violent opposition between men and women, my focus is different. I agree with the goal of deconstructing heterosexualism and the categories 'man' and 'woman'. But in my opinion there can be slaves without masters, there can be women without men. Thus, even though 'lesbian' is a concept beyond the categories of sex, nevertheless we tend to embrace the existing categories both in assimilation and in resistance. More often than not, we embrace the values of dominance and subordination.

We tend to seek meaning by subordinating ourselves to a higher order or system because we seek the semblance of security in something constructed outside of us in which we can participate. Heterosexualism is such a system. In another context Marilyn Frye writes of the "mortal dread of being outside the field of vision of the arrogant eye":

> We fear that if we are not in that web of meaning there will be no meaning: our work will be meaningless, our lives of no value, our accomplishments empty, our identities illusory.[125]

My concern is involved with the sense in which it is true that there are no 'masters' without 'slaves', for in that same sense there are no 'men' without 'women'. A king cannot be king without his messengers attending him. And patriarchy cannot persist without female complicity, regardless of how that complicity is commandeered, complicity that persists as women and lesbians back away from our power to invent.[126] My concern in pursuing withdrawal or separation, both ethically and politically, involves pursuing lesbian agency outside the dominant/subordinate values of heterosexualism. To separate, withdraw, refocus, is to cease attending to the existing system. As Alice Molloy wrote:

> return no thing to evil, that is the basis of separatism. give it no energy, no time, no attention. no nourishment.[127]

The no-saying and the struggle are essential, but so is the ability to withdraw from the existing ground of meaning. If we remain riveted on their categories, we will not succeed in creating new ones.

Thus, separatism is, most importantly, a refocusing, a focusing on lesbians and a lesbian conceptual framework. Through our focus, our attention, we determine what is significant and what is not. Attending is active and creative. And by focusing on ourselves and each other as lesbians in all our diversity, we determine, not that we exist in relation to a dominant other, but rather that we can create new value, lesbian meaning. By focusing on ourselves and each other, we make lesbianism possible. In calling for withdrawal from the existing heterosexual value system, I am calling for a moral revolution.

Now, beginning with the first aspect of separatism, by withdrawing or separating from the conceptual framework of heterosexualism we can understand a number of things central to lesbian moral agency and the creation of new value. We can realize male domination persists through both predation and protection. We can realize that what it means to be a woman is a creation of the patriarchy, and that 'femininity' makes male domination appear natural. We can realize that what men call 'difference' is actually 'opposition', and that women have resisted male domination, though not necessarily by challenging heterosexualism. We can perceive women as moral agents, making choices as best they can within the

Lesbian choices

framework of heterosexualism. And we can also understand that lesbians have made other choices, choices not among the designated options. Describing her first trip to a gay bar, Judy Grahn writes:

> Nothing distinguished the Rendezvous Bar from any of the others except that its reputation among queers was that it was "ours." . . . In those days homosexuality was so closely guarded and so heavily punished that it might as well have been illegal just to gather in a bar together. . . . But the sleazy Rendezvous was where we bottom-of-the-world overt Gay people could go and be "ourselves."
>
> I went there one night with another Lesbian I had met in the service; I remember the fear I felt on the bus ride downtown. The bus passed through a dark tunnel and the driver had a black curtain wrapped around his seat. I felt I was on a journey to hell and had to laugh at my young self for undertaking such a perilous journey. There would be no turning back for me once I had entered such a place; I knew very distinctly that I had "crossed over."
>
> From the minute I entered the doors of the Rendezvous . . . and gaped in thrilled shock at the self-assured, proud Lesbians in pants and the men in makeup and sculptured, displayed, eerily beautiful faces, I saw myself as part of a group that included some very peculiar characters and characteristics. I ceased then to be a nice white Protestant girl with a tomboy nature who had once had a secret and very loving Lesbian relationship with another nice girl who was attending college to become a teacher. That definition no longer applied as I stepped into my first Gay bar to become a full-fledged dike, a more-than-a-Lesbian.[128]

The choice to act on lesbianism was a solitary one, as Audre Lorde describes:

> There were no mothers, no sisters, no heroes. We had to do it alone, like our sister Amazons, the riders on the loneliest outposts of the kingdom of Dahomey. We, young and Black and fine and gay, sweated out our first heartbreaks with no school nor office chums to share that confidence over lunch hour. Just as there were no rings to make tangible the reason for our happy secret smiles, there were no names nor reason given or shared for the tears that messed up the lab reports or the library bills.[129]

The choice was based on lives that went before, as Elana Dykewomon writes:

> These women, I think, are my true foremothers. They became strong and independent in isolation. They may seem to me all caught up in roles, they may never agree with me about what's important, what a political act it is within the state to be a lesbian, an act of defiance — nevertheless, they committed that act and gave me the courage to commit mine. I love them for it.[130]

And it was a central choice, as Caryl Bentley describes, one involving integrity:

> I think coming out is a life-long process. It consists for me of connecting feelings, ideas, and experiences to my identity as a Lesbian through naming and perhaps acting on them. In the mid-1950s, when I, like other Lesbians my age, was alone, claiming my Lesbianism meant recognizing and owning my feelings of love for one other woman. Refusing to bury and deny my feelings was a matter of integrity to me; this stubborn claiming is something I still respect myself for.[131]

But it was also not without consequences. From Beth Brant:

> The word *lesbian.* Lesbian. The word that makes them panic, makes them afraid, makes them destroy children. The word that dares them. Lesbian. *I am one.* Even for Patricia, even for her, *I will not cease to be!* As I kneel amidst the colorful scraps, Raggedy Anns smiling up at me, my chest gives a sigh. My heart slows to its normal speech. I feel the blood pumping outward to my veins, carrying nourishment and life.[132]

It was a revolutionary choice, as Cheryl Clarke notes:

> For a woman to be a lesbian in a male-supremist, capitalist, misogynist, racist, homophobic, imperialist culture, such as that of North America, is an act of resistance. . . . The lesbian has decolonized her body. She has rejected a life of servitude implicit in Western, heterosexual relationships and has accepted the potential of mutuality in a lesbian relationship—*roles* notwithstanding.[133]

Yes, these were political choices. In her essay on butch-fem relationships in the 1950s in the u.s., Joan Nestle articulates the political nature of many lesbians' choices:

> In the 1950s this courage to feel comfortable with arousing another woman became a political act.
>   Butch-fem was an erotic partnership, serving both as a conspicuous flag of rebellion and as an intimate exploration of women's sexuality.[134]

In reply to the charge that lesbians were merely copying heterosexual choices, Joan Nestle argues:

> Since at times fems dressed similarly to their butch lovers, the aping of heterosexual roles was not visually apparent, yet the sight of us was enraging. My understanding of why we angered straight spectators so is not that they saw us modeling ourselves after them, but just the opposite—that we were a symbol of women's erotic autonomy, a sexual accomplishment that did not include them. The physical attacks were a direct attempt to break into this self-sufficient, erotic partnership. The most frequently shouted taunt was:

"Which one of you is the man?" This was not a reflection of our Lesbian experience as much as it was a testimony to the lack of erotic categories in straight culture.[135]

In other words, lesbian relationships of the 1950s were a challenge to existing values. Lillian Faderman adds that

> there were in several eras and places many instances of women who were known to engage in lesbian sex, and they did so with impunity. As long as they appeared feminine, their sexual behavior would be viewed as an activity in which women indulged when men were unavailable or as an apprenticeship or appetite-whetter to heterosexual sex. But if one or both of the pair demanded masculine privileges, the illusion of lesbianism as *faute de mieux* behavior was destroyed. At the base was not the sexual aspect of lesbianism as much as the attempted usurpation of male prerogative by women who behaved like men that many societies appeared to find most disturbing.[136]

Of course, to claim the prerogative of men is not necessarily to try to become men. Judy Grahn argues that the point was not to be men but to be butch and get away with it:

> We always kept something back: a high-pitched voice, a slant of the head, or a limpness of hand gestures, something that was clearly labeled female. I believe our statement was "Here is another way of being a woman," not "Here is a woman trying to be taken for a man."[137]

Joan Nestle adds:

> The irony of social change has made a radical, sexual, political statement of the 1950s appear today as a reactionary, non-feminist experience.[138]

Nevertheless, there has been copying of heterosexual roles. Some lesbians worked to become like man and wife; some even became transsexual men. And that is to say that the choice to affirm lesbianism does not make lesbians immune to heterosexual social organization. Further, the choice to affirm lesbianism does not make lesbians immune to racism. As Audre Lorde writes:

> Being gay-girls without set roles was the one difference we allowed ourselves to see and to bind us to each other. We were not of that *other* world and we wanted to believe that, by definition, we were therefore free of that *other* world's problems of capitalism, greed, racism, classism, etc. This was not so. But we continued to visit each other and eat together, and in general, share our lives and resources, as if it were.[139]

Nor are lesbians immune to deeply internalizing heterosexual value, the value of dominance and subordination, as Julia Penelope notes:

Just as I based my own sense of power on making love to other wimmin, I perceived their willingness to let me make love to them as a "giving up" of power. When they yielded to me, surrendered themselves to me passionately, made themselves "vulnerable" to me, I became powerful. I was absorbed by the anticipatory thrills of the "chase," and my sexuality was dependent on the sexual charge I experienced when I made a new "conquest." By identifying my own sexuality with power, and making satisfaction dependent on controlling another Lesbian's body, I'd bound myself to the constant need to rekindle that "charge" over and over again. Because I saw sex as a way of empowering myself, I saw the wimmin I made love to as giving up *their* power to me, and it was never long before I had to find another "conquest." If I was "getting" power, then my lover of the moment must be "losing" power, and I would begin to disengage myself from a Lesbian I'd begun to despise because I perceived her as "powerless" and "weak." The very "femininity," the softness, that had first drawn me to her would now repulse me, and I would refuse to make love to her. My refusal, like my previous love-making, became an assertion of my "power over" her.[140]

The need to control and be controlled in relationships is central to the dominant/subordinate values of heterosexualism, and, as I will argue, it is central to the values of the anglo-european tradition of ethics.

Through all of this, I am not trying to argue that heterosexualism is the "cause" of oppression. I do mean to suggest, however, that any revolution which does not challenge it will be incomplete and will eventually revert to the values of oppression. Heterosexualism is the form of social organization through which other forms of oppression, at times more vicious forms, become credible, palatable, even desirable. Heterosexualism— that is, the balance between masculine predation upon and masculine protection of a feminine object of masculine attention—de-skills a woman, makes her emotionally, socially, and economically dependent, and allows another to dominate her "for her own good" all in the name of "love." In no other situation[b] are people expected to love, identify with, and become other to those who dominate them to the extent that women are supposed to love, identify with, and become other to men.[141]

It is heterosexualism which makes us feel that it is possible to dominate another for her own good, that one who resists such domination is abnormal or doesn't understand what is good for her, and that one who refuses to participate in dominant/subordinate relationships doesn't exist. And

The need to challenge heterosexualism

---

b   The situation of the mammy is similar. Racism and the politics of property intervened, however, to keep her from being quite so close to the master or mistress as woman is to man. Nevertheless, this did not make her situation any more palatable, and in many respects, it was worse.

once we accept all this, imperialism, colonialism, and ethnocentrism, for example, while existing all along, become more socially tolerable in liberal thought. They become less a matter of exercising overt force and more a matter of the natural function of (a) social order.

Heterosexualism is a conceptual framework within which the concept of 'moral agency' independent of the master/slave virtues cannot find fertile ground. And it combines with ethical judgments to create a value whose primary function is not the moral development of individuals but rather the preservation of a patriarchal social control. Thus I want to challenge our acceptance and use of that ethics. And I will continue, in the next chapter, by discussing the feminine virtues of altruism, self-sacrifice, and vulnerability, and how we use them to gain control in relationships.

In discussing what I call Lesbian Ethics, I do not claim that lesbians haven't made many of the choices (heterosexual) women have made or that lesbians haven't participated in the consensus of straight thinking or that lesbians have withdrawn from the value of dominance and subordination and the security of established meaning we can find therein. I am not claiming that lesbians have lived under different conceptual or material conditions. I am claiming, however, that lesbian choice holds certain possibilities. It is a matter of further choice whether we go on to develop these possibilities or whether instead we try to fit into the existing heterosexual framework in any one of a number of ways.

Thus I am claiming that the conceptual category 'lesbian' – unlike the category 'woman' – is not irretrievably tied up with dominance and subordination as norms of behavior. And I am claiming that by attending each other, we may find the possibility of ethical values appropriate to lesbian existence, values we can choose as moral agents to give meaning to our lives as lesbians. In calling for withdrawal from the existing heterosexual value system, I am calling for a moral revolution, a revolution of lesbianism.

2
The Feminine Virtues and Female Agency

IN THIS CHAPTER I want to discuss the concepts of 'altruism', 'self-sacrifice', and 'vulnerability'. I begin here because very often discussions of ethics begin here. For example, philosophers will argue that if human beings are not altruistic, then morality is not possible.

Among lesbians, more importantly, after the initial burst of this wave of the women's liberation movement, many of us began to focus on the kind of society we hoped for among womyn. We talked of learning to be more "open," and by that we meant vulnerable. And as we found our interactions were less than utopian we began to talk about the need for a feminist ethics. Those discussions often began with declarations of how (some other) lesbians were selfish, together with assertions of the importance of self-sacrifice. In other words, while fighting the fathers' politics, we began reaching for their ethical concepts to interpret and judge our interactions.

I want to suggest that when people begin to talk about the importance of altruism and self-sacrifice, it indicates they perceive an inherent conflict of interests among those involved. Such a focus represents a narrowing of ethical attention to only certain kinds of interactions. Further, to resolve the conflict of interests, those with lesser institutional power will be expected to be altruistic. In this respect, altruism and self-sacrifice are considered "feminine virtues." 'Femininity' is a concept which makes female submission to male domination seem natural and normal. As such, the "feminine virtues" function to preserve the relationship of dominance and subordination, facilitating the access of those with greater institutional power to the resources of those with lesser institutional power.

However, within a relationship of dominance and subordination, the power of control can be exercised both from a position of dominance and from a position of subordination. Within a limited range of activity, considerable manipulative power can be exercised from the feminine position. Because of male domination, over time women have developed the ascribed feminine virtues into survival skills and created of them tools for control. And this power of manipulation is the essence of female agency promoted under heterosexualism.

When lesbians use these virtues among each other, we wind up using our survival skills against each other; thus our survival skills go awry. I want to suggest that the feminine virtues are a means of exercising control in relationships – whether as lovers, friends, or collective members – and that as a result they function to interrupt rather than promote lesbian connection.

Egoism and Altruism

Altruism as the prerequisite of ethics

OFTEN WHEN SOMEONE approaches the question of ethics and moral possibility, she will begin by asking whether people are naturally selfish or whether they are capable of thinking of others. The idea is that a person is unscrupulous and immoral if the only one she cares about is herself. Philosophers, too, seem drawn to this question, suggesting that if selfishness is part of human nature or if people aren't naturally altruistic, then ethics is impossible.[1] The philosophical question of altruism concerns whether "men could choose to act for the interests of others, even to their own personal harm."[2] The idea seems to be that unselfish thinking of others, or altruism, is a prerequisite for moral behavior.[a]

I find it significant that the possibility of ethics rests with altruism rather than self-awareness or self-understanding. For many professional philosophers as well as those not schooled in the tradition, the possibility

a Some philosophers will talk of impartiality rather than altruism. Nevertheless, in the long run, such a focus includes the idea that people must be willing to give up their interests as a prerequisite for the possibility of ethics. On the other hand, some have argued that egoism is the basis of ethical decisions, that pursuing only one's own good will lead them to friendship, cooperation, love. Perhaps the most famous proponent of this argument is Ayn Rand.[3] Often, however, this position is self-contradictory or it translates into views consistent with ethical altruism and utilitarianism or, philosophers will argue, it abolishes ethics.[4] More important to my argument, such a focus still accepts the modernist framework that centers ethics in a concern with conflicts of interest.

of ethics rests with our being prepared to abandon our own interests in favor of the interests of someone else. Now, what kind of conceptual framework is operating which would make such a consideration central to ethical possibility? That is, under what conditions would our interests be regarded as in conflict with those of others to such an extent that the resolution of the conflict by sacrifice is considered necessary to the *possibility* of ethics?

This has not always been an ethical focus.[b] It was not until the seventeenth and eighteenth centuries that egoism and altruism became central to anglo-european ethical thought.[5] Neither Aristotle nor Plato included altruism or self-sacrifice among the virtues. Even during anglo-european philosophy's christian focus of the middle ages, there did not appear a special concern that individual and group interests might be in conflict. The good of the individual was not then regarded as essentially in conflict with the general good, the good as such, or religious good. There were, of course, particular conflicts of interest, but there was not a general theoretical problem which threatened the possibility of ethics.[c] Basically, the classical views of ancient greece focused on the character of a person and the religious views of the middle ages focused on obedience/loyalty to a master (god).

Modern ethical thought

Starting with Machiavelli (1469–1527), another shift in anglo-european thought began. Machiavelli captured men's minds by portraying them as motivated by greed and fear – a natural development given the church's power and the concepts of 'heaven' and 'hell'. Galileo (1564–1642) developed a method of scientific explanation whereby to explain something is to isolate its parts and show how they must be combined to form the whole. Applying this to the social sphere, we find the idea that individuals per se lack qualities which would permit them to function in a society. As a result, *how* individuals can be made to cooperate becomes a central problem of social organization.[7]

b   In discussing the modern anglo-european focus on altruism, I do not mean to imply that women, either wives or slaves, fared better under heterosexualism in ancient greece, for example. I mean merely to discuss this refinement in heterosexualism, where women's subordination is partially secured through the ethical dictates of altruism, self-sacrifice, and vulnerability.

c   There were debates in medieval times concerning self- sacrifice and when it is applicable – debates central to christian, moslem, and jewish thought during that period. The debates concerned differences between an individual and a god, between individuals and society, between civil law and religious law, and so on.[6] However, the idea that ethics is not possible unless humans are altruistic is the result of the shift from religious to materialist motivations for civic action.

By the seventeenth century, the anglo-european imagination was ready for Hobbes (1588–1679). Hobbes was deeply affected by the fact of civil war (apparently different in its implications about mankind than previous religious crusades). He argued that from man's equality—that is, any man's ability to kill any other man—arises man's hope of attaining his desires. He felt that all men's desires emerge from bottomless pits. Further, since men (allegedly) desire the same things, they are inherent enemies of each other. He claimed that the state of nature is a state of war. Thus Hobbes and other, less rabid, social-contract theorists held that man's basic drive stems from greed and fear, and is a drive to control others.[8] In other words, men are aggressive and competitive by nature.

This portrayal of man's nature first depicted self-interest as inherently in conflict with others' interests and with group interest, and catapulted the resulting problems to the center of ethics. Given Hobbes's whole scenario, as well as his focus on men, we might indeed wonder how basic social cooperation could ever be possible.

The answer lies, for many anglo-european philosophers, with the state. The idea is that, while nasty and brutish, men are still rational. Hence they can realize that it is in their self-interest to give up their natural rights (such as the right to pillage, plunder, and kill) to a state which will provide a check against man's "presocial" drives and, through impartial judgment, regulate him (social control).[d] Further, while man starts with his own self-interest, ideally he will use his rational (moral) ability to overcome, or at least regulate, his presocial drives and develop his own impartiality and altruism. Thus altruism appears, ultimately, to be a prerequisite for ethical behavior.

In reality, as Marilyn Frye notes, man perceives the rationality of letting the state regulate his drives and he doesn't need to overcome them. As a result of this social contract, he need develop no ethically altruistic ability.[10] Further, challenging social contract theory, Virginia Held notes:

> As descriptions of reality [conceptions of contractual thinking] can be seriously misleading. Actual societies are the results of war, exploitation, racism, and patriarchy far more than of social contracts. Economic and political realities are the outcome of economic strength triumphing over eco-

---

d Bett Farber suggests that what appears to be the individual self-seeking that results in submission to the state actually invokes a hierarchically organized power structure which is designed to prohibit self-confrontation and which is comprised of a herd of individuals who flee being alone, being in pain, taking risks, making mistakes; who flee growth and joy; who flee being mortal.[9]

nomic weakness more than of a free market.[11]

Now given that (patriarchal) societies do not emerge through negotiation of mutual needs, it would seem social contract theory concerns not the creation of societies but rather the maintenance of existing power structures, replacing religious justification and the "divine right of kings." And since both 'conflicts of interest' and 'altruism' are concepts central to the theory, we may ask how, in the maintenance of the power structure, altruism functions to address conflicts of interest.

The anglo-european shift from medieval feudalism to mercantilism and then modern industrial capitalism paralleled the shift from a spiritual/religious focus to a modern materialist focus. The accompanying shift in anglo-european ethical thought singles out one type of situation as a model for the entire range of human action and motivation:

> All too often from Hobbes on, a special type of human situation has been treated as a paradigm of the whole of moral life – that is, a situation in which I and someone else have incompatible aims and my aims are connected only with my well-being. Of course such situations do arise, but the clash between self-interest and benevolence which characterizes them is only one case out of many in which incompatible aims have to be resolved.[12]

In other words, as a result of the shift from religious to materialist concerns, anglo-european ethical attention shifted from its medieval focus on loyalty to a master and became riveted on clashes between our own and others' needs and desires. Given this focus of ethical attention, we have inherited a dichotomy by which actions are characterized as either egotistical (selfish) or altruistic.

Consequently, anyone's attempts to pursue her life in consideration of her needs, with understanding of her limits in relation to the context and her abilities, and in recognition of her talents, either have no ethical import or are perceived as selfish and hence unethical. If she takes herself into consideration, she is regarded as if she had no concern for others.

I am *not* leading up to a suggestion that in a lesbian society there would be no conflict of interests. Nor do I believe that in lesbian community *Conflicts of interest* there should be no significant differences in interests; I couldn't stand the boredom. After all, coming up against our boundaries and noting how they rub others' boundaries is one source of creative growth. So I am not naively exploring a world without differences in interests and strategies and goals, some of which conflict with others. My interest lies in the centrality of our focus on only certain types of conflicts.

My suggestion is that concern with altruism and self-sacrifice actually signals an underlying belief that the interests in question are inherently or essentially in conflict. That is, when there is a strong focus on altruism and self-sacrifice, it is an indication that the interests of those involved are already perceived as being in conflict. And given this, we may suspect that whenever we find an appeal to self-sacrifice or altruism, we will uncover an attempt to resolve that conflict by getting one party to drop their interests in favor of the other for the purpose of achieving and maintaining a certain social order. At any rate, in paradigm cases involving concepts of altruism and self-sacrifice, we can expect to find an underlying, possibly inherent, conflict of interests; and it is worth examining just what these interests are, and how the conflict is resolved.

Unrestricted power   Consider a situation in which one person possesses relatively unlimited authoritative power—Nixon and watergate come to mind. One line of reasoning goes like this: If people are not capable of thinking of more than just themselves, then ethics is not possible because when one of them is successful at pursuing his interests and climbs to the top of the power structure, we will be at his mercy. If people are not naturally altruistic, then there will be nothing within him to restrain him, there will be nothing to make him be a "good" person and so not take "unfair" advantage of others.

Significantly, however, Nixon's self-seeking became a problem of this magnitude only as he gained fairly unrestricted authoritative power, the power of the state. And yet the state is the very institution most social contract theorists claim exists to reduce the threat of conflicting interests and to restrict individual self-seeking.

What allowed Nixon's self-seeking to become a threat to the interests of others was a power structure which directs people's interests by having them submit to authority, obey rules, and set aside their "presocial" interests "for their own good." It was the state which put Nixon in the position of having relatively unrestricted power. In this case the state not only failed to reduce the threat of unrestricted self-seeking, the state actually created the real possibility of it. The actual problem was created by the solution.

Further, in the watergate case the ultimate conflict of interests lay, not between individuals, but between individuals and the state. By Nixon's pardon the interests of the state and its hierarchy won out over certain individual ethical interests and even rights. And this resolution occurred, I would suggest, because of a general desire to maintain a certain social order and resulting hierarchy. Nixon was not guilty of unrestrained self-seeking. He was guilty of lacking subtlety and of getting caught, thereby no longer being an effective head of state.

In other words, in one situation in which altruism comes to mind as a significant prerequisite for ethical behavior, the self-seeking excesses of one who has relatively unlimited power are essentially excused for the sake of preserving the power structure of the state. And our focus on altruism and self-sacrifice is reinforced and heightened in one grand ideological self-fulfilling prophecy.

A second model involving altruism and self-sacrifice as central to ethical behavior, and so as essential to the possibility of ethics, emerges in the lives of women as determined in patriarchal society. Altruism and self-sacrifice are considered feminine virtues – virtues either especially peculiar to women or of special concern when apparently lacking in women. *Altruism as women's virtue*

Now, given that a heightened concern with altruism and self-sacrifice indicates a general social perception of an underlying inherent conflict of interests, it would seem that the focus on altruism and self-sacrifice in connection with women indicates that people generally regard the interests of men and children, in particular their alleged need of women, as essentially in conflict with the interests of women.

Further, it is significant that the individual self-seeking of men and children is *not* in question. That is, self-sacrifice is not a general (nuclear- or extended-) family virtue, even though other members of a family may engage in it. It is a feminine virtue. Self-sacrifice is expected of women; this is the sense of female agency promoted under heterosexualism. Those women who don't act in ways that are perceived as self-sacrificial and altruistic are regarded as morally deficient and reprehensible.

In other words, the perceived conflict of interest between men and children, on the one hand, and women, on the other, has been resolved in favor of men and children to such an extent that self-sacrifice and altruism are feminine. The possibility of ethics in this case seems to rest on the willingness of women to devote themselves to men and children by acquiescing to male authority and by bearing and being responsible for children whether or not they choose to.

So, in a second situation in which altruism and self-sacrifice come to mind as significant prerequisites for ethical behavior, concepts are developed to encourage/coerce women to give up pursuit of their own interests and to adopt the interests of men and children. And this occurs, I would suggest, in the creation and maintenance of heterosexual social order.

That is, the self-seeking excesses of men in relation to women are generally excused for the sake of preserving the structure of the family and hence of the state. Our focus on altruism and self-sacrifice is reinforced and heightened by the excesses of men and the state, and we turn to the idea of women as essentially altruistic and self-sacrificial (nurturing, unconditionally loving, and so on) in a romantic desperation for assurance of the possibility of grace and goodness in this world.

Notice, however, that altruism accrues to the one in the subordinate position. Nixon was punished only because he was so obvious he got *Altruism and subordination* caught, was not subtle enough, was not polished enough as a master. But there has been no effort to make sure heads of state henceforth act with greater altruism. As long as those in power *say* they are altruistic (there to serve the people[e]), as long as they *say* they submit to a higher authority (a constitution and an alleged god[f]), then citizens are to trust them, giving up pursuit of their own interests if their interests conflict with those of the state. In the nixon case, the conflict of interests was resolved by getting one party, citizens, to drop their interests in favor of the dominant party, the state.

In the case of the conflict of interests between women and men, altruism is expected of women but not essentially of men. While those in the subordinate position may hope for altruism from those in the dominant position, those in the dominant position extract it from their subordinates. That is to say, 'altruism' becomes a relevant concept when conflicts of interest are a central part of a social order. Further, altruism mediates conflicts of interest in that it accrues to the one in the subordinate position: those with lesser power are expected to drop their interests and concerns in favor of those with greater power. This is one reason altruism and self-sacrifice are considered feminine virtues.

The appeal of altruism as a prerequisite for ethics is connected with the
Capitalist value power of the state and the maintenance of heterosexualism, both of which involve ritual enactment of the relationship of dominance and subordinance. And all this is closely connected to the materialist values of modern-day capitalism as well as modern-day socialism (or state capitalism[g]). Modern-day socialism, as practiced in the u.s.s.r., for example, is blatant in portraying individual interests as being in conflict with the state: individuals are expected to be altruistic and put aside their own interests under the 'dictatorship of the proletariat'.[13]

Capitalism as we experience it today includes the values of self-interest in the form of atomistic individualism and competition for the purpose of dominating others. As such, it nourishes the idea that our interests are in-

e   Of course, *they* define the needs of the people and *they* decide which peoples' needs they will serve.

f   Many think men are basically leaders. I perceive them more as followers. In general, they seem to warm to hierarchies, feeling secure when there is a structure they can fit into. Most want to dominate others – but only if someone above them can be appealed to. Thus, they find someone higher – if not another man, then a god – who validates them.

g   By 'state capitalism' I mean that the state owns the means of production.

herently at odds.[h] And when we perceive individuals' interests as inherently at odds, we appeal to altruism.

Thus, we have a third model involving an ethical focus on altruism: namely, economic exchanges. My discussion will focus on capitalism as practiced in the u.s. One line of reasoning goes like this: given the values of capitalism, in particular the profit motive, if altruism isn't part of human nature, then ethics in the marketplace is not possible. (Such claims are prevalent with regard to insider trading in the stock market.)

In other words, within the system of capitalism, profit is a central motivation for choices. By 'profit' I mean, not fair salary or a living from our work, but rather financial gain beyond payment for any work we do and at the expense of others simply because we have the power to get it, because we possess the means of production or otherwise have some advantage over others. Modern-day capitalism sets us up, not to seek fair exchange and barter, but rather to try to gain advantage over others and exploit them. Given such values, the appeal to altruism is this: if people are not naturally altruistic, then there will be no inner restraint operating in those who gain advantage at the marketplace to make them be "fair." So unless people are altruistic, ethics is not possible.

Again, most social-contract theorists maintain that the state is needed as a check on those who pursue unrestricted self-seeking. We tend to appeal to the state for regulation, that is, to enforce altruistic behavior. (Of course, once the state can restrict free trade and apply sanctions to force those with "undue" advantage to show some self-restraint, their compliance becomes not a matter of altruism but rather self-interest.)

For example, the heads of oil companies gaining windfall profits, when found out, were expected to exhibit some self-restraint and altruism, even though their actions were perfectly in order with the values of the capitalist marketplace. And when they did not show restraint, the state was expected to intervene and force them to share their profits.

The problem is that the higher authority, an institution such as the state, takes on a life of its own. We tend to believe that the state is or can be impartial (whatever that may mean), that it has no interests of its own, and that it functions to serve individuals and their interests. In fact, the state, in enforcing justice, will act to protect itself and its own interests (particularly its interest in continuing to exist), and it will evaluate every-

---

h Complicating this is the phenomenon of multinational corporations, which thwart the "free enterprise" system. Rather than follow the laws of supply and demand, they engineer demand years in advance. For example, oil companies could hold onto oil and hence drive up the price of cars which get high gas mileage ten years down the road.[14]

thing in those terms. The state controls the interests of those it governs by defining their needs, regulating them, limiting them, and in general reinforcing a dominant/subordinate relationship between state and citizens.

This relationship, in turn, gives rise to the need for the competition of capitalism (conquest) as a motivation of human action.[i] Modern-day capitalism gives individuals a reason for engaging in the world when they are otherwise bound by a system which has ultimate control over them: it allows them a chance to gain advantage over their peers and perhaps surpass their superiors.[j] And when gaining advantage over others becomes a basic motivation for individuals in a society, altruism indeed appears to be the prerequisite for ethics.

An ethics centered in altruism, one focused on conflicts of interest, is natural to societies which embrace modern-day materialist value. Further, when we appeal to altruism in an attempt to achieve moral reform, we come full circle: we actually wind up reinforcing the dominant/sub-

---

i   When fear is not a primary factor, both capitalism and nationalism are needed to bind members to the modern state. Nationalism is used for state cohesion (i.e., to justify maintaining the state and to engender a sense of meaning and purpose in individuals by defining those outside the state as different, other, and hence as a threat). Modern-day capitalism gives men purpose by giving them the chance to gain power and advantage over others within a system which has ultimate control over them. Thus, the pull in the u.s.s.r. – as a result of the dominance of the state (which has no intention of withering away) – is toward freer individual capitalist enterprise to stimulate (motivate) individuals and the country. Of course, it is crucial that women in democratic states not gain too much advantage (motivation) in the marketplace (equal rights), for if there were an obvious influx of competition, middle- and working-class men might perceive their chances as diminishing and so revolt against the system. Women's participation is primarily as consumers and commodities.

j   Basic myths behind capitalist motivation include "survival of the fittest" and "advancement based on merit." And we are acknowledged as useful persons by being "allowed" to work. However, in a dominant/subordinate hierarchy, of course, someone decides who is "fit," someone determines "merit," and someone is in a position to "allow" us to work. By dangling jobs and "merit" in front of us, those in power suggest that their recognition somehow means we're a better person – that even if we can't gain profit by participating in the system, at least we can gain "acknowledgment" and hence meaning through our work and advancement. But this means, of course, that only those who are working have value; if we aren't working, it is because we are lazy slobs. Yet even in theory, capitalism requires that there be unemployment to depress labor prices. When we aren't working, it is in fact because the system requires it.

The protestant work ethic holds that if we work hard, we will "make it." But this implies that if we didn't "make it," we didn't work hard or hard enough. This is not true. What is true is that if we do "make it," we will have worked hard. But it is also true that in a system requiring a pyramid structure very few can "make it" – and only by beating out and exploiting others.

ordinate relationship which gave rise to the need for capitalism as a human motivation and hence for altruism to curb its excesses. By appealing to altruism, we buy into a context in which individuals' interests are regarded as inherently at odds. Then we perceive the need for a state to control us, and the relationship of dominance and subordination appears appropriate – while altruism accrues to those with lesser power.

Within u.s. lesbian communities we are, at the present time, being drawn to the idea of altruism in connection with lesbian projects turned businesses. For example, it would seem appropriate to community concerns, as well as to the needs of individual lesbians, to expect those involved in lesbian businesses to exhibit altruism and refrain from being motivated by profit and a desire to mainstream lesbianism into heterosexualism. And within the framework of capitalist enterprise, the logical response of the business owner is a resounding "No." When some who own businesses do pursue economic advantage to what is perceived as an extreme degree, when they do not "sacrifice" their business interests to lesbian community ideals, community members call for sanctions against those who betray lesbian "trust." These responses all bury, rather than unravel, the confusion we feel among ourselves when we find our interests apparently clashing with our ideals.

Lesbian businesses

Further, in the long run, it is not the more powerful but the less powerful who will be expected to be altruistic. If lesbians use capitalistic values in an attempt to control what lesbian businesses do with lesbian material – for example, through economic boycott – then shortly the lesbians boycotting will themselves be asked to be altruistic. They will be expected to stop the boycott on the grounds that it is more important to have some lesbian businesses, imperfect though they may be, than to have none. And it will be pointed out that lesbians don't boycott straight businesses which are, politically, far worse. Thus lesbians will be asked to set aside political interests in the name of consistency and the need for lesbian businesses.

In this respect, the appeal to 'altruism' helps maintain a certain economic order rather than challenge injustices arising from it. As a result, we will ultimately begin to wonder why we bother to involve ourselves in community. I hear concern now such as, "Why should I engage in lesbian community unless I can make a buck?" And given that sentiment, the idea of contributing to community out of altruism begins to emerge as an ideal in a grand, self-fulfilling prophesy. Thus, those lesbians operating centers or coffeehouses may begin to regard their work as altruistic, rather than as central to their existence, and so guilt-trip other lesbians and also burn out.

Now, these were not sentiments we had at first. This was not our motivating energy. When there was no movement, finding, identifying, and enacting community was part of what it meant to be a lesbian. This was not altruism. And with the bursting forth in the u.s. of the gay liberation movement and of this wave of the women's liberation movement, we gave meaning to our lives by creating lesbian projects and expanding lesbian community, particularly in order to have economic alternatives. This was not altruism. Nor, in starting lesbian projects, were we motivated by existing capitalist values – by viewing the dollar as a god or by a desire for economic conquest.

The first businesses were created by lesbians coming out of consciousness-raising groups searching for ways to put politics into action, to create the possibility for lesbian expression in a world which silences us. This was not capitalism – while there was the desire to own the means of production, it was in order to be able to produce lesbian focused material, not to exploit and gain profit from others' labor. Nor was 'altruism' a relevant concept. We were giving meaning to our lives and trying to find ways to survive as lesbians. What fueled us was neither profit nor altruism but our anger and our lesbian desire.

Now if, at this point, we are tempted to appeal to altruism in discussing differences among us, it means we have come to regard different interests – say the interests of a lesbian in business and the interests of individual lesbians using the business – as essentially in conflict. Thus, a question we can ask in the community is, How did the interests of these lesbian ventures come to be in conflict with the interests of individual lesbians?[15] Why did the creation and exchange of goods develop into conflicts of interests?

As Anne Throop Leighton points out, what started in the community as a desire for economic survival and flexibility has transformed into a process of embracing u.s. economic values: To start a business we must pay taxes, we will need to borrow money, we will need equipment beyond what is currently produced by lesbians, and so on.

Thus we enter the marketplace, and then we slowly begin to internalize its values. The problem arises, as Anne Throop Leighton argues, when we come to believe that we entered the marketplace to make a profit, when we come to regard making a profit as a good. The problem arises when, over time, we come to believe we entered the marketplace to play the game, to engage in competition for the sake of conquest, to gain more material goods than our neighbors, to gain power over others. The problem arises when we forget our agenda and accept the values of the system in order to fit in.[16]

If we decide to pursue economic exchanges within the existing capitalist value system, then the development of events will be fairly predictable: without a lesbian focus on community, ultimately we will come to interact in the system just as everyone else does, valuing profit. Again, by 'profit' I do not mean barter or fair exchange or gaining a fair wage for our work or being paid for what we do so we can survive economically and continue to pursue our goals. I am referring to economic exchanges which yield the economic gain of a few as a result of the exploitation of many. Of course, within the community we are economically nowhere near such a possibility. Nevertheless, we are beginning to lapse into the thinking and values that go along with such economics.

I want to suggest that the solution to this trend is not to appeal to altruism. Appealing to altruism will only fuel the problem since altruism presupposes an inherent conflict of interests and so perpetuates that context. If we did not perceive our interests as being *essentially* in conflict, we would not consider altruism a value to embrace.

We need a moral revolution.

Instead of appealing to altruism, we can begin to seriously evaluate our individual and collective interests, particularly the differences among us. And given that we live in a capitalist as well as a patriarchal, racist society, we can explore ways to keep our economic exchanges out of the capitalist value framework. I want to suggest we begin weaving a new concept of lesbian economics.[17] As long as we subscribe to existing values, perceiving them as essential to our survival and well-being, altruism will appear to be an ideal. And, concomitantly, the marketplace will continue to render it the choice of fools or subordinates.

I believe it is possible to weave a lesbian economics independent of modern materialist values.[k] We have started, actually, through the exchange of goods among lesbians. But that exchange is slowly becoming immersed in modern capitalist values. We need to discuss economic factors among lesbians, examining both our needs—particularly, what we need in order to grow and to weave in this living—and our fears, for ex-

---

k   For example, anarchist achievement prior to the fascist invasion of spain was phenomenal. Myrna Margulies Breitbart writes: "Anarchist peasants did not believe that efficient agricultural production required hierarchical management or structures of domination and subordination which characterized feudal and capitalist production modes."[18] And she notes: "Anarchist decentralism was based upon an entirely new philosophy of life. Its characteristics—self-management, integration of economic and social activities, smallness of scale, and federalism—were aimed at developing positive human qualities. That Spanish anarchists succeeded in doing this is indicated by the personal traits of its adherents—people who were anxious to cooperate with others at all levels, who seemed to understand the needs of others and want to respond, who maintained interest and enthusiasm in their work in spite of long hours, who lived close to and respected nature, and who managed their complex lives responsibly without entrenched forms of authority."[19]

ample, being left without money or growing old in (greater) poverty. In this respect, self-understanding, not altruism, is the prerequisite of ethical behavior. I think such discussions can help us begin to interact without control and manipulation despite our economic differences. But we will not be able to develop a lesbian economic revolution without also weaving a lesbian moral revolution—a set of values among ourselves which further develop female agency away from the dominant/subordinate relationship of heteropatriarchy.

The Feminine Principle

The virtues of subservience

WE APPEAL TO altruism, to self-sacrifice, and in general, to feminine virtuousness in a desperate attempt to find grace and goodness within a system marked by greed and fear. However, while these virtues may herald for us the possibility of ethics—the possibility of some goodness in an otherwise nasty world—nevertheless, as Mary Daly has pointed out, they are the virtues of subservience.[20]

Under modern phallocratic ethics, virtue is obedience and subservience,[21] and the virtuous are those who remain subordinate (accessible).[m] The function of phallocratic ethics—the master/slave virtues— has been to insulate those on top and facilitate their access to the resources of those under them. For example, the highest virtue ascribed to a servant in victorian england was "loyal family retainer"—not unlike the "pro-life" loyal family (disposable) container. As John Kenneth Galbraith observes:

> The convenient social virtue ascribes merit to any pattern of behavior . . . that serves the comfort and well-being of. . . the more powerful members of the community. Inconvenient behavior becomes deviant behavior and is subject to the righteous disapproval or sanction of the community.[23]

Again, altruism, together with self-sacrifice, accrues to those with lesser institutional power.

Men have designed the feminine virtues and the resulting sense of female agency, to promote their own interests. I include here 'vulnerability'. While vulnerability is not usually called a virtue, still a virtuous

---

m   Thus, an elementary school is considered to be successful if it produces children who are well-behaved, that is, children who can sit for hours without going to the bathroom or otherwise fidgeting, who learn discipline through learning the disciplines (the "basics"), who perform according to the teacher's will without asking questions, and who obey rules and authority. The goal of education is discipline, not understanding, for our thoughts are supposed to fit into the categories developed by preceding patriarchs. We are taught to accept the hierarchy of dominance and subordination.[22]

woman must make herself vulnerable by being nonreciprocally open, loyal, and dependent. For if self-seeking is a central concern that thwarts ethical possibility, then one who is open and vulnerable and not watching after her own interests and needs is virtuous. Altruism, self-sacrifice, and vulnerability – as virtues of subordination – function to channel women's energy and attention away from their selves and their own projects.

Despite this, and because of the effects of men's behavior, we can be tempted to regard the feminine as more valuable than the masculine. Many suffragists defended votes for women by appealing to women's "moral superiority." Today some women suggest pursuing feminine vulnerability, for example, as an antidote to masculine aggression. *Women's moral superiority*

In describing the ideology of what she calls 'heterosexual virtue', Jeffner Allen notes:

> Women are held to be better than men, either wholly or in part, precisely because women are nonviolent. Women's superiority is frequently attributed to feminine qualities of nurturance, understanding, and concern for others.[24]

She points out, however, that we ignore the history of nurturance – "in which women give freely, expect nothing in return, and remain powerless while partaking in unsatisfying relationships." And she notes:

> Obliterated, as well, are women who have rejected feminine qualities as false virtues that are restrictive and useless for women's daily lives.[25]

Currently, some women are developing an ethics based on the feminine. For example, Nel Noddings has developed an ethics based on 'caring' in which she appeals to 'the feminine', in particular, feminine receptivity. Caring includes what she calls engrossment and motivational displacement on the part of the one who cares and reciprocity on the part of the one who is cared for. As carers, we are to apprehend the other's reality – a welcome contrast to phallocratic ethics – but we are also to allow our motive energy to be put at the service of the other: "I am impelled to act as though in my own behalf, but in behalf of the other."[26] Those who are recipients of this caring are to exhibit reciprocity, however this merely amounts to acknowledging the caring – a baby wiggling in delight as she is bathed, for example. Further, our ethical selves can emerge *only* through caring for others.[27] As a result, this description appeals to 'the feminine' in that the one who cares is, ethically, always focused on the other and the other's projects.[28]

Carol Gilligan has argued that, in ethical matters, women tend to focus on interpersonal relations while men's ethical considerations involve principles.[29] In the process, she has attempted a vindication of what she perceives as women's morality.

Claudia Card has written a significant critique. Among other things, she argues that Carol Gilligan does not take into account women's oppression and, consequently, the damage to women of that oppression. And, she argues, the fact that women have developed necessary survival skills under oppression does not mean these skills contribute ultimately to women's good.

For example, while Carol Gilligan revalues women's concern for approval as actually a concern for maintaining relationships, Claudia Card reminds us that the approval women seek is usually male approval, which is granted for "obedience to conventions requiring affiliation with men, respect for their views, empathy for them, etc." Or again, while Carol Gilligan revalues the so-called weak ego boundaries of women as a capacity for affiliation, Claudia Card reminds us that only certain affiliations are pursued. Lesbian relations, for example, are more often than not a source of terror for women.[30] Thus, for example, Gene Damon (Barbara Grier) opens her contribution to *sisterhood is powerful* this way:

> Run, reader, right past this article, because most of you will be women and you are going to be sincerely concerned with women's rights, and you are going to be frightened when you hear what this is all about.
> I am social anathema, even to you brave ones, for I am a Lesbian.[31]

In addition, it may be that women have a greater capacity for empathy, however women tend to direct that empathy to men of their own race and class, not to women of other races and classes, or even women of their own race and class. (Early radical feminists called this male-identification.)

Further, Claudia Card points out that intimacy has not cured the violence in women's lives; instead, it "has given the violent greater access to their victims." She goes on: "Without validation of success in separating, we may learn to see our only decent option as trying to improve the quality of bad relationships." She adds:

> More likely to be mistaken for a caring virtue is a misplaced gratitude women have felt toward men for taking less than full advantage of their power to abuse or for singling them out for the privilege of service in return for "protection."[32]

Claudia Card argues that misplaced gratitude is a form of moral damage women have suffered; and she suggests there are others such as women's skills at lying, being cunning, deceit, and manipulation.[33]

Men and women under heterosexualism   Actually, I go a step further and argue that, while men have designed 'the feminine' for their own purposes, women have refined these virtues in defense and resistance, developing them as a means of obtaining some control (individual and limited) in situations which *presume* female self-sacrifice. Women have developed the "giving" expected of them into survival skills, strategies for gaining some control in situations where their energy and attention are focused on others.

That is, the power of control can be exercised from the subordinate position, and under heterosexualism women have refined and developed the feminine virtues for just that purpose. Under heterosexualism, female agency involves manipulation and cunning – for example, a woman getting what she needs for herself and her children by manipulating a man in such a way that he thinks it was all his idea.

I will add here that manipulation, cunning, and deceit are not peculiar to women. Men are also extremely manipulative and deceitful, and can exhibit considerable cunning, for example, in keeping their dominance over their peers or subordinates from appearing overt, or in enlisting women to support them. The difference, finally, between men and women under heterosexualism may lie in who maintains dominance – though not, in every instance, in who maintains control.

Dominance is maintained by violence or the threat of violence – which, in the long run, means by destruction or the threat of destruction.[n] If nothing else works, men will disrupt or destroy what is going on. Thus, to be different from men, women stress nonviolence. Under heterosexualism, manipulation and control are not challenged; what is challenged is only the threat of disruption or destruction. Women want men to "play fair" in the game of manipulation and control by not resorting to the one-upmanship of destruction.

While many claim that there is a feminine principle which must exert itself to counterbalance masculinism pervading world cultures, what they seem to ignore is that the feminine has its origin in masculinist ideology and does not represent a break from it.[p] Further, the counterbalanc-

---

n   Such threats range all the way from, "If you won't let me pitch, I'm going to take my ball and go home," to "I'm not going to abide by the salt ii treaty." And while terrorists have the power of disruption, those who dominate have the power of annihilation.[34]

p   This dualism is related to the manichean good/evil dualism and the taoist yin/yang dualism. The manichean approach holds the two opposites in constant conflict, each attempting to dominate and vanquish the other. The taoist approach embraces the conflict but strives for harmony and balance of the two opposites. And while the taoist ideal involves harmony and balance, the nature of the opposites is significant: yin/yang, female/male, dark/light, black/white, cold/heat, weakness/ strength. The one is the opposite of the other because it is the absence of it. Thus, strength is the absence of weakness as weakness is the absence of strength. Further, one of the pair is the absence of the other because it is a

ing works both ways. Because of the non-discriminatory nature of feminine receptivity, that is, a lack of evaluating or judging what the feminine responds to, the feminine requires the masculine to protect it from foreign invasion.

Within lesbian community, many lesbians embrace a feminine principle and suggest that self-sacrifice and vulnerability, as well as a romantic ideal of mothering and all-embracing nurturing, are desirable ethical norms in our relationships. I want to challenge this.

'Selfishness' and 'Self-Sacrifice'

Selfishness and conformity

CONSIDER, FIRST, THE use of the label 'selfish'. Those who are judged to be selfish are often those who do not respond to demands from others: the question of selfishness is a question of whether a person thinks only of herself. This consideration often develops into a complaint that the person deemed selfish does not act in ways that contribute to a social structure such as the nation, the family, the synagogue or church, the corporation, the sewing circle, or the collective. Significantly, when a person goes along with the group, even if she is only thinking of herself—being "selfish"— she may well be considered ethical for doing the "right" thing. Further, someone who is perceived as selflessly opposing the group nevertheless often is judged immoral and unethical. Thus someone can be "selfish" and yet "good"—as well as "unselfish" and yet "bad."

Apparently, the relevant factor in judging a person to be selfish is, not whether she considers herself first, but whether or not she goes along with the group (or conforms to a higher order) in one of a number of prescribed ways.[q] It seems that selfishness is not of prime concern; rather, the label is used as an excuse to manipulate our participation toward someone else's end.

---

void. While there are two opposites, in the long run, there is only one essence. The dualism is actually a monism.[35]

In discussing the new spiritualism, Susan Leigh Star argues that the new mystics have managed to mask male identity beneath the guise of androgyny. Further, she points out, "Amidst the escalation, it is vital for us to understand that the new mysticism has to do with the control of women; that it may be seen as a sexual as well as a spiritual phenomenon; that it represents a subtler form of oppression, not a form of liberation."[36]

q As a result, we find that there is really no room for anyone who finds the group, the social structure, or the higher order unacceptable and does not wish to go along in any of the prescribed ways. If she separates from the group or the structure or the order, she is judged unethical and ostracized by those caught up in the structure. Such judgment can come from those who would bring change through reform as well as from those who would retain the status quo.

Secondly, masculinist ideology suggests that true female nature affirms itself through self-sacrifice. Mary Daly defines 'self-sacrifice' as the handing over of our identity and energy to individuals or institutions.[37] This ethical value encourages a woman to give up pursuit of her needs and interests in order to dedicate her efforts to pursuing others' needs and interests, usually those of her husband and children. *Self-sacrifice under coercion*

Self-sacrifice appears to be a sacrifice of self-interest. Yet women face limited options: men limit women's options through conceptual, physical, and economic coercion. As a result, when a woman engages in self-denial, acquiesces to male authority, and apparently sacrifices her own interests to those of a man in conformity with the dictates of the feminine stereotype, she may actually be acting from self-interest, doing what she deems necessary to her own survival.

Drawing upon Kathleen Barry's analysis of the strategy men use in female sexual slavery, Marilyn Frye suggests that when women who are trapped in actual conditions of female sexual slavery, or who are caught up in masculinist arrogant perception, apparently sacrifice their own needs and interests by aligning their resources in support of a man, they nevertheless are not acting selflessly or unselfishly. She argues, rather, that women facing such conditions are intently involved in acting in their own self-interest:

> The slave, the battered wife, the not-so-battered wife, is constantly in jeopardy. She is in a situation where she cannot, or reasonably believes she cannot, survive without the other's provision and protection, and where experience has made it credible to her that the other may kill her or abandon her if and when she displeases him. . . . [W]hat she does "for the other" is ultimately done "for herself" more consistently and more profoundly than could ever be the case in voluntary association.[38]

The point is that because of coercion under patriarchy, the woman realigns her choices to focus on the man. While she is not working on her own projects, nevertheless she is intensely involved in acting in her own self-interest.

One consequence is that, except perhaps in extreme cases of female sexual slavery, when a woman is in a situation in which she is expected to shift her identity to that of a man or a child, the stage is set for her to work to control the arena wherein her identity is located. She has not sacrificed her self: by altruistically adopting another's interests, she has transferred that self, or rather it has been arrogated by the man.[39] And while she may have given up pursuit of her own unique interests and needs in favor of those of her husband (and to a lesser extent those of her children), she will pursue their interests and needs as her own.

This, in turn, gives rise to a double bind of heterosexualism: While she is expected to attend to everyone else's projects, she has no final say in how they are realized. She thus becomes the nagging wife or the fairy-tale stepmother. For example, mothers may "live vicariously" through their children and some wives may be "domineering." And those mothers who pursue their children's needs and interests too enthusiastically are criticized for not being passive enough. The stereotype of the jewish mother attests to the trap self-sacrifice sets up for women.

Use of the terms   Thirdly, the concepts of 'self-sacrifice', 'altruism', 'selfishness', and 'self-interest' may appear to be factual descriptions, but the implications we can draw from sentences containing these words depend significantly on how we use them. For example, independently of male coercion, 'self-interest' could be used in such a way that any act, even an act of altruism or self-sacrifice, is actually a matter of self-interest. Someone who "self-sacrifices" may feel better about herself when she focuses on what she can do for others rather than having to assess her own needs; thus she might choose to engage in such behavior out of self-interest.

We could even argue that 'self-sacrifice'—acting with regard for another's interests to the exclusion of our own interests—is a matter of refusing to take risks or, even, is selfish. For if I disregard my own interests, I can live through someone else's choices, enjoying the fruits of their power if they are successful, for example, while if they fail, not being responsible for failure but only for bad choice. So I'm being selfish in not taking my own risks.

Further, if I actually self-sacrifice, I leave the task of caring for myself to someone else. I may become a burden to others (and thus selfishly inconsiderate of them); or if no one accepts the burden, I will become of no use to the one for whom I was self-sacrificing and hence, again, selfish. We can play around with these concepts and come up with all sorts of interesting results; and through all this, acting in consideration of our own needs and limits becomes lost in the shuffle.

Fourthly, the selfish/selfless (or egoism/altruism) dichotomy does not accurately categorize our interactions. Often we do not consider our interests and the interests of others as being in conflict.[40] Concern for ourselves does not imply disregarding the needs of others. For example, if we go to a healer when we are ill, work hard at our projects, take showers and baths, we are acting in our own self-interest. But this is hardly a matter of selfish conduct.[41] In addition, doing good for others need not involve disregarding ourselves. If I decide to help you build a frame for your futon, I may be taking a break from my work. But sharing this with you does not mean I thereby disregard my own needs or interests. It might be that sharing your project is just what I need at this time.

Now, fifthly, in challenging the concept of 'self-sacrifice', I do not mean to suggest that the sort of "selfish" behavior which self-sacrifice is sup- *Egocentrism* posed to counter does not exist among lesbians. For example, a lesbian may consistently act as if her feelings are the only ones, that she is warranted in interrupting anything else going on to demand attention (the strategies for this are many and varied). However, while the problem is real, the solution does not lie in advocating self-sacrifice. When a lesbian is acting this way, often it is because she hasn't a firm sense of herself in relation to others and is threatened; advocating self-sacrifice will only compound the problem.

Egocentrism is the perception that the world revolves around oneself. Now, it is important to have a healthy sense of oneself, centered and in relation to others. But egocentrism is our judgment that those around us have no other relationships, needs, commitments, or identity than that which they have with us. Egocentrism is perceiving and judging others only in relation to ourselves. Hence it is a confusion of our needs, reactions, and choices with those of others. Egocentrism is a form of "selfishness," for it entails a lack of consideration for others – it involves a lack of awareness that others are different and separate from us, and have needs distinct from our own. (Marilyn Frye has explored the phenomenon in terms of "the arrogant eye" of masculinist perception.[42])

Actually, there are at least two versions of egocentrism we engage in. In one type, we use attention from others to bolster our self-esteem: we connect our egos to others' responses; and when others do not always act as we planned, we regard this as a reflection on ourselves, confirming our own lack of worth. For example, we may tell another we'll be at a certain place, presuming she will show up but not directly asking her, thus relying on a commitment that was never made. If she doesn't show up, we consider this a betrayal – without any regard for her choices, which may have nothing to do with us. Actually, the fact that her choices may have had nothing to do with us is part of the problem – it proves we weren't important. In this case we use others to determine our value when we have been unable to do so for ourselves.

In another type of situation, we construct the basis for our self-esteem by creating a story about the world, particularly our immediate environment. Then we interpret everyone's actions in terms of how they fit into that construct. For example, we may plan an event and decide we are doing this for others. We then expect them to interact and contribute in ways we specify. If the others don't go along, they will have betrayed our gesture. In this case, rather than allow their behavior to reflect back on us as in the first case, we determine their value only as they fit into our framework.

In general, when others don't play by the rules we've used to construct our reality, we reinterpret what they are doing to fit our game plan. As a result, we do not allow others their own responses and reasons. Rather than talking out our differences of judgment and attending what each other has to say, we simply avoid such engagement and construct our own reasons for the other's reactions. This involves a distortion because, while we create value by interacting, nevertheless we are not the only ones contributing to the situation; we are not the only ones involved.

In the community we tend to promote self-sacrifice as a virtue and a proper antidote for behavior resulting from egocentrism. However, self-sacrifice cannot solve the problem because egocentrism involves a confusion of needs similar in form to the confusion that occurs with self-sacrifice: my perception of my needs and concerns becomes so entwined with my perception of others that anything relating to the other must relate to me and vice versa.

The difference is that in the case of self-sacrifice we cease to have a distinct sense of ourselves. In the case of egocentrism we cease to have a distinct sense of the other. Thus, advocating self-sacrifice as a corrective measure to selfishness really feeds an underlying problem of ego boundary: the solution actually nurtures the problem.

Sixthly, another's "self-sacrifice" is not particularly helpful when we *Self-sacrifice is not* are pursuing our goals. Some of us joke about wanting a wife. Yet in con- *helpful* sidering what most contributes to the development of my work, I find that it is *not* those around me giving up their goals to pursue mine. What helps me is others vitally and intently pursuing *their* goals – their music, their writing, their photography, their pottery, their editing, their collective and organizational work, work through which they weave their own meaning as lesbians – work, thus, which contributes to our lesbian ground of be-ing. Certainly I want encouragement and criticism – an exchange of ideas which feeds us both. I need and want attention; but this comes from those who are actively pursuing their own goals, who have ideas which rub against mine, and who spark and are sparked by an exchange. This pursuit of goals is neither a matter of self-sacrifice nor of selfishness. It is a matter of weaving tapestries of lesbian value, it is a matter of creating meaning in this living.

Someone might argue that self-sacrifice is important in certain political situations; that under certain conditions, sacrificing ourselves to the feminist or lesbian struggle is feasible and acceptable. Yet lesbian burn-out results from self-sacrifice in political projects, especially when the project does not develop in the direction or as quickly as the lesbian imagined – burnout which in turn results in virtual or even complete withdrawal from lesbian community. If a lesbian devotes herself to a project in such a way that her identity merges with it while her life goes on hold, and she does not gauge her own needs and limits, she may become unable to pull back at times and so become devastated if things don't go exactly and immediately as she believes they ought to. She may work frantically, as if responsible for the whole situation . . . until something snaps and she ceases to care, ceases to be able to respond. Self-sacrifice is not a means of engaging.

When we engage in political work, or projects and relationships, we need not regard this as taking us away from our everyday concerns, as being in conflict with our personal goals, and hence as a sacrifice. Nor is it useful to believe we must sacrifice in order to feel we are truly struggling. Rather, we can regard our work as a matter of pursuing our needs and interests, as part of our means of living in heteropatriarchy, as our means of creating meaning in our living. Ours is a choice of where to engage our energy, and as a result we can understand why we find the project valuable, gauge our abilities and needs, understand our limits, consider at what point the work would cease to be meaningful for us. In this way we make choices, take risks, make mistakes, revalue our commitment as things progress, but we do not so easily lose our self in self-sacrifice and burn-out. (And the prerequisite for this is self-understanding.)

And this brings me to my seventh point. We tend to regard choosing to do something as a sacrifice. I want to suggest, instead, that we regard *Choice as creation* choosing to do something as a creation. From heterosexualism we tend to believe that any time we help another, we are sacrificing something. Thus, we might regard helping a friend fix a carburetor, spending an evening listening to her when she's upset rather than going to a party, or helping her move, as a matter of self-sacrifice. But these acts do not necessarily involve self-sacrifice. Rather, they involve a choice between two or more things to do, and we will have reasons for any choice we make. Often we have choices to make. But that we have to make choices is not itself a matter of sacrifice.

Certainly, at times a lesbian might set herself against another's project, forcing the other to choose between herself and the project in order to gain "proof" of the other's love. Further, it is certainly possible that a lesbian may become so dependent on one friend that, in attempting to meet the lesbian's needs, the friend ultimately will have to set aside her own goals. (And at that point the friend will likely begin to demand authority over the lesbian's choices.) But, in general, helping others is not a matter of self-sacrifice.

There is another way of approaching this: we can regard our choosing to interact as part of how we engage in this living. Such choices are a matter of focus, not sacrifice. That I attend certain things and not others, that

I focus here and not there, is part of how I create value. Far from sacrificing myself, or part of myself, I am creating; I am weaving lesbian value.

As I engage in lesbian living, I make choices – to start this relationship, to work on this project, to withdraw now, to dream now. I make daily choices; and at one time I may choose to help another, at another time not. But in choosing to help another, I am not thereby sacrificing myself. Instead, this is part of what I involve myself in. When we regard interacting with others as a sacrifice and not as an engagement, it is time to reassess the relationship.

Nor, when we make a choice to engage here rather than there, do we need to regard ourselves as sacrificing or compromising parts of ourselves. When we interact, we pursue certain interests. We may have other interests, and we can choose which we want to develop, involving ourselves elsewhere for some. In any given engagement, what is possible exists only as a result of how those involved connect – as a result of what each brings to the engagement and of how it all works out. So when we decide to interact, we do not need to regard ourselves as compromising or losing anything, but rather as embarking on an adventure.

For example, a lesbian develops a friendship with another lesbian. They may have a common interest in the martial arts and work out together. In the process, they create possibilities that were not there, maybe eventually deciding over time to open a lesbian martial arts school. They may develop strategies specific to women and lesbians. And in the process they have created a connection between them, one that changes over the years. During this time, they are not opening a bookstore, writing a book, building a house – actually, they may take on another project, but there will be things they do not do. And they may create other possibilities with other lesbians, their lovers, for example. My point is that in making their choices, they have not sacrificed themselves or other projects. They have created something that did not exist.

What we choose is what we've decided to try to create. And we may change our minds, find that what we thought we were working for isn't what emerges, find it has emerged but that we don't really like it, find it is what we want but later find ourselves wanting to go on to something else, find that over time it changes significantly and so leave it. But even this is not a sacrifice. For as we change, what once existed also changes; if we leave it, we are not leaving what we originally created but rather something different. Thus, our choice to go on to something else is also not a sacrifice.

There is an idea floating about to the effect that if we cannot do everything, if we have to choose some and let other things go, then we are sacrificing something. Given traditional anglo-european philosophy and u.s.

imperialist ideology, u.s. lesbians, in particular, tend to think the whole world exists for us, that everything is potentially ours (or should be), so that when we have to choose between two or more options, we feel we are sacrificing something or that we have lost something. But everything is not ours; everything is not even potentially ours. In fact, nothing out there that exists is ours. Thus in acting, engaging, making choices—in choosing one thing rather than another—we are not losing anything. In acting, engaging, making choices, we are creating something. We create a relationship, we create value; as we focus on lesbian community and bring our backgrounds, interests, abilities, and desires to it, we create lesbian meaning.

What exists here as lesbian community is not some predetermined phenomenon which we opted for but rather a result of what we've created. And the same is true of all our relationships. Thus, the choice to engage here rather than there is not a sacrifice of what's "out there"; to engage is to create something which did not exist before. I want to suggest that revaluing choice is central to Lesbian Ethics.

Now, if we decide to regard choice as a creation, not a sacrifice, situations requiring difficult decisions will still arise between us. However, we can regard our ability to make choices as a source of power, an enabling power, rather than a source of sacrifice or compromise. Thus by revaluing choice we begin to revalue female agency: female agency begins to be, not essentially a matter of sacrifice and manipulation, but rather a process of engagement and creation. (And the prerequisite for this is self-understanding.)

Understanding choice as creation, not sacrifice, helps us better understand choices we make typically considered "altruistic." We often are drawn to helping others. That's one reason so many are drawn to healing, to teaching, to volunteering to work at shelters, to practicing therapy, to working at community centers or in political campaigns, to going to nicaragua—to all kinds of political work. In doing such work, we feel we are creating something, that we are participating in something; we engage and we make a difference.

However, there remains the danger that we treat choice and engagement as "handing our identity over to individuals or institutions," or even as "acting as though in my own behalf, but in behalf of the other." To choose and engage, we are both separate and related. In heteropatriarchy, engagement and creation for women amounts to mothering. Mothering, perhaps, most clearly embodies the feminine virtues, is itself a feminine virtue. And appealing once again to the 'feminine', we tend to romanticize 'mothering' as women's function and regard it as unconditional loving, as a matter of selflessly protecting and nurturing all life.

In the first place, mothering is women's *function* only given the values

Mothering as women's function

of heterosexualism. Church fathers (inspired by Thomas Aquinas among others) and state fathers (such as Hitler and Mussolini) argue that the function of a woman is to bear and raise children. They thereby conclude that women ought to bear and raise children.

Certainly it is true that some women have borne and raised children, many women are capable of it. Nevertheless, we cannot conclude that something a woman is capable of is women's function or that women ought to do it unless we add a premise to the effect that women ought to do what they're capable of. Now, women are capable of many things, and women actually do many things—kill battering husbands, for example, or avenge the rape of daughters. Yet christian fathers are not prepared to assert that women ought to do all they're capable of, they are not prepared to add any such premise. As a result, what appears to be a factual statement about women's function is actually a disguised value statement in that men have picked one of the many things women do and decided to call *that* women's function.[43]

If I were to pick one thing and claim it is women's function these days, I would suggest it is amazoning. Some women do it, and many women are capable of it. And, in my opinion, it is far more necessary than mothering. While some might focus on mothering, the vast majority might answer the call to amazon. Further, they would accomplish through amazoning what they keep trying to accomplish through mothering—appropriate atmosphere for children, self-esteem for girls, caring, room to grow and flourish.   .

Other fathers in patriarchy, scientific fathers, claim that women's function is to bear and raise children because, they claim, the species will not survive otherwise.[r] As a result they target women who cannot or who do not bear children as "abnormal" women. Given the population, we can only conclude that these fathers are actually thinking of maintaining dominance of their race (which they equate with its survival) and—to touch on finer points—maintenance of their class. Concomitantly, white men institute programs of forced sterilization against women of color. Further, as Marilyn Frye writes:

> In the all white or mostly white environments I have usually lived and worked in, when the women start talking up feminism and lesbian feminism, we are very commonly challenged with the claim that if we had our way, the species would die out. (The assumption our critics make here is

---

r   Not surprisingly, from sociobiology comes the idea that rape and infanticide are an ethical necessity for preserving the species.[44] Indeed, rape and infanticide have been called altruistic.[45] It simply warms the heart to realize men have been altruistic all along.

that if women had a choice, we would never have intercourse and never bear children. This reveals a lot about the critics' own assessment of the joys of sex, pregnancy, birthing and motherhood.) They say the species would die out. What I suspect is that the critics confuse the white race with the human species . . . What the critics are saying, once it is decoded, is that the white race might die out. The demand that white women make white babies to keep the race afloat has not been overt . . . [White] women have generally interpreted our connections with these men solely in terms of gender, sexism, and male dominance. We have to figure their desire for racial dominance in their equations.[46]

Men stress women's breeding function when they want cannon fodder or a larger pool of unemployed through which they can drive wages down and exploit the labor force. Women may find that the species will survive only if women refuse to bear and raise children, particularly when under pressure from men to breed. Certainly, as Sally Gearhart convincingly argues,[47] the survival of the species may depend on women reducing drastically the number of male children they bear.ˢ It is not at all clear that the survival of the species depends on women bearing and raising children. As Elsa Gidlow writes, "ask no man pardon."[49]

The idea that mothering is women's function also appears in women's spirituality, which is rushing to claim the 'feminine'. Women's spirituality embraces mothering as nurturing and as an ideal for all women.ᵗ

s Many feminists are caught up with the nature/nurture debate. I consider it a ruse. It may be that men do what they do because of a genetic deformity. Alternatively, the society they control may well have conditioned and produced them. But for purposes of feminist choices, it is irrelevant which view, if either, is accurate. On the one hand, just because something is genetic does not mean it is unchangeable; we treat asthma, for example. On the other hand, just because something is conditioned doesn't mean it can be changed or that it can be changed quickly or even in a lifetime. We are aware of how long it takes to unravel aspects of our own conditioning. In fact, whatever battle wounds we have will remain with us during our lifetimes, at the very least as scars. So whichever leaning we have in the nature/nurture debate, change involves time, a long time, and what we have to deal with is what there is now. If men ever decide to change their behavior, it is possible that they will succeed; but even if they do make such a decision, they will be acting the way we understand them to act for a long time. And our choices must take that into account.[48]

(One may wonder whether it is conceivable that men could change in such a way as to be able to function in the framework of lesbianism. I think it is possible. For example, if men changed themselves to become like dolphins – playful, intelligent, non-intrusive creatures – they could well fit.)

t Billie Potts asked me to distinguish between lesbian spirituality and women's spiritual-

Mothering, for many, is the paradigm of women's creativity and power, whether mothering takes the form of nurturing children (boys or girls or men) or saving the world and being the buttress of civilization.[u] As one author writes:

> Women's power is the power to give birth whether we are birthing children or ideas. Our power is the power to nurture, to nourish, to take care and protect all life.[52]

The idea that all women are or should be mothers in one way or another is not only not challenged, it is pursued.

To begin with, actual mothering is not simply a matter of protecting and nurturing all life. The choice to feed children is the choice to interrupt the life process of something or someone else (whether or not that action is with its consent). The choice to mother is also a choice to protect one's own against others when necessary. The choice to mother can involve the choice to destroy destructive forces, from bacteria to batterers: a mother, like others, may have to kill to survive. Mothering may also involve the choice not to bring a child into the world so long as society won't let a lesbian be the kind of mother she chooses to be.[53] The choice to mother can involve the choice to abort.

I think mothers can claim both the power (enabling) of life and the

Mothering versus amazoning

---

ity, pointing out that lesbian spirituality has been almost wholly coopted and that we have participated in the cooptation, for example, by calling our spirituality 'womanspirit'. By referring to lesbian spirituality, I do not mean to suggest there has been a well-defined tradition, though Z. Budapest and others such as Jean and Ruth Mountaingrove and Billie Potts worked to define a womon-centered tradition during the early u.s. women's liberation movement.[50] Much of what is called 'women's spirituality' comes from the craft of europe and went underground during the burning times. And while that tradition has a history of oppression and persecution, it nevertheless adheres to the dualism I'm challenging and which much of early lesbian spirituality challenged.

Several elements are involved in the dissolving of lesbian spirituality. One is the embracing of the 'eternally feminine'. A second is accepting a christian influence and setting up churches and highly structured institutions. A third involves embracing the light/dark dualism. A fourth involves letting go of a political analysis of the context we live in when pursuing the idea that we choose what happens to us. Fifthly, women's spirituality embraces a mothering metaphor of creativity, as if the goal of this living is or could be all-nurturing and all-embracing. Finally, women's spirituality itself is dissolving into humanism.

u   Marilyn Frye notes that as a result of the anglo-european and u.s. women activists of the nineteenth century, women's anger on behalf of great moral causes became tolerated in the public realm. However, she notes, this represents an historical and logical extension of women's "right" to mother: permitting women's anger only in behalf of others.[51]

power (enabling) of death. Many feminists, for example, attempt to deny the depth of the choice to abort by claiming that a zygote is nothing but a clump of cells or that, while a fetus may be a potential person, it is not morally significant. I think this an error. The choice to abort a fetus is morally significant. To legitimize the choice we need not deny its moral import. As a moral agent, a mother who makes such a choice is making a choice about what is possible.

Mothering is one way of embracing and developing one ability to make a difference in this living; it is creating a quality of life through choice. As such, it does not always involve protecting living things, nor is the energy involved only nurturing energy. More significantly, we must challenge the concept of mothering as it is institutionalized in heteropatriarchy.[54]

As Jeffner Allen notes, mothering reproduces patriarchy and serves men.[55] And as Monique Wittig and Sande Zeig note, mothers are separate and distinct from the amazons. "Then came a time when some daughters and some mothers did not like wandering anymore in the terrestrial garden. They began to stay in the cities and most often they watched their abdomens grow. . . . Things went so far in this direction that they refused to have any other interests."[56] Thus some lesbians who have given up on the movement have turned to mothering as an alternative, presumably to work on the next generation. Further, as Baba Copper suggests, "heteromothering cannot break away from the heterosexualism of female socialization into subjugation." She argues that only through "lesbian group-mothering can we begin to rear daughters who will be capable of female bonding."[57]

In many lesbian communities there is resentment between those who have children and those who do not, with both groups feeling unsupported by the other. If we acknowledge bearing and raising children as only one among the many things we might choose to do, then I think problems would ease some. We might then acknowledge that some lesbians just are good with kids and like them, while some don't. And we might acknowledge that lesbians, including those who bear children, have other projects which are equally important. A great deal of communicating is needed, a great deal of revaluing. But talk won't ease the tensions until we divest ourselves of the idea that mothering is women's function and fulfillment. Perhaps then we can begin to make lesbian group-mothering a real possibility – and by this I do not mean improved childcare, I mean pooling the children and having those lesbians who are drawn to this project participate in shifts. Maybe then, those who are called mothers will again ride with the amazons.

Baba Copper suggests that lesbians can develop a cosmology which can explain to a female child how she can learn to differentiate from and identify with others without dominance and subordination. She adds, "we will have to do all this without motherly domination of those same daughters in their infantile dependence, and without self-sacrifice on the part of the lesbian mothers and shareholders."[58] It may be that we come to deconstruct 'mother' as we do 'woman' and 'feminine'. Again my suggestion is that amazoning is more appropriate for girls and others to experience than mothering.

The ideal of 'mothering' appeals to 'unconditional love'. So we must ask *Unconditional love* whether we want an ideal of unconditional opening or giving. Perhaps the paradigm of unconditional loving lies in the stereotype of the mammy. Bell Hooks writes:

> Her greatest virtue was of course her love for white folk whom she willingly and passively served. The mammy image was portrayed with affection by whites because it epitomized the ultimate sexist-racist vision of ideal black womanhood—complete submission to the will of whites. In a sense whites created in the mammy figure a black woman who embodied solely those characteristics they as colonizers wished to exploit. They saw her as the embodiment of woman as passive nurturer, a mother figure who gave without expectation of return, who not only acknowledged her inferiority to whites but who loved them. The mammy as portrayed by whites poses no threat to the existing white patriarchal social order for she totally submits to the white racist regime. Contemporary television shows continue to present black mammy figures as prototypes of acceptable black womanhood.[59]

Certainly, as lesbians we are tempted to embrace an ideal of 'unconditional love', for we live in a society whose members, including our blood family, are expected to turn from us if they find out who we are—that we are lesbian. If we can count on someone showing unconditional love, at least we may find some care and affection in an otherwise hostile and dangerous environment. Yet the ideal of unconditional loving is that we can be loved no matter how rotten we are. Thus to pursue such an ideal under oppression is to accept the judgment that we are or might be rotten.

Further, if care and affection were truly unconditional, then they would be amorphous and indiscriminate. And that really isn't care or affection. We tend to appeal to a romantic idea of unconditional giving or opening or love which, ultimately, makes no sense and which works only to distort a relationship. Unconditional love is like unconditional perception—for example, seeing under no conditions of light or color.[60] There are always conditions of perception, they are the means by which we perceive. What and how we perceive are relative to those conditions.

Similarly, there are always conditions of love, though I do not mean to suggest that these conditions are criteria by which we love. Rather, they are the means by which we love. That our attention is focused and particular is part of what makes it caring. (Not incidentally, it is lesbians we love.)

More importantly, as Baba Copper argues, the unidirectional ideal of mothering undermines reciprocal interaction between mothers and daughters and so encourages incompetency and ageism among us.[61] In discussing Barbara Macdonald's thesis that children and husbands combine in exploiting mothers, helping to create ageist responses to older women,[62] Baba Copper describes her own experience:

> The children learned an assumption of privilege from their father, and he in turn became one of the children – legitimately passive, irresponsible. . . . [M]y older daughters never witnessed an *exchange* of nurturance. In their view of how the world worked, mothers gave, and men/daughters received. Ours was such an isolated nuclear family that they literally never had any opportunity to witness me being nourished, sustained, taken care of, or emotionally supported. . . . My own daughters, now in their thirties, are dutiful wives but still do not know how to extend nurturance to me, or to negotiate when we have a difference of interest. . . . As the children grow up, they continue to relate to older women with the clear expectations of service. By then they have laid claim to a place of privilege in the power hierarchy.[63]

In other words, the ideal of 'unconditional loving' as embodied by the stereotype of the mammy is not a distortion of unconditional loving but rather an accurate realization of it. To pursue the ideal of mothering as unconditional loving or total nurturing, to pursue this sense of female agency, is to pursue oppression. The masculine and the feminine are not significantly different in what they engender.

Mothering as unconditional love is self-sacrifice. And in general I want to suggest that when we equate self-sacrifice with virtue – something we must exhibit to be considered ethical – and we act accordingly, control begins to enter our interactions as a logical and acceptable consequence. For if we do not perceive ourselves as both separate and related, we will be off-center and forced to control or try to control the arena and those in it in order to retain any sense of agency, of ability to act.

Control and female agency

If my identity rests with another and her actions, then I am going to have to try to affect her choices and actions because, at the very least, they reflect back on me. For example, I may choose to help someone who is ill. Now, if I regard my choice as self-sacrifice, then who I am will be caught up in whether, how, and how soon she gets well. As a result I may well go beyond helping, to attempting to control her choices in certain key ways. And in exercising such control, I may not be allowing her time to heal in her own way, on her own terms, by her own means.

My goal in exploring the feminine virtues lies in uncovering the kind of interacting we enable – the sense of female agency we promote – when we believe that self-sacrifice, altruism, and vulnerability are part of ethical behavior. The feminine virtues, virtues which accrue to the less powerful, are developed as strategies for manipulating and gaining control in a relationship of dominance and subordination. When self-sacrifice and altruism – rather than self-understanding – are regarded as prerequisites for ethical behavior, control – rather than integrity – permeates our interactions.

I am not simply saying that at times we don't behave as well as we might. I am saying, instead, that the *structure* of the feminine virtues will thwart even our best efforts because these virtues don't function to promote a female agency which stems from self-understanding and which is both related and separate. And far from facilitating our ethical interaction, the feminine virtues actually interrupt attempts among lesbians to connect and interact ethically by promoting control and distance and by erecting barriers.

In her introduction to *the coming out stories,* Adrienne Rich asks: "And why is our common, 'moral and ordinary' . . . love not enough to create of us a māedenhēap – a band of female warriors, a movement? . . . Why are we still so rent among ourselves?"[64] In "Women and Honor: Some Notes on Lying" she notes: "There is a danger run by all powerless people: that we forget we are lying, or that lying becomes a weapon we carry over into relationships with people who do not have power over us."[65] I believe that part of the unraveling of these concerns lies in an exploration of the feminine virtues.

If, as a matter of survival, women have developed the feminine virtues into strategies for gaining some control, strategies which promote distance and erect barriers, we face a problem. Since we have not fully perceived and named these strategies as part of our resistance to male domination under the rule of the fathers, they can operate among us automatically, as habitual reactions in various types of situations. This is particularly obvious with the concept of 'vulnerability'.

Vulnerability

THERE IS A belief among lesbians, not only that engaging and making choices is a matter of sacrifice, but also that the way to engage and establish trust among ourselves is to make ourselves vulnerable to each other. Many lesbian-feminists plan for a world in which we can be "safely vulnerable" to each other. I myself once had this idea and argued that so long as a society exercises power as control, vulnerability will be confused with impotency. Thus, one who is vulnerable is a target of attack, a victim. However, I went on, in a womyn-identified space – a space in which power can develop as ability, not control, can emanate from the dark core, and is a power of processes and changes – vulnerability may come from strength, not weakness. Then when we choose to make ourselves vulnerable, I thought, it will be because we are strong and flexible enough to absorb what may come.

That was my argument, and while superficially the idea sounded plausible, I soon began to wonder about it. I imagine a time when we can be open to each other with less caution and greater flexibility because we allow greater honesty to inform our exchanges. But I no longer believe this connects in any way with 'vulnerability'.

When playing with the dictionary one day, I discovered that 'vulnerable' comes from the latin *vulnerābilis*, meaning "to wound." An allegedly obsolete meaning is "having the power to wound." Current usage connects 'vulnerable' with either being wounded or being open to wounding or attack. I do not believe a concept tied this way to attack and wounding can involve any form of agency but the power of control and its resulting presumption of access – the resulting relationship of dominance and subordination.

The context of making ourselves vulnerable in order to establish trust emerges from the dynamics of all forms of oppression. Those who have been captured, conquered, colonized, enslaved, and exploited in any form are expected to show themselves to be non-threatening to their masters once the overt violence of conquest is over. At this point, covert forms of violence begin, and the oppressed are expected to make themselves vulnerable through the concept of 'cooperativeness' in order to gain their masters' trust in return for a few privileges the master might bestow such as freedom from overt forms of violence. *The context of vulnerability*

Thus, for example, "blue" and "pink" collar workers in the u.s. are expected to be open and completely honest with their employers about anything related to their job such as pregnancy, health, drug use, etc. And such honesty is supposed to indicate the willingness of the worker to work. Workers who conceal such non-reciprocal information are considered sullen, uncooperative. Employers then use this information, not to determine their employee's best interests, but rather to determine who will be promoted, demoted, or fired – in order to determine their own ability to gain profit. The protestant work ethic encourages vulnerability in workers and maintains the power imbalance between employer and employee.

As this point in time, vulnerability is perhaps most intricately embedded in our lives through the concept of 'love' that emerges from heterosexualism. Women have been forced to make themselves vulnerable to men, to open themselves to wounding by extending themselves appeasingly and displaying their weakness or their alleged helplessness, during initial contact and ever after at regular intervals in order to prove they're not like Eve, Cleopatra, or Delilah. Women thereby reassure men that they would never be able to threaten men, that they understand the necessity of remaining loyal to men, and that men are beings who warrant such reassurances. Vulnerability and granting undue access to men—so matter of course that men often do not even need to solicit it—have evolved under the rule of the fathers, forcing women to establish that they are exceptional (that is, not like other, dangerous, women) and hence worthy of a man's attention and trust. Thus, the idea of making ourselves vulnerable in order to establish trust emerges from a context in which women have been forced to deny their common connections in order to survive, that is, in order to attain male acceptance and approval under the rule of the fathers. Such a sense of female agency does not promote lesbian connection.

Aside from constant appeasing postures, the primary way for a woman to prove to a given male that she is exceptional is to derogate the women around her. While waiting in new york's la guardia airport, I watched a young woman arrive and greet her boyfriend, who was there to meet her. She had been to a family gathering, and for the next twenty minutes of conversation she derogated each female member of her family, beginning with her grandmother. In the process, she was making herself vulnerable in two ways: In the first place, she was dissociating herself from her female bloodline and from women in general in order to prove, indirectly, that she, at least, could be trusted by him. This is the result of male-identification; she exposed herself to wounding by cutting herself off, and she will be wounded by the isolation—has been wounded already. And she was doing so in an attempt to survive by aligning herself with a male.

More interestingly, she was using vulnerability as a tool. She was exposing herself by exposing the weakness of the women of her bloodline to show that she could recognize their qualities as weaknesses and that she abhorred them as much as any man would. The case is interesting because she was using vulnerability in an attempt to gain security and avoid risk. She was exposing herself by exposing the weaknesses of her bloodline in order to ward off an attack on herself and in order to gain male approval—trust. If her boyfriend later hurls a charge at her that she, too, has these weaknesses, he will have betrayed her—she will affirm his male supremacy as long as he affirms her exceptionality. By giving him information that could be used to hurt her, in order to establish exceptionality and gain his trust, she was using vulnerability to gain some security and even a bit of control from a position of subordination.

There is a related pattern among heterosexual women who deny connections with feminism or with lesbians. There is also a related pattern among liberal or socialist feminists who take pains to deny connections with radical and separatist lesbians in order to make the men of their politics feel more comfortable. And there is a related pattern among women and lesbians who attack lesbians or women more vehemently than they would attack men in order to gain credit with whichever exceptional men they have chosen to engage.

After a heterosexual liaison has been established, vulnerability can be used in another way; it can become a means whereby a woman controls a man's access to her life in certain respects and forces him to keep his distance emotionally, if not physically. This way he can't consume her. One woman described her parents' relationship this way: The wife is submissive, vulnerable, and needs protection. As the husband is the dominant member of the pair and she has no separate means of self-realization, he is supposed to guess what she needs and, on occasion, wants. (Since he's supposed to be superior, let's see just how much he really knows.) She makes herself vulnerable by depending on him to guess and provide for her needs; if he fails, he wounds her. As inevitably he does fail at second-guessing her needs—while she is a whiz at guessing his since she has had to learn to observe him—she feels hurt and eventually angry owing to his fatuousness. In the process she makes him feel guilty. He is thus distanced and must attend to her even more closely (or have a nagging feeling of guilt), trying to guess her innermost needs while she goes competently about her business. Then at crucial moments she can call in her due; she can call certain shots in their relationship while keeping him at a distance.

This is but one heterosexual scenario. Given the power imbalance of the social mechanisms accompanying heterosexualism, vulnerability can be a way of gaining token, minor, individual control. And while the control may be minor relative to masculine autonomy, the *conceptual* difference between regarding the vulnerable woman as submissive, on the one hand, and regarding her as *resisting* total dissolution within the dominance/subordination scenario of heterosexualism, on the other hand, is significant for us; for this manipulation is the sense of female agency promoted under heterosexualism.[66]

One revealing television perfume commercial, aired around the turn of the decade for the december holidays, exhibits a seductively dressed white woman with a french accent who states, "I crave vulnerability; I think too much intimacy is dangerous." This is a significant contrast.

The message is that she craves control and thinks too much openness dangerous. She makes herself vulnerable but does not permit the sort of understanding of herself which one who is intimate would have.

Yes, openness is dangerous for a woman trying to gain some control over her circumstances in a context denying all remnants of female independence. And out of this context emerges the idea of wrapping a man around the little finger — right or left, as the case may be. She keeps him at a distance, maintaining the mystery. If the mystery is dispelled through intimacy (knowledge a man often begins to gain when a woman continues to let down her defenses after first engaging in sexual intercourse with him), she becomes ordinary and hence no longer exceptional. (Then she may resort to other means to maintain her exceptionality.) Yes, in this context intimacy is dangerous, and vulnerability is a strategy for gaining control.

Again, under the rule of the fathers, women have fashioned the giving and vulnerability expected of them into various strategies for survival. And it is important to herald these strategies for what they are. However, because women as well as lesbians have so refined and perfected them, they may have become for many of us a matter of reaction and defense rather than a carefully planned course of action. Or, at least, very often we can resort to them without fully considering other options. Making ourselves vulnerable to gain control can be a matter of habit, and as a result we are in danger of using vulnerability unthinkingly against those who have no real power (control) over us.

Lesbians and vulnerability   Among lesbians, if I make myself vulnerable in order to establish trust, if I open to a lesbian in ways that invite her to wound me, if I open up before we have found a common ground of respect and hence a basis for trust, my opening is most likely an attempt to gain control in the relationship without acknowledging either the attempt or any control I might succeed in gaining. Further, even if this isn't my intention, it will likely be a consequence of my choice.

For example, if I share doubts about myself with a lesbian before we have grounds for trust, I am revealing to her what I am defensive about. If she then criticizes me for the very thing I am defensive about, she has declared open war because I "trusted" her with this information which I am sensitive about; she has betrayed my trust. This then acts as a constraint on her: so long as we remain friends she cannot openly criticize me in these areas; she must support me (i.e., not challenge me).[v] From the other

v   In making these remarks, I am not suggesting that a lesbian who grew up learning to always hide her emotions should never open up.[67] What I am talking about here is a means of exercising control, not a means of growing.

direction, we often respond to others who share their doubts with us by feeling bound not to criticize them, even when protection from criticism was not their intent. Our engaging has thus become a binding; and our friendship has become, not an open, honest exchange of ideas, empathetic critiques, sympathetic suggestions, and perceptive support, but rather a means whereby we have enlisted someone to insulate (protect) us from our fears and pain (as opposed to holding us through them).ʷ

For example, a white lesbian might come to a gathering to connect with lesbians of color. And she might choose to interact by making herself vulnerable in an attempt to undermine the dominance/subordination relationship of racism. She may confess past racist ideas she's had or acts she's committed, which she only just now has come to understand, in order to expose herself and thus disavow the power of her skin privilege. In the process, by admitting her racism she may expect a lesbian of color to feel grateful, surprised, relieved, even hopeful, and to regard her, thus, as trustworthy for having exposed herself, admitted her sins, and thereby somehow ensured that with this new found knowledge and understanding, such acts and ideas will never occur again on her part or in her presence without interruption. In the process, the white lesbian is nevertheless exercising control. She has put a constraint on the relationship which she is attempting to establish with the lesbian of color by "trusting" her with this information. If the lesbian of color chooses to pursue the relationship and later wants to explore her feelings in connection with racism or even calls her friend's actions racist, she will have "betrayed" the "trust" that was established by reopening the white lesbian's exposed wounds.

In a related fashion, we might use vulnerability as a means of constructing barriers and setting up protection. For example, a lesbian of color may use vulnerability in an attempt to gain control in the racial dominance/subordination relationship. She may tell of her experiences of racial oppression in order to ensure that a white lesbian doesn't get too close or in order to protect herself from a white lesbian's questioning of certain political choices she's made or to block (rather than elucidate) critiques of aspects of her culture. Her use of vulnerability in the latter case invites partial examination of her culture, but suggests that full examination would wound her, and hence betray the trust she exhibited in opening

---

w   While I am suggesting these ways of interacting emerge from survival skills developed from a position of subordination within heterosexualism, they are neither peculiarly "fem" nor peculiarly "butch." Both those who claim the label 'butch' and those who claim the label 'fem' can use vulnerability to erect barriers and gain control in a relationship.

up. While it is crucial that we continue to dismantle the dominance/subordination relationship of racism between us, this project will not succeed by means of vulnerability, particularly not through confession and absolution.

Vulnerability can also become a way of gaining undue access to another lesbian's life. In exchange for becoming vulnerable to you, I may expect automatic time priorities and constant explanations about what you are doing.[68] Or I may make assumptions about your willingness to do certain things which I would not make about other close friends. This is the taking for granted, the presumption, of lovers.

Further, if I attempt to establish closeness by using my vulnerability, then later on if I find your interests or needs changing, I will be more likely to perceive such a change as a betrayal of my "trust." But then my "trust" amounted to trusting that you would not change.

Finally, vulnerability can be connected to egocentrism. For example, I make myself vulnerable by telling you that something you do hurts me, that since we have begun our relationship, you continue to play poker with your friends every other friday. You may consider this, be concerned that I am upset, and yet decide to continue. It may have other meaning for you, it may involve part of the way you want to act in the world. I may then decide that the reason you do this is to hurt me, perceiving your actions only in relation to me, ignoring the fact that other factors may be involved. The one who makes herself vulnerable expects this to override all other considerations.[69]

Now, I do not mean to encourage using another lesbian's vulnerability as an excuse to avoid attending her in her pain or anger. There must be spaces where we can explore our wounds and the injustices done to us. And we must be able to ask for help. However, the other must also be able to refuse. What I am concerned with is our use of vulnerability as a means of engineering closeness or as a means of gaining access or (paradoxically) as a shield. And what we might watch for is the power play, the coercion.

In general, when we open to wounding for a purpose, we are in a sense holding ourselves up for ransom (the redemption of a political prisoner). And the price another must pay to redeem us is to refrain from criticizing us in certain areas. We *trust* the other will not hurt us; and if she does, even by just withdrawing because of her own wounds, then she can become a scapegoat for all that goes wrong in the relationship, thereby enabling us to avoid examining ourselves. More importantly, we can use vulnerability to avoid examining the values we affirm through the choices we make.

All of this does not always happen in our relationships. My point is that using vulnerability (to establish trust, to gain access, to obtain control) sets up constraints against change and growth and, especially, against connecting and intimacy.

An appeal to vulnerability has surfaced from a context which its proponents call lesbian-feminist, an appeal which openly embraces the full *Submission* force of the word's etymology as an end in itself and not even as a transforming power. Some lesbians claim that to be a lesbian-feminist in the fullest sense we must engage in sadomasochism, in particular in masochism, because emotionally and physically submitting to another lesbian (though not to a man) is the ultimate act of trust. By opening ourselves to wounding, by inviting another lesbian to wound us (say, by humiliating us), so the argument goes, we are allegedly expressing the ultimate trust.

In the first place, by asking another lesbian to dominate her, a lesbian is forcing the other to be supremely attentive: she is becoming the center of attention, and she is thus gaining some control. Further, to do so, she must be willing to accept the dominance/subordination context established by the fathers; she must be willing to embrace subordination. This line of reasoning buys into heterosexualism by equating trust with submission.

Hailing vulnerability—the specific opening of ourselves to wounding— as a desirable virtue effectively obscures the fact that we live under the rule of the fathers, a rule of dominance and subordination, and that our survival is itself profoundly political because it means survival as lesbians, on our own terms. And, as Audre Lorde reminds us, we were never meant to survive.[70]

The appeal to vulnerability also buries the fact that turning the other cheek is an act of violence.[71] In turning the other cheek, we are inviting *Nonviolence* the other person to do us violence. (We may also be egging on an attacker, encouraging him.[x]) The belief that this action does not merit the name of violence stems from the same mode of thought exhibited by a wisconsin police officer who refused to alert the community to a rash of rapes, refused to warn women that a rapist was striking often and obviously, because he didn't want anyone to get hurt. It stems from the belief that violence done to women doesn't hurt anyone, or that breaches of women's integrity or health are not violations.

In questioning an ideal which involves a devaluing of our selves, Jeffner Allen connects "nonviolence" to the ideology of heterosexual virtue:

---

x   Of course, such a strategy may work to stop an attack, as can happen for example in street fighting. Nevertheless, when such tactics are necessary, they are not a matter of opening or connecting but, rather, of avoiding violence.

The ideology of heterosexual virtue forms the cornerstone of the designation of women as nonviolent. The ideology of heterosexual virtue charges women to be "moral," virtuously nonviolent in the face of the "political," the violent male-defined world. The ideology of heterosexual virtue entitles men to terrorize – to possess, humiliate, violate, objectify – women and forecloses the possibility of women's active response to men's sexual terrorization.[72]

She points out that, constrained to "nonviolence," women are precluded from "claiming and creating a self in the world."[y]

At every turn women have been encouraged not to take themselves seriously; and while one side of vulnerability in a situation of dominance is a power play, an attempt to gain control, the other side perpetuates a devaluation of female existence. Jeffner Allen notes that the heterosexual prescription of female "nonviolence" continues to give first priority to not killing rather than to keeping free:

> To continue to place nonviolence above freedom suggests that my aversion to violence must be stronger than my aversion to my own death.[74]

She suggests that the reason for doing something need be neither a principle of violence nor a principle of non-violence, but rather, consideration of lesbian survival on specific occasions.[75] Jeffner Allen goes on to state that

> the freedom of a lesbian world originates from a specific form of violent activity: the passionate energy to tear apart and put together anew almost everything we believe and live.[76]

Thus, embracing "nonviolence" – and, more generally, femininity, the "trust" of subordination, and vulnerability – as a means of being moral leads us to undermine lesbian agency, even when we are trying to establish connections and trust among ourselves.

Vulnerability and feminist utopia   Even in a space free of patriarchal rule, a feminist fantasy space, I find myself leery of using vulnerability to establish trust. A good example occurs in Sally Gearhart's *The Wanderground*. A woman, Margaret, who had escaped from the city after having been raped and dressed in armor as a joke, meets Seja, a hill lesbian. Failing to reach the woman in armor either through language or with a mind stretch, Seja makes herself vulnerable, saying, "If you do not understand my words or my mind, then understand my body. I do not wish to harm you. You may kill me if you

---

y   Following Ellen Willis, Melanie Kaye/Kantrowitz notes that men don't take us seriously because they are not physically afraid of us.[73]

like, I trust you will not."[77] With that Seja exposes her neck to the woman in armor, showing her she could kill Seja with her sword, that Seja was willing to take this risk with her, that Seja, therefore, was not the enemy.[78]

First of all, the image is based on the practice among some animals of exposing their bellies, throats, or genitals to other members of their pack. The problem is that such behavior, when it occurs, appears to establish an order of dominance, itself a form of security; but it does not establish trust among equals.

Secondly, I think the woman in armor might well have struck Seja. Men had just brutally raped her and dressed her in armor as a mockery. She was wounded and violated, and wounded animals strike out regardless of the intentions of those approaching them.

In conversation late one evening in minneapolis, Sally Gearhart pointed out that the hill lesbians have a concept of death different from our own, so that taking such a risk would not have the political significance it does in terms of lesbian survival in patriarchy. While the feminine virtues function to feed women's energy and strength to men, it is not true that in the wanderground those we live with fear and hate us. In this respect, then, vulnerability becomes a strategy to be used in a certain type of rescue mission in order to transform fear of an external force into trust of our own kind.

Although the idea is appealing, I question the strategy. While vulnerability may transform a woman's fear, it will not transform her personality. Suppose, once recovered, Margaret turns out to be the sort of person Seja just does not get on with. Suppose in five years Margaret makes political choices Seja strongly disagrees with; suppose she chooses to go back to the city. It is possible that Seja might eventually come to resent Margaret – not because Seja helped her and now doesn't get on with her, but because Seja risked her own life in the process of helping Margaret, and her heroism seems to have made no difference. Seja's act of making herself vulnerable *presumes* that Margaret will choose to pursue and develop her own agency independent of heterosexualism. But what if she does not? In evaluating the transforming power of trust, we must again ask whether there is ever any such thing as unconditional giving or opening – and, again, whether such an ideal is desirable. Why do we connect with particular others?

There is another important consideration in the use of vulnerability as a rescue strategy. By using vulnerability to transform Margaret's fear, Seja is forcing Margaret to choose between killing a lesbian and letting loose her own armor, her defenses. And in choosing to let loose her armor, Margaret must quiet her anger, contain it. Yet it may be too soon for

Margaret to do this; it may be time instead for her to vent her rage and thus begin to assuage her wounds.

Now, someone might argue that Seja is providing a safe situation in which Margaret can vent her rage if necessary. But what does that mean? If I expose myself to someone who has been seriously wounded in order to gain her trust, I provide her with an inappropriate target for her anger. If she hurts or kills me, she must later live with that. So Seja is not providing a safe situation in which Margaret can vent her rage. Even though the risk of Seja's life does not have the political significance it would under the rule of the fathers, still her life is not without meaning or value. Had Margaret killed Seja, Margaret would have had to live with this loss, a loss that was not a goal of the expression of her anger. In effect, Seja is providing Margaret with an occasion for exercising great self-restraint and intense emotional and intellectual effort in order to read the situation and respond with "humanity." When forced, that is not exactly healing.[79]

Further, turning our rage on each other when the other is not the appropriate target, whether consensual or not, may relieve tension and frustration and hence momentarily feel good. But we are not thereby dealing with the source of anger. And if, in one way or another, we cannot address the source to our satisfaction, our tension and frustration will build again and again and must be relieved again and again in a recurrent pattern that proscribes healing and change.

The problem is compounded when this process is defended in the sadomasochistic arena, and the temporary relief of tension is associated with sexual orgasm. The recurring process of building tension and then seeking relief is not perceived here as a failure to break out of the cycle and deal with the source of tension. Those who pursue sadomasochism attribute it, rather, to the natural recurrence of sexual appetite. The process is thereby embraced in the name of feeling good, and those who push for growth and change are judged puritans.

To return to the wanderground and Seja's strategy of aiding Margaret in her anger and pain: wounds take time to heal. The hill lesbians instead could have left Margaret alone, watching from a distance as they did with the gentles (political faggots), leaving food nearby and protecting her from extraneous forces while she focused on her self, giving her time and space to discover and name her own needs including venting her anger. There are ways to deal with someone else's anger and pain other than by risking our own lives.

Further, trust does not have to be established immediately. In forcing Margaret to respond to her by choosing to trust or to kill, Seja may be placing an additional burden on Margaret and cutting short a needed process instead of aiding her in addressing her anger. Even in the best of contexts, to use vulnerability as a tool is to take a "short-cut through another's personality."[80]

Intimacy and Self-Understanding

IT IS IMPORTANT that we examine the belief among lesbians that the way to open and to establish trust is to make ourselves vulnerable to each other, that this is an ethical or feminist ideal. It is also important to examine the converse belief: that in order to retain power, we can never really open to another lesbian, never share our full selves. I do not mean to suggest that, because of all the problems I've discussed, we be aloof, keep at a distance, remain independent to avoid dependency. I do not mean to encourage shallow relationships—or, even, no relationships at all. I do not mean to suggest that we take no risks with each other. *Taking risks*

I mean to encourage deep evaluation of our risks. And I am suggesting that using vulnerability is itself a way of avoiding risk, a way of maintaining distance and control. I am suggesting that independence and dependency, while perhaps being opposites of a sort, are actually two sides of the same coin.

We tend to go to one of two extremes in our relationships. Either we open and presume access in a way that manipulation in all its many guises, from whining to ultimatums, becomes a common aspect of our interaction, or we hold ourselves at an emotional distance in order to maintain our autonomy and independence. Both extremes involve controlling the other, both undermine female agency outside the framework of the master/slave virtues, both interrupt lesbian connection, and both undermine intimacy.

Certainly, if I remain aloof, never really engage emotionally, and never extend myself to others, then I will take no risks. Controlling ourselves this way is a survival skill, one many of us learn in resisting the dominance of sexism as well as of racism and classism. We learn not to expose ourselves in situations where it will be used against us. But even among equals, self-exposure is not a form of genuinely engaging with others.

Risk, in our relationships, is not a matter of opening to another and simply exposing our wants and needs. If I regard risk as simply a matter of exposing myself, then my goal is control, and my risk is that I will lose control. Further, if I open from vulnerability, I am not really opening. For while I open myself to exposure, I am not open to you, to your needs and changes.

For there to be the risk of engaging, instead, we can regard ourselves as having one part in an interaction, and leave those with whom we engage their own parts. For example, if I express something serious to a friend or lover, she may reject me or she may attend and consider what I've stated or she may express something equally serious on her part. Depending on her response, our relationship will now develop in one of several possible directions. In other words, the relationship changes.

The real risk of connecting lies in a willingness to take the next step, to change the relationship, to let go of the "security" of static predictability. The risk lies, when we connect with another, in letting go of control and embracing the unknown. And such risks are important when we begin relationships, as well as after we've been connected for years.

As you come to understand me more intimately, you will come to understand what is most capable of wounding me. However, once intimacy and trust are developed, *if* they are developed instead of a forced closeness, we are less likely to use that understanding to hurt or control each other. Hence we have less need to use our vulnerability as a defensive weapon. And we may find the space to grow in ways that make us less vulnerable and therefore more open.

The closeness of intimacy takes time. As Janice Raymond writes:

> Discretion taught that to know a person you have to grow and take time with her and that there is no such thing as instant intimacy. It cautioned against sharing intense emotions and thoughts with those with whom one is barely acquainted. And it cut through the easy rhetoric of quick recipes for breaking down barriers between people by revealing how facile friendships can set up new barriers and create new forms of alienation based on false intimacy.[81]

Intimacy involves connecting through sharing affection and understanding, through sharing interests, politics, experiences, despair, and desires. One meaning of 'intimate' is "requiring few words." When I understand someone that well, when we are that psychically attuned, few words of explanation need pass between us (though we may be rapt in hours of conversation). Along with the development of trust, this takes time. And it is not something anyone can set out to construct or can guarantee. The most we can do is to be clear on our part.

If I pursue the closeness of intimacy, of greater understanding, and embrace the risk of change, if I let go of control (which does not mean therefore being out of control), I will less likely restrict my growth through distance ("independence") from you or restrict yours through manipulation ("dependence") for fear of losing something valuable in my life. Intimacy cannot be lost, though our intimate relationships may well change. Thus, even if we grow apart, the real value can remain solid—we don't have to destroy it for fear of losing it.

Intimacy involves deep understanding of another, and another's deep understanding of us. And the prerequisite for that is not altruism. The *Self-understanding* prerequisite for that is self-awareness: If you are going to understand me intimately, then I must understand myself so that I am not threatened by your understanding of me. For before I am really able to respond to you, I need to be clear on at least some things about my self–including those things I am confused or defensive about. I also need to be clear that I will not be intimate with everyone, that I will not get on well with everyone.

The feminine virtues do not serve us. Altruism focuses us on conflicts of interest, self-sacrifice distorts relationships, vulnerability is a way of pursuing a forced closeness which maintains a certain control, precludes self-awareness, and presupposes dependence. Mothering reproduces patriarchy. Developing the feminine virtues undermines our connections. Self-understanding, choice as creation, amazoning, and intimacy are altogether different matters.·

Finally, I am concerned with the focus of ethics. Self-understanding, which is the prerequisite for genuine intimacy in our lives, seems also to be the prerequisite for a moral revolution, the natural starting point of Lesbian Ethics. It is here, in deep understanding of self and in relation to others, that lesbians hold the possibility of female agency independent of heterosexualism.

3
Power, Paternalism, and Attending

IN THIS CHAPTER I want to challenge our idea of power as control. When we believe that to be political or good or effective we must control a situation, we wind up instead trying to control ourselves and each other. In this way we undermine rather than enhance each others' abilities. And when we find we cannot control a situation, often we will turn on those involved in one way or another, undermining our own responsiveness in the process. Rather than try to control situations for each other, I suggest we attend each other as a way of increasing both our own and each other's moral agency. As it stands, we tend not to respect each other, and as a result we perpetuate the power of privilege as well as confuse lesbian connecting and engaging with binding.

Power

The personal and the political

THEORETICIANS WITHIN traditional anglo-european ethics have remained largely silent on the topic of power as a factor in ethical choice.[1] Presumably, they think that the concept of power is adequately covered by the discipline of political science; they think of power as more of a political than a moral issue. When men consider questions of power, they focus on state authority, police and armed forces, control of economic resources, control of technology, and hierarchy and chain of command. They think moral considerations, on the other hand, concern personal choices, such as how to treat others, how to conduct our affairs, how to be good, and how to help others.

Of course, they might bring certain moral considerations to bear on certain political decisions. Thus, following the utilitarian principle that one ought always to act in such a way as to bring the greatest good to the greatest number, those in power argue that it was morally appropriate for the united states to annihilate hiroshima and nagasaki because with such an exercise of power, fewer lives were lost than would have been in a drawn-out, less dramatic war.[a] The idea that we are morally (not just legally) obligated to obey the laws of the state also reflects a typical interaction of ethics and politics in traditional thought, as does the idea that the state has a duty to protect the individual and the individual a duty to obey the state.

Nevertheless, men generally regard politics and ethics as distinct, and power the proper subject matter of politics alone. As a result, when they consider ethical questions, they tend not to regard differences of power as relevant. The closest they come to addressing questions of power involves considerations of how we should treat others in hierarchies: our duty to those above us, whereby the feminine virtues are brought to bear; and our responsibility to those below, whereby paternalistic justifications of domination abound. Such considerations reinforce institutional power and privilege while treating the power difference in hierarchies as morally irrelevant.

Modern anglo-european philosophers have discussed 'free will', and we might expect them to concern themselves with ways people can act responsively under oppression. But their exploration of 'free will' does not involve any such consideration. Rather, they analyze the question of whether the existence of a planned universe or a mechanistic universe means that our actions are all predetermined. They do not acknowledge power differences, nor do they analyze the use of power as an element which deserves consideration when we make or evaluate ethical choices.

If we depended on traditional anglo-european ethical theory to evaluate choices people make under conditions of oppression, we would focus on the immediate and personal factors of their lives, such as how they got themselves into the situation or what they might have done to avoid facing such choices. We would not consider the political context they lived

---

a   Actually, if we follow that principle, then we should simply annihilate every human on the planet (or at least every man), since in the long run fewer lives would be lost than if man continued engaging in war after war through the centuries.[2] In developing her notion of 'testeria' – "the ability of the male ruling class to efficiently, calmly, and maturely carry out planetary catastrophe" – Juli Loesch noted in 1972: "Since the turn of the century, over 50 million human beings have been slaughtered in war by psychiatrically normal people."[3]

in nor the fact that their options were limited. We would not consider that their decisions might be reactions to the oppression they faced. Nor would we consider that the concept of 'moral choice' simply might not apply in certain cases, that the situations some have faced are ones in which they had no status as moral agents. In traditional ethics, the personal and the political are generally thought to be separate domains.

Significantly, it was feminists who argued that the personal is political.[4] Simone de Beauvoir started many women thinking about the category of 'woman', particularly how women are defined essentially as the other in relation to men.[5] Betty Friedan started a number of women thinking about men's control of the media, in particular the portraits of women prevalent in popular magazines during world war ii (when women were needed in the work force) and portraits prevalent after world war ii, during the back-to-the-household movement, when the government forced women out of jobs and gave those jobs to men.[6] Kate Millett brought attention to the fact that the relationship between the sexes is political. Expanding the definition of 'politics' from "methods or tactics involved in managing a state or government" to "a set of stratagems designed to maintain a system," she argued that "politics refers to power-structured relationships, arrangements whereby one group of persons is controlled by another."[7] Mary Daly brought attention to how the power of naming has been stolen from us, particularly by religious fathers.[8] And the anthology *sisterhood is powerful,* edited by Robin Morgan, was a major inspiration for the upsurge of the u.s. women's movement.[9]

Women emerging from civil-rights and antiwar activism, as well as from the left, brought what they had learned: from socialism,[10] how the material conditions of our lives affect our choices; from anarchism,[11] how violence done by the state is not qualitatively different from violence done by outlaws (it is different only in degree of organization and extent of its effect). Consciousness-raising groups sprang up, and women began articulating how what happens to one woman happens to the vast majority of women. Detecting patterns which suggested these events were political and occurred, not because of individual moral choices a woman made, but instead simply because she was a woman and despite her choices, feminist theoreticians began focusing on connections between the personal and the political, especially on the power structures in heterosexual interactions.

As a result, feminists recognized power as a factor not only in matters of state but in the privacy of personal interactions; and we began exploring the manifestations of power permeating the lives of women and lesbians which were more subtle and more insidious than military and economic force: the power of language,[12] the power of suppressing images,[13] the

power of expectation and perception,[14] the power of access and definition.[15] We began to understand how these means were used to constrain
our personal choices. We also began to claim our own powers: the power
of communicating, of consciousness-raising,[16] of organizing, of produc-
ing, of healing. And we found the essential connection in our lives. As a
character in June Arnold's novel *The Cook and the Carpenter* tells it:

> Look, I really don't believe that anyone can work for a revolution separate
> and distinct from [one's] own personal happiness or love-needs. Such a per-
> son wouldn't have any way of knowing the difference between what is true
> and what is false. It isn't that we're trying to do two things at once – set up a
> counterlife and work for a revolution; the two are halves of the same whole
> and the absolutely essential thing is to keep juggling them.[17]

In our individual and collective interactions, we ran up against the
more subtle forms of the dominant power we'd been exposing. We found
we were using it against each other in the forms of racism,[18] anti-
semitism,[19] classism,[20] ageism,[21] ablebodyism,[22] sizeism,[23] as well as sexism and heterosexism. This took the form of blatant prejudice as well as
the more insidious power of privilege – the privilege of ignorance, even
arrogance. We then tried to control each other with political rules, and
that resulted in a lesbian backlash. Further, our breast beating, as well as
our use of vulnerability and self-exposure, resulted not in growth and
transformation so much as in guilt-tripping and manipulation. Finally,
we tried to prove our good intentions, if not our purity, by pointing the
finger at others. We argued we were powerless, yet we had and still have
quite an arsenal of weapons.

Now, it is not my intention to offer an analysis of the concept of
'power' – or perhaps I should say the concepts of 'power', since my use of *Power-over and*
the word in the previous paragraphs includes several different ideas. But *power-from-within*
there are certain key elements of the concepts of 'power' which I find significant to lesbian interaction and hence to Lesbian Ethics. Those exploring lesbian and women's spirituality often distinguish between 'power-
over' and 'power-from-within'.[24]

'Power-over' is a matter of dominance and subordination, of bending
others to our will through a variety of overt and covert methods.[b] It is the
power of control; and while it can be exercised both from a position of
dominance and from a position of subordination, our attention is riveted
on those who blatantly exercise it from a position of dominance, for it is

---

b   Thus, using feminine wiles is an exercise of power-over in that it is an attempt to impose one's will on someone, albeit someone dominant, and from a position of subordination.

then backed by threats of disruption and continuing acts of destruction.

'Power-from-within', on the other hand, is a matter of centering and remaining steady in our environment as we choose how we direct our energy. 'Power-from-within' is the power of ability, of choice and engagement. It is creative; and hence it is an affecting and transforming power, but not a controlling power.

Of the two general categories, 'power-over' is a main focus in u.s. society and tends to be the only form of power we recognize. Interestingly, the word 'power' comes from the latin *pōtere* and the old french *poeir*, later *pouvoir*, the spanish and portuguese *poder*, and the italian *potere*, all of which refer to ability. Current dictionary definitions focus on three ideas: (1) power as ability, (2) power as control or authority, and (3) power as strength or force. However, in one way or another, all these ideas tend to be played out in our society as control, as one person imposing their will on others through various means.[c]

We tend to assess strength or force, for example, either in terms of destruction or of controlling others. Those in positions of power tend to amass strength and force and transform them into means (sanctions) which they can use to maintain and enhance their position. They thereby impose their will on others through authority and control. Thus, those who use the power of strength or force tend to play it out in terms of control.

The idea of power as ability is important and suggests that we recognize and acknowledge 'power-from-within'. It suggests some rich and exciting ideas such that our powers are a matter of our energy and abilities, and that we can exercise power through what we weave as we focus our attention and engage in this living. As we develop our abilities, we become adept: we practice crafts; we weave tapestries.

Yet this is not how power-as-ability is developed in dominant u.s. social thought. Within this society, 'ability' has come to be associated with 'power-over' through the concept of 'cause': we assess ability in terms of our capacity to perform "effectively"; what I am able to do is measured by what I can cause to happen. We put less stress on how we engage – and the effects on others of our engaging – and more stress on how much we produce. Since our output quantitatively increases if others help with our projects, 'ability' comes to be connected to our talent for getting others to

---

c Significantly, imposing one's will on others takes precedence over economic exploitation when the two are separated. Those with economic advantage will perpetuate certain structures in order to feel in control even when such structures are not economically feasible. For example, in labor/management disputes in which turning over some of the decision making to labor would be profitable, management fairly consistently refuses.[25]

lend their efforts to our projects. Insofar as we perceive ability as actual power, we tend to evaluate it in terms of whether we can get others to do what we want.

Our ability, if perceived as power, is measured by the extent to which we're able to control others and get results. In other words, the ability we tend to recognize in this society as power is administrative, not creative ability.[26] Ability as power in the dominant society is the ability to designate tasks, to make assignments, to manage, to direct, to handle or control others – sometimes called "leadership."

In one way or another, 'control' or 'power-over' seems to be fairly central to the concept of 'power' in use in mainstream society. And it is the prevalence of this notion – the idea of controlling, of power-over, of imposing our will – that I am interested in challenging in lesbian interactions.

Patriarchal justification for exercising power in the sense of 'control' or 'power-over' or imposing one's will on others ranges all the way from the blatant "might makes right" to the subtle ideology of protection of the "weak" and "defenseless." Both extremes are used in colonialism and racial domination as well as in "love" relationships between men and women. Within lesbian community we tend to agree, in theory at least, that "might" does *not* make "right." On the other hand, we do get caught up with the delicate cohort of brute force – paternalism. Paternalism is perhaps the most pervasive justification for exercising power over another's choices and controlling, or trying to control, a situation. In political terms, paternalism is "a practice of treating or governing people in a fatherly manner, especially by providing for their needs without giving them responsibility."[27]

Paternalism

Philosophers and statesmen usually discuss the issue of paternalism in terms of the conditions under which the state has a "duty" (the right) to intervene in a citizen's life when the citizen is not harming others. Typically, liberal justifications for restricting or coercing a person's choices involve the idea that the state has the right to interrupt a person's activities if they interfere with other individual or group rights.[d] But paternalism as a justification for state intervention has a different focus. The idea is that under certain conditions the state has a duty to intervene in a citizen's affairs, although not for the good of others nor for the good of the whole nor for the good of the state. Under paternalism, the state intervenes for

---

d Of course, who has what rights is an altogether different matter: it gets played out in terms of the good of the whole – that is, the good of those in power, of the state.

the individual's own good.[e]

The concept of 'paternalism' is significant because it extends the notion of 'authority' beyond simply that of a dominant regulator or one who has the power to make (legislate) or enforce decisions (e.g., the police force). Paternalism involves the idea of a citizen or agency who is actually in a better position than the person herself to determine what is best for her *and* who, thus, *should* decide for her what she will do. In essence, paternalism (1) justifies interrupting or even abrogating a person's integrity "for her own good"; (2) validates the idea that someone has a right, indeed an obligation, to dominate (protect, coerce, and so on) someone else under certain conditions and so force her into a certain dependency; and (3) gives credence to the idea that such dependency benefits an individual.

Paternalism involves the idea that someone else knows better, not just in the sense of having information we could well use in making our decisions, but in the sense of being in a better position to define our own needs and interests and, because of that, determine what we will do. Of course, at certain times someone else may realize better than I what is "good for me." But it doesn't follow that therefore they should determine what I will do. Paternalism encourages us to cease relying on our own ability to judge[f] (and learn from our mistakes); hence, it encourages the loss of moral agency.

Control versus Attending

LESBIANS ARE CAUGHT up with the paternalistic idea that to help someone in pain or trouble, we must try to control the situation for her, that when she is in crisis it is appropriate for us to take over for her. My first concern is that in taking over for another, we are undermining her responsiveness (her ability to respond[31]) and hence her moral agency.

It has been said that the oppressed may comfort each other but they do

---

e   Typical examples of paternalistic policies that professional philosophers address include social security, mandatory use of seat belts, and smoking restrictions (because of harm to oneself – these arguments were developed before the awareness of problems of passive smoking).[28]

f   For example, by "knowing what's best," doctors can destroy health. Lynn Mabel-Lois describes her own experience of doctors repeatedly prescribing uppers to "help" her lose weight, despite her attempts to explain she'd been addicted to the drugs before and had broken the addiction only with a great deal of difficulty. The repeated reply was, "We'll worry about that when you're thin."[29] As Vivian F. Mayer points out, it is doctors who make fat people sick and psychiatrists who make fat people crazy.[30]

not empower each other. I think this happens in lesbian communities. We may make each other feel better at times, but we don't often interact in ways that encourage growth, healing, and transformation. We may be adept at comforting each other, and we may be good at guilt-tripping and manipulating each other, but do we *enable* each other? Or rather, when we enable each other, what exactly are we enabling?

Under the concept of 'enablement' as developed by alcoholics anonymous and similar self-help groups, those close to alcoholics often enable an alcoholic's dependency rather than her abilities to dry out, stay sober, and engage in the world from out behind the haze of liquor. As Celinda Cantu explains, enablers become co-alcoholics, those who are as "dependent on the alcoholic as the alcoholic is on alcohol," for they "get a fix by taking care of and being needed by the drunk."[32]

When interacting with each other, it is important to ask what we are participating in and what we are enabling. Under oppression we may get a fix from someone else being dependent on us in any of a number of ways. We tend to believe that to be effective in a situation we must control it; that to be good, or sisters, to another we must end her pain and make everything all right; that this is what being powerful means. In the process we discourage her ability to make choices, to respond within the limits of the situation she faces. We assure her that everything will be all right even when that may not be the case.[33] And we enable her vulnerability rather than her ability, we condescend. As a result, we undermine her moral agency.

Taking over a situation

Two lovers, one chinese american and one white american, separate. The chinese american lesbian goes to friends for comfort and to process her pain.[34] The friends, mostly white, upset and wanting to make her feel better, take sides: they stay away from the other lover, isolate her, possibly even verbally attack her. Intervening this way seems the right thing to do. After all, if one finds a friend in pain, it seems only natural to try to lessen the pain. We become protective of our friend. We try to take over for her. In this case it seems our efforts can be successful, we can control the situation. We comfort her, we turn on her ex-lover . . . but do we empower her? And are we empowering ourselves? I mean to ask whether we have really exercised power in this situation. I mean to ask whether anyone is growing more adept or learning anything in this situation.

A lesbian may want someone to understand what she feels, perhaps giving her another perspective, at least providing a check as she sinks into her pain. But if her friends are likely to try to "even things up" and she does not want this, then she cannot go to them to explore her pain. Further, if they are likely to intervene, they are also likely to get caught up in the outcome and so have a vested interest in it beyond the care and concern of friends. Should she eventually reconnect with her ex-lover, the friends who intervened may feel used or even betrayed.

On the other hand, the lesbian who is hurt may be going to friends to seek their intervention. She may ask them to hurt her ex-lover in some way. More likely she will covertly encourage them to hurt the ex-lover. Rather than create her own circle of protection while she soothes her pain and heals, she may encourage her friends to do so for her, ignoring the ensuing consequences, as if the ex-lover could simply vanish from the community. While the ex-lover may expect the lesbian to do what she must to deal with her pain, including cutting off, if the friends also cut off, they are treating the ex-lover as if they were the injured parties. By intervening in the situation, they may be comforting their friend, but they are taking on something that is not theirs and they are not empowering their friend.

In addition, if we continually protect a friend or lover like this, putting ourselves in the middle of problems she faces, over time we will begin to lose respect for her. We will begin to regard her as unwilling or unable to make her own decisions. In order to maintain respect for her, despite her apparent inabilities, we will then have to begin perceiving her as a victim who is totally helpless and under attack as is no one else in the lesbian community. This, of course, may be the case in extreme situations. But if perceiving her as a victim becomes the essential dynamic between us, we must encourage and maintain it at all costs in order to keep meaning in the relationship. And this will undermine her own abilities.

Undermining responsiveness Now, aside from problems arising when we can and do take over a situation, I want to suggest that when we find we cannot make a difference this way, we begin to lose our responsiveness – our ability to respond. When we regard power as an ability to control things and it turns out that we can't control a situation, we are left facing our own apparent powerlessness. Often we will then step back as if we'd failed and assume blame (guilt) for the entire situation as if we had created it; alternatively, we will turn our back on the situation or otherwise deny that there is a real, continuing problem.

Either of these reactions is a matter, I believe, of attempting to deny our powerlessness, under the dominant concept of 'power', by affirming that we can and do make a difference. By blaming ourselves, we affirm that we could have made a difference if only we'd tried harder, been quicker or more skillful. By turning on the other, we deny that in this instance there was a problem to solve. Thus, regarding power as the power of control and finding we can't control a situation, we are likely to break down in ways that undermine our responsiveness, our ability to interact with others – we undermine our moral agency.

A white upper-class woman is raised to be charitable to those less fortunate than she, but she is insulated from experiencing economic oppression. Finally, her life brings her to a place where she can no longer be protected from the stark reality of poverty. She has been taught that a good woman is one who relieves suffering, and the task here is so great that even if she were to give away all she had, putting her own family in the same situation, it would make no other difference. Her response is to deny her powerlessness by refusing to notice poverty. Or a working-class chicana lesbian who has been close to poverty all her life, too close, but who has gotten out by schooling herself at night and working jobs, one before school and one after, may lay claim to power by turning on those left behind and blaming them for their situation. As in both these cases, when we cannot control a situation and yet somehow feel we should, we may cease to notice the oppression or may possibly even blame the victims.

A white feminist works as best she can to make a space safe for lesbians of color. A black lesbian points out that the space is still racist—or, at the very least, predominantly white. The white feminist, feeling trapped and realizing she is unable to control the space, retreats into denial. She verbally attacks the black lesbian, accusing her of being divisive. Growing up female, she has been drilled in feminine ineffectiveness, and this situation opens a raw wound. When someone brings her face to face with her own powerlessness, she responds with the force of her own pain. Defensive, feeling guilty because she is unable to immediately control the situation, the white feminist shuts down—"I can do no more," said in frustration and anger.

A black lesbian tries to make her space safe for a long-time white friend and lover who is coming to visit and has serious physical ailments. Her efforts, worried and careful as they are, are not enough. The space still contains elements which trigger her friend's disease. When the friend points this out, the lesbian turns on her in anger, for she has been brought face to face with her limitations. Her friend's presence reminds her of her own powerlessness, of her inability to fully control her environment for those she loves. As she is unable to cease noticing her friend's suffering, she instead attacks her, saying in anger, she has done all she can.

I think that lesbians, along with others, have absorbed the concept of 'power' prevalent in masculinist thought which implies that if we have any power, we can control a situation and aspects of the people in it. Yet if we accept this idea, then as long as we are not in control, we assume we are powerless and that nothing we do makes any difference. Or, if we accept this idea, then we may conclude that there is no difference between us and imperialists, the klan, nazis, or the john birch society because the effects of our actions are, apparently, the same—the continuation of oppression.

Assuming responsibility for a situation

Yet we are alive and making choices and connecting and making changes; and I believe the frustration that is building is making us tear apart each other (and ourselves) with manipulation, guilt-tripping, coercion, and scapegoating. As long as we articulate our suffering, our voices are strong and beautiful and we can take pride in ourselves and how we have broken from the dominant ideology, which would have us graciously accept oppression, graciously submit. But just as we begin to feel our strength, take pride in our accomplishments, and begin to sense some ability, some meaning, we come up against our limits and respond in any one of a number of ways—many of which involve, I suggest, attempts to deny that we are powerless, to deny that what we do makes no difference.

Consider the following situation: A white lesbian is seated on the el (subway) with a bag next to her. There are many empty seats around her. A black man boards the el, looks around, and heads toward the seat in which she has placed her bag insisting she move it. She complies, but then she asks him, "Why can't you sit elsewhere?" He begins to harass her and continues until she moves. Later she gets angry at herself. She begins to worry that she was reading too much into the situation, that she was projecting her bad feelings onto him. At the same time she gets upset at herself because she gave in, because she was not as assertive as she should have been.

A number of things can be said about such a situation. For example, had there been a white authority present, he would likely have sided with her, for reasons having nothing to do with justice. Given that this is a racially divided u.s. city in the late 1970s, how can she be nonracist in the situation? In her concern not to be racist, what happens if she treats the black man differently than she would a white man, especially if that means she is not adequately protecting herself? In some situations there may be no clear-cut right and many wrongs—or, at least, many traps within which there are no fully acceptable alternatives.

Now, what I find significant is that she evaluates the situation by considering only her own behavior, ignoring his. She does not judge him; she judges only herself. She blames herself. She claims all responsibility.

Notice that if the situation is fully her responsibility, then she is not helpless, even though she may have felt helpless at the time. There is something she could have done differently to determine the outcome. If she is wrong in such a situation, then she can go on in the world without fear of random violence; she can be sure of sense and meaning in events. Taking the blame herself makes her an agent; it implies that she has power and that she could have avoided what happened. For the same reasons, in many rape cases the woman blames herself—she should have been somewhere else, wearing different clothes, and so on. One who blames only herself is, among other things, denying that her actions were irrelevant.

A sixteen-year-old white woman in a straight middle-class household watches her mother divorce her alcoholic father and then take on a high-stepping boyfriend, who is father of the sixteen-year-old's own boyfriend and who subsequently molests her sister. The young woman helps her sister return to the father, who has been sober now for several years; and she gets child services to bring charges against her mother's boyfriend. Later the young woman begins to feel guilty: she has been unable to get her younger brother away from this man, who is also a batterer, and from her mother, who is lying to her brother and refusing to give him messages or presents from his family. She is estranged from her mother, who continues to love the boyfriend; and she feels sorriest for her mother's boyfriend, who himself has a string of previous disasters, including the death of a wife in a car accident. She feels guilty because she cannot make everyone's life better. She does not consider the fact that what lies within her power is the ability to keep herself from also becoming a casualty in this mess. Because she cannot control the situation, she begins to feel powerless as well as responsible for it.

A girl stops eating. Those around her become concerned that she is anorexic and urge her to face "her problem." In fact, she is facing too many problems. She responds to the trauma and pain of those around her. She talks of how she can't get away from everyone else's problems; to gain peace of mind and stop feeling guilty, she feels she must control the situation by solving their problems. That is not possible. However, one thing she can control is her own body—she stops eating. As those around her notice and try to force her to eat by guilt-tripping her, she loses her appetite entirely and food becomes repulsive. Yet, given the idea that power is control, she has affirmed some power in a situation in which she feels totally out of control.[g]

Consider another example. A lesbian is sick and withdraws. Her friends do not understand, but it is because she cannot cope with their feelings of helplessness. She needs all her energy to face her disease. They want to help; but if they can't do that and notice improvement, they have

The ability to connect

---

g   Many believe that lesbians and women who are anorexic or bulemic are simply bigger dupes than everyone else in internalizing the messages of the diet and clothing industries. This is inaccurate in my experience. At least some anorexic lesbians and women began not eating as children in response to physical, sexual, or emotional abuse from parents or other authorities.[35] Not eating is a means of exercising control in a context in which someone feels out of control.

no way of simply living with her illness. Ultimately, they may withdraw in guilt and then never feel comfortable about reconnecting with her. Or they may turn on her in frustration, saying, "If you really wanted to be well, you would be."[h]

Because of our concept of power as power-over, we lose the ability to connect, to attend, to learn from each other, and hence to contribute to the ground of our lesbian be-ing. As a result, we are vulnerable to internalizing the belief system of those who dominate.

A white lesbian is losing her job because she is lesbian. The community can organize and pressure her employer to change his mind. But if he doesn't want to, they have no power to make him change. They may use psychic powers and attempt to will disaster. But if he is dead-set on his decision, they cannot bend his will to their own. Ultimately, the lesbian may feel contempt for her friends and her community. They cannot, it seems, make a difference. She may then settle into her employer's conceptual framework and internalize it.

Another lesbian is ill and feels contempt for her friends, contempt for their inability to stop her pain. Because of her idea that power means making pain or oppression end by intervening in a situation and immediately controlling it, she turns to those who do seem to have the power to inflict pain and oppression on others, regards them as harbingers of reality, and thus turns from lesbians and pushes away support.

We want someone to make it all better for us—and are furious when they can't—for oppression is not something we chose. And we want to make things right for those we care about. Paternalism as a way of thinking is an understandable response to living under conditions of oppression, of dominance and subordination, particularly of heterosexualism. But is this how we become adepts? As a way of thinking, paternalism does not help undermine, but rather reinforces, the conditions of oppression.

Attending as enabling Throughout the previous discussion I have been suggesting that it is inappropriate to try to control events for someone we care about. We would never think of intervening to control or terminate a process that was joyful. Trying to end a friend's pain, or to remove its source, encourages violation: by acting for her because we believe we are in a better position than she to handle the problem, we undermine her process and set aside her integrity. In other words, we indulge in paternalistic thinking—a comforting justification for imposing our will on another. The power of control is not an enabling, adepting power.

h It may be that some illnesses are ways of working through certain things. The point here is that the other, in judging her choices this way, thereby implies that the one who is ill is doing nothing or that what she is doing is not worthwhile.

I want to suggest a different approach to our interactions, an approach which encourages and weaves a different concept of power: power-from-within. I want to suggest that attending our friend in her pain, lending support, but not intervening to control, is powerful in that it is empowering, enabling, adepting.[36] Under the fathers' conception of power, we feel helpless as we watch her pain, and we want it to end. But if, instead of trying to control things, we attend her, our action empowers her in that it enables her to gather and focus her own strength. Such attending is often what we do when we share joy.[37]

As Alice Molloy writes, "attention is the coin of our realm."[38] When we attend someone or something, we focus on them or it and hence we give them or it our energy. Mostly we focus on and attend the agendas of those who dominate. Because of their power – that is, their ability to disrupt and destroy – our attention is riveted on them. But of course it is because we attend them that they can continue with their agendas.

When, instead, you attend me, our channels of communication are open and we are sending and receiving energy. When I attend you, I stretch toward you, I am present to you, I engage with you. I focus my energy on you, my rhythms. By attending one who is in pain, I can help steady her. When she is off-center and in crisis, I can help stabilize her nerves and fluctuations, perhaps acting as a beacon or a magnet. When we attend each other, we can create between ourselves an enabling, adepting power.[i]

She says her lover is leaving, she says she is sick, she says she is discriminated against on her job. I understand what this means to her because I understand something of politics, because I have my own similar experiences, and because I am intimate with her – I understand much of what goes on within her. And because of that I become a witness. I know how she feels because I understand how she has felt in the past – I understand her living.

If I focus on her and attend her process, she realizes that someone else understands what she is going through; and this in itself is empowering. As Juana María Paz writes: "I cannot go it alone. I need someone who re-

---

i Dayo notes that attending is the central ability of that "ancient and prepatriarchal path," midwifery: "Midwifery is a particular form of attendance. . . . The attendant cannot control the birthing womon's process – to interfere physically brings the kind of disaster with which obstetrics has made us so familiar. Physically, small measures of soothing are possible. On the other hand, doing anything other than attending will absolutely get in her way – disempower her. And yet, for most wimmin, this attention is utterly required. And if she is attended, her labor, her work, progresses. . . . I am suggesting that this . . . knowing is within our grasp, that the old, old ways are not forgotten."[39]

inforces my reality, who shares my dreams and visions."[40] That another lesbian realizes what I go through can keep me centered and sane. I do not have to remain in the craziness of isolation, believing that no one realizes what is happening to me. I am not isolated. I am part of a group and recognized;[j] I am being taken seriously; I make a difference.

Whenever we face something alone, we must constantly reaffirm that what we think is happening actually is happening. Or we must continually make sure our responses don't stray too far from what is actually happening. When our friends attend us, they provide reality checks; and this is empowering. It does not mean that we become dependent on them to determine for us what is real but rather that we can use their responses as added information with which to evaluate the reality. As a result, we do not have to use our energy and attention to constantly monitor our situation. Instead, we can address our feelings, our needs; we can focus our energy on processing our pain, on making decisions about how to proceed, and on growing.

This is not to say that the friends make no judgments in the situation. In fact, in attending we very much bring ourselves, our experiences, our perceptions, our advice—our energy. Nor is this to say that the friends should never do anything (for example, when a lesbian asks for help in a custody case or in a case of job discrimination). Rather, I am asking us to question the heroine in us: our urge to rush in and try to control things, the urge to find our essential value in someone else needing us, being dependent on us.

Thus, I am not trying to suggest a hard and fast rule for interacting with others. What I am trying to suggest is not a rule of right behavior but a way of approaching each other, a different perception and evaluation of our choices, a different understanding of power. I want to suggest that when we regard control of situations and of others as the appropriate mode of action in crises, we perpetuate a foundation of dominance and subordination, for we give substance to the idea of taking over for another and treating her as a victim. Alternatively, I am suggesting that if we focus our actions on attending her as she makes her choices—perceiving what she is experiencing, understanding her situation, making suggestions, but leaving the choices to her—we will begin to weave a different concept of power. Enabling a friend's abilities, not protection of victims and control of situations, would motivate our interactions.

---

j Many loners, I believe, carry on through difficult times by imagining competent attenders—mind spirits—who perceive what is happening even though mortal fools perceive nothing.

I am also not saying that we will never have occasion to intervene in a friend's processes. We can come up with all kinds of baffling cases. What *Intervention* if a relationship is an increasingly violent battering relationship? What if our friend has a seizure? What if she is arrested? What if she is about to step, unknowingly, into the middle of a busy street? What counts as taking over another's processes, abrogating her integrity? And if intervention is always coercive, is it nevertheless always the thing to avoid at all costs?

I am suggesting that we approach the idea of helping a friend (lover) from a different perspective. A different approach will affect what we consider as reasonable options available in a situation. It will also determine what actions or choices we regard as needing explanation.

Thus, we might choose to intervene for a friend, but we would do so only in very dangerous situations. And rather than regard our action as heroic, we would regard it as a very serious assumption, even presumption, because it would be first and foremost a choice to abrogate our friend's integrity. Under such a different perception of intervention, rather than explaining a decision not to intervene, as is called for under the heroic model, we would feel a need to explain our intervention.

Further, if we chose to intervene, it would not be appropriate to simply leave at the end of the crisis, considering our action as praiseworthy and complete. We would be prepared to stay in our friend's life until she was centered, able to again act for herself. We would be prepared to work to undo the violation of our initial intervention and any resulting dependency on us as heroines. And we would be prepared for the likelihood of her frustration and anger at the intrusion, at the (temporary) loss of her integrity and agency, and our part in it.

Being able to attend each other means that we can steady ourselves and each other as we face our individual situations. And that steadiness, I *Success in action* want to suggest, is what will help us actively resist oppression. It takes understanding and tremendous inner strength not to panic. We live in a world governed by male threats of destruction; we live by a time bomb. And the time bomb is ticking. But the successful dismantling of a time bomb is not accomplished by rushing in. Those who dismantle time bombs work meticulously with the small parts of the bomb, attending to one at a time, not letting themselves be uncentered by the magnitude of the task or the lack of time, giving each small part their full attention, keeping themselves steady even though surrounded by impending disaster. And the bomb may well explode before they're through. But their attention is not focused where they may seem helpless.[k] Their attention is

---

k   According to Machiavelli, to keep power one must keep others in fear. Men's power of

focused where their abilities can make a difference if a difference is going to be made. The work we face is not heroic or climactic; we can settle down to how we are going to live our lives through this, developing our own abilities and encouraging those of others so that transformation can occur.

Thus, we may decide to demonstrate because a friend is fired. But how we approach it makes a difference. Our focus could involve a do-or-die energy such that if we don't block this instance of oppression we've failed, we've made no difference. Alternatively, we can shift the focus of our attention to our friend and how this action enables her and us. Partly, this shift involves clarifying what will count as success in the endeavor. If the friend chooses to bring suit, must winning it be the only gauge of success? Success may be a matter of simply thwarting the smooth functioning of the master's plan as in sabotage, only this time open and clear-cut. Success may be a matter of our friend finding the means to fight back, to cause trouble, to make the employers acutely aware that we are not willing to accept the situation. Viewed in this way, success is in her hands: she can make a difference with her living; she is a moral agent; she moves here, and things are no longer the same.

Now I do not mean to suggest that we ought always to be attended.[41] *Limits to attending* Sometimes privacy is essential, especially when the one in pain does not trust herself not to manipulate her friends into taking over for her. And sometimes we just want to wallow in our grief, not having to worry about how we appear to others. This is especially true if our friends are extremely uncomfortable with our pain and hence want first and foremost for it to end. Or we may want to be alone if we feel our friends are watching us, curious about how we respond. (There's nothing wrong with such curiosity, but the one in pain may not want to satisfy it.) Privacy may be what a lesbian needs and wants in a given situation.

Further, there are limits to attending. In the first place, it may be important that I shield myself as I attend another, whether I am gaining new understanding or going over old territory. Thus, while I can come to understand another's situation, still I do not *absorb* it as if it were my own. Sally Gearhart's depiction of shielding before entering the remember rooms in *The Wanderground* is an important concept.[m]

domination backed by force and the threat of destruction is their ability to keep us riveted on them, unable to do anything but respond in terror to their agendas.

m   In this episode Clana, a seven-year-old, goes to the remember rooms, where, along with others and with the help of women remember guides and cats, she steps behind the "eyes and ears of a long-dead hill woman and made her memory [her] own." She learned of

Secondly, if attending another lesbian means we absorb her pain, particularly if that manifests itself as an attack on us in the form of misplaced anger, then remaining and giving our attention empowers neither her nor ourselves. When we accept attacks from a friend or lover, we expect nothing of her—we condescend. Absorbing the attacks only feeds her low opinion of herself, confirming her internalized oppression—her belief that she is mean, or that those who bother with her aren't worth much, that she lacks integrity, and so on. To remain in her presence at these times, particularly when she is trying to manipulate us, does not empower but further disables.

Thirdly, while I may decide to attend another in her process of making decisions, there may come a time I can no longer be party to the choices she is making. For example, she may decide to repeatedly get drunk to ease her pain. If she is not an alcoholic, I may attend her through one or two drunks; should she begin to make this a habit, I can argue that I think this is not really helping her. However, if I cannot convince her to stop, and if collaborating with her or trying to bend her will to mine are my only choices in attending, then I may choose to withdraw my attention. Attending involves energy; and if I cannot accept what my energy is contributing to, then I can withdraw it and cease to be a part of the events.

It is also important to realize that 'attending' carries its own dangers. A lesbian may in attending add burdens to her friend's process simply *Dangers in* through her own ignorance. She may not be able to understand the *attending* depths of what her friend is going through, and hence she may respond in ways that diminish the situation or that lend it an air of melodrama. The danger is that she becomes unreliable in her attendance.

A working-class lesbian responds, for example, to her upper-class friend who is acutely and chronically ill by assuming her friend's mind is as debilitated as her body, not realizing that her friend doesn't have the energy to maintain and defend herself but still absorbs the energy and games around her. Or a white middle-class lesbian responds with incomprehension to a black working-class lesbian's lack of emotional display at some tragedy in her own life, not realizing that, in her friend's life, expression of emotion carries dangers of exposure.

The danger is that she who is attending, in attempting to make sense of what she does notice, creates another story, a category in which to place

the experiences of women under patriarchy—"episodes about the city, the Purges and Hunts, to understand the last Revolt of the Mother." The girls and women spent time in ritual preparation for this event, the women teaching the girls to shield themselves so they wouldn't feel all the stories in their "hardself."[42]

her friend's suffering; and her friend now has not only her own problems but the other lesbian's distorting perceptions to deal with as well. Thus, as diane hugs writes:

> No longer can I be in public and not be aware of the roles society imposes on me. Often times just being out in public with my emotions feeds into one of the pre-existing stereotypes of disabled people. If I am angry it feeds into the bitter crip stereotype. If I am sad or depressed the poor pathetic handicapped B.S. comes in. Accomplishing a normal life task which may be considered brave or bold by those who have never been confronted with any similar barriers in their lives, then I'm seen as the courageous crip. If I'm being athletic then of course I must be a super crip. Leaves little space for me to be myself, to be seen as a whole being whenever I am in the public view.[43]

That is, attending is itself a skill, an ability, which we need to learn to develop.[44]

This is not to say that lesbians who make the best attenders are always those who have first-hand experience of what their friends are experiencing. Sometimes a lesbian without past experience of our situation can be our most helpful attender. If we need to clarify for ourselves what we are going through, her questions may aid us in that process.

Further, lesbians with first-hand experience of what another lesbian is experiencing can also add burdens to her process. One lesbian may be fired from her job and trying to collect support to bring pressure on her employer, perhaps raising money for lawyers to file a discrimination suit. Another lesbian, to whom she turns for support, may have been through one or more firings already, and her friend's situation simply calls up old nightmares. She may turn from her friend because her own wounds are too raw. If she doesn't make clear that her withdrawal is owing to her own unresolved pain, she may seriously undermine her friend's perception of her situation. After all, if someone knows by experience what we are going through and still ignores us, then we will likely find ourselves questioning whether the discrimination we think is happening to us actually is happening.

Now, while there can be problems if the one who attends has too little *Impartial observers* or too much experience, I do not mean to suggest that attending is a matter of being or having an impartial observer. What I am suggesting here is not the humanistic psychology of the '60s and '70s that pretends to be nonjudgmental. I am not talking about the disengagement of an allegedly impartial observer, for to make no judgment is still to make a judgment. For example, the alleged nonjudgmentalism of rogerian therapy merely discourages awareness of our environment and of the values of the status quo—in therapy, often the value of blaming the victim. ("What I hear you saying is that you think you've been raped and that you feel it is your fault and that you feel you must have invited it.") Simply "objectively" "validating" someone else's pain affirms one set of judgments over and against other judgments (in this case, masculinist rather than feminist perceptions of rape). The allegedly nonjudgmental humanistic psychology affirms status-quo politics.[n]

Further, attending is an engaging interaction, and so I caution against the dynamic of regarding therapists as professional attenders.[p] The patient-therapist relationship formally designates one as in need of help while designating the other as having the "objective" ability to help by virtue of her training. As I've been suggesting, this is not what attending is about.

Attending is not a matter of being or having an impartial observer. Nor should it be. For as we attend, it is *our* energy we add to the situation. We come with our agendas and dreams. We come with our experience and judgments. We come with our needs and limitations. If a friend is losing a job, it is not just anyone who notices, it is *we*. As we attend, we involve our energy and our perceptions in the situation. Our attending gives it a different perspective. The situation thus changes; it involves her and us and what we all can make of it. Attending is not impartial or disengaging. It is profoundly engaging. (Thus, of course, it is fraught with mistakes as well as successes.)

We are tempted to go to someone who acts as a therapist because therapists are professionals and so must be "objective":

---

n   Or, another example: "Nonjudgmental, impartial observation in place of attendance was responsible for a short-lived 'caesarian birth movement' which tried to make caesarian sections as comfortable and as much like vaginal birth as possible. This has been replaced through very intense effort (especially by one particularly adept attendant, Nancy Wainer Cohen[45]) by the caesarian prevention movement which advocates natural vaginal birth except in the most extreme of situations."[46]

p   In criticizing therapy I am not necessarily criticizing the desire to become a therapist. I think that desire, at least at times, emerges from a desire to help others, not as a matter of altruism or self-sacrifice, but as a way of creating value and making a difference in each others' lives. It also stems from a desire to be self-employed while at the same time maintaining connection with other lesbians and women.[47] On the other hand, the desire can emerge from a desire to be in control. My main criticism, however, is of the institution and its structure. In my opinion there are other ways of engaging with each other which are more enabling, adepting. And in connection with economic considerations, I think we can work to find other ways to exchange money and so help to support each other economically. I will add that I am not denying that some have been helped by therapy. I am talking about therapy as a movement phenomenon.[48]

I do this believing that the person has no hidden agenda, no reason to betray me or to try to mold me in her image. In short, I believe she is objective. But what is objectivity? Is it disinterest, detachment or nonpartisanship? If so, do I want someone who is not interested in my well-being?[49]

"Objectivity" is nothing but a collection of perceptions which agree. One who acts as a therapist nudges our understanding of particular "inner feelings" into a particular world view – one which varies according to the school of therapy she adheres to. And while the depth of our feelings gain meaning from a context, one who acts as a therapist appears, through her "objective" professional status, to not participate either in creating that context or in being limited and focused by it. She is "impartial," thus, and she doesn't have to get caught up with our feelings or her own feelings; she can simply show us (or let us discover) how our feelings fit her model ("reality").

In challenging the idea of an "objective" observer, I want to suggest we also dispense with its foil, "subjectivity." Certainly in consciousness-raising groups, for example, we each bring our personal experiences. But invoking the concept of 'subjectivity' implies we have private, totally separate perceptions which need the mediation of a judge (someone "objective"). The meaning of our feelings and interactions develops in a social context. And therapy focuses us on "subjective" inner states rather than the social context in which our personal experiences take on meaning. In this respect, it has displaced consciousness-raising groups.

What we have done in c-r groups, as well as by focusing on each other as *Therapy versus c-r* lesbians, is neither a matter of being "objective" nor "subjective." Rather, it is a matter of challenging the patriarchal context and creating a new ground of meaning from which we can develop different perspectives about our interactions.

The therapeutic model encourages a lesbian to go to one who acts as a professional to deal with "her problem." It reinforces liberalism by promoting the idea that the meaning of our feelings is introspective. And it encourages the idea that first we become strong and then we act.[q] So we get angry, for example, and then focus on coping with our feelings.

The problem here, Anna Lee suggests, is not that therapy focuses us on our selves – we attend our selves as well. Rather, the problem is that ther-

---

q Joanna Russ reports a conversation between two lesbians "one of whom was living openly as such and one of whom was afraid to leave her marriage. The married one said, 'I can't leave my husband because I'm not brave, like you,' To which the other (who had left *her* husband only two years before) said, 'Don't give me that. I was just as scared as you when I left my marriage, but I did it anyway. *That's what made me brave.*'"[50]

apy encourages individual solutions to nonindividual problems.ʳ Citing Naomi Weisstein, Anna Lee reminds us that studies investigating the outcome of therapy for "neurotics" indicate that people do better without therapy.[51] Further:

> For the most part, wimmin who emerge from therapy lasting longer than six months have less resilience. Even if one is in therapy under six months, an unquestioning acceptance of therapy's focus on individual solutions can occur. Also, it is my observation that almost any problem will send the womon back to a therapist for the quick fix. It is conceivable that we can have many therapy-free years—if we narrow the focus of our lives to our immediate environs: a relationship with a lover or decorating our homes. In these ways, then, we are accepting and acting on the lessons learned in therapy—to reduce the scope of our lives to that which we can control. That which we cannot control, i.e. oppressive forces, we allow to continue without any struggle on our part. In disregarding outside forces, we have accepted individual solutions to societal problems.[52]

In other words, the institution of therapy encourages our belief that power is a matter of control and so discourages our moral agency, our ability to go on and make choices in situations, particularly situations we can't control.

Consciousness-raising groups involve lesbians getting together, discussing what's bothering us, noticing how similar things bother others but may affect them differently, calling each other on well-known avoidance tactics, and developing an analysis of what is going on—challenging the patriarchal meaning of all this in order to develop our understanding, to work our way out of a patriarchal context, and to develop lesbian meaning. While such interacting has its own set of problems (for example, a group may be intent, not on making changes, but merely on complaining and comforting), still our understanding of oppression has developed within such groups and does not come from therapy. As Anna Lee argues:

> The early second wave of feminist revolt began by friends coming together to talk about individual experiences, and realizing those experiences were similar and not isolated or crazy. Consciousness-raising groups were absolutely opposed to degenerating into therapy sessions. . . . Feminist analysis of rape didn't come from the human potential movement . . . Feminist analysis of racism didn't come from therapy.[53]

ʳ At one feminist event on therapy, for example, a woman asked how she could get her children to not be upset by the fact that her boyfriend occasionally beat her, and the therapist proceeded to suggest ways to help the children cope.

That is, therapy interrupts the process of lesbians creating lesbian analysis and meaning which emerged through c-r groups. It replaces the kind of community engagement through which we have developed new value.

In discussing our growth and development, Anna Lee introduces the idea of a 'focus muscle'. Learning to focus, we develop an ability to challenge the fathers' agendas: we develop an ability to detect the programs of the fathers as well as an ability to create value outside their agendas. Anna Lee argues, however, that when we go to someone we regard as an authority whom we pay, then someone else is directing our attention and we are not learning to develop our focus muscle. More importantly, such a focus muscle is not a private, individual matter. It is a matter of creating meaning outside our patriarchal context. And that involves the interaction and "agreement" of attending, not individual introspection.

Anna Lee also suggests that the therapeutic relationship undermines our ability to weave friendships:

Therapy and friendship

> Some wimmin argue that the feminist therapist is not an expert but a paid friend. . . . The therapist becomes just a womon who bears witness, while the other womon discovers what she needs to know. . . . [T]his argument for feminist therapy claims that [therapy] can truly empower wimmin through professional friendship. But what is the nature of this friendship? . . . If friendship is conducted on a paid basis, then it becomes a relationship subject to the laws of the marketplace. The value is determined by the price set and paid. By this law, a relationship without a price is not a relationship at all. Once we succumb to the belief that friendship can be paid for, we begin to distort the nature of not-for-profit friendship. . . . We bring the most intimate parts of ourselves to paid friends, while offering the most superficial parts of ourselves to our nonpaid friends. The excuse is that burdening our friends with our pain or anger or sorrow is unacceptable. But if we can only bring our joy to our friends, how can we value them? When we exclude our most intimate selves from our friends, we weaken the bonds between wimmin that are necessary to fuel a social movement.[54]

In fact, as both Janice Raymond and Caryatis Cardea argue, feminist therapy is an obstacle to or substitutes for female friendship.[55]

Therapy and the therapeutic process do not replace friendship; nor do they replace group process. Our ability to make choices and go on in situations is something we develop by acting and engaging with each other. Therapy allows us to separate from this process; in this way it fosters the idea of power as control. So I want to suggest that what I am calling 'attending' is a matter for friends and lovers, for lesbians in community, and for those who join groups in common cause, not for professionals.

So often we either withdraw because our energy can't control, or we face a situation but use it for some other end, romanticizing and objectifying others in the process. Attending can be especially hard on us because we have had to learn selective perception for survival and also because the lesbian telling is not always honest. But the point of attending is not for either us or her to control a situation; the point is empowerment, enablement, within a situation.

There's a difference between controlling a situation and acting within it. The point of attending a friend is, not that she can better control herself or her own situation, but that she can better act *in* the situation. The point concerns her ability to go on, to make decisions as a moral agent, as an agent who makes choices, who creates value. And if the focus of our energy is, not control, but rather attending, then there can be growth and enablement through engagement. Juana María Paz writes: "Flying Thunder had not been able to give me the dream I saw with her or the strength I saw in her, but she gave me the time and space to develop these things on my own."[56] Or as Harriet Ellenberger writes:

> A friend sat me down – a woman that I've lived with for eleven years now and am separating from – and what she did for me is I think what lesbians consistently do for each other, when we are doing our jobs well. She sat me down and said, What are you trying to say? *What are you trying to say? What are you trying to do?* But she did that sitting down of me at the kitchen table, and that questioning of me at the kitchen table, in this utter faith that she has always had, that something significant eventually issues out of the confusion of my thought.[57]

Thus, as Mary Daly notes in *Pure Lust*, "Be-Friending is the creation of a context in which acts/leaps of metamorphosis can take place."[58] In attending, we are helping create a context in which our choices can take on new meaning.

And there can be growth and enablement even if there is no resolution at first and even if there is misjudgment and error. In a group of lesbians, *Growth in attending* both lesbians of color and white, a lesbian of color declares she cannot relate to white lesbians because the questions in her own mind only become greater and more confused when she tries to talk about them. The understanding of intimacy, at this point, is just not occurring. The white lesbians have proved to be unreliable in their attention, and not only does she have to explain much to them, they just don't get it. She decides that to address her own needs she must withdraw.

If we value this development in terms of control, it could be regarded as a failure of all the other lesbians – white and lesbians of color – to make a space in which she could explore her questions. Her choice could throw the others back on their inability to control things, their apparent helplessness; and they might shut down or shut themselves off from her for a variety of reasons. Reacting in this way, they would fail to attend her pain and learn from what she is saying.

If, on the other hand, the others can touch their own pain and fear from this development in the situation, they may be able to understand that theirs was a context in which she could clarify her needs sufficiently to withdraw. They may be unable at this point to attend her because they don't have the ability to perceive her questions and confusion without blocking or crumbling before them, thinking they ought to have answers now. But they can perceive her reactions and attend the pain their ignorance is causing, and they can learn from the situation. This understanding, rather than leading them to react helplessly, empowers them to go beyond blocking or liberal guilt, to gain further understanding.

Gaining understanding   In other words, attending is interactive, it is a two-way exchange, unlike the dynamic of "authorized" relationships, unlike relationships in which one person is the authority and the other is the patient/client. Of course, those in positions of authority learn things from their patient/clients. Nevertheless, what they learn never challenges their authority. In attending, no one is the authority. Thus it may be that she who attends at any given moment helps steady the one she attends. It may also be that she who attends at the moment is the one who grows and changes in the process.

For gaining understanding is another part of attending. Not only does attending enable the one who is attended at any given time, it empowers, enables, the one who attends. While a prerequisite for lesbian ethics is self-understanding, our understanding grows and develops through interacting with others.[s] The one who attends is gaining understanding – understanding of other situations, understanding of different but essential perspectives, understanding of her self in relation to those perspectives, understanding of different energies. And she is also learning to act in situations. Attending dispels ignorance.

Ignorance for lesbians and for lesbian community is a life-and-death matter. It may be that ignorance feels comfortable, but it is the comfort of numbness, not the comfort of centering when reality is confirmed and we have the understanding we need to go on, to make the best decisions possible within the circumstances. We may need to withdraw for a while, but that is quite different from numbing ourselves.

---

s Sheila Mullett argues that some things we learn about our selves only in relation to others, things which involve gaining perspective on our selves and developing our relational capacities.[59]

Living on the fringe of a patriarchy, we realize our jeopardy and rush around in a panic trying to make things happen. We are led to believe that she who sits and observes is ignorant. Yet ignorance is not inaction. Ignorance, rather, is goal-oriented behavior that is unconsidered and unthinking.[60] As we realize that the dominant culture's knowledge is unreliable and does not yield what we want, we find we have no one to learn from but each other.

This means we learn as we go, and considered action means carefully attending each other and resisting the impulse to work for control. If we do not think to attend each other but instead are thrown reeling back on our own fears, we will not use our time to pull ourselves out of ignorance. If we feel helpless and guilty because our only concept of power is control, we begin to shut down in one of a number of ways. One who attends, on the other hand, takes and learns as an attender and then acts in her own capacity, contributes her own part.

That I am aware of what another goes through can help her remain centered. If she is attended, she is not isolated; thus she can focus on her process. That I attend what she goes through helps me to address the unknown. Though I do not share her exact process, I can affirm her reality and come to know beyond intellectualizing, come to *feel*, something that is not my experience.[t] Attending thus increases my ability to respond; it is one way lesbians of vastly different backgrounds can work together.

I have been arguing that paternalism does not serve us; it leads us to pursue power as control and as a result we undermine our own and each other's moral agency. Not surprisingly, there is a connection between paternalism and patriarchal privileges: race privilege, class privilege, able-bodied privilege, for example; part of what these privileges offer us is the ability to ignore those without them. Paternalistic thinking, the belief that it is appropriate to act for (not with) someone, keeps us believing that we can do things without knowing others or understanding their perceptions and world-view in relation to our own (often called "objectivity" in science), it encourages atomistic individualism. Paternalism and the belief that power is control encourage the arrogance, indeed contempt, of ignorance. As a result, it undermines our ability to undermine dominant values.

Addressing white women, Ellen Pence writes:

Dominant privilege

---

t As Bett Farber points out, attending is a specific instance of the conceptual agreement which makes up lesbian political analysis. She goes on to note that it is a function of our location in the history of lesbian politics that our analysis begins with attending pain rather than, say, intuition or strength.[61]

Knowing that we grew up in a society permeated with the belief that white values, culture, and life style are superior, we can assume that regardless of our rejection of that concept we still act out of that socialization.[62]

Paternalistic values function to keep all lesbians from working out of our socialization by encouraging us to believe that we can be responsible without understanding those with whom we act, or those on whose behalf we act. Attending as a value encourages us not to act for but to attend, not to assume always the author stance but rather to step aside and learn from. Barbara Smith writes:

> It's not white women's fault that they have been raised, for the most part, not knowing how to talk to Black women, not knowing how to look us in the eye and laugh *with* us. Racism and racist behavior are our white patriarchal legacy. What is your fault is making no serious effort to change old patterns of contempt.[63]

Or again, from Judit Moschkovich:

> I do not hold any individual American woman responsible for the roots of this ignorance about other cultures; it is encouraged and supported by the American educational and political system, and by the American media. I do hold every woman responsible for the *transformation* of this ignorance.[64]

I will add that attending in such situations, as is true in all situations of attending, does not mean simply accepting something the other states because she states it; that, too, is a way of ignoring her, of not really having to deal with her, of not attending her.

Paternalism encourages lesbians to indulge our fear of the unknown,[65] to resist this transformation, to not make the serious effort; it leads us to believe we can act in the world without understanding anyone. As a result, in addressing movement white tokenism, Lorraine Bethel writes: "What chou mean *we*, white girl?"[66]

In terms of race, many white lesbians have begun to dispel ignorance. Paternalistic values still function, however, because they encourage us all to believe that to act responsibly toward someone of another group, we must act to control and make the situation all right. And while I noted above how that can make us break down and turn on each other, there is another aspect. If we pursued the enabling power of attending rather than the controlling power of paternalism, we would be interacting, engaging. But that is not the form responding to difference among us has taken for the most part.[67] Instead, we continue to be tempted to act *for*. And this translates into arrogance, even contempt.

In describing humanism Marilyn Frye writes:

We feel it is morally acceptable, even laudable, to treat members of other species with contempt, condescension and patronage. We supervise their safety, we decide what is best for them, we cultivate and train them to serve our needs and please us, we arrange that they shall be fed and sheltered as we please and shall breed and have offspring at our convenience. And often our concern for their welfare is sincere and our affection genuine.[68]

She argues that phallism is a form of humanism: men meet women with humanist contempt. And she adds:

An arrogation of rights and duties fully analogous to humanism is carried out in relation to infants, the aged, the ill, those labeled insane or criminal, and by members of dominant races in relation to members of subordinate races.[69]

What has happened among many white lesbians in terms of race, among many able-bodied lesbians in terms of disability, among many middle- and upper-class lesbians in terms of class, for example, is an arrogation of rights and duties toward those perceived as different. Again from Ellen Pence:

I began to see how white women ignored the need to reexamine the traditional white rigid methods of decision making, priority setting, and implementing decisions. Our idea of including women of color was to send out notices. We never came to the business tables as equals. Women of color joined us on our own terms.[70]

Mitsuye Yamada writes:

Women's organizations tell us they would like to have us "join" them and give them "input." They are the better ones; at least they know we exist and feel we might possibly have something of interest to say to them, but every time I read or speak to a group of people about the condition of my life as an Asian Pacific woman, it is as if I had never spoken before, as if I were speaking to a brand new audience of people who had never known an Asian Pacific woman who is other than the passive, sweet etc. stereotype of the "Oriental" woman.[71]

In other words, in acting to be inclusive, in this case white lesbians concerning racism, lesbians for the most part have yet to undermine the arrogance of ignorance, indeed, the arrogance of dominance.

María Lugones argues that this is connected to the idea of responsibility — the idea of being a responsible decision-maker: "Being central, being a being in the foreground, is important to your being integrated as one responsible decision maker."[72] Paternalistic values, the power of "benevolent" control, encourage lesbians to act to stay in charge. (In this way, the therapist is not able to attend.)

One white lesbian academic administrator develops and produces a women of color series. At a surface level, the basis of her decision is reasonable, even valid, given the institution she is working in. Two other white lesbians write a grant to fund a conference and then invite women of color to participate. From the perspective of these directors, they are creating opportunities, where there were none before, for women of diverse backgrounds – they are being politically responsible, they are doing grunt work: handling the organizational details so that others may have the opportunity to communicate, interact, learn.

As Anna Lee notes, from the perspective of those on whose behalf they act, they are simply representatives of the white patriarchal structure. They may offer goodies, and they may be sufficiently manipulable through liberal guilt to provide everything demanded, but they are still in control from the perspective of those whom they "serve." Paternalism encourages lesbians to try to control a situation to be sure the right thing is done, thus to use each other in the rush for political correctness. As a result we wind up controlling, or trying to control, each other. In other words, we show each other contempt, not respect.

We also try to remain in control of ourselves. María Lugones argues that we block identification with those we perceive as different because fully attending each other includes perceiving how the other perceives us, and that may not yield a reflection of ourselves we like. The interaction of attending is a self-conscious interacting: we are aware of the other not only as other, but as she herself becomes subject and reflects us back through her perceptions. María Lugones suggests, thus, that we are afraid of plurality, particularly in ourselves as reflected by others. Addressing white anglo women, she writes:

> You block identification with that self we mirror for you because knowing us in the way necessary to know that self you are requires self-conscious interaction. Your fear of duplicity directs you to forget all interaction that we have had because that interaction, when lived and remembered as interaction, reveals yourself to yourself as a duplicitous being. So you are inattentive to our interactions. You are not keenly attentive to what our interactions might reveal.[73]

In my experience, lesbians also block identification because we are afraid of what we imagine we would find in the other's perceptions; and what we have conjured in our imagination is almost always worse than what we find in the other's perceptions of us. Or, perhaps, once it is faced, it is never as bad as we imagined in our avoidance. In general we embrace control in order to acknowledge only those parts of our selves we approve of.

Letting go of control is perhaps the most terrifying thing to ask anyone under oppression. But control does not serve us. I want to suggest that revaluing our energy from control to attending is central to Lesbian Ethics.

Attending contributes to the moral agency of both the lesbian who attends and the lesbian who is attended in any given situation. In being attended and refusing to accept power as the ability to control, we increase our responsiveness—our ability to respond. We are enabled to act in a situation and go on; we find we do make a difference. Thus we can begin to undermine the debilitating effects on us of paternalism as well as other forms of domination. That we learn to focus on and attend each other can make our ground of choice more solid.

And in attending we also increase our responsiveness. For when we do not accept power as the ability to control, we will less likely shut down and numb ourselves, internalize oppressive ideology, ignore difference, objectify others for a political end, or turn on another and deny her situation. Secondly, we gain in our ability to respond because we gain awareness, understanding. Thirdly, we will be able to realize how we replicate dominant values and have a way to begin dispelling the dominance of privilege. And understanding increases our ability to make choices.

Up to now the power we have been using has involved strategies of control such that our collective resistance has been simply in our survival—in "only not dying."[74] I believe that by regarding our power instead as a power-from-within, as an ability to create new value through our choices and interact with others, we can increase our resistance to the point that we begin also to undermine (some) structures of oppression.[u]

Engaging versus Binding

THUS, I CHALLENGE the idea of control in our relationships regardless of the justifications. I have argued against control from a position of *Autonomy* subordination through the feminine values, and I have argued against control from a position of dominance through the masculine value of paternalism. From heterosexualism, we tend to regard controlling others and being controlled as acceptable. And I have been arguing that when

---

u Beyond personal relationships, attending can be empowering as a community function. While I believe we're still too caught up with power as control for attending each other in a group ritual to be fully enabling, even within spirituality circles, still there is a power here we can eventually develop. The movie *Witness*, although damaging in elements of its portrayal of the amish, nevertheless hints at one aspect of the empowerment of groups witnessing, attending.

we regard controlling other lesbians and being controlled by other lesbians as desirable ethical norms, we undermine lesbian moral agency.

However, in making these arguments, I do not mean to suggest we remain independent of each other. I mean to suggest, rather, that dominance and subordination are not the only way of interacting. Thus, I am not suggesting that we work to develop autonomy. 'Autonomy' comes from the greek 'auto', meaning "self," and 'nomos', or "rule." Thus the word actually means "self-rule" and usually applies to states or national groups. Now, the idea of 'self-rule' conjures up the idea of 'other-rule' and independence from it. But as lesbians in patriarchy we are not independent of other-rule; and a central aim of Lesbian Ethics is to develop a sense of ourselves as moral agents independent of the values of heterosexualism, even though we are also subject to other-rule. In this respect, embracing the concept of 'autonomy' leads us in the wrong direction. For if we base our sense of moral agency on being autonomous, when we find we are not, we may feel we can't be moral agents – or, again, that nothing we do makes any difference. Further, when we can act, we will act to stay in charge.

Secondly, when 'autonomous' is applied to individuals, it suggests separation and independence from others – the orphan hero who has no ties and is self-sufficient in nature.[75] Thus, one who is "autonomous" has no connections; one who is "autonomous" does not interact with others. Actually, if we are autonomous we can do things to or for others without being affected by them.

Thirdly, in religious contexts 'nomos' ("rule") is used to name the subordination of reason to faith, and this is regarded as a form of love – the subordination of oneself to a divine law beyond man's understanding. 'Autonomy' ('auto' plus 'nomos') thus comes to mean "self-love" through the subordination of oneself to one's own law. And yet I am conjuring a framework wherein the concepts of 'dominance' and 'subordination' make no sense. 'Autonomy', it seems, is the "androgyny" of human interaction: with 'autonomy' one can ameliorate a little dominance with a little subordination in the concept of the 'self'.

Along these lines, a fourth difficulty arises. 'Autonomy' begins to imply the idea of self-control: if we are autonomous, we are able to control our selves; the one who is autonomous is the one who can rise above her nature and exercise self-control through will power. Yet control of self no more fits within the framework I am conjuring than does control of others, either from a position of subordination or a position of dominance.

'Autonomy', it seems, is a thoroughly noxious concept. It can invoke anything from self-subordination to self-isolation. And it encourages us to believe that connecting and engaging with others limits us (such that we "sacrifice" when making choices) and undermines our sense of self. While some of us may be tempted to invoke 'autonomy' in radical contrast to the feminine of heteropatriarchy, I find it is born within that context and nurtured by it.

Each of us is unique in what we focus on, move away from, create, challenge, and connect with; and yet we live under and are affected by oppression. Further, what it means to be a lesbian is deeply connected with lesbian networking and the possibility of community; who we are emerges through our interactions with others. Our growth as lesbians is essentially related to the values that emerge in lesbian community. Thus the sense of self I mean to invoke is not one which fails to engage with others. *Autokoenony*

Nevertheless, I do mean to invoke a sense of our selves as not essentially *defined* in terms of another. I mean to invoke a self who is terrified neither of solitude nor of gatherings, a self who is both elemental and related, who has a sense of herself making choices within a context created by community. I mean to invoke a self who is both separate and connected. So I create a word for what I mean: 'autokoenony' (ô´ to kēn o´ nē) which I take from the greek 'auto' ("self") and 'koinonia' ("community, or any group whose members have something in common").[76] What I mean by 'autokoenony' is "the self in community." The self in community involves each of us making choices; it involves each of us having a self-conscious sense of ourselves as moral agents in a community of other self-conscious moral agents. And this is not a matter of us controlling our environment but rather of our acting within it and being a part of it.

Thus, being autokoenonous does not involve isolation, nor does it mean not being influenced by or not depending on others. By 'autokoenony' I do not mean that we strive to act independently of each other such that we either refuse to depend on someone else in time of need (thus becoming unreliable) or work to keep ourselves from being dependable. An autokoenonous being is not one who foolishly acts as if no one else exists, asking for no help and connecting not at all — as if engaging may limit her. An autokoenonous being is one who is aware of her self as one among others within a community that forms her ground of be-ing, one who makes her decisions in consideration of her limitations as well as in consideration of the agendas and perceptions of others. She does not merge with others, nor does she estrange herself; she *interacts* with others in situations.

So in challenging control in our interactions and yet appealing to the concept of 'autokoenony', I am not suggesting a community in which we never depend on each other. I am suggesting that there is a difference we do not currently acknowledge, perhaps even perceive, between depending on someone and being dependent on her. If I depend on someone and she is unable to meet her commitment, I may be set back, but I can carry on. Carrying on may involve replanning the scope of my venture, finding someone else to help me in the particular capacity my friend was unable to, joining with some larger project, or at times abandoning the project and moving on to something else. But I am the subject, still, of my choices. If, on the other hand, I am dependent on someone and she cannot keep her commitment, I fall apart: I cannot carry on; I am the object of events, the one to whom things happen. I am not one who makes choices, and so I am not a moral agent.

Further, if I am dependent on someone rather than depending on her, when over time things change and in evaluating her situation, she must also be aware that should she be unable to continue as before, I might fall apart. Thus she becomes responsible for me; and if she needs to slow down, she may respond with guilt feelings around my dependency when she really needs to focus her energy on herself for a while.

I am not proposing a rule, such as "Never be dependent." In the first place, in any given case it may be unclear whether we are dependent on another or whether we are depending on her. Secondly, rules are easily abused in moments when we are dishonest or in moments when we are threatened and fall back on old habits of manipulation. My concern is that we regard and approach and affirm each other as both separate and related, lesbians who act in community as well as in a context of oppression – not as total victims of circumstances and, equally, not as beings totally responsible for a situation.

In discussing the possibility of lesbian community, Julia Penelope *Subculture versus* makes a distinction between a subculture and a community. A lesbian *community* subculture is a group we become part of automatically by declaring ourselves lesbian – but a group "wholly defined in negative terms by an external, hostile culture that sees us as deviates from their 'norm'."[77] In contrast with this is lesbian community. And while in writing her essay Julia Penelope holds that no such association exists yet, she suggests certain features that would distinguish it from lesbian subculture:

> First and most important, membership in a community is a voluntary act. One joins a community because she finds companionship, support, and commitment to common ideals within that community. Second, a community, as such, is internally defined by its members on the basis of shared experiences and common interpretations of events in the real world.[78]

Julia Penelope goes on to suggest that it is difficult to make the transition from subculture to community: "The struggle against oppression may create *alliances*, but it will not automatically establish *bonds* that will prevail beyond the immediate oppression."[79] And she argues that we have failed to distinguish between bonding and binding. Bonding "is the process of establishing a kind of intimacy, . . . a process of creating strong links between and among women based on mutual respect for the wholeness and strength of other women."[80] Binding, on the other hand, is a state of dependency, and it can involve very little understanding of each other. Thus, the process of moving from subculture to community is the arduous process of moving from binding, or being thrown together by an outside threat, to bonding, or choosing to engage, as a result of attending, based on shared values, respect, intimacy. Actually, I use the terms 'engagement' and 'connection' because the word 'bond' carries its own sense of something that binds, holds, or fastens together.

In working toward lesbian community, we have not yet come to fully attend or respect each other, we do not yet fully interact. Instead, we often act to control each other, and we confuse 'support' with 'approval', 'needing' or 'depending on others' with 'dependency', 'intimacy' with 'vulnerability', 'helping others' with 'self-sacrifice', 'empathy' with 'pity', and 'engaging' with 'binding'. The distinctions are difficult to clarify in given instances. How, for example, do we support another lesbian in such a way that she does not come to depend on our approval rather than on her own judgment? How do we keep our needs from becoming habits, dependencies? How do we resist attempting to manage the decisions of lesbians whose problems or even just agendas and goals are of concern to us? How do we open from centering and choice rather than from weakness and fear? How do we resist the potential in illness for manipulation? As Juana María Paz writes in *The 'La 'Luz' Journal:* "There is a fine line between love and dominance, and between nurturance and control."[81]

My concern with these distinctions involves the difference between attempting to control a situation, on the one hand, and the process of empowerment, enablement, within a situation, on the other. For example, there is a significant difference between 'support' and 'approval', one which traditional morality erases. Traditionally, to say I approve of something is to say I would do it if I were in that situation, if it were up to me.[v] We are often taught that there is only one right way to do something; this is an idea necessary to competition and to standardized tests.[w] Such

Support versus approval

---

v   Thus, one reason given for not passing laws which would prohibit discrimination against homosexuals is that the legal acknowledgment is tantamount to approval which in turn is tantamount to advocacy.

w   In the case of i.q. tests, for example, children may have excellent reasons for picking other answers than the one designated as "correct" by the test designers. For example, one

an approach allows for no recognition of differences. Thus, to approve of something is to affirm that it is the "right choice," that is, that anyone with good judgment would choose it.

In this respect, to approve of something someone does is to claim power over her. It is to claim that we are an authority, that she can depend on us to know what is right. For example, if I approve of your work, you may cease depending on me for my honest opinion, which you can evaluate and use to further your own project, and instead become dependent on my praise. Thus, you might slowly and subtly change what you are doing, gauging your choices according to certain things you realize I like in order to continue pleasing me.

In a skit designed to expose some of the power games middle-class lesbians play with working-class lesbians, dolores bargowski and coletta reid have one working-class character say:

> Whenever you tell me how good I am I start expecting it from you. I stop believing in myself and look to you for what I know I already have. I feel like I have to keep behaving then so you won't take your support away. You make me dependent on you when I don't need to be. You make me pay for the support you give to me.[83]

When approval has been the form of support, for you to grow in your own direction there will have to be a serious break between us; and, as a result, you or I or both of us will feel betrayed.

The other side of the coin is the idea that withholding approval of what another does is oppressive.[84] And withholding approval can be oppressive in a relationship of dominance and subordination. For example, often the relationship between parent and child is one of dominance and subordination, that is, one in which the parent controls the child rather than one in which the parent interacts with the child and, while acknowledging the child's limits, nevertheless respects and acts to preserve her integrity. When a dominating parent withholds approval from a child, that can be oppressive. But in a relationship where there is mutual respect, giving a negative judgment is not oppressive. As Marilyn Frye points out in another context, the mark of a voluntary association is that one can survive displeasing the other.[85]

By suggesting we interact with each other in terms of support rather

---

question used shows a cup, and the child is to pick what goes best with it – a saucer, a table, or a flower. The "right" answer is the saucer. But some children's homes have no cups and saucers, only mugs; and they are taught that cups go on tables rather than on the floor. And some know that cups are most beautiful when they hold a flower.[82] To have one "correct" answer, we must arbitrarily designate it and discount the richness of a variety of approaches as well as embrace classism and ethnocentrism.

than approval, I am not appealing to what Joanna Russ calls "that amorphous, judgment-less, uncritical, and ultimately meaningless 'emotional support' which all too often passes among women for real love and real respect."[86] Amorphous support means we aren't really attending what the other says; we're not taking her seriously. A highly attentive critical evaluation of our work can be very supportive. But if the critique is given in the form of approval or disapproval by someone who has become the "authority" on what is good and what is not, then it becomes a problem. When a critic has an axe to grind, when her words are treated as if she is a moral authority, or when her message, besides being critical, also trashes the other, what she says can be devastating.

There are serious abuses in our evaluation and criticism of each other's work. Nevertheless, I think the key is not to set up rules whereby we critique each other only in certain ways, according to certain polite standards. I think the key is that we not regard the critics as impartial arbiters of truth, beauty, and political analysis. Thus, we regard the one who critiques our work as making a statement as much about herself as about our work: her critique becomes as much a reflection of her interests, defenses, focus, ability, and limits as it is a comment on our interests, defenses, focus, ability, and limits. It is a statement from where she stands, from her own center and connected to her own needs; and we can use the information we gain from it to further consider what we are doing from where we stand, from our center. We can take what we find useful and, if we're not dependent on her approval, leave the rest. (Of course, once this is articulated on paper, it is a snap to enact it in practice!)

Confusing 'empathy' with 'pity' is yet another way we confuse enabling power with power-over in our interactions. To pity someone else is to remove ourselves from her reality; it is to distance ourselves without acknowledging that is what we are doing. By pitying her, we fail to understand how or even that she is a moral agent—someone who is making choices from within her circumstances, sometimes making mistakes, reacting and acting in her own way and with reasons. To pity her is to regard her as a victim, as less than us because of the particular limits she faces which we don't; thus it is to expect less of her than we expect of ourselves. To pity her is to avoid identifying with her, hence to avoid understanding her.[x]

Empathy versus pity

Alternatively, when we act from empathy, we attend her, give her our attention, while also expecting her to make choices and function within

---

x   Thus, some upper-class ladies could give charity to lower-class women precisely because they pitied them and hence could avoid identifying with them, avoid knowing them.

her situation. Actually, I mean to invoke something more than empathy. For when we empathize, we try to understand how we would act if faced with that situation. I am suggesting that we understand what is going on in all its complexity, hence that we understand the situation not only as we would address it but as she perceives it.[87] (Thus we also meet our selves as she perceives us.[88])

For example, two lesbians go to a city to enjoy an exhibit. One is able-bodied, the other a paraplegic, requiring a wheelchair. Where they live, the community is able to help and the lesbian who is paraplegic has sufficient resources to meet her needs. When the two embark on this overnight adventure to the city, the able-bodied lesbian helps the lesbian who is paraplegic get around. Because her actions stem in part from pity and in part from trying to be in control, the able-bodied lesbian pushes herself past her own limits, reasoning that the lesbian who is paraplegic is dependent on her. After a time exhaustion sets in, and she begins to resent her friend's situation; by evening she withdraws in silence, sleeping in a separate room. The lesbian who is paraplegic, aware of all this, is thrown back on her own trauma of dependence in a strange and hostile environment.

We may approach another as if she were helpless because we feel we'd be helpless in her place. Thus rather than attend her and acknowledge that she is not helpless, we close down, embracing our own assumptions and fears. Rather than trying to understand her self in her situation and how she perceives us, we distance ourselves, objectifying her, and act from duty and obligation toward her. Thus, in a circumstance in which we have extended contact, we fail to interact. In the above example, if both lesbians attend each other, gauge their needs and abilities and discuss the situation as it progresses, they may decide to simply cut the trip short. But they will be enabling each other to act in the situation.[y]

When we attend, we work to understand the other, move past our own circumscribed assumptions. However, this does not mean we make no judgments. It means we are in a better position to make judgments. To pity someone, for example, can be a way of avoiding assessing and judging a situation. Consider a lesbian acting out. In some cases a lesbian in pain or crisis will strike out and attempt to hurt another, perhaps one who

---

y I think we need, in our discussions, to distinguish (at least) between acute illness, chronic illness, terminal illness, and disability. Some things expressed to someone who is acutely ill are not appropriate to the situation of one who is chronically ill. And some things expressed to someone who has a disability are not appropriate for someone who is terminally ill or who is acutely ill. We need a lot of discussion to sort this all out.

has been a source of pain for her. For example, one lesbian breaks up with another, and the other, devastated because the relationship was "the best thing that ever happened to her," turns on her ex-lover. Friends watch as she plans to be in places where she knows her ex-lover will be, in order to threaten or even hurt her ex-lover. Often our temptation is to pity her and tolerate her excesses because of the pain she has gone through. In this case it may seem as if we are sympathetic and attending her.

However, if our approach to the one who is acting out is to accept her behavior because we understand how badly she's been hurt, we pity her; we are not really attending her because we ignore or discount her excesses and perceive only an object of pity. In understanding how it goes with her, we also evaluate, judge, the situation. If, in the process, we expect nothing of her, we imply that she is not capable of the value we hold for ourselves. Hence we affirm her alleged worthlessness. To expect nothing of her is to treat her as if she were expendable.[89]

When someone is acting out, we may attend her more closely than usual. But we can remain aware of what is going on, noting her attempts to hurt and where they come from, as well as understand, even feel, the pain she is in. But to pity a lesbian is to treat her as a victim, as someone to whom something happened. Alternatively, to attend her is to respond to her by acknowledging that she is a living, active being who makes choices, some of which are mistakes, a being who is integral and account-able (who can give reasons, or at least consider the reasons, for her choices), a moral agent. The difference between 'empathy' and 'pity' is a difference in the attitude with which we approach each other.

We can approach the difference between 'need' and 'dependency' by further considering the difference between depending on someone and being dependent on her. The idea, in asking for help, is to focus on how we can avoid letting our needs become habits whereby we presume, we begin to take the other for granted. For example, between lovers a need may become a presumption—I need this, so of course you will give it.

Need versus dependency

One working-class white lesbian is attending school, and the financial-aid office once again is holding up her payments. She is thus dependent on her working-class white roommate (and ex-lover) to cover food and rent until her money comes through. This has happened several times over the last three years. The roommates have had several fights about it, with the one feeling she must support the other and the other offering to leave. This time the lesbian in need, feeling trapped, simply announces that she will repay the money when she gets it, leaving no room for dis-cussing the matter (for there really are no alternatives except going to friends' houses for a few nights at a time). So of course there is a fight. The lesbian in need later admits that she had given her roommate no room for a choice. She had not tried to find the money elsewhere nor even asked her roommate if this time she could cover her.

Our economic situations are bottom-line, but so are our relationships. We cannot survive without friends; we cannot afford to take them for granted. They may want to help or they may not. Or they may not be able to help. Or their helping us may not really help us, if our choices have been taking us too close to the edge and it is time for us to face change — their help may enable poor choices. They may even be unable to help us find help elsewhere. But whatever the case may be, they are acting, choosing, reacting beings too, with their own needs and limits, as unique moral agents.

Our presumption is that if there is a need, then it must be met. The reality is that there is a need, and it either will or will not be met. And the trick is that the need does not specify who is to meet it. Presuming that the lover or the roommate will meet the need comes from an aspect of egocentrism — an energy that operates on the assumption that this need is the only one in the world, that the lover or roommate hasn't her own agenda and concerns, that there is no one else who can or should meet this need. But the one who is close needs space for choice. There is a difference between engaging and binding.[z]

From the other direction, often it is only when we reach our limits that we feel we can say no to others' needs, and then we may turn our backs in exhaustion; it is often only when we fall apart that we let go of trying to control a situation — meeting her need, not experiencing her disappointment. However, if we die, she will get her needs met elsewhere . . . or she will not. But it is no longer our concern. Similarly, if we are in the intensive-care unit of a hospital, we are unable to meet any needs of others, and others cease to expect things of us while we're there. Now if we can say no at this point and turn to take care of ourselves, why not two days before we get that sick? And if we can understand this, we can also understand another saying no to us.

---

z   The same sort of presumption can occur, for example, when one roommate has a child, or when two lesbians become lovers and one has a child and the mother presumes the lover will have a parenting relationship with the child. Certainly that a lesbian is a mother is part of who she is. But that the lover is not a mother is also part of who *she* is. The lover or the roommate may want to co-parent, but that is her choice; it is not a matter of the logic of the situation. For example, until lesbian amazoning develops, as some lesbians do, we could find someone to co-parent with and be lovers with someone else.

This is not to say that the lover has no relationship with her lover's child. When we become lovers or good friends with others, we can set up our own relationships with those close to our lover or friend — her children, her friends, and of course her companion-animals. (When we ignore the companion-animals,[90] we make a grave mistake!)

We feel we either have to be in full control or visibly out of control to be at ease with the world. But this is not adepting. Can we find a way to go on, to interact within circumstances, to make choices—to be moral agents? To say yes sometimes to the needs of others and also to say no? When we need help ourselves, to give the other room for choice, taking the risk that she will say no? Otherwise, guilt and manipulation become the means by which we interact with each other. When our needs become dependencies, we can't afford to take risks and grow.

When we interact on the basis of guilt and manipulation, we are not acting from center but rather are thrown off-center and so we act to control. And under such conditions the other will likely also attempt to control the arena. For example, if it is presumed she will give financial aid, then the roommate will likely start hassling the lesbian in need about whether she was responsible in getting her form in on time, whether she filled it out neatly and legibly, whether she "copped an attitude" with the financial-aid officer, whether she did everything possible to be a "good girl." In this way the roommate starts checking the friend's choices in terms of the roommate's needs, not allowing her friend her own reactions to the debilitating situation of having to beg for money.

Within patriarchal thought this dynamic of beginning to insist that the other act according to our dictates if our help is to be taken for granted, is referred to by the phrase "there is no such thing as 'no strings attached'" or "there's no such thing as a free lunch." Such sayings emerge because the structure of relationships within the dominance/subordination framework of heteropatriarchy is essentially one of defined roles in which debtor/creditor interactions are the standard of appropriate behavior: he brings home the bread, she owes him sex; she provides a home, he owes her loyalty or at least discretion. Yet we need not evaluate dynamics among ourselves in these terms, presupposing these values. Relating need not be a matter of dominance and subordination. In the case of the lesbian needing financial aid, if the two attend each other rather than try to control each other, they may be able to work together to develop a plan; they interact, and so can enable each other.

In working to attend each other, we can learn to realize each is separate and also connected. We cannot accomplish much if we each go it alone, but we will also not accomplish much if we simply take each other for granted. For one thing, we can realize that when we engage another in our concerns, what we can create *changes*. Another brings her own agenda and evaluative ability to a situation. She does not pursue the project exactly as we would, rather she brings a new dynamic to the situation, one which will change it. When we acknowledge this, then it becomes clear why attempting to control her or the situation merely perpetuates the fathers' values—we treat each other as means to ends rather than as integral beings with whom we engage.

When we start entwining our lives with others as if there were no boundaries, no differences, as if another being involved with us makes no qualitative difference to a project or the situation, we will perceive any distinctiveness or difference as threatening and any distancing as abandonment. Our interactions thus become manipulative and operate from guilt, and we start talking about how so-and-so owes us something or betrayed us. It is then that attempts to coerce each other by any number of strategies can become rampant. For we want guarantees that we will be there for each other. "Strategies of intimacy," it has been called in another context.[91] And its function is group cohesion through guilt and manipulation.

In conversation one spring in new york, Alix Dobkin suggested that we can regard all the fighting we do among ourselves, not as a negative indication that we're disintegrating, but rather as a positive indication that we are focused on each other, that we care about each other. And she cited Barbara Myerhoff's *Number Our Days* as indicating that a group could engage in serious infighting and still cohere. In certain respects I agree: as long as we focus on each other, we at least acknowledge each other. On the other hand, acknowledgment by itself does not transform our networking from subculture to community. *Number Our Days* is a thoughtful and provocative book, but it offers a central idea about group cohesion I question.

Barbara Myerhoff explores the lives of the elderly of the aliyah senior citizen's center in venice, california, mostly eastern european jews who escaped the holocaust and immigrated to the u.s., where they worked and married and raised children who successfully assimilated into u.s. culture. The old people of the center operate from a long tradition of jewish separatism, of jews realizing they cannot depend on goyim in a world laced with antisemitism, but also of jews focusing in on themselves, caring for their own, celebrating their own kind, developing and carrying on their own tradition, creating meaning by focusing on themselves. Billie Potts writes of this tradition, one which despite the resurgence of antisemitism, "has almost vanished from the american scene."[92] It is a tradition of buying jewish, of the hand-me-down network, of saving all that is useful, of creating jewish institutions to help jews from birth to death, of an entire people being self-sufficient unto themselves.[93]

Barbara Myerhoff's thesis is that the group's "strategies of intimacy" hold them together. She argues that the center old people transformed survivor's guilt into a sense of responsibility which manifested itself through guilt and manipulation, and that this was their way of gaining control over each other and their destiny, and hence affirming meaning in their lives.[94] Nevertheless, Barbara Myerhoff's foil in the book, Shmuel, one of the center old people, argues that when Barbara Myerhoff finds the guilt-tripping and hurting and manipulating behavior "interesting," she asks nothing of the center old people, shows no respect.[95]

I agree that these strategies indicate an intense caring among the center's members and keep them riveted on each other, but I disagree that the strategies are what holds them together. What holds them together is rather the strong tradition of jewish separatism, of focusing on and attending each other as jews. And what keeps them tolerating the "strategies of intimacy" is fear of outside threats, threats so serious that the members bypass directly dealing with conflicts and difference because the risk of splits in the community is too great and because their mutual trust is "too thin to support disclosure to each other of their greatest hurts and needs."[96] Their goal is not diversity and growth but survival and persistence.[97]

As lesbians we, too, can embrace separatism, and we, too, can focus on each other to forge meaning in our lives. But we are not bound together in the same way by an outside threat. And our guilt-tripping and manipulation and attempts to control will not hold us together. While we do face outside threats, many of us have nevertheless turned our backs on community simply because the manipulation in many of the political exchanges became more intolerable than the lack of validation in heterosexual society. Others of us left because our ethnic heritage presented a more meaningful, certainly a more familiar, culture. An outside threat can hold us together only in extreme conditions and even then not for very long. In part this is because of the outside threats we face: identification on the basis of outside threats creates serious loyalty splits and contradictions which simply cannot be ignored or bypassed within community. Further, given the pervasiveness of heteropatriarchy, we haven't yet managed to be strongly lesbian focused; we haven't yet a rich and complex enough culture with which to attract each other and give comfort past the contradictions.

If we are to form an enduring community, it will not be on the basis of outside threats. Further, it will not be on the basis of a rich tradition nor of what we find here (though we do have a crone-ology[98]). If we are to form an empowering community, it will be on the basis of the values we believe we can enact here: what we bring, what we work to leave behind, and what we develop as we engage with each other. If we are to transform subculture to community, it will be on the basis of what we create, not what we find. And attempts to control each other won't hold us together; instead, they actually undermine our ability, particularly our moral agency.

Thus, I am interested in engaging, not binding—in choosing to interact with each other rather than being forced to try to control each other because of an outside threat or internalized fears. I am not suggesting that we ignore the outside threats which do exist, but I am suggesting that they need not be the reason we stay together.

Given that we are trying to develop a diverse community, paternalistic and feminine values do not serve us. Trying to control each other replicates patriarchy, and keeps us ignoring each other. I am suggesting that by attending rather than controlling each other, we can interact in such a way that within limited circumstances we can empower ourselves and each other, and undermine (some of the) values of the fathers.

4
Integrating Reasoning and Emotions

IN THIS CHAPTER I want to discuss the split between reasoning and emotions, and the subsequent belief that one must control the other, which informs traditional anglo-european philosophy from ancient greece to the present and which we as lesbians perpetuate in our interactions. I want to suggest that accepting the split keeps alive the idea of power as control and keeps our selves fragmented and isolated. My overall argument is that our moral agency is encouraged by integrating and so politicizing reasoning and emotions within the community, for this is how we get back in touch with the energy that moves us, energy which is deadened when we separate reasoning and emotions.

Reason versus Passion

THE SPLIT BETWEEN reason and passion has been a central element of the rule of the fathers beginning as far back as ancient greek culture. *In the tradition* Mary Daly notes:

> The Aristotelian theory of moral virtue, which was assumed into Christian theology, centered around the virtue of prudence, the "queen" of the moral virtues. Prudence presumably is "right reason about things to be done," enabling one to judge the right and virtuous course. . . . Since moral virtue was understood as the mean between two extremes, prudence was understood as a virtue in the intellect which enabled one to steer between two opposite vices.[1]

Virtue was, loosely, a matter of common sense, and the virtuous person was one who chose the mean between two extremes. Thus, one who showed the virtue of courage steered between the extremes of cowardice and foolhardiness in assessing given situations. For example, a man who fled his house when it was attacked by one or two others was a coward, while he who remained to defend it alone against an army was a fool. Those who were prudent (virtuous) could moderate and control their passions by exercising reason; being neither foolhardy nor cowardly, but rather courageous, they would take risks when it was reasonable to do so. Mary Daly reminds us that a theory focused on prudence presupposes the emotions to be inferior to reason; for what takes us to extremes on this view are our emotions, and what helps us to be prudent is our reason.

In other words, within this framework passion could, and often did, go to extremes and had to be controlled. The virtuous person exercised control, and 'reason' itself became synonymous with 'stability', 'moderation', and hence 'virtue'. Thus the conceptual split between reason and passion involves the idea of something being out of control (passion) and something which can control it (reason). Man, therefore, had a choice and, using reason, could exercise his will or will power to control his excesses.

It is this disintegration of reason and emotion and the implicit idea that one can and should control the other which brings control through paternalism, as well as control through the feminine virtues, into the realm of ethics and makes them credible, acceptable. We are given to understand that the way to achieve good is through control, beginning with reason controlling emotion. The idea is that drives and desires are at best amoral, at worst inherently evil, and that through reason we can use our will power to control them and so gain control over our selves. Those who fail to do so are showing a weakness of will, an indication of human frailty – the original sin. This lack of control is a source of further sin and a crucial factor in the human tragedy.

Mary Daly goes on to argue that, following Aristotle's influence, the church established itself as the moral authority – church fathers claiming to be in the best position to determine which choices were prudent – for, they said, evil results when passion runs out of (their) control. Through this assumption of paternalistic authority, the church slowly eroded individual moral agency, shifting moral focus from prudence to obedience by affirming that a virtuous person would accept guidance from the church on faith. Thus, the ethical goal of self-control transformed into one of religious obedience as ancient greek patriarchal culture gave way to roman pagan patriarchal culture which in turn gave way to christian patriarchal culture. The myth of the fall gained prominence as christian fathers named women 'passionate' or 'emotional' while naming themselves 'reasonable'.[a]

The patriarchal reason/passion/control ideology has provided ground for the conceptual framework which makes male control of women (and nature) prudent, reasonable.[3] Thus under the fathers emerged the fundamental order of civilization, heterosexualism, which eventually yielded Nietzsche, who pointed out that while women's cunning humility implies a condition of slavery, nevertheless slavery is a mark of a "higher" civilization.[4]

The idea that we need self-control so we can rise above our nature, while stemming all the way back to ancient greek ideas, perhaps reached the height of expression with Kant. He argued that the moral individual is one who uses pure reason (logic) to determine what to do and then, by exercising his will, acts from duty alone to rise above his emotions or inclinations and hence his nature. Kant called this "autonomy."

From the other direction, but preserving the reason/emotion split, Hume argued that the emotions control reason: the emotions are what drive us to act, motivate us. Thus in moral matters we use reason to obtain our (emotional) desires; moral judgment comes not from reason but from a special moral sense, a capacity to feel. This later developed into a theory that what we call 'moral' is nothing but that which we desire or find desirable. Thus "you ought to do x" really means "I want you to do x" (not entirely inaccurate within heteropatriarchy).

In discussing Nietzsche's conception of the will to power, Walter Kaufmann notes that the common generic element in moral codes is self-overcoming:

> Morality always consists in not yielding to impulses: moral codes are systems of injunctions against submission to various impulses, and positive moral commandments always enjoin a victory over animal instincts.[5]

The idea of reason controlling emotion or emotion controlling reason or a will separate from and so controlling both is prevalent among lesbians. We tend to believe that to do anything we must be in control and that to feel anything we must be out of control. This fragments us, and it encourages us to psychologize our emotions while regarding political correctness as a set of rules with which to control ourselves and each other.

---

a   Thus, it is in men's interests to perpetuate the severing of emotions and reasoning, making their own propensity to wantonly destroy life appear a purely rational endeavor. And men can, as in a street fight, go out of control, all the time counting on other men to break it up.[2]

Thus, we set ourselves up to use ethics to gain safety and protection. I want to explore the effects of all this among lesbians.

Deep e-motion   To begin with, we can gain further understanding of the patriarchal severing of reasoning from emotions by considering Mary Daly's argument in *Pure Lust*. She uses the term 'passion', rather than the more modern 'emotion', to stress the movement involved; and she coins the term 'E-motion' to name the "dis-covery of deep elemental Passion":

> E-motion designates that Fire which moves women out beyond the Foreground and its fatherly fixes, into Pyrogenetic ecstasy.[6]

Real passions or deep e-motions "are movements within us, and they move us." As such they are different from the plastic passions:

> In contrast to real passions, plastic passions are free-floating feelings resulting in more and more disconnectedness/fragmentation. Since they are characterized by the lack of specific and nameable causes or "objects," they must be "dealt with" endlessly in an acontextual way, or within a pseudo-context.[7]

In other words, real passions or the deep e-motions have a clearly defined object or cause while the plastic passions have no specific object or cause. And because they have no specific object or cause, the plastic passions contribute to blaming the victim. (After all, if we feel something is wrong in our lives but don't name those who are the cause of that wrong, we will ultimately blame ourselves and each other.) Mary Daly argues that the process of naming the agents or causes of oppression is essential to breaking out of the plastic passions, which include anxiety, guilt, depression, hostility, resentment, resignation, and fulfillment.[8] She also distinguishes deep e-motion from the potted passions, or "twisted and warped versions of genuine passions," which are stunted and artificially contained. Potted passions are incomplete and hence substitutes for genuine e-motion.[9]

Her stress on the movement of e-motion is central to lesbian moral agency, as is her idea that often e-motions are connected to something outside the person—an object, or as I will suggest, a subject. And while I agree with most of her analysis, my focus is slightly different.

In the first place, I think it is important to distinguish between object and cause of our emotions.[10] Someone else may be the target or object of my emotion—the subject of my perception and judgment—but they are not thereby the cause. Men justify raping women by equating object and cause, for they claim that a particular woman "caused" them to attack her by her "seductive" dress. Thus they claim they are not responsible for their emotions or resulting action when in fact their action is their response—how they respond—to a woman. I distinguish between object and cause of emotions because we are agents of our reasoning and our emotions.

Secondly, Mary Daly uses the word 'passion' to indicate the power, the energy, of our emotions. I prefer to reclaim 'emotion', adopting her suggestion of the movement in strong emotions, or e-motion. For 'passion' comes from the late latin *passiō*, translated from the greek *pathos* meaning "suffering" or "submission," as in "the passion of christ," and derivative of the latin *passus*, or "suffered," "submitted." It is hypothesized that the word comes from the proto-indo-european root *pēi*, meaning "to hurt."[11] From this etymology, it can be inferred that one who is passionate either suffers or causes suffering—thus emerges the idea that passion must be controlled. In current usage 'passion' is "any emotion or feeling as love, desire, anger, hate, fear, grief, joy, hope, etc. especially when of a compelling nature."[12] Thus, when we are passionate, we are being compelled or acted upon by our emotions. As a result, the idea persists that passion is something which can overcome reasoning and hence could or should be controlled by reason.

'Emotion', on the other hand, comes from the latin *ēmovēre*, "to move out, stir up, excite." Women have been accused of being too emotional (though as I will discuss shortly, anger is the one emotion denied women), and men have gone about reasonably controlling women's emotions. I want to reclaim 'emotion' and the wonderful energy that goes with it, for with emotions we move out, stir up, and excite; and while this involves suffering at times, it does not have suffering as its root. Mary Daly's concept of e-motion, deep e-motion, the movement within us which also moves us, is the focus I am interested in.

Significantly, Gertrude Stein distinguished between passion and emotions:

In her ideal completeness she would have been unaggressively determined, a trifle brutal and entirely impersonal; a woman of passions but not of emotions, capable of long sustained action, incapable of regrets. In this American edition it amounted at its best to no more than a brave bluff.[13]

This suggests a distinction between passion and emotions similar to the distinction between vulnerability and intimacy: both vulnerability and passion—as Gertrude Stein is referring to it—can be used to close off and distance rather than to connect.

Thirdly, emotions are sources of movement. And I agree with Mary Daly that the plastic passions have no specific object (subject) and hence contribute to blaming the victim. Still, some genuine emotions may not have a subject either. For example, I may wake up with a feeling of joy, and it can be a source of motion while there may be no specific subject of my joy.[14]

The problem arises when, for example, I feel depressed and this is not simply an energy to bring me down from hyper energy. The problem arises when the depression is connected with our oppression and I am unable to recognize either the agents of oppression or that I am responding to the conditions of oppression. That is, the problem arises when our reasoning and emotions are separated, fragmented; for that involves an inability to fully perceive, to judge – in this case, an inability to name names. As a result we wind up with endless processing, spinning in place, or with resignation and assimilation, rather than with political movement. ment.

When our feelings become e-motions – energy that moves us – we move toward,[15] we engage, we interact with others who become the subjects of our e-motion. We focus. Now, it is important that we not be always focused; sometimes it is necessary to unfocus, disconnect our attention, and simply space out. But when we interact, we attend and connect. Ours is an engaging energy – toward a subject and in a context. This is part of our power-from-within, and it involves our reasoning and emotions, our whole selves, not just fragments.

Emotions are not private objects We tend to regard emotions and feelings as private, separate from our reason, and discoverable only by introspection. Naomi Scheman challenges this idea. She argues that emotions (such as being in love or angry), beliefs (such as believing that amazons once rode between the black and caspian seas), intentions (such as intending to apologize), and expectations (such as expecting a woman to come out) are not simply individual states:

> This largely unquestioned assumption, that the objects of psychology – emotions, beliefs, intentions, virtues and vices – attach to us singly (no matter how socially we may acquire them) is, I want to argue, a piece of ideology. . . . It is deeply useful in the maintenance of capitalist and patriarchal society and deeply embedded in our notions of liberation, freedom, and equality.[16]

Although we tend to think of beliefs and intentions, for example, as discrete entities, they exist in relation to our social context (for example, capitalist patriarchy) where they develop in focus and complexity.

Naomi Scheman points out that we are liable to resist the idea that they make sense only relative to a framework because we tend to regard psychological states as simply aspects of our inner lives which we discover. She notes that certain sensations may be discovered through introspection, "but most of what we care about – emotions, beliefs, understanding, motives, desires—are not such particulars":

> We can, I think, maintain that our twinges, pangs, and so on are particular events no matter what our social situation, but it does not follow that the same is true for more complex psychological objects, such as emotions, beliefs, motives, and capacities. . . . The question is one of meaning, not just at the level of what to call it, but at the level of there being an "it" at all. And questions of meaning and interpretation cannot be answered in abstraction from a social setting.[17]

In other words, we are in certain respects social beings. While we experience urges and pangs and leanings, for example, we develop those inner states into full-blown emotions and beliefs and intentions through interacting with others who react, reflect back, and themselves engage, and against the backdrop of our social and political context. Our emotions, beliefs, abilities, desires, exist in a "social web of interpretation that serves to give meaning to the bare data of inner experience and behavior."[18]

Naomi Scheman goes on to point out that this view is essentially incompatible with a liberal view that regards social groups as "built on the independently existing characteristics of individuals."[19] Under a liberal view, even if we acknowledge that psychological states are social constructions, political respect would demand that "evenhanded consideration be given to all these states."[20] In this respect, of course, the whole enterprise of therapy reinforces liberal ideology. Naomi Scheman suggests that we actually don't value all our feelings and inclinations equally, and that we need to evaluate our psychological states, not only in terms of our own true nature, but also in terms of how we can be self-deceived or victims of false consciousness or just muddled relative to our social context.

Under patriarchy, specific meanings have been given to our psychological states. For example, women's and lesbian's anger is named and developed as "madness," women's and lesbian's resistance is nonexistent, and those instances of resistance which are undeniable are called, again, instances of "insanity." At times women are said to be "frigid," at other times to be "hot mamas." Women's gratitude for protection is called "love"; lesbian love, a "perversion"; and so on. Within patriarchy, women's and lesbian's feelings and beliefs and desires are regularly constructed. And, most importantly, this has affected not only how we act in the world, but how we feel about and understand ourselves, our own feelings, and what we respond to.

Now, the patriarchal definition of the meaning of our feelings has its limits. It was socially constructed, and we broke the social agreement when we broke our collective silence. Our twitches and pangs suddenly erupted; we began to name problems that had no names. We created consciousness-raising groups and began to articulate our anger. We created new meaning, and this changed the way we felt; it changed what we understood about ourselves. This was not an individual, isolated, or private endeavor. We explored our lesbian desire, for example, and through lesbian interaction and political analysis, we changed the meaning of our desire from an illness and source of shame to a source of pride and joy. This is something we did, but we did it through lesbian engagement and in consideration of our social and political context, not through private introspection.

When we begin to evaluate our feelings, begin to name the context through which they emerge, by refocusing and interacting we begin to develop a complexity of understanding which in turn affects the texture and depth of our feeling. And we also begin to understand that feelings can be shaped, developed, and changed.

The meaning of our emotions, beliefs, intentions, intuitions, is developed in a social context, and we can challenge or develop that context and so challenge or develop meaning. This is not an individual project, neither the challenge nor the development. It involves the interactions of lesbians who question and analyze and evaluate. And that means it is a political endeavor – an endeavor which involves interacting and in which reasoning and emotions are not perceived as distinct entities.

Desire and Political Perception

CONSIDER, FOR EXAMPLE, patriarchal definition of sexuality and desire. Within the dominant ideology, sex is heterosexual or male homosexual. Elements of the meaning of sex in patriarchy include the beliefs that (1) sex is necessary to a man's health, (2) sexual desire involves a death wish (eros), (3) male sexuality is a powerful and uncontrollable urge, (4) rape is natural behavior, (5) sex is an act of male conquest, (6) sexual freedom includes total male access to females, (7) sexual feeling is a matter of being out of control, and (8) sex is a natural phenomenon such that women who resist male sexual advances are "frigid."[21]

Patriarchal sexuality

Audre Lorde has begun challenging this dominant meaning of our desire. She argues that the erotic is power, that it is a resource within us and a source of knowledge. She opposes the erotic to the pornographic, since the pornographic emphasizes sensations without feelings, without engagement, and hence perpetuates the fragmentation of our energy. She argues that the erotic is nonrational, and suggests that "the erotic is not a question only of what we do. It is a question of how acutely and fully we can feel in the doing."[22]

Desire as power

Thus, Audre Lorde has begun to revalue our desire by naming it a power-from-within, and she points out that it is life-invoking. This is central to lesbian thought, and while I agree with most of her analysis, my focus is slightly different.

In the first place, I think it a mistake to characterize desire as nonrational for the very reasons I've been discussing. Attraction does not exist in a vacuum, the meaning of our feelings and responses is developed in depth and complexity through the social context in which we realize them. That we desire lesbians is not incidental; our desire is focused. And that focus results from integrating reasoning and emotions.

Secondly, I want to suggest that there are problems with calling our desire 'erotic', problems with invoking the concept of 'eros'. 'Eros', as developed in the homopatriarchal greco-christian tradition, is quite the opposite of life-invoking; it is death or other-world oriented. Mary Daly has explored the necrophilic focus that defines eroticism in patriarchy.[23] 'Eros' is the will to get and possess, it is a force which strives for perfection, for immortality. It is associated with priestly desires and male sadomasochistic death wishes as well as heterosexual procreation; it involves the idea that men lose their vital fluids by engaging in sexual intercourse. (Thus, before a "big game," men are to lie alone.) In religious terms, 'eros' represents an ecstatic loss of self, a love which is directed toward a god and whose climax, in christian mysticism, is self-annihilation (perfection). (Thus christian mysticism and sadomasochism embrace the same ideology, share the same erotic roots.)

Patriarchal love

In the homopatriarchal greco-christian tradition, a tradition which permeates our thinking, in addition to 'eros' there are essentially three other kinds of love: 'agape', 'nomos', and 'philia'.[24] 'Agape' is unconditional giving, total and unevaluated—so-called christian love or motherly love—and particularly devoid of desire. It bestows grace on its object, thus implying that its object by itself has no reason to merit such love. 'Agape' is a love in spite of the person, not because of them.

'Nomos', properly meaning 'law', involves a love which subordinates reason to faith; it is a submission to a divine law and order "beyond" man's understanding. Under this concept, it is not man's place to question the will of a god; thus we gain the idea of love being acceptance of authority. And under this concept, reason is a threat because it implies independent will and possible rebellion. Reason creates doubt and insecurity; faith, on the other hand, gives confidence and peace (comfort, numbness).

And, finally, 'philia' is brotherly love, giving rise to the unity of things, a communion among men. In this case, the saving force is that which unifies, connects, and draws all together into one indiscriminate mass. It is a universal love for mankind without any attention to particular individuals, differences among individuals, or the complexity and distinctness of the conditions of their lives. That which separates, differentiates, alienates, is the destructive force.

I find *all* these concepts—'eros', 'agape', 'nomos', and 'philia'—fragmented and fragmenting. I think we can weave our own concepts of lesbian love and desire and energy and power.

Sex   I will add here some thoughts about the word 'sex'; there are problems as well with using it to talk about our desire. The word 'sex' comes from the latin *sexus*, akin to *secus*, derivative of *secāre*, "to cut, divide," as in 'section', and itself suggests fragmenting or severing. As a result, Mariel Rae suggests that 'sex' is a term which erases lesbian desire, sensuality, and orgasm.[25]

In discussing the meaning of 'sex', Claudia Card asks whether sex is a purely biological phenomenon like eating and drinking and sleeping, or whether it is something whose meaning emerges through an institutional context, as is the case with breakfasting, dining, or going to potluck dinners. She suggests that if we regard sex as a purely biological phenomenon, then "when one tries to abandon a phallocentric conception of sex, it is no longer clear what counts as sexual and what does not."[26] She suggests that the only preinstitutional sense of sex she can make out is a biological one that refers in one way or another "to reproductive capacities of members of a species that reproduce sexually rather than asexually." In this respect, of course, the clitoris is not a sexual organ:

> In short, I do not see how it is possible to give an account of what it means to call ... clitoral pleasure ... *sexual* without reference to the institution of sexuality. If there is such a thing as "plain sex," which does not mean simply "femaleness or maleness" but which is ordinarily pleasurable and had only intermittently and is independent of the institution of sexuality (logically prior to it), it seems also to be a purely androcentric phenomenon.[27]

In other words, if one refers to 'sex' as a purely biological phenomenon, such as eating, rather than an institutional phenomenon, such as potlucking, then clitoral pleasure is not part of sex.

Thus, understanding sexuality is not just understanding a "drive" but understanding the context, indeed the institutions, which gives our urges and responses depth of meaning. Now, in evaluating the patriarchal institution of sex, Claudia Card notes that it sanctions hatred and domination—they are integral rather than peripheral to it. Further, the institution of sex, even imagined outside a patriarchal context, remains essentially a male phenomenon. As Marilyn Frye has pointed out, sex is a phenomenon which requires having one or more male sexual organs present such that penetration of almost anything counts as having sex.[28]

In considering the Philip Blumstein, Pepper Schwartz survey on sex,[29] Marilyn Frye notes that it was brought to her attention that what 85% of long-term heterosexual married couples do more than once a month (which lesbians, according to the studies, do far less frequently) takes, on the average, eight minutes to do.[30] She goes on:

> I know from my own experience and from the reports of a few other lesbians in long-term relationships, that what we do that, on the average, we do considerably less frequently, takes on the average, considerably more than 8 minutes to do. It takes about 30 minutes, at the least. Sometimes maybe an hour. And it is not uncommon that among these relatively uncommon occurrences, an entire afternoon or evening is given over to activities organized around "doing it." The suspicion arises that what 85% of heterosexual married couples are doing more than once a month and what 47% of lesbian couples are doing less than once a month is not the same thing.[31]

Marilyn Frye wonders what violence lesbians do to our experience when answering the same questions heterosexuals answer, as though they have the same meaning for us. She notes that in her experience and reading of the culture, heterosexuals count what they report in these surveys according to the man's orgasm and ejaculation. And she suggests that the attempt to encode our lustyness and lustfulness in the words 'sex' and 'sexuality' has backfired: "Instead of losing their phallocentricity, these words have imported the phallocentric meanings into and onto experience which is not in any way phallocentric."[32] For example, the joy lesbians can feel in swirling a lover's vagina and in having our vaginas swirled as a potter swirls a pot has nothing to do with banging and penetration, and the male organ is inadequate to the task.[33] I want to try to leave behind the word 'sex' and focus instead on 'desire'.

Our attraction to each other and our desire take many forms. Yet the institution of sexuality portrays all desire as leading to orgasm, and that, too, is inadequate for us. The point of desire is not necessarily orgasm. As JoAnn Loulan writes:

> Even those of us who usually have orgasms find ourselves tyrannized by this supposed goal of sex. When we constantly work towards having an orgasm, we are unable to experience each sexual encounter for the pleasure it can give us. Our preoccupation with this particular muscle spasm echoes our general approach in a consumer-oriented society: striving for a goal, while disregarding the pleasure (or lack thereof) that we experience in the process. For women who never reach that goal, there often may be little reason to have sex.[34]

The institution of sexuality portrays all sensuality as "foreplay," as simply part of the trek on toward orgasm.[35] This diminishes all our sensual abilities. I mean to suggest that orgasm, along with all other aspects of our sensuality and desire, ceases to be powerful when we work to make it conform to homo- and heterosexual meaning: we will remain fragmented so long as we regard orgasm as the focus and point of all lesbian desire and sensuality while everything else remains mere excuses.

Claudia Card reminds us that the language of what she calls eroticism is different from the language of sex. She distinguishes what she calls eroticism from sexuality, suggesting it is an emotional, not a biological category. She notes that the patriarchal institution of sexuality presents the erotic as sexual "by construing erotic play . . . as a sexual invitation."[36] Pointing out that the "erotic" may or may not be "sexual," Claudia Card suggests that it is a way of touching, one which does not succeed unless the other is also touching. In other words, it is interactive. Further, "erotic" interchange "can work like super-glue—just a little bit can have one hooked for years. This is not true of sexual activity in general."[37]

We need new language and new meaning to develop our lesbian desire, especially as we explore and develop what draws us, where our attraction comes from, what we want to keep, what we want to change and why, how our attractions vary, how our desires change over time, and so on.[38] And this is an interactive, not an introspective matter. We need a lot more discussion and exploration among ourselves in something like consciousness-raising groups, certainly among intimates—lovers and friends—to develop the meaning of lesbian desire, and to heal our fragmentation.

Fragmentation   One indication of our fragmentation is that we have severed and continue to sever our lesbian desire from our work, our interactions outside the bedroom. Or we pretend our desire is not present anywhere but in the bedroom partly out of a false belief about what commitment to a lover means. Our lesbian desire is present in our work, in our meetings, at take-back-the-night rallies, in the bars, in heated debates, as well as in the bedroom. And to separate these aspects of our lives is to fragment our power; for our desire enables us, as lesbians.

Another indication of our fragmentation is that at times we find ourselves attracted to lesbians we don't especially like. We also are attracted to difference as exotic, not as something to discover and learn from but rather as a mystery and hence something we objectify and keep at a distance. As a result, we use vulnerability or alternatively a stoical approach with each other, rather than developing intimacy. Perhaps we are afraid that if the other is no longer a mystery, we will find ourselves reflected back as ordinary, not special. We often opt for melodrama to create meaning.

Further, we tend to believe that to be safe we must be rational and in control but to feel anything we must be emotional and out of control. Thus we regard desire as a matter of 'eros' (ecstatic loss of self) and success as a matter of being either in or out of control. And we often try to separate desire from feelings for a particular lesbian in order to avoid the risk of connection—being momentarily and allegedly out of control (during "orgasm") while still maintaining strict control over our feelings. This way we think we can have the "goodies" while remaining "safe."

I want to suggest that desire is neither a matter of being in or out of control, nor need it be a matter of being "safe" or "in danger." Desire is a matter of connection. It is our lesbian desire which moves us to connect with each other. And when we open deeply to another through desire, we create channels which will remain with us through this living—even when the desire changes.

Again, the depth of our feeling expands through the meaning developed in our social context. As we begin to revalue our lesbian desire, I think we will be less likely to be attracted to difference as exotic, as that which is a threat to who we are and hence a thrill, or as an arena for conquest.[39] We may also be less likely to move toward sameness just because it offers the apparent security of familiarity. Thus, we can come to embrace more fully both desire and difference as biophilic, not necrophilic.

A third indication of our fragmentation is the idea prevalent among us that making love can ruin a friendship. We are intent upon maintaining a distinction between friends and lovers. I think this is because, to varying degrees, our love and desire have been oriented toward eros in patriarchy, toward the necrophilic. Under the homopatriarchal construction of the erotic, desire becomes a threat to us, can steal (sweep) us away—we *fall* in love, we go out of control.[40] Thus we don't want to muddy or threaten our friendships with desire. We keep very strict limits on what counts as appropriate engagement with those toward whom we direct our desire, whether they be insistence on the distance of one-night stands or whether they involve moving in forever and ever with someone we've made love with. And we act to protect our friendships so when our lover relationships blow up, we have a haven, a resource, with our friends.

A fourth indication of our fragmentation is that we seldom laugh while making love (or if we do, we're keeping quiet about it). Kate Clinton connects humor to lesbian desire, suggesting those hilarious moments of laughter come from the same source as our desire:[41]

Feminist humor . . . is a deeply radical analysis of the world and our being in the world because it, like the erotic, demands a commitment to joy. . . . The demand for our presence in the moment is another way in which our sense of humor and the erotic are entwined. For full participation in the erotic, you have to be there.[42]

As Marilyn Frye notes:

Attention is a kind of passion. When one's attention is on something, one is present in a particular way with respect to that thing. The presence is, among other things, an element of erotic presence. The orientation of one's attention is also what fixes and directs the application of one's physical and emotional work.[43]

That is, presence is central to engaging. And Anna Lee suggests we claim our desire for the sheer lesbian joy of it.

What does it mean to say I want a womon? I must acknowledge what I feel is real. Unclouded by attaching forevers to it. What is happening is surely powerful and is sexual. It is the smell, touch, the rhythm of the womon's body exciting my senses. All of them. Fully engaged. Full. My senses become stretched to their limits and beyond.[44]

She adds that our desire "is the underlying river often silent, frequently diverted, that connects one to another."

Thus as Harriet Ellenberger suggests, our lesbian desire helps us move out of conditions of oppression and want to live. She notes that "we have what we need if only we look in the right places, if only we pay attention to what goes on between us," adding:

I think that's what goes on between lesbians – that we somehow bring each other into [meaningful] existence.[45]

Our lesbian desire includes humor and joy, both of which involve presence. And being present to each other, attending each other, interacting, is part of how we bring each other into meaningful existence.

The issue of presence brings up another indication of our fragmenta-
Jealousy tion – namely, the question of jealousy. When we engage with someone, we may regard anyone or anything else she focuses on as a threat. I want to challenge this. I think there are serious problems involved with how we attend each other. However, I don't think the solution lies in trying to slot our relationships into a preconceived form such that we believe we must find the one and only and that no other meaningful engagement, including work and play outside that form, must enter our lives.

When someone spends time with another, does the fact that she also spends time with a second affect the quality of time she spent with the first? Does the fact that she spends time with another by itself *change* the nature and quality of her interactions with the first? In certain respects it may. That I interact with one enhances my framework which I bring to my interaction with another. But I am present or I am not at any given moment, and that I am later present elsewhere does not change the nature of my earlier presence. At least in my experience, attention and presence are not quantitatively measured. Of course we are limited by energy, space, and time. And we cannot engage intimately with a large number of other lesbians. But, in my experience, that I am present at one time with one in no way diminishes my presence at another time with another.

The question of jealousy concerns questions of trusting our interactions. If she attends only me, then it would seem I have no worry about whether her love is "true." (This, of course, is not so.) But if she also attends another, she may be lying to me. Now there is the possibility that another may be playing us for a fool. But so what? If another plays us for a fool, it was she who wasted her time. Once we find she is lying, of course we can withdraw. But as to evaluating our time spent before that moment—well, *we* were engaged; she was, thus, the fool. So another may be dishonest. Nevertheless, that a lesbian cares deeply for someone else (a mother, a child, a lover, a friend) does not in itself diminish her care for or her presence with us.

My general point is not restricted to relationships with others. For example, one lover may be happily and intently although exhaustingly involved with her job or project. And this can as easily become a source of comparison and jealousy as can another lesbian she might be involved with. But such jealousy is unnecessary. Interacting with others and engaging in other projects enhance what we bring to a relationship. What matters is that there is quality time between us.

Some lesbians couch the issue in terms of monogamy/nonmonogamy. I think this is a mistake. As Julia Penelope argues, "Both terms name heteropatriarchal institutions within which the only important information is: *how many women can a man legitimately own?*" The terms 'monogamy' and 'nonmonogamy' presuppose that women are the property of the men who marry them.[46]

The issue is not how many lovers someone has. It may be that two lesbians want to share intimacies—physical desire as well as secrets and hopes and joys and pain—only with each other, and that this best suits their needs and wants at the time. Or it may be that lesbians want to explore intimate desire with more than one other, thereby changing the dynamics of the lover relationship. There are vehement arguments decrying the pitfalls of one choice or the other. The truth of the matter is that each focus carries its own problems and its own joys. What works is different for different lesbians as well as for the same lesbians at different times. What matters is the quality of presence.

Engaging is not all-encompassing; rather, it is a selection of focus, the result of what each of us brings to the engaging. When you and I engage, at whatever level, it is a unique engagement because it involves entwining your energy and mine. While it gains meaning from a context – patriarchal or lesbian – it is not just a matter of form. Something special happens, as a result of our attentiveness, when you and I engage. Sometimes we forget this specialness, that this energy is here now, in this living, and that it is unique. You and I need times to focus fully on each other, special time we plan together.

And no one else provides for just that. Nor should they. For when you engage with someone else, whether as lover or friend or co-worker, you focus on, attend, respond to her. That, too, is unique. What you and I have cannot be replaced by what you and she have. I think we can move away from heterosexual stereotypes.

In developing the meaning of lesbian desire, we can revalue the distinction between friend and lover together with the idea that the point of all true sensuality is orgasm and the judgment that whether one reaches orgasm with another is the significant factor in defining a relationship. Often we now act as if a lover were the only one meant for us, and we stifle desire in our relations with others and in our projects. While friends may be important, our responses to them go secondary, even with close or best friends; their wants and needs go on hold automatically. Alternatively, they become the only ones we'll be intimate with while we pursue superficial sexual engagements; we maintain "freedom" and thrills by opting for the anonymity of objectification. Maintaining these firm distinctions means we really don't have to make choices in certain situations. We simply respond according to the dictates of the form.[b]

Friends and lovers

---

b   One form is butch/fem. I have not talked about the categories 'butch' and 'fem' directly because, like 'monogamy' and 'nonmonogamy', I think the terms focus our attention away from deeper concerns. Certainly, we are affected by heteropatriarchy's categories of 'masculinity' and 'femininity'; we have internalized these values. Certainly, too, butch/fem are not exact replicas of masculinity/femininity. (For example, while women are expected to be responsible for the sexual satisfaction of men, it is butches who are responsible for the sexual satisfaction of fems.[47]) And certainly, to simply dismiss butch/fem is to miss a great deal of our past.

However, 'butch' and 'fem' are simply conceptual boxes and not very accurate ones at that – many lesbians must strive to fit the mold. Further, both butches and fems can be fully obnoxious and arrogant; both butches and fems like to cook; both butches and fems can fix flat tires, repair plumbing, do electrical wiring, like flowers, lift weights, wear jewelry, and so on. In a particular relationship, that one lesbian likes to cook and the other likes to clean up is fine; in another relationship, the cook may retire to something else. But we don't need the labels 'butch' and 'fem'. Like any stereotypes, if we perceive the world through them, the world will come to be that way. Nevertheless it doesn't have to be that

Further, if we find our feelings change and don't fit that form, we conclude the relationship has ended, that we no longer care, no longer are able to respond. For example, many lovers will go through times when they don't take each other to orgasm, nevertheless they cuddle, give back rubs, and in general are very physical with each other. Now if one feels a lack but the other doesn't, then a problem may arise. However more often in my experience, both are quite happy with this. If they start to feel they must regularly reach orgasm because they believe that lovers are supposed to do that, then they may decide something is wrong with their relationship when that is not the case.

When we focus on a form rather than the energy dynamics of those involved, we tend to think of relationships—whether as lovers, friends, collectives, or community—as static and not dynamic, as unchanging. As a result, when we do observe change in a relationship because someone is changing, we believe the relationship is ending, that only nothingness will follow; or if we suppress that change, we ultimately force the relationship to end because it has become stifling.[c] We reach for a form into which to fit ourselves to make the relationship rather than regarding ourselves as the form, the limits, and the substance, while regarding the relationship as fluid interaction. I think if we regard orgasm not as the goal or defining factor of all encounters while, of course, continuing to delight in it, and if we overlap the concepts of 'friend' and 'lover', our connections in community and community itself will become stronger, particularly through extended relationships.

Actually, we have developed far more complex relationships than the distinction between friend and lover acknowledges. I mean to suggest that we consider the energy involved in all sorts of connections. We engage in different ways with different lesbians. With some there is a chemistry that is magnetic. It may not last long, and there may not be much else in the connection, but it is engaging and fun; it becomes painful only

---

way; that the world *is* that way is a result of our perceiving, agreeing, that it is that way.

In the long run, I don't focus on the issues of monogamy/nonmonogamy and butch/fem because I believe they are covers for an underlying issue. The real issue involves our urge for a code to tell us what to do, not because it yields the best possible good (since there are no guarantees), but simply because it is familiar, and uniform, and helps us fit in so we don't have to think about it, and because creating everything as we go is so arduous and takes so much energy. . . . But then we didn't take the easy path; we're lesbians.[48]

c   In general, fear of change inevitably leads to support of the status quo for no other reason than that it is familiar. This then becomes a conservative force: order becomes the single most important goal of the administrative mind regardless of the effects on the lives and health of those involved.

when we try to make it something it is not. With others there is an immediate connection as if we were old friends; there is a recognition of each
other and a comfort almost from the moment of meeting. And with each
new meeting we can take up as if no time had passed since the last meeting, even when that time involves years. With others there is the challenge of constantly covering new ground. With still others there is the engagement of living together, of sharing space that weaves the pleasures of
companionship. Besides companionship, this engagement involves each
being able to find solitude without either one feeling threatened.

With some there is the pleasure of doing certain things together, working on a project or going camping, for example. Over time the connection
grows. We may or may not be pursuing orgasm, but the engaging is intense. With others there is the utter joy of dancing with abandon, or
wrestling, without either necessarily being a prelude to orgasm. With
some we may be lovers and find thrill and joy in connecting and yet not
live together because old habits would make the effort a disaster. With
others, we may have been lovers and our relationship changes. Nevertheless at times we spend nights together, snuggle and hold each other, finding comfort in a deep connection that changes over time. Lesbian
mothers may co-parent and be able to respond in very intimate ways with
lesbians who are not their lovers. With other lesbians we have "affairs."
When this occurs over time and each is "brutally honest" with the other,
it can be a very stable and comforting element in our lives. Or again, some
lesbians – actually many lesbians – we may want to reach out and touch in
a particular moment, and, without changing the main focus of our lives,
share something intimate as a way of connecting, of embracing, for the
sheer joy of their presence in our lives. Or a group of lesbians may make a
home together and not be lovers. To live together well, whether or not as
lovers, takes very special attention. This is also true of working together.

Our connections are many and varied. And I believe we can continue to
vary them and stay closely connected to a number of lesbians throughout
our lifetime. Our connections are a matter of our attention, our presence,
and our interactions, including our lesbian desire. I think we would do
well to dissolve the rigid distinction between friend and lover. What matters is our circle of intimates and their circles and so on.

Now, while we have developed more complex relationships than the
Patriarchal values distinction between friend and lover allows, nevertheless we are still
deeply caught up with the models developed by men, particularly in
terms of the meaning of attraction and attractiveness. Again, too often
difference is pursued as erotic, whether in terms of roles or in terms of
race or in other terms, because it is perceived as exotic. Or we play a numbers game either with ourselves or with others, as Kate Moran notes:

As a fat lesbian I am so seldom seen as a possible sexual partner that I long ago stopped obsessing on how many women I would like to be involved with. It's not a relevant question for me. I don't care how many times thin, cute, small amazons sleep with each other trying to prove they are thin, cute, small amazons, or, if they meet at a softball game, buy matching running shorts, and are only seen when they run out of tofu. I'm not interested in judging other Lesbians on the basis of how they choose to structure (or not structure) their intimate relationships. What I do care about is how other Lesbians perceive me and deal with me.[49]

She goes on:

Proving worth through sexual conquest belongs in the stag parties of the heteropatriarchy. It certainly tells us nothing about a dyke to know how many wimmin she sleeps with or how exclusively committed she is. Looking at numbers is a game. What's important to me is talking honestly about how we deal with each other and starting to take seriously the anti-fat prejudice of many Lesbians. Quantity simply isn't an "issue" for me or for the Fat Dykes I know, but quality, and the lack of it in our relationships, certainly is.[50]

As Baba Copper notes in addressing the prejudice enacted in the community against older lesbians:

Patriarchal standards of taste – rules of esthetic and erotic choices – perpetuate male structures of power. If we allow male-defined standards of choice to be our default standards, then we maintain female powerlessness. We waste the opportunity which our lesbianism provides: to choose how to choose. . . . Unless old lesbians are re/membered as sexual, attractive, useful, integral parts of the woman-loving world, then current lesbian identity is a temporary mirage, not a new social state of female empowerment.[51]

Other forms of erasure result in objectification. As diane hugs writes:

Being disabled I get treated differently, not better, but often more oppressively. I have never been approached sexually by so many women than since I ended up using the wheelchair. It scares me to think others may be attracted to me because they assume that since I am disabled I will be submissive in nature. Also the physical presence thing really gets to me. It's as though as an able-bodied lesbian I was average looking from the feedback I got from others, now that I'm in the chair I hear that others think I'm beautiful. It's as though I'm exceptional looking for a crip. I really get tired of it all.[52]

Our desire is connected to our attention and our choices: who we attend, who we ignore, and *why* and *how* we choose to ignore or attend. Our desire in a certain sense is a microcosm of the macrocosm of our oppression: it has been erased and/or used against us to such an extent that we turn against ourselves and suppress it; and yet when we do manage to overcome what's been done with our lesbian desire and explore it in joy and discovery, it comes out all preprogrammed by the patriarchal institution of sexuality and still erasing, fragmenting, destroying. Perhaps one aspect of healing our fragmentation lies in reconnecting desire with caring — real presence and attention — not the romantic haze of happily-ever-after.

> We both sat there, two disabled lesbians in our wheelchairs, each on opposite sides of the bed. Sudden feelings of fear and timidness came over us. But once we finished the transferring, lifting of legs, undressing and arranging of blankets, we finally touched. Softly and slowly we began to explore each other, our minds and bodies. Neither could make assumptions about the sensations or pleasures of the other. It was wonderful to sense that this woman felt that my body was worth the time it took to explore, that she was as interested in discovering my pleasure as I was in discovering hers.[53]

In revaluing our lesbian desire, Audre Lorde argues that it is essentially

Desire as choice   biophilic, not necrophilic:

> The erotic offers a well of replenishing and provocative force to the woman who does not fear its revelation, nor succumb to the belief that sensation is enough. . . .
> The erotic is a measure between the beginnings of our sense of self and the chaos of our strongest feelings. It is an internal sense of satisfaction to which, once we have experienced it, we know we can aspire.[54]

And thus our desire yields a metaphor for choice:

> Within the celebration of the erotic in all our endeavors, my work becomes a conscious decision — a longed-for bed which I enter gratefully and from which I rise up empowered.[55]

That is, the focus of our love and desire, not the pseudo-focus of discipline or self-control or the pseudo-intensity of being out of control, is the source from which we actively engage in depth of feeling and connecting in this living. Our desire informs our interactions as we choose where and how we focus and direct our attention. This is not a question of being either in or out of control.

Audre Lorde goes on to expose the impetus of traditional anglo-european duty-centered ethics which excludes desire:

> The principal horror of any system which defines the good in terms of profit rather than in terms of human need, or which defines human need to the exclusion of the psychic and emotional components of that need . . . is that it robs our work of its erotic value, its erotic power and life appeal and

fulfillment. Such a system reduces work to a travesty of necessities, a duty by which we earn bread or oblivion for ourselves and those we love.[56]

That is, appeals to duty are necessary to motivate us to work because our desire has been severed from our work; thus when we find ourselves appealing to duty, as well as to self-sacrifice, it is an indication that we have lost the focus of our desire. We can acknowledge our lesbian desire as power, power-from-within—particularly, a powerful source of connection, engagement, and focus.

From Adrienne Rich:

> Whatever happens with us, your body
> will haunt mine—tender, delicate
> your lovemaking, like the half-curled frond
> of the fiddlehead fern in forests
> just washed by sun. Your traveled, generous thighs
> between which my whole face has come and come—
> the innocence and wisdom of the place my tongue has found there—
> the live, insatiate dance of your nipples in my mouth—
> your touch on me, firm, protective, searching
> me out, your strong tongue and slender fingers
> reaching where I had been waiting years for you
> in my rose-wet cave—whatever happens, this is.[57]

Desire involves choice, it is a judging that integrates reasoning and emotions and all our faculties. From Mary Daly:

> Primarily, then, *Pure Lust* Names the high humor, hope, and cosmic accord/harmony of those women who choose to escape, to follow our hearts' deepest desire and bound out of the State of Bondage . . . As [she who is moved by this desire] lurches/leaps into starlight her tears become tidal, her cackles cosmic, her laughter Lusty.[58]

When each of us came out, we invoked lesbian desire and we turned our attention to lesbian existence. It was a choice, a judgment. Now, what part was the "pure" emotion? What part the reason (or was there none!)? What part the intuition? What part the dreams? What part the psychic? And what part was purely private? These parts were not separated. Our lesbian energy emerges from an integration of our selves and our interactions with each other. And that integration involves both judgment of context and interaction with subjects. As such, that choice is political. Another way of putting this is to note that the whole lesbian being is greater, far greater, than the sum of the parts. This is perhaps most obvious in terms of anger.

Anger and Political Perception

WITHIN THE DOMINANT ideology, with the exception of the stereotype of "a woman scorned," women's anger is virtually non-existent. We are all familiar with the way that men undermine women's anger with such statements as "You're so cute when you're angry" or "The bitch is crazy." When men regard women's anger as inappropriate, they label women "insane," "mad." And the concept of 'femininity' obscures female resistance to domination by characterizing as "normal" the woman who remains submissive to men and characterizing as "insane," "mad," the woman who gets angry and fights back.

With the rise of the u.s. women's liberation and gay liberation movements, we began to collectively discuss in consciousness-raising groups what we got angry about and, as a result, began to name names and so change the meaning of our anger from insanity to outrage. In the process we integrated our reasoning and emotions – we began to realize that emotions are cognitive – and we began to change our lives.

Anger is cognitive Vicky Spelman argues that regarding emotions as involving reasoning rather than as being distinct from reason helps us to articulate their political significance. She focuses her discussion on anger, pointing out that while the fathers have depicted females as emotional and not rational, anger is the one emotion they don't discuss. She argues that someone who gets angry is not having an arational reaction – a simple matter of stimulus-response – but rather she is reacting to a situation by assessing it, by making judgments.

Thus, Vicky Spelman argues that anger is cognitive, that if someone is angry, she is making judgments – in particular, the judgment that the person she is angry at is wrong in some way. Vicky Spelman goes on to argue that anger is threatening when subordinates direct it toward those who dominate. The threat comes from the political judgments in the anger, in particular, that subordinates have a right to judge superiors and hold them accountable. She argues that subordinates have a right, possibly even an obligation, to get angry, and suggests that those who dominate censor the anger of subordinates as a way of short-circuiting subordinates' moral and political judgments.[59] If this is accurate, it means that getting angry is a way of challenging the dominant/subordinate relationship – thus, that anger can transform consciousness.

Audre Lorde has suggested that when one person is angry at another, it implies that they are on equal ground and that the one expects the other to change:[d]

Anger is the grief of distortions between peers, and its object is change. . . . It implies peers meeting upon a common basis to examine difference, and to alter those distortions which history has created around difference.[60]

And as Marilyn Frye notes, anger is a reaction to being thwarted, frustrated, or harmed, combined with a perception that this is an offense: when one person gets angry at another, she is implying that the other unfairly obstructed her in certain respects and she is demanding respect which that obstruction showed a lack of.[61] As a result, getting angry involves orienting ourselves toward another, and that in turn requires a response. Without an appropriate response (which may include the other claiming our anger is not justified), our expression of anger is simply an expression of feelings. Marilyn Frye goes on to argue that others' concepts of us are revealed through their reception of our anger – heterosexual women, for example, can get angry at men on behalf of children or in the kitchen, but not on their own behalf or in the bedroom: "To expand the scope of one's intelligible anger is to change one's place in the universe . . . to become something different in that social and collective scheme which determines the limits of the intelligible."[62]

By getting angry at another, the first is implying that the second is accountable for actions in relation to the first and also that the first is in a position to make a judgment about the second. If this implication holds, then it follows that when a subordinate gets angry at a superior, the subordinate is by that very action interrupting (if only partly) the dominant/subordinate relationship. Or again, when a woman gets angry at a man outside the domain of women's sphere, she is beginning to change her place in the universe. Thus, men undermine women's anger in order to block the political judgment of that anger and to avoid questions of accountability to subordinates. And, given all this, it follows that anger as an emotion is not independent of reasoning. Rather, combined with our reasoning, our understanding, anger is cognitive, it is a perception, a judgment.

As lesbians, we have developed the meaning of our anger through consciousness-raising groups and at political rallies and through constant communication with each other. We understand at many levels that anger is political. Together with love and desire, it has been a major source of motion in the emergence of lesbianism – of lesbian perspective

---

d Audre Lorde's argument emerged from the context of women responding to racism. Her concern is with racism in the women's movement, in this instance, in the national women's studies association. And she argues that her response to racism is anger because it is energy which, when focused with precision, can induce racial change.

and projects – and in the transformations of consciousness which we have so far undergone. Our lesbian desire and anger at oppression have fueled what exists now as lesbian community – lesbian sensibility, networking, interaction, celebration, development: lesbian connection.

Coping   But within community, I believe we now focus more often than not on how to cope with anger rather than addressing and evaluating the political judgment of our anger. We either use our reasoning to control our anger, or we expect the emotion of it to control our reasoning. We expect to be either in or out of control. As a result, we wind up with stunted perceptions and perpetuate the fragmentation of our selves. This is not the way to move under oppression.

Consider one case of anger between two white lesbians, one working class and one middle class. Whenever the first is harassed by a man on the street, she gets angry and goes after him. Her lover, in turn, gets angry at her for her lack of control and claims that the working-class lesbian's anger is abusive. In trying to resolve the tension which the situation produces in them both, they go to therapy to work on how the working-class lesbian can better control her anger and the middle-class lesbian can best cope with it.

Or consider a second case. Lesbians, mostly white but also of color, are sunbathing in a predominantly lesbian area of the lake shore. Two take off their tops (getting ready for michigan), feeling relatively safe among so many lesbians. A heterosexual couple strolls through the area; and, as they notice the two who have taken off their tops, like a tourist, the man readies his camera to take a picture. One of the two lesbians looks at him calmly and says, "I'll break your camera." The heterosexuals leave. When later this story is told among lesbians, discussion centers on whether this was a good way to deal with her anger.

Or consider a third case: A black lesbian has a party at her home. Lesbians of varying colors attend. Toward the end of the party a white lesbian takes her leave. Shortly she returns, angry and upset, because a group of neighborhood boys threatened her. Lesbians from the party accompany her to make sure she reaches her car safely. However, at the same time a cop car appears, patrolling the area. Still angry, she goes to the police and complains of the boys' harassment. After the police leave, the black lesbian gets angry at the white lesbian for encouraging the police to go after boys in her neighborhood, claiming that the way the white lesbian chose to act on her anger endangered her – claiming, therefore, that her friend's anger was abusive. The general energy of the party turns to soothing angry feelings.

Why do we consider these cases primarily matters of dealing with our feelings? Why do we focus on these lesbians' choices about how to deal with men in given situations as matters of coping with their emotions rather than as matters of political judgment? That is to say, why do we focus on the psychological element of our emotion to the exclusion of the political?[63] Why do we address a situation by asking whether we coped well with our feelings, or whether we did the most "sensible" thing, rather than asking questions about the politics of the situation, the judgments of our anger? For it is in discussing our emotions and exploring their subjects that we develop the meaning and complexity of our feelings.

I believe we avoid exploring the political judgments of our anger in part as a reaction to our earlier attempts to control each other and control situations with political correctness. Our initial exuberance from naming our oppression turned rapidly to impatience with those who did not seem to perceive what could be perceived. After all, everything was so immediately obvious there was almost nothing more to be said. Those who were wary must merely be trying to hold on to privileges which were bought with loyalty to men. Analyses came fast and furious, shocking us into consciousness like buckets of ice water. As we grew impatient with each other, analysis gave way to rules, and those lesbians who followed the rules were trustworthy, even if they didn't fully understand the ideas behind the rules, while those with reservations were regarded with suspicion if not outright distrust.

Political correctness

For example, lesbians were to wear short hair as a sign that they were not intending to gain approval from men by playing to men's fantasies. But for some jewish lesbians, short hair was too close to shaved heads in the camps. Or, in one effort to ensure that the general lesbian perspective was not a white, middle-class perspective, white lesbians were to give greater credibility to any statements made by lesbians of color than to statements made by white lesbians. We relied on rules to bring change. As a result, we were unable to accommodate each other when someone's responses came from places foreign to others; and we were unable to evaluate many responses.

Now, in questioning the development of political correctness into rules, I do not mean to echo the lesbian response to political correctness that takes pride in being politically incorrect by pretending that politics are irrelevant and that nonradical choices aren't political. Nor am I suggesting that we not criticize each other or not insist we each consider certain changes. Our political analyses are significant and crucial. As Julia Penelope argues in the context of butch/fem relationships:

Yes, early second wave lesbian-feminists trivialized role-playing in Lesbian relationships and, yes, they didn't really understand what they were attacking. But the kernel of truth that I perceived in their analysis started me on a decade of growth and change.[64]

Political correctness involves attempts to create a framework in which nonoppressive value can emerge.[65] And its central focus is on risk, change, and breaking out of the framework of heterosexualism. However, that new value must be chosen, woven, developed, embraced – not enforced. If it is enforced, it will cease to be the value we began to weave.

In questioning the development of political correctness, I mean to question the strategy of trying to weave political transformation through the use of rules. The problem with political correctness is not the politics but the correctness, the rules. A rule applies indiscriminately. And that doesn't work among lesbians. It backfires and results in backlash: many decide to drop the politics.

Significantly, while as a group we have dropped the politics, we have not dropped the correctness – our dependency on rules. And hence we are still caught up with social control in community, even though we think we've "gotten beyond" political correctness. Yet, without the reasoning, without the analyses, it appears that questions concerning anger reduce to coping with feelings or burying them.

The influence of therapy   The increasing influence of therapy as a way of life is another indication that we've turned to psychologizing and coping with our emotions. Again, the institution of therapy reinforces the idea that our issues are individual and our feelings private; it focuses us on inner states rather than on the context from which our feelings gain their depth of meaning. And it ignores the interactive nature of growth, healing, and change. As a result we ignore the political nature of our anger: that its meaning emerges both through our interactions and in a social and political context.

Consider again the three cases. There are significant judgments in the anger. In the second situation, the lesbian has decided that the actions of the man with the camera are intolerable and that she will take a stand. That this was a lesbian area of the lake shore is not significantly different from a similar action in a lesbian coffeehouse or even in the bedroom, for privacy and discretion are not the issue. The point concerns lesbian space, times of enacting lesbian value and gaining relief from heterosexual energy.

Now, rather than discuss this case as a psychological matter concerning whether she effectively dealt with her anger (for example, Did she still feel frustrated after her action?), we can begin again to ask: Under what circumstances and by what means do we claim lesbian space? Under what circumstances and with what kinds of actions can we address random male violation or heterosexual intrusion into lesbian space? Will we find and help create lesbian value only at the womyn's music festivals, the bars, the coffeehouses, and our homes, or can we also enact it elsewhere? How do we maintain lesbian space/value alone on the street, alone on the job, alone in the classroom, alone in the bedroom? Can we continue developing an energy, especially a collective energy, which disintegrates heterosexualism and does not attract male posturing? How do we develop such a collectivity? These have virtually ceased to be vital community questions.

In the first case, rather than focusing on the differences in how each lover handles her anger, we can focus on the differences in the political judgment which gives substance to the anger of each. For example, the working-class lesbian has decided that she will claim her space on city streets even at the risk of retaliation. She has decided that the threat of retaliation is less dangerous to her than the damage which would result if she let a man's harassment stand unchallenged, thereby confirming his low opinion of her. Her middle-class lover, on the other hand, has decided that under no condition will she willfully put herself in (more) danger on the streets. She is unwilling to react to every man who irritates her; she would rather use her energy to maintain focus on her own agenda. In considering the implications of their anger, and hence the judgments involved, we become aware not that they approach anger differently so much as that they approach politics differently. And the approaches involve considerations of safety, of identity, of expenditure of energy, and of enacting lesbian value – elements which affect the meaning and depth of our anger.

In the third case, the white lesbian believes that men harass us because they can get away with it, and she has decided that under no conditions will she allow male harassment to go unchallenged. Whenever possible, she uses greater force to retaliate. The police afforded such an opportunity. On the other hand, the black lesbian lives in the neighborhood. The harassers will still be there the next day and the next week, after the other lesbians have gone home. Further, white cops seize any opportunity to harass neighborhood residents. Both lesbians' judgments are political and significant, and how these judgments affect the other lesbian as well as lesbian value needs to be discussed. To focus only on dealing with our anger is to miss a great deal.

Again, when can we take off our shirts, our covers? When can we uncover, dis-cover our values? When can we weave and enact lesbian space? Where? And how? And what does that mean? As therapy and individual "dealing with feelings" has come to replace what consciousness-raising and group discussion and political analysis once provided for us, so have we ceased developing such questions.

I am suggesting that our emotions develop in complexity as they gain their meaning from a context. In this respect they are judgments, judgments within a context which in turn affect how we feel about and understand ourselves and the choices we make. When we try to separate reasoning and emotions, especially by coping, we fragment our energy, we undermine our ability to make choices, and we perpetuate the idea that power is control. To integrate reasoning and emotions is to politicize them.

Resistance to Healing the Fragmentation

YET I FIND significant lesbian resistance to that integration, to healing the fragmentation of our reasoning and emotions. And I think several factors are involved.

Being in or out of control   Our ideas about reasoning and emotions come from the fathers in whose society we find we must exercise self-control merely to survive:

> She must use her mind. She must think to keep her fingers free of the machine. She must think to keep the seam sewn straight. She uses her vision. She must see if the pieces of cloth fit together. She must see the fabric slide through the machine. She uses her will power. She must keep her mind on this work before her, she must stay here, she must not let her eyes wander, she must not let her mind wander, she must keep her thoughts on the work before her, she must keep working, she must not think of standing up and walking out the door, she must not think too often of the time, she must keep her eyes in focus, she must not think of where she would like to be, she must not dream, she must use her will, her power, here.[66]

Many of us have been taught that to get on in this world, we must exercise self-control. What Susan Griffin exposes in this passage, among other things, is that self-control, will power, involves shutting down both reasoning and emotion.

And we are constantly told that we must exercise will power, self-control, and discipline. The exhortation to exercise self-control, for example, is the single most prevalent taunt hurled at fat people, particularly by parents, teachers, and members of the medical profession. Rather than address how the diet and clothing industries affect how we feel about our bodies, and how antifat ideology connects to classism and very effective measures to get us to assimilate, instead we turn on our selves and each other, undermining our ability to enjoy lesbian bodies as well as our ability to maintain health.[67] At this point, both reasoning and emotions have been "transcended." Some of us exercise phenomenal control in the false belief that if we exercise control we will do no harm; we come to believe that discipline is the key to accomplishing anything.

As a result, we gain a false expectation about the function of reasoning in emotions. I suspect many of us have felt that if we use reason, we will be in control and will not have to or will not be able to (depending on the situation) feel emotion, that reason will protect us from being "out of control" with emotion such that if we do feel something we didn't plan or don't want, then reason was ineffective or useless.

Thus we learn to exercise self-control in order to force to the front only certain aspects of ourselves, keeping others under wraps. We try to maintain strict control of ourselves in order not to let show some part we don't approve of. One result is that we can block identification with those who are different or who we perceive as different. Rather than realizing that development of our selves proceeds through interacting with others (for example in c-r groups) who give us perspective, instead we withdraw in isolation, or possibly to a therapist.

Further, we are told that creativity—actually, they call it productivity—is a matter of will power and self-discipline. Discipline is "training intended to produce a specified character or pattern of behavior."[68] The disciplines of academia are designed to fit our reasoning into predetermined categories— the "conceptual boxes supplied by professional educators."[69] And when our reasoning doesn't fit those boxes, discipline becomes punishment. Thus to create/produce, we must discipline ourselves, punish ourselves, deprive or sacrifice ourselves for example (rather than choose how we will focus our energy at given times), and force a product to emerge.

In reaction to all this, we tend also to believe that to really feel or express something, to be authentic, we must be out of control. The idea is that true desire or true anger is a matter of how intensely we feel, that such feeling only happens when we've shut off reason, and that such a state involves losing control of ourselves. Certainly, when we are out of control, we have a definite intensity—for example, being drunk or strapped down and screaming—but it doesn't follow from this that we are experiencing or expressing any greater depth of feeling or any complexity and intricacy of emotion. While I have been arguing in favor of letting go of control, letting go does not mean being out of control. Nor does it mean giving up the ability, the power, to act. Both being in and out of control are illusions, the dichotomy a false one.

The tapestries we weave—our selves, the poems, the relationships, the research, the stews, the quilts, the networks, the images—are not a matter of discipline, nor are they a matter of conforming to the existing disciplines, nor are they private, nor are they a matter of losing control. Our creativity involves times of engaged focus as well as times of dreaming, daydreaming, imagining, opening to psychic energy, musing (processes virtually impossible to sustain in patriarchy). This is not discipline. Nor is it loss of control. Both being in and out of control are agendas of the fathers.

Reasoning is not a substitute for emotions. Reasoning is part of the substance, direction, and perspective of emotions just as emotions are part of the texture, substance, and quality of reasoning. Trying to fragment them, even if at times it seems a relief or safer, or more intense, will only fragment our abilities. Trying to address only one is like trying to appreciate art by focusing only on color. Creativity does not emerge when we fragment our selves.

Assimilation   A second reason we resist healing the fragmentation of our reasoning and emotions emerges in our attempts to assimilate and survive. Finding we can't control patriarchy, we try to separate our emotions from our intellect and address politics purely at an emotional level, or purely intellectually. For example, we may decide to rest in our emotions – to be simply angry or in pain in reaction to aspects of patriarchy. In this way we gain acknowledgment from those who attend us without anyone expecting anything. We can focus on our feelings and not have to act in the situation, particularly when it is a situation we do not control. This way we take risks only insofar as we are acknowledging our feelings; we are not taking the risks of engagement. Alternatively, we may try to find safety by backing off from our emotions and intellectualizing a situation. In this case we may risk engaging, making the most reasonable choice in a situation; but we don't have to risk integrating our deep emotions.

Consider, for example, a student new to feminist material entering a women's studies class which presents radical material. She begins to learn of patterns of violence committed against women worldwide and gets angry. She also begins to regard other women differently. She then starts noticing all that goes on around her from a different perspective. She tells boyfriend, parents, friends, about this, at times ranting, and she continues to point out each newly discovered offense or victory. Most of her friends ignore or ridicule her. This goes on for several weeks, but finally she can no longer take the tension and she comes to class saying, "I can't be angry all the time."

At this point in her journey, if her resolution is to drop her anger altogether rather than, say, to transform it into motion, she will soon also back away from the political judgment, ceasing to notice what goes on around her by numbing herself or denying the politics altogether. My point here is that when we back off from the emotion, we also back off from the judgment which informs it. We aren't going to have pure intellectual understanding of oppression – or of anything, for that matter. Without the emotion, the judgment of the emotion wanes. Mary Daly calls this 'dissociation'.[70]

In other words, emotions and reasoning aren't so easily separated. We may well want to back off from some emotion or from some judgment. That is a matter of choice in consideration of a number of factors. My point is that the two go together. Thus, efforts to rest either in the emotion without the judgment or in the reasoning without the emotion will fail. When we engage our lesbian being, the whole is far greater than the sum of the parts. Hence, parts can't be subtracted. Instead, the energy, the entire being, changes.

Often we choose not to become angry at those who dominate because we believe the ramifications are too great, for example losing a job or being beaten up. We back off from the emotion to avoid the political judgment and feel safer. However, I would like to suggest that the choice is not between getting angry or not; the choice is between making one judgment or internalizing a different one. And these choices, affecting our energy, involve different transformations of consciousness.

Consider the following case. A boss repeatedly harasses a lesbian, who is in the closet, on the job. She can get angry or not. Suppose she chooses not to, fearing the loss of her job. If she is isolated and without a political support network, she has to assimilate the energy of that experience by herself. Assuming she perceives harassment as wrong, if she chooses not to blame the boss, she must perceive the fault as hers. Since she cannot then "reasonably" be angry at him, she may turn her energy to whining or resentment or frustration. She feels bad. So to end the hurt and isolation, she may go to the source, seeking comfort in the form of forgiveness – or at least reaffirmation and approval, either verbal or nonverbal.[71] In other words, she's now in the position of asking for male approval because he harassed her. As Mary Daly notes, "women under the sadostate are continually confessing guilt and begging forgiveness."[72]

In backing off from her anger, she is not avoiding political judgment. She is dropping one political judgment in favor of another political judgment, perhaps owing to fear – fear that is quite specific or even fear that is nonspecific and amorphous.[73] Backing off from political judgment does not provide a haven of peace. It may, however, provide numbness, dissociation. My point is that seeking safety by trying to sever reasoning and emotions, or by trying to back away from one or the other, results in a transformation of our energy, a transformation of who we are.

Nevertheless, both the feeling that we can't be angry all the time and the consequences of getting angry remain. Getting angry involves tension, and we only wear down our abilities and effectiveness and burn out when we are constantly tense over a long period of time with no movement. Given that the changes we seek will not occur within a year, ten years, or even our lifetime, these concerns are important to address.

A state of anger

In evaluating this problem, Jeffner Allen suggests we consider the difference between getting angry and being in a state of anger.[74] When we get angry, we are reacting to a situation. Often there are physiological changes — our blood pressure rises, adrenalin flows, blood rushes to our face, and so on. This type of reaction typically occurs when a sore point is struck and takes us by surprise. Something has occurred which we weren't expecting, and we are caught off-guard.

Being in a state of anger keeps us from being caught off-guard as easily. Having gotten angry on a number of occasions and having evaluated the situations and the judgments of our anger, we begin transforming our perceptions, forming a consciously political perspective. Transforming our energy to a state of anger means we can face those who dominate, separating from their values, and work to maintain our own integrity, even though we do not control the situation. We may not be able to change certain situations alone — for example, the conditions of our employment — but we do not have to accept the dominant frame of reference as our own. Thus, though a boss may harass us, we do not have to internalize his judgment, the judgment of his emotions; we don't have to resign ourselves. Being in a state of anger is maintaining our ability to name names and so keep alive our memory of our deep selves. As Mary Daly notes, this time the war against women is not simply a physical massacre. "It is killing of consciousness and integrity in women."[75]

A state of anger under oppression is a state of political judgment and hence a state of political awareness. It is a state of maintaining and developing the meanings which emerged from the women's liberation movement. And it is a crucial element in the transformation of consciousness and the possibility of collectivity, for collectivity requires planned — not reactive — movement.

I do not mean to suggest that we should now always be in a state of anger and so never get angry. Nor do I mean to suggest that we learn to be nice girls in expressing our anger.[76] In coming to awareness, getting angry is the other side of depression; getting angry is the beginning of fighting back. My point is that getting angry in some cases is a matter of discovering and understanding oppression at a superficial (first) level. In the case of the women's studies student, she discovered oppression but hadn't yet incorporated it into her general judgment and perspective.[e]

---

e   This is in marked contrast to the beginning of women's studies. Students and teachers and community consciousness-raising groups alike knew of oppression; an awareness of it

She hadn't yet fully revalued what she had considered valuable (both her restrictions and her privileges). She hadn't yet touched her deep elemental memory.[77] If she begins a process of transformation, especially if she is able to do so collectively with others, she begins to entwine her intellectual knowledge and her feelings, healing the fragmentation of her self.

She may continually get angry at first. However, if that does not bring about the desired change, then she may move toward a state of anger, a state of shifted perception. Those who turn back have been unable to incorporate the information in their everyday perceptions and instead seek the comfort of numbness.[78] For example, the women's studies student may meet continual resistance from those closest to her. If she has no one else near her who perceives what she now perceives, who attends her, and if she doesn't want to lose her friends, she will have to stop communication and eventually stop judging.

Getting angry, of course, in and of itself, may instigate change. When others are operating from habit — unconsidered and unevaluated — or from ignorance, getting angry may well be all that is needed to get their attention and begin the process of transformation. Basically, moving into a state of anger is a useful process when our getting angry is ignored and brings no change. A state of anger becomes a state of separation when our anger is censored. This is as true among ourselves as lovers, friends, co-workers, or community members as it is in our response to the dominant society. If done in isolation, it becomes a state of insanity within a patriarchal context. If done collectively, in consciousness-raising groups, at rallies, in study groups, in political action groups, to name but a few, it becomes political transformation.

I am suggesting that we continue transforming our reactive anger into political anger by developing the judgments of our emotions, particularly through continued collective discussions and political analyses of our situations and our parts in them. In this way we become less isolated and helpless, we continue to transform ourselves from victims to movers, we choose our strategies and moments of action.

For example, suppose a particular subway stop in the city is known for the heterosexual men who harass women. In articulating the judgments of our anger, we may work out a plan, not necessarily to directly challenge them, for example, but to interrupt the flow of their habit. This becomes not just an action in reaction but an action for our selves.[79] And we can

permeated our beings. We were already angry and were looking for form and understanding. Today a woman's studies teacher has to first get women students angry (aware) and then try to do something with their anger, all in too short a time.

focus our success, not on controlling them, but rather on our energy in interrupting them and thwarting their intended effect on us. Thus, even if they continue for a time, it will not be on their terms. In this way we begin to exercise our power, our ability, without having to either control the entire situation or drop our anger from exhaustion. We learn to make a difference through our actions. Most importantly, we continue to collectively create a context in which we develop the meaning of our anger, break out of the plastic passions, and develop our abilities—particularly our collective ability—for other, more far-reaching situations. We develop our moral agency.

Of course, all this is no guarantee of safety. But then, there is no guarantee—only an illusion. The question is how to go on under oppression; and survival concerns are certainly relevant. But survival includes, in part, being able to make choices and act within situations, and our ability to do this is not increased by severing emotions and reasoning.

Feelings and privacy   I find yet a third reason behind lesbian resistance to healing the fragmentation of our reasoning and emotions: it stems from a need and desire for privacy and it involves the idea that our feelings are private. To suggest that our emotions are cognitive and that their meaning is developed in a social context, is not only to imply that they involve judgment and are not simple reactions. To suggest our emotions are cognitive is also to imply that our emotions might be open to challenge in some way. To acknowledge the judgments of emotions is to acknowledge that there is something that can be questioned by those we engage with; for any time I make a judgment, I may make mistakes.

Consider statements such as, "These are just my feelings; I wouldn't be honest if I didn't say them to you. But they're just feelings; they're not what I'm thinking." Such claims are often designed to make our expression of feelings off-limits, to ensure that others in the community do not question the judgment or perceptions embedded in our emotions. In other words, we tend to regard emotions as private feelings: if I'm feeling something, I'm feeling it and no one else has a right to say I'm not really feeling it or that I shouldn't or that I'm wrong in some other way. I've already suggested that our feelings are not private in that the meaning and depth of our feelings are developed in a lesbian context (and also in patriarchy). Still, there is a strong sense in the community that each lesbian has a "right" to her feelings.

Now, certainly each lesbian has her feelings. If she is responding to a situation, thereby making a judgment of energy, those feelings are coming from somewhere. And she may not be willing to have her feelings/judgments challenged, for example when she is shaky and vulnerable or just plain tired, or by those who haven't experienced where she comes from – particularly if they have learned little about her background. For example, lesbians who don't have to walk or use public transportation in an urban area may be ignorant of the overt violence that is a daily part of that experience. Or lesbians who live in neighborhoods where violence is not overt and immediate may be ignorant of the ramifications of attracting attention. Or lesbians who do not work in companies where white-collar employees are perceived as part of a family (that is, where one has to be cordial, grateful, and attentive in a dominant/subordinate economic relationship) may have no understanding of another lesbian's on-the-job survival skills and choices.

These examples multiply, emerging from every different background and present situation lesbians face. If others were constantly evaluating, even challenging, the judgment, the perception, of our emotions – anger, for example – we would have to acquaint our friends and other peers with the context we face in all its complexities. And we may not have the time or think that addressing their ignorance is worth the effort. Or we just may not yet understand our situation well enough ourselves.

Further, each lesbian needs space for her feelings. Not all expressions of feelings are designed as critical theses to be evaluated. At times, just expressing our feelings, making a statement without the intention of starting a discussion, is all we need to regain our balance. Sometimes we just want the comfort of being perceived.

Beyond that, if our feelings are challenged by others before we are ready, our being forced to defend our position will likely interrupt any process of growth and transformation we are engaging in. We may not benefit from being rushed through our feelings. We may well be stuck in one place for a long time, and we may be staying there for a purpose – because we are absorbing all the aspects of the lesson so we won't have to repeat it. For example, some lesbians remain in a relationship that isn't working long after all their friends have perceived its destructiveness. Sometimes a lesbian stays because she is trying to understand why it is not working or what it is that draws her. Defending herself to those around her because they are impatient does no one any good. At this point, she may claim privacy and insist her friends not challenge her feelings (choices).

As for friends attending such a situation, the option of withdrawal is important. It may be that our friend keeps saying she's going to do something about the situation, but what seems to be happening instead is that she comes to us for relief and then goes back, renewed, to the same old thing. If we are enabling her to remain in a situation we want no part of, withdrawal is one way we can respond to her choices. As Granny explains in Anne Cameron's *Daughters of Copper Woman:*

A woman would come to the circle as often as she needed, but the circle wasn't there to encourage a woman to only talk about her problems. The first three times you came with the same story, the women would listen and try to help. But if you showed up a fourth time, and it was the same old tired thing, the others in the circle would just get up and move and re-form the circle somewhere else. They didn't say the problem wasn't important, they just said, by movin', that it was *your* problem and it was time you did somethin' about it, you'd taken up all the time in other people's lives as was goin' to be given to you, and it was time to stop talkin' and *do* somethin'.[80]

Feelings are not isolated, private events. They do not arise in a vacuum, nor are they expressed in a vacuum. They exist in a context, are a perception of events. Certainly, it seems incorrect to suggest that I might be mistaken about what I feel. Further, it seems ludicrous to suggest that the statement "I feel that . . . " could be mistaken. To precede a statement with the words "I feel that" seems somehow to make the statement inaccessible, nonchallengeable. Isn't that what we mean by "safety" when we ask for safe places to explore our feelings? Yet if emotions are also judgments and so not distinct from reasoning it would follow that they are somehow challengeable.

Feelings in perspective and context

I want to suggest that our feelings are not private – that is, they are open to assessment and challenge – in that (1) they are not isolated and can be considered in perspective, (2) they may be inappropriate to a particular context or situation, and (3) our expression of them is not private.

Consider the following situation. Two lesbians are long-time friends. One comes to visit the other and starts a relationship with another lesbian in town. The visiting lesbian is nervous and tense about this, for she is taking risks she has not taken before. When she and her new lover have an encounter that goes well, she is on the crest of a wave. However, when there is major miscommunication, she becomes extremely upset. Her attention is riveted on her pain to such an extent that her stricken energy permeates her friend's apartment. At first her friend attends her, and the situation poses no real problems. But if the situation goes on for a long time, or recurs each time the visiting lesbian returns, then the friend must either stop her own agendas and attend the visiting lesbian almost exclusively since she can't get away from the energy, or find ways of ignoring the visiting lesbian thereby possibly increasing the visiting lesbian's insecurity and sense of isolation. Either way, the friend is affected by the visiting lesbian's energy. If the visiting lesbian is not in touch with her own fear and pain, then she may perceive her friend's withdrawal as abandonment and lack of caring. If the friend tries to explain to the visiting lesbian that she is tired of the tension, the visiting lesbian may respond by saying, "If I hid my feelings, I wouldn't be honest."

Now, I want to suggest that in this situation, feelings are open to evaluation and even challenge in certain ways. Regardless of what is going on with the new lover, there is the matter of the visiting lesbian's interaction with her friend. Her friend wants her own engagement with the visiting lesbian: while she may be willing to concern herself with the visiting lesbian's trials and tribulations in forming a lover relationship, there are other elements of the visiting lesbian's life which the two of them share as friends.

Thus, the visiting lesbian's feelings are open to challenge, in the first place, in that her friend can expect her to consider them in perspective (the friend and her lover are not the only ones in the world). This is not to say that the feelings themselves are "wrong" or "mistaken." It is simply to say that a friend can ask us to consider the effects of our choice to focus exclusively on certain feelings rather than, for example, also focusing on our feelings toward her, allowing us to spend some good time together.

My second suggestion is that, while our feelings come from very real places, they are open to challenge in that they may be out of context.[81] Again, I am not suggesting that the feelings themselves are mistaken — whatever that might mean — just, in this case, that they may be inappropriate to the situation. For example, a lesbian taking risks by engaging with another may feel off-center and react out of habit, judging certain actions on the other's part as a sign of danger because such actions have been in the past. However, the present situation may differ in crucial ways from ones she has faced before. Our feelings include an evaluation of situations which may be mistaken — and thus open to challenge from friends.

Thirdly, there is a difference between feelings and choosing to express them to someone else. There is a tendency in lesbian communities to think that it is appropriate to express feelings at any time and in any place, even to anyone. Thus, if someone is angry or in pain and we won't hear her or we insist that she explain her anger, she may argue that this is stifling and hence oppressive to her. And in certain cases, it may be.

Expression of feelings

The problem is that the expression of feelings is not an isolated, individual, private act. For example, if you get angry or come crying to me and I sit there watching television as you express your feelings and I only look up when you stop, saying, "Are you done now?," this is not likely to be acceptable to you. Or again, if you enter the room and begin to hurl accusations at me, I doubt you would find it acceptable if I yawned and said, "Oh that's interesting." In other words, expressing our feelings is not a matter of yelling into a vacuum. We expect certain reactions. And regardless of how minimal they might be (in expressing my feelings, I might be satisfied if you just understood me, even if you didn't agree with my judgment), a relationship is involved.

The statement, "Those are just my feelings," involves not just one lesbian expressing herself but also another responding in certain ways. The expression of feelings is designed to secure a response. Hence it involves a relationship. And insofar as one has engaged in a relationship by expressing her feelings, what she says is open to evaluation and even challenge from the other.

Part of our resistance to healing the fragmentation of our reasoning and emotions is a resistance to the possibility of such challenges, for, if we can't feel safe in heteropatriarchy, at least we can work to feel safe in the community. Within heteropatriarchy the deepest parts of our selves have been under attack. Insofar as we engage in lesbian community we want to be free of such asaults and attacks.

Safety versus taking each other seriously

As a result, we tend to focus on safety as a central element of community. In particular, we tend to believe a viable lesbian community is one in which it would be completely safe for us to express our feelings. I want to suggest that, not only is safety an illusion under patriarchy, it is not a useful goal among ourselves – for attempts to guarantee safety involve attempts to control.

When we claim that we need a community in which it is safe to express our feelings, we often seem to be imagining a situation in which we can blow up while others restrict themselves to a range of acceptable responses. The belief that we have a right to express our feelings in any way at any time is the belief that we have certain automatic rights of access and connection to others in the community. The one who is the recipient of the expression of feelings is being asked to respond in certain ways – she is being told how she must be responsive. And my suggestion above is that this is open to evaluation and even challenge. For insofar as the one may need to express herself, the other may need to refuse to attend, to withdraw. Appealing to a goal of safety obscures the possible conflict here. In making a space safe for one to express her feelings, we may be making it dangerous for another who is, for example, the subject of attack or of ignorance. What becomes of safety if that translates into a guarantee of one lesbian's access to other lesbians at any time and only on her own terms?

The appeal to safety as a community goal may at times be an attempt to ease the risk of interacting; for whenever we approach someone else, there is a risk of rejection. (I don't mean a risk of not getting what we want – although there is the risk of that too; I mean the possibility of being reflected back in others' judgments as insignificant, incidental.) The issue of safety among lesbians in community mostly involves not being laughed at, put down, ignored, out-shouted, or in general taken for granted. And this is a matter of taking each other seriously.[f] Consequently, I want to suggest that, rather than working toward safety, we work on taking each other seriously as a goal. In weaving lesbian community, I think we might work to create a space in which every lesbian can be attended, taken seriously, and valued for herself—where she can be acknowledged.

The difference is one of focus, and it becomes most obvious when we are not acting with full integrity or when we are in conflict. For example, if we are focused on safety, we can be tempted to tolerate absolutely anything another lesbian does. If a lesbian is acting out or scapegoating others, we may believe that she needs a safe space where she can express herself. Yet tolerating absolutely anything a lesbian does may not be taking her seriously at all. It may be, rather, confusing empathy with pity, to have no expectations of her and hence to regard her as less than ourselves. This is condescending, and such a space really isn't safe for her. (In this respect, to take another seriously does not necessarily mean respecting her choices.) Taking another seriously means attending her and then evaluating, judging, the situation for ourselves, and making choices about our response.

In a space in which we are taken seriously, "safety" is not defined only on our own terms. Being taken seriously involves community; it involves engagement with others. I am suggesting, thus, that being able to express our feelings and have others respond to us is also a matter of being able to respond to others. Both aspects are integral to our being taken seriously.

I have been arguing that the split between reasoning and emotions does not serve us: It leads us to perpetuate the fragmentation of our selves *The whole lesbian* thereby undermining our energy, our power-from-within, and our ability *being* to assess situations. It encourages us to depoliticize our judgments. It leads us to regard the meaning of our feelings as private and hence our selves as isolated. It encourages atomistic individualism. When this occurs, we are more susceptible to absorbing the dominant society's values and perceive our feelings accordingly, and we are less able to collectively undermine those dominant values.

The idea that emotions are independent of our reasoning can only come from a political perspective that depicts individuals as isolated, solitary, and competitive; a political perspective that pretends we do not develop in relation to each other and presupposes that social groups are

---

f Often the charge of racism among lesbians is a charge that white lesbians aren't taking lesbians of color seriously.[82]

built on "independently existing characteristics of individuals." Again, as Naomi Scheman suggests, our inner states develop into full-blown emotions and beliefs and intentions through interacting with others and within a context. Healing the wound enables us both to better understand our selves and to interact with others. As a result, we will less likely feel the need to be either in or out of control.

In *Witches Heal,* Billie Potts connects integrity with healing and notes that healing our selves is a "personal act of empowerment."[83] I believe that what we are involved with in the community we've created is massive healing at many levels – an integrating of the parts of our selves which is crucial to surviving and developing our moral agency. Throughout this chapter I have focused almost exclusively on the fragmenting of reasoning and emotions. However, far more than this is involved.

In a creative writing workshop, Toni Cade Bambara noted that those in power discredit other crucial parts of our selves, particularly our dreaming, our intuition, our imagination, and our psychic faculty. I would add our humor. She suggested they do this because they cannot control these parts.[84] They can control them only by disintegrating them: through terrorization, derogation, and objectification they fragment all our faculties and so disintegrate us. Toni Cade Bambara's concern is to reconnect our parts – to let our dreams touch our daily thoughts, for example – so that when we focus, our whole being is engaged. In this way we are far less likely to be controlled. Thus we create, we create a poem, a relationship, a casserole, a collective, a revolution.

Through consciousness-raising groups we have developed the complex meanings of our anger. We can develop in the same way our psychic faculty. We need to explore our intuition, develop our humor. We can find the power of our dreams through speaking them to each other.[85] And we can explore new spaces by enacting and sharing our imagination. We can also develop depth and complexity by engaging in consciousness-raising concerning our fears, our anger at each other, and our lesbian desire.

My concern with healing the fragmentation of our reasoning and emotions, finally, is this. Our anger is the movement by which we express frustration at having our lives obstructed or denied.[86] And our lesbian desire brings the connecting – lover relationships, friendships, collectivity, companionship. In reality our emotions and reasoning as well as our dreams, intuitions, instincts, hesitancies, nuestra facultad,[87] observations, humor, psychic awarenesses, valuations, imaginings – judgments emerging in lesbian community against a background of racist, imperialist, heterosexual culture – are all we have to guide us on our lesbian journey. Our abilities to make judgments – all these faculties – directed and encouraged our initial choices. And they are still our guides, our warning signals, our outposts, our trailblazers, our campsites, and our maps – that which we use to notice, consider, and make our choices, as we go. And they change and they develop in complexity and meaning as we interact.

As we travel our lesbian journey, our reasoning and emotions will undergo transformation, particularly as we learn to integrate them with our other faculties and as we develop lesbian meaning by engaging with each other. As Edwina Lee Tyler shows us any time she touches a drum, it is the flow of energy and understanding back and forth among us that centers, transforms, and gives back again, that creates meaning.[88] And as we heal by integrating and politicizing our fragmented selves, I think we will become more adept, particularly at laughing.

It is said we lack a sense of humor. In the last 30 years, at least, there has been very little to laugh at. But we are beginning to create our own humor. As Kate Clinton writes:

> Fumerists [feminist humorists] make whys cracks. We ask our own questions and they have the potential of splitting the world apart. . . . We fumerists say we are not staying in some happy holding pattern, passively waiting until it is over. We say we are going to laugh and by our laughing, change things. It is a very active ethic of withdrawing the seriousness of our beliefs from men's enterprises. We are saying that the joke is no longer on us. We say we are not going to die laughing at their stories anymore.[89]

The possibilities of lesbian meaning emerge among us. And the whole lesbian being is greater, far greater, than the sum of the fragmented parts. Integrating our selves – centering so we can engage in this living, respond to others, and develop our lesbian meaning rather than exercising self-control by trying to sever our emotions and reasoning – affects the choices we make and helps us to declare ourselves moral agents. Thus in the next chapter I want to explore and develop the concept of 'moral agency' among lesbians.

5
Moral Agency
and Interaction

IN THIS CHAPTER I want to explore the idea of 'moral agency', moral be-ing, particularly under oppression. Within ethics as we define it now, the idea of being a moral person or agent is tied primarily to the question of whether we freely choose our actions. In certain respects this question involves the idea that to be ethical we must be able to control external forces or, at the very least, that a proper moral choice would be one in which there were no constraints on us, no limits. Traditionally, philosophical concern involves whether we could have done otherwise or whether our actions have been determined in some manner – the focus is almost exclusively on whether we can blame or praise others for what they have done and whether we can be blamed or praised for what we have done. Hence there is a strong emphasis on excuses, accountability, and justification. My suggestion, on the other hand, is that moral agency involves enacting choice in limited situations, avoiding de-moralization, and working within boundaries rather than trying to rise above them. I want to suggest that the focus of Lesbian Ethics be, not praise and blame, but judgment at a deeper level and "the morale of survival."[1]

'Free Will' and Excuses

'Free will' WITHIN RECENT ANGLO-EUROPEAN tradition, the question of moral agency begins with an abstract conflict between the concepts of

'free will' and 'determinism'. The idea is that we are moral agents in that we are morally accountable for our actions, and we are morally accountable only if we could have done otherwise. If we could not have done otherwise, if our actions were determined, then we had no choice. One formulation of that problem is this: If, from a religious context, an all-powerful god (who is thus all-knowing) already knows what we're going to do, or if, from a scientific context, under mechanistic laws of cause and effect, our actions are merely effects of previous actions which caused them, then our actions are not really free. They are determined in that we could not do otherwise. And this is the case, so the argument goes, even if at the time of acting we are under the illusion of having freely chosen our actions. (Significantly, anglo-european philosophers are only concerned with whether our actions are determined by a benevolent god or an indifferent mechanistic universe. The idea that they could be determined by an oppressor does not seem to have occurred to them.) This way of addressing the issue of moral agency yields problems which seem unresolvable almost before they've been addressed. For given a belief in an all-powerful god or a belief in traditional science, it appears that all our actions are determined and none are freely chosen.

Interestingly, while the traditional problem of free will appears to yield the conclusion that all our actions are determined, something of the opposite conclusion emerges from existentialist philosophy and also from areas of lesbian and women's spirituality and witchcraft. According to proponents of these areas of thought, we have total 'free choice'. That is, according to these views, everything we do or that has happened to us – in the case of women's spirituality, even our birth – is something we have chosen. *Existential choice*

Apart from this shared central thesis, however, there are important differences between the two areas. According to Sartre's existentialism, we always have a choice because we can get out of a situation (by suicide at the very least). If we don't choose to get out of the situation, then it follows we have chosen it:

> Thus there are no *accidents* in a life; a community event which suddenly bursts forth and involves me in it does not come from the outside. If I am mobilized in a war, this war is *my* war; it is in my image and I deserve it. I deserve it first because I could always get out of it by suicide or by desertion; these ultimate possibilities are those which must always be present for us when there is a question of envisaging a situation. For lack of getting out of it, I have *chosen* it.[2]

Sartre argues that we have not *chosen* our birth, we have not chosen to be "thrown" into the world at a particular time and place and as a particular type of person (for example, a jew in nazi germany).[3] However, he argues that to be authentic we must embrace the situation in which we find ourselves. Moreover, we are responsible for everything we do or that happens to us subsequently.

Now, there are elements of Sartre's concept of 'choice' which are refreshing. He was concerned with 'choice' in wartime, among other things, and he challenged those who pretended they had no choice under such conditions – those who claimed they were simply following orders, or who claimed they were following what their priest, for example, told them. (In the latter case, we still choose whom we pay attention to.) Nevertheless, in the long run, Sartre's concept of 'choice' does not acknowledge oppression, and as a result his discussion of inauthenticity in women as a group and in jews as a group, blames the victim.[a] He does not acknowledge the reality of coercion or admit his inability to control the outcome of some situations. He claims it is *his* war, not everyone's war.

Further, a christian moralism (apparent in the idea that those involved in war deserve it) informs Sartre's existentialist notion of freedom. While he does not believe there are any ultimate principles of right and wrong or a god to justify such, he certainly labors within a conceptual framework in which both ultimate principles and dominant deity are needed to make sense of events in the world. (He was, after all, constructing his philosophy during the despair of a world war.) Sartre's 'freedom' is an absence, an absence of a dominant deity to ensure the perpetuation of ultimate principles – an absence which, while throwing us into choice, also results in absurdity and is terrifying. Thus, while he holds that we create meaning with our choices (there is no preexisting meaning given to the universe by an anthropomorphic god), he finds this an indication of absurdity, a cause for despair, and a prelude to nausea.[7]

Some authors in the areas of women's and lesbian spirituality and witchcraft also hold that we choose whatever happens to us. But their development of the idea doesn't carry with it the heavy guilt-trip that Sartre's existentialism does. (Most authors also tend not to focus on choice during wartime or consider the problems of collaboration which Sartre was concerned with.) According to this view, choices are made in

Choice in women's spirituality

----

a   For example, while he argues that we must embrace our situation, he depicts women who embrace their situation and conform to heterosexualism as models of inauthenticity.[4] As Marilyn Frye notes, Sartre insists that a woman who claims she feels pain from coitus and dreads it actually fears pleasure and is self-deceived.[5] And his book *Anti-Semite and Jew*,[6] an intriguing discussion of the persona of an antisemite, essentially portrays a jew who flees persecution as inauthentic.

other lifetimes which affect this lifetime, and insofar as we choose to come back in a particular life, we do so in order to learn something, to work something through, to effect change in relationships begun in other lives, and so on. Thus once we are born into a given life, much informs our choices, and the idea is to try to understand this. If we do, we can begin making choices to counteract or modify the direction and events of the course we are on.[8] 'Free will' in this life, then, means that we can strive to understand the events that surround us, work on the problems they pose, and once we arrive at an understanding, choose to make changes. Under some views we keep coming back until we achieve "perfection."

Insofar as there is a determinism in this line of thought, it is spiritual and not the mechanistic determinism of traditional anglo-european philosophy. Karma functions deterministically only when we are unaware, and the course of events can be changed by our spiritual will (which is significantly different from the disciplinary and controlling mind-over-body will of the patriarchs) through integrating our whole being, understanding our situation, and then making our choices.

While these ideas provide intriguing ground for exploring a concept of moral agency, they need to be more carefully developed than I have found them to be so far. For example, one traditional admonition is that what we do comes back three times over, so of course we should never do harm. But such a motive for choice in action could conflict significantly with motives stemming from the belief that we are here to work through our karma. Certainly, it would discourage risks; for if in trying a new pattern of action we make a mistake and harm results, then we're stuck with triple its effects. Secondly, this admonition doesn't really deal with the fact that the consequences of our actions are complex, with some "good" and some "bad" resulting in most cases. Thirdly, I don't accept the energy of the holocaust coming back three times over to anyone. And finally, I don't find such a motive, which is a check on our actions based primarily on fear, very interesting or especially useful in constructing lesbian value.

Or another example. The theory would seem to suggest that some jews had a chosen destiny that took them to the holocaust, or that some blacks were on a chosen course that took them into slavery, or that women who are raped chose a course that took them there, and so on. And while I think it true in certain circumstances that we attract a particular kind of energy by the energy we put out in the world (it is Ronald who must barricade the white house), I think a great deal more analysis of oppression needs to be completed within women's spirituality before any such theory can be accurate or useful in helping us address the terms of our lesbian lives under oppression. Too often spirituality simply ignores the reality of oppression or otherwise discounts it.

Now, while all these theories about 'free will' and moral choice are interesting, it is not clear that they really help us understand moral agency, especially under oppression. It is just not clear what saying either that all our actions are determined or that we choose all that happens to us, *means*. 'Freedom' is an abstract concept, and we should thus be wary when working with it.

One approach to abstract concepts in philosophy, such as 'freedom' or 'reality' or 'truth', is to address, not those concepts themselves, but their denials. Thus, rather than approaching 'freedom' in action by trying to define it, we might begin by considering those situations in which we would be regarded as not acting freely. The idea is that 'freedom' is not the name of a quality which we, or our actions, or our choices, possess. It is not the name of a characteristic of actions but rather the name of a dimension in which actions are assessed.[9b] To say some act was freely chosen is to exclude certain specific ways in which it might not have been freely chosen.[11]

In understanding moral agency, we might thus consider under what circumstances we would not be held responsible for the consequences of something we did or failed to do. In particular, we can consider whether any excuses apply. Appealing to Aristotle, J. L. Austin suggests:

> Questions of whether a person was responsible for this or that are prior to questions of freedom. . . . [T]o discover whether someone acted freely or not, we must discover whether this, that, or the other plea [of excuse] will pass—for example, duress, or mistake, or accident, and so forth.[12]

Austin is suggesting that by determining whether excuses apply, we have already addressed the question of whether the person freely chose to do what they did: if there is no excuse for something they did, then they are responsible for it. Thus the question of moral agency is a question of accountability in action, and is centered, not around the problem of free will, but, more common-sensically, around whether or not one has excuses.

Suppose, for example, I promised you I would meet you at a given time, but I did not show up. In deciding your response to the situation, likely you would attempt to find out why I did not show up. If I simply found something better to do or even forgot about our agreement, likely you would get angry, perhaps attempting to make me realize I had done

---

b   Similarly, 'reality' is not the name of a characteristic of things nor 'truth' the name of a characteristic of assertions.[10]

you an injury. Or you might distance yourself, regarding me as someone who held commitments lightly and hence as someone you didn't want to develop a friendship with. However, if I had an excuse, likely you would not blame me for hurting you; I did not freely choose to break our date.

So to understand moral accountability and thus what it might mean to suggest that someone is a moral agent, we can begin by evaluating how excuses function. Aristotle suggests two general categories of excuse: ignorance, and constraint or physical restraint.[13] For example, if I were physically restrained in certain ways—if I had a car accident and could not keep our appointment because I was hurt, couldn't even get to a phone to let you know—likely you would not blame me for breaking the date with you; likely you would not regard me as having freely chosen to miss the date. Through this type of consideration we can understand what it might mean to say I chose to break the date with you. In this case the question concerns whether or not I was restrained by a car accident or a similar prohibiting event.

A second category of excuse is ignorance. Suppose, for example, I am driving my car when my brakes give out and I hit a pedestrian. If I realized my brakes were going but just hadn't gotten around to taking the car into the shop, likely you would regard me as responsible for the accident. On the other hand, suppose I had just had my brakes fixed—in fact, was driving the car out of the shop when the brakes went and I hit a pedestrian. In this second case, likely I would not be held morally responsible for hitting the pedestrian, since—short of gaining technical expertise and checking a professional mechanic's work myself—I had no way of realizing anything was still wrong with the brakes. In this respect, ignorance can function as an excuse.

These examples offer another way we can understand what it might mean to say you chose what happened. Of course, rarely do we choose to hit pedestrians. However, if someone realizes their brakes are faulty and just hasn't gotten around to having them fixed, then if they choose to drive the car anyway, we tend to consider them responsible for the consequences of their choice. So freedom of choice can be a question of whether you were aware of what you were doing.

In this way, by examining particular situations and considering excuses, we can begin to develop an understanding of moral accountability and thus moral agency; the concept of 'freedom' as presented in the problem of free will is far too unclear and unwieldy. For my purposes, considerations about 'freedom' as it relates to 'moral agency' involve considerations about our day-to-day moral choices from where we stand—as finite beings who will die (who will end this life) and who live within the boundaries of a finite world as well as under significant restrictions, including oppression. That is, my interest concerns what we as lesbians face, as we make choices, given the parameters of this life. And it is from such a day-to-day, mundane perspective, rather than from a grandiose theory of free will, that I wish to proceed.

Choice and creating value   Focusing on choice in situations, Simone de Beauvoir develops an interesting concept of 'choice' and thus of 'moral agency' in *The Ethics of Ambiguity*.[14] Developing aspects of the existentialist tradition, she connects choice with the creation of value. She suggests that children find themselves in a world they did not create and so do not have to assume responsibility for creating value. They can accept as ready-made and absolute the values adults have created and simply choose to obey or rebel against the limits of that world. However, as children grow and gain awareness by asking why they must do as adults demand, they undergo an identity crisis. At this point they find themselves in a world no longer ready-made but rather one which has to be made. They must determine for themselves what is valuable and what is not — what to accept of their parents' values and what to reject. In this way, they move to a moral plane.

From this point on, people become moral agents, creating value through the choices they make. (By engaging as lesbians, for example, we create lesbian value.) And there are numerous opportunities for avoiding choice, for being inauthentic. (Being inauthentic by avoiding choice is an existentialist's version of moral error or sin.) For example, the 'serious man' pretends value is ready-made and hides behind a role. He is not a person but a father, for example, or a soldier. As a result, he claims he is compelled to do certain things — it's his duty. He pretends his choice has unconditional value, hence denies making a choice, and so becomes a tyrant. He pretends the value he chooses is outside him and that he is subordinating himself to it. Thus, he feels justified in forcing those he dominates to also submit to the value (by submitting to his authority). Or again, the nihilist, understanding there is no objective value, remains a cynic, pretending nothing he does makes a difference and so remaining comfortable in his "powerlessness." He refuses to engage in this living himself, instead simply criticizing those who do.[15]

Simone de Beauvoir argues that the value we create through our choices is the value that exists, there is no value against which we can justify what we choose. What we choose, is, simply, the value that will emerge. (This is obvious in terms of lesbian community: the values that are emerging among lesbians are a result of what we enact.) The ambiguity of this state of affairs, in part, is that the value we create is not eternal. We will die, and others' choices can transform what we have created (just as we can transform what others have created). Nevertheless, to be authentic we must engage in this living, embrace our finiteness, and make our choices as if what we create were eternal – with that degree of emotion, energy, and commitment.

Significantly, given that Simone de Beauvoir allows for no absolute value against which we can justify the value we choose (since we create, rather than discover, value), and given that the value that exists will emerge from the choices we make, it is nevertheless, by her argument, not possible to choose just anything. It is not possible, for example, to choose nazism. And that is because, as her argument goes, nazism is not a choice of value but a fleeing of choice. That is, to be a nazi is to be a 'subman', as she terms it. The subman is one who loses himself in a label – 'white supremist', 'antisemite' – for he seeks to have meaning determined for him. He is terrified of taking the responsibility to act in the world. Instead, he finds a scapegoat to blame for all the world's ills and thus needs do nothing himself about changing them. He is one who is afraid of choice and so pretends he has none by becoming a fanatic and submitting to a higher order, one he pretends is outside himself.

Evil results, for Simone de Beauvoir, from people who pretend they are not creating value by the choices they make, who pretend there is an absolute value outside of themselves to which they must submit and which justifies them in forcing others to submit to it by forcing others to submit to them. The nazi program is just such a program.

To be ethical, according to Simone de Beauvoir, we must not only embrace our own freedom and create value through our choices, we must also choose the freedom of others. For we don't create value in isolation, independent of others. We realize our freedom by engaging in action, and that means interacting with others – others who must also be free, for if they are not, we are not able to really interact with them. Thus, Simone de Beauvoir deals with human choice in particular circumstances and notes that choosing such freedom means we must work for the liberation of those who are oppressed – not as an altruistic act, but rather to enact our freedom, to enact moral agency. We cannot be fully moral agents alone. Our freedom and moral agency require that others also be free.

I find this discussion of creating value through our choices and of inauthenticity thought-provoking. However, given the influence of Hegel and Sartre, among others, on Simone de Beauvoir's work, it is still not clear what the term 'freedom' means in the particulars of moral choice given the problem of constraints on our choices. So in order to approach moral agency by discussing everyday choices, I want to return to considering the way excuses function in our interactions. *Ignorance as an excuse*

As I noted, exploring excuses is a way of approaching moral agency by exploring what it means to say a person is morally responsible for her actions. Nevertheless, there are serious problems with both categories of excuse I have mentioned—ignorance and constraint. And understanding some of these problems can help us get a better sense of what it means to be a moral agent.

Consider first the question of ignorance and the example of faulty brakes. If I didn't understand that having to push the brake pedal completely to the floor meant my brakes were almost worn out, and I lived in a place with hills like san francisco's, you would likely not regard my ignorance as excusable. We expect people to educate themselves in certain respects. Thus, ignorance does not always excuse us for harm which results from something we did or failed to do.

Within the lesbian community, ignorance as an excuse has been challenged around major issues and found lacking. These issues include classism, racism, antisemitism, ablebodyism, ageism, sizeism, specieism, heterosexism, sexism, and at times, capitalism, socialism, and imperialism. As Cherríe Moraga exploded: "What each of us needs to do about what we don't know is to go look for it."[16] The degree to which this challenge has been met has depended on a number of factors: the general openness and sensitivity (even without understanding) of the community to the particular issue, the risk involved for those describing immediate experiences, the degree of vulnerability of community lesbians concerning the issue, and the degree of ignorance still prevalent in the community about the issue.

For example, working-class lesbians have challenged middle-and upper-class lesbian presumptions; analyses have been offered to the effect that middle- and upper-class lesbians have grown up with class privilege. This means in the u.s., that, among other things, most middle- and upper-class lesbians have grown up ignorant of the effects of classism on the working class, ignorant of working-class culture and methods of interacting, and, in the case of middle-class lesbians, unconscious of middle-class values as specific, limited values.

We have developed less analysis and maintained greater ignorance (at least in many communities) about the differing effects of racism on various ethnic groups. Our attention has focused almost exclusively on black/white relations, which nevertheless continue to exhibit much of the dominant ideology (both conservative and liberal). Little work has been done on the effects of the pressure to assimilate on native americans and hence on native american lesbians while the u.s. prepares to celebrate the 500th anniversary of the "discovery of america."[17] And little work has been done on the effects on asian-american lesbians of the stereotype in the dominant culture of asians as the "perfect minority," hence, according to stereotypes held in other oppressed cultures, as "just like whites" (and so as having nothing significant to say), or the stereotype of all asians as being "alike" and not coming from vastly different cultures.[18]

Or, along another line, there remains much work to do on the effects of aging on older lesbians, on the fact that 'over the hill' means 'out of sight' and that the increasing inability of older lesbians to participate in the community is a change, not in the capacity of older lesbians, but rather in the status ascribed to them by other lesbians.[19] From the other direction, we continue to ignore the effects of ageism on young lesbians, how older lesbians discount young lesbians, how this, too, is connected to power, and how young lesbians are excluded and so cease to care. Examples abound.

Ignorance can be dispelled by a combination of political analysis, consciousness-raising, humor, and genuine experience through attending and other interaction. As doris davenport writes:

> To begin to end some of the colossal ignorance that white feminists have about us, we (black and white feminists) could engage in "c.r." conversations about and with each other. If done with a sense of honesty, and a sense of *humor*, we might accomplish something. If overcoming our differences were made a priority instead of the back-burner issue that it usually is, we might resolve some of our problems.[20]

Ignorance persists, however, despite the best of intentions, because ignorance is generally unaware of itself. It also persists when we believe we have a vested interest in it.

As Marilyn Frye notes, "one need only hear the active verb 'to ignore' in the word 'ignorance'" to appreciate that ignorance is not a passive state.[21] As I noted in chapter three, an aspect of the power of privilege is to ignore. Within the lesbian community, in part because of our awareness of the ignoring involved in ignorance, we tend not to regard ignorance as an excuse in these matters and in many other matters concerning ways we interact. In fact, over time we come to realize that much ignorance is the result of ignoring. Given our experiences with stereotyping and cultural boundaries, we expect each other to attend and learn both about each other and from each other. Being ignorant about our differences is not an acceptable excuse for choices which result in harm, particularly when we hide our needs and fears behind it.

This attitude toward ignorance results, I believe, from our increasing understanding of how ignorance plays a major role in perpetuating oppression, from our growing awareness that no one is "pure" or "blameless," from our increasing responsiveness in divesting ourselves of the ignorance nurtured under oppression, and from our understanding of the danger of ignoring under oppression. To survive we must be aware of our surroundings, develop that awareness. As Baba Copper writes and as others before her have written in other contexts:

> The way to respond to *all* accusations of ageism is identical to how we must respond to accusations of racist, classist, physicalist or sexist behavior. Do a lot of listening, both inwardly and outwardly. Resistance, excuses or rationalizations only compound our problems. There are basic questions which fifteen years of feminism have taught us to ask: Who profits? What are the hidden assumptions? Why have we ignored it? This is not necessarily to say that the action or absence of actions has been correctly named. But when an older woman raises the issue of ageism, do not explain to her what you *really* meant. Listen. [22]

I will add that the same is true when a younger lesbian raises the issue of ageism. In this case, while there can be ignorance as a result of different youth cultures with each generation, still the ignoring is not the result of being unaware of the situation for lack of having been there. The ignoring and avoidance involved in ageism against both the young and the old suggests that the ignorance which fosters and is fostered by all oppression involves much more than lack of experience. It involves avoiding what we've been taught by the dominant society to fear, and it means trying to hang on to the tidbits the patriarchy throws us. But the tidbits, the "privileges," appear as privileges only in a context of dominance and subordination where we need power over others to gain status. In the long run, it is the fathers who profit from our ignorance and ignoring.

A central part of working out of oppression involves divesting ourselves of ignorance and its effects. This process can be traumatic: aside from facing things we fear, in divesting ourselves of our ignorance we will make mistakes with each other; and by the very setup, the situation is not one that involves being excused for our mistakes. That these mistakes are made in ignorance separates us from those who do such things with full understanding of what they are doing. But our mistakes still result in harm to others. So we're in a difficult position.

Nevertheless, the process of such mistakes is part of what moves us on toward lesser ignorance, toward dealing with the issues, and thus toward more informed choices. We don't divest ourselves of our ignorance by hiding or by refusing to engage in order to avoid mistakes. Thus, the other side of deciding that ignorance is not an excuse is the idea of going on and engaging despite the fact that we will make mistakes. In these ways, ignorance, excuses, and subsequent counteraction take on a different texture in the community.

Constraint as an Excuse   The other general category of excuse – physical restraint or constraint – is also taking on a different texture. Consider how constraint functions as an excuse. Aristotle offers the following definition:

> An act done under constraint is one in which the initiative or source of motion comes from without, and to which the person compelled contributes nothing. [23]

One example involves someone on a ship which is blown off-course. Generally, the idea is that we are not responsible for what happens to us when we are constrained or when we fail to commit acts because we were physically unable. This definition is narrow, to say the least. For example, what about acts committed at gunpoint? If someone holds a gun to me, demanding I hand over my keys and I do so, I am not doing so under constraint by Aristotle's definition. Generally, while the category of ignorance permits too much, this category of constraint permits too little. The problem is that constraint, so understood, applies to a fairly narrow range of situations lesbians face and does not in any way take into account conditions of exploitation and oppression.

Consider two examples of "choice" under oppression. One case was popularized by the novel *Sophie's Choice*. Sophie is a woman in a concentration camp who is told she must choose which of her two children will die, and that if she refuses to choose, both children will be killed. As soldiers reach for her son, she grabs him and her daughter is taken to her death. Some might regard her situation as an extended matter of constraint, under the above definition, since the "initiative or source of motion comes from without." However, some might also insist that she did act, she did contribute something, and in so doing she is at least accountable, if not responsible, for her daughter's death.

The second example involves Lucy Andrews, a free black who in 1859 petitioned the south carolina legislature to allow her to enter slavery. She was sixteen years old with two children and could find no employment, nor could she stay anywhere longer than a week or two at a time.[c] Her

---

c   Glennon Graham, having done his dissertation on free blacks in south carolina during the time in question, is familiar with Lucy Andrews's case. She was of mixed parentage; her mother was white and her father, while unknown, was black. As the daughter of a white woman, Lucy Andrews was born free, but white women who slept with black men were treated as black at the time. Further, Lucy would have been considered fair game for any man, which is likely why she had two children by age sixteen. Escape to the north would have been almost impossible as many northern states had laws by then restricting the emigration of free blacks. She was living in a rural area and so had little access to other free blacks, who tended to congregate in the cities. She was also caught in a fight between large plantation owners, who supported free blacks, and small plantation owners, for whom any free black was a threat. Large plantation owners supported free blacks in certain "democratic" values: for example, free blacks could own property, and the majority of

choice really doesn't fit under 'constraint' as defined above. After all, she petitioned the courts two years running (the first time she was refused) — no one actually put her in iron chains. Thus, some might be tempted to conclude that she freely entered both herself and her children into slavery. In this case some might argue that she is morally responsible for enslaving herself and her children.

Marilyn Frye points out that under the line of reasoning surrounding such definitions as Aristotle's definition of 'constraint', if a person physically does anything over and above muscle contraction, then she acts voluntarily and of her own accord.[26] Such reasoning is inaccurate, and doesn't begin to acknowledge the complexity of our lives as we live them. Marilyn Frye suggests we reevaluate this concept, and she offers her own analysis of coercion:

> To coerce someone into doing something, one has to manipulate the situation so that the world as perceived by the victim presents the victim with a range of options the least unattractive of which (or the most attractive of which) in the judgment of the victim is the act one wants the victim to do.[27]

Marilyn Frye goes on to suggest that exploitation, oppression, and enslavement involve even greater refinements of domination by those in power:

> What the exploiter needs is that the will and intelligence of the victim be disengaged from the projects of resistance and escape but that they not be simply broken or destroyed.[28]

In other words, oppression functions, not just by those in power limiting our options, but by those in power successfully getting us to contribute our efforts toward the maintenance of those oppressive conditions (now named something else such as social organization or national security). This is the central goal of neo-colonialism. And domination is totally successful when someone, in being coerced to lend their efforts to maintain those oppressive conditions, internalizes those oppressive values, comes to believe those values are good and right — or even that they are fact (reality).

---

black slave-holders owned themselves and their families, while nevertheless being unable to vote. During the 1850s there was a great debate between those who would make free blacks choose between becoming slaves or leaving the state (small plantation owners) and those who would protect free blacks' "rights." The legislature (supported by large plantation owners) may have turned her down the first time out of a sense of "justice" or because no one wanted a sixteen-year-old female with two children — more expensive than productive. Nevertheless, by her second effort, forty prominent whites of lancaster county signed her petition and "supported" her entry into slavery.[25]

So while a person may physically perform certain acts, may actually make certain choices, she nevertheless may be coerced in that her options are manipulated by those who have power over her. In Sophie's case and in Lucy Andrews's case, the options were manipulated in just such a fashion. Further, a person may have been subject to domination in such a way that her will is disengaged from resistance, and she is forced instead to attend to the interests of those who dominate. In creating a situation in which Sophie was forced to "choose" which of her children would die, clearly the commandant's goal was to break her will. However, this was not likely the goal of those responsible for the system under which Lucy Andrews found the choice to enter slavery plausible. Lucy Andrews was not simply broken or destroyed, but her will and intelligence were disengaged from the projects of resistance and escape.

Now, we can borrow Marilyn Frye's extended definition and analysis of coercion to broaden the concept of constraint as an excuse, arguing that neither Lucy Andrews nor Sophie is morally responsible for the results of her choices, since her choices were clearly coerced. That is, Lucy Andrews did not freely choose to enter slavery, nor did Sophie freely choose to send her daughter to her death.

Yet saying simply that neither freely chose her actions because she had an excuse is not satisfying, for it does not begin to characterize the situation. Nor does it begin to address what moral agency could mean in these circumstances. To conclude simply that Sophie did not freely choose to send her daughter to her death because she had an excuse, and that Lucy Andrews did not freely choose to enter herself and her children into slavery because she had an excuse, says too little. While Marilyn Frye's analysis of coercion and exploitation helps us understand how constraints function under oppression, it is apparent, now, that trying to analyze moral agency under oppression by considering excuses is simply inadequate.[d]

My suggestion is that the concept of 'excuses', whether in the direction of ignorance or of constraint, though central in recent ethics, is inadequate for developing a notion of 'moral agency' under oppression. While it is important to explore the particulars of our moral choices, doing so by considering whether excuses apply does not acknowledge the complexity of our lives, particularly when we have to make decisions

---

d Marilyn Frye's purpose in analyzing coercion under oppression is not to develop a concept of excuse under oppression. I am making the connection myself to show the inadequacy, not of Marilyn Frye's analysis, but rather of focusing on excuses to understand moral agency.

under coercion. Oppression is not a matter of excuse but rather a dimension within which we make our choices, a dimension which involves constructed ignorance, coercion, exploitation, and at times, enslavement. My concern is with our going on and making choices within this dimension.

Avoiding De-moralization and Claiming Moral Agency

De-moralization

ANYONE WHO IS manipulated and yet who has to act will be affected by the situation she faces. There are consequences regardless of excuses. The options available to Lucy Andrews and Sophie were manipulated in such a way as to de-moralize them—to undermine their moral agency, their ability to make choices as moral agents. I am concerned with countering this de-moralizing. I am concerned with what Alice Molloy calls "the morale of survival."

There is, of course, the fact that someone coerced both Sophie and Lucy Andrews, either directly in Sophie's case or indirectly in Lucy Andrews's case. There are agents involved in oppression, exploitation, and in the de-moralization of domination. But I am not focusing on them, since oppressors are already in the business of undermining others' moral agency and we can't count on them to cease once the folly of their ways has been pointed out (over and over, I might add). The oppressed still go on under oppression and make choices even when coerced and exploited. To conclude simply that Sophie and Lucy aren't to blame for their choices because they are oppressed isn't helpful. For they still have to go on with their lives and make further choices, as do all under oppression. Thus my interest concerns avoiding de-moralization under oppression—preserving our ability to go on and make choices as moral agents.

According to the dictionary, to demoralize someone is (1) to deprive them of spirit, courage, discipline; to destroy the morale of; (2) to throw into disorder and confusion; and (3) to corrupt or undermine the morals of.[29] In discussing the parallels between the english domination of the indigenous peoples of ireland and of native americans, George M. Fredrickson describes english colonial action all the way from outright extermination to de-moralization. When indigenous people resisted english encroachment and domination, the english countered with extermination, expropriation, and the image of the "treacherous savage." He describes the puritans, an intensely ethnocentric new england community that was "planted" in the 1630s, noting that more than other colonists, the puritans believed they had a god-given duty to stamp out native american religion. He goes on:

> In other colonies threats to the integrity of the Indians' way of life came less from systematic cultural intolerance than from the ravages of European diseases against which they had no immunity and the demoralizing effect of contact with traders who plied native americans with alcohol, made them dependent on european trade goods, and induced them to carry on the disastrous practice of extirpating the wildlife within their territories to provide furs and skins for the white market.[30]

In this case native americans were de-moralized in that they were coerced into turning against the very things they valued.

In introducing the concept 'de-moralization', I mean to invoke much more than low spirits. I mean to focus on the undermining of someone's ability to make choices and her ability to perceive herself as being able to make choices, even in difficult situations. The phenomenon I am concerned with involves someone finding herself in the position of having to betray herself or someone else or some values she has honored. Under such conditions, we might give up, our will broken, and act as if what we do next doesn't matter anyway. And sometimes it doesn't. At a less stringent level, de-moralization occurs when we find ourselves coerced into "minor" betrayals, for example, when we accept the dominant/subordinate framework in which we don't exist as lesbians — staying in the closet, denying our lovers, being sociable to heterosexuals who make antigay jokes, and so on.

Beyond the betrayal of what we hold valuable ourselves, when oppressors coerce our choices, they de-moralize us. 'Moral agency' involves 'autokoenony', a sense of self in community. Those who undermine our autokoenony undermine our sense of self and hence our ability to make judgments and choices.

If in going on and making choices under oppression we begin to internalize the values of dominance and subordination, we are, on that account too, being de-moralized. Such a framework encourages us, not to evaluate a situation and choose for ourselves, but rather to accept the dictates, whether benevolent or malevolent, of those higher in the hierarchy. While, despite all this, we are still moral agents making choices, nevertheless, our *ability* as moral agents is being undermined. Hence we are being de-moralized.

My concern is with how we focus on ourselves and each other, how we come to understand the parameters of our lives through analyses such as Marilyn Frye's, how we begin to question underlying values which are presented as reality, how we learn to make choices without claiming responsibility for and so trying to control the entire situation–in other words, how we assess our choices understanding our options are coerced under oppression. This is no simple task. If we are going to develop a concept of 'moral agency' under oppression, while analyzing the coerciveness of oppression, we need to focus, not on excuses, but rather on how to avoid de-moralization and how to claim our moral agency under oppression as best we can.

Separation   In *Dreaming the Dark,* Starhawk describes a situation in which women's options were recognizably manipulated while the women were nevertheless tempted to blame themselves. A group of women were crowded together in prison as a result of blockading the diablo nuclear power plant in california.ᵉ They were given a number of unacceptable options regarding incoming women and were given fifteen minutes to choose among those options. They came up with their own options–which, of course, the guards rejected–and they then proceeded to feel they had failed. As a result they were de-moralized. Starhawk goes on to write:

> Yet in reality we did not fail, we were manipulated. Even though we could see at the time that we were being set up to be divided, we didn't see how to stop the process. Looking back, however, we could have recognized, when our solutions were turned down, that we were not actually being given the chance to make a decision that would suit us. We could, at that point, have refused to cooperate any longer with the illusion that was being perpetrated. Our withdrawal would have made the reality of the situation clearer–that the guards, not us, were responsible for the conditions we were forced to endure.³¹

It is important to work to avoid being de-moralized. And in some circumstances, when domination is institutionalized one aspect of avoiding de-moralization can be accomplished through separation. By separating ourselves, at least from the illusion that we are equal participants in these events, we can avoid claiming responsibility for something over which we have no control. Thus, we can go on to make choices as best we can with others who share the same values. Viewed this way, separation is not a matter of hiding from reality by pretending it doesn't exist. It is a way of acknowledging reality. Nor is it a way of avoiding struggle. It is a way of struggling.

When we become de-moralized, we cease to be moral agents independent of the dominant/subordinate framework of heterosexualism. When we become de-moralized, we have lost the focus of our anger and our de-

---

e   This nuclear plant, a masterful and daring chapter in man's struggle to control nature, is built right on the san andreas earthquake fault line.

sire; we have de-politicized our emotions such that we blame ourselves or each other, not just for our choices, but for the circumstances themselves. Or we cease to notice that there is anything wrong. When we become de-moralized, we lose belief that our actions make a difference – some differ-ence – hence we lose our selves. This is no way to move under oppression.

By ceasing to participate in the dominant belief system – particularly in the lie that we have any acceptable choice in certain situations – we may be able to resist de-moralization and go on to realize, to create, the values which will undermine oppression. I am not saying that we can suc-cessfully separate ourselves and resist de-moralization in all oppressive circumstances. But separation is an aspect which may help us under cer-tain circumstances. We can imagine that Lucy Andrews may well have succeeded in separating at a certain level, thus avoiding complete de-moralization and continuing to live her life and provide for her children as best she could. From the portrayal of Sophie in the movie *Sophie's Choice,* Sophie's return to "normal" life after the war and her subsequent breakdown and apparent suicide suggest she did not.

Notice that these considerations about Sophie and Lucy Andrews are not judgments of praise and blame; they are more basic. They are judg- *Praise and blame* ments about the energy and transformation, within particular circum-stances, of the moral agents involved, judgments about their ability to go on and make choices in pursuit of their goals. They are matters of the morale of survival. Now, given that discussions of free will and excuses are inadequate for developing a concept of 'moral agency' under oppres-sion, I want to examine some problems with the related ideas of praise and blame; for while we have moved away from a focus on excuses in the community, we nevertheless are caught up with questions of praise and blame as central to moral agency.

Once we begin considering questions of praise and blame among the oppressed, we find the extremes of blaming the victim or victimism. As it stands now, someone who is harmed under oppression is held responsible for everything that happens to her – not only for her choices, but for the situation itself (women invite rape, slaves never resisted slavery, jews were willing victims, and so on). Alternatively, she is perceived as a total victim, as if she were not making choices and trying to survive and go on. (And, either way, praise for choices of survival and resistance never ac-crues to those acting under oppression unless we romanticize particular individuals or groups; and then we still distort their lives.) Moral ac-countability as we understand it – centrally focused on 'praise' and 'blame' – does not present us with a viable concept of choice under op-pression. Thus, it contributes to our de-moralization.

Now, I don't want to suggest that a more adequate concept of moral agency involves a more sophisticated treatment of praise and blame. I want to suggest, rather, that—just as we have moved away from excuses in our ethical thinking—we also move away from praise and blame in order to get at a deeper, more complex sense of moral judgment.

The problem of moral agency under oppression—of resisting being demoralized by those constructing the social organization—becomes confusing when our choices under oppression result in harm to others, when we realize ways we collaborate in our own or others' oppression. It is here we find appeals to excuses, together with the desire to assign praise and blame. The appeal of excuses stems in part from the idea that our intentions are relevant in moral matters. That is to say, when someone does us an injury, it generally matters to us whether or not she intended to harm us. If someone's choices result in harm to me, but I find out she had no idea what she was doing, that matters. Certainly, if she intends me harm, that matters. Further, if feminists who make mistakes are not significantly different from successful nazis, birchers, or klansmen, then what is the use of even trying to talk of ethics or effect political change?

Nevertheless, it is not another person's intentions which hurt me. A bigot, after all, may be inept or otherwise lacking the power to act in ways which harm me (either physically, emotionally, psychically, or mentally). If I am harmed, it is another person's (or group's) actions which harm me; and that is so whether they act intentionally, from ignorance, or are coerced in certain ways. Further, if I make certain choices which result in harm, the consequences are there regardless of whether I intended them. I believe concern with intention and hence excuses has dwindled with our growing political awareness. But I think our urge to focus on praise or blame when we detect an injury has not. And I want to challenge our attraction to praise and blame.

To claim the ability to praise and blame—especially if that involves the idea that we are in a position to excuse—is to identify with the perspective of one who has the power to excuse or not excuse, a judge.[32] Then, since we are not focusing on excuses, the one blamed is held forever unexcused, forever guilty.[f] This happens, for example, when someone is called a racist or a batterer. And when we can't accept such a harsh judgment of another, we deny that she did what she did. For example, one lesbian, because of her feelings about lesbians who batter, denied that a friend of hers had ever battered her lover because she wanted to continue to regard her friend as a friend.

---

f   Thus I distinguish between making judgments or assessing situations for ourselves as we determine a course of action, on the one hand, and being a judge, on the other.

We tend to rivet on praise and blame. When we praise someone, we tend to worship her, to have unreasonable expectations of her – and when it turns out she is ordinary and picks her nose like the rest of us, we turn from her in bitter disappointment. (This is connected to what Joanna Russ calls the "magic momma" syndrome.[33]) When we blame someone, we tend to hold her up before the community as the epitome of evil and try to find other nasty things about her to confirm our opinion.[34] We obsess over whether so-and-so actually did such-and-such, and try to get others to admit that she is a bad person or a good person. Alternatively, we obsess over making sure that, no matter what else, we cannot be blamed for any bad behavior. This doesn't move us anywhere.

I am not suggesting we cease getting angry at each other. That exchange must continue as we unlearn the patriarchal scripts among ourselves. What I am talking about goes beyond anger – when the pack senses blood and closes in.

In the first place, pointing a blaming finger is not likely to induce another to change long-time patterns. She will more likely go on the defensive – and by that, I mean sense that she is being forced to respond to someone else's agenda while also sensing that what she has to say may not fit it. And pointing the finger leaves no room for complexity. We may be clear on how she is wrong, but what about the elements in her judgment that are right? Radical surgery, cutting out "bad" parts, does not yield transformation. Pointing the blaming finger and focusing on the idea of a static character portrays us inadequately. It separates us inaccurately; she whom we blame becomes different from us. While we may need to withdraw from her to break certain patterns, she is not essentially of a different type (a devil to our angel).

Blame and change

Secondly, while getting angry at each other in the community stimulates change, the obsession with confession and absolution before the community doesn't move us anywhere.[g] If we move under such conditions, I want to suggest it is in spite of such a focus and not because of it. Further, this focus has us riveted on how others judge us rather than understanding the dynamics of a situation. Then, because excuses and intention are considered less and less in the community while we focus heavily on praise and blame, we are setting ourselves up to avoid taking moral or political risks such as getting to know someone different from

g Often the ones we choose to point our finger at are not the worst "sinners," nor even necessarily the most perceptible, but rather the ones who irritate us the most or whose "sins" we most identify with and so feel threatened by or whose "sins" we find most prevalent in ourselves.

us. In discussing racism and classism among white anglo women, María Lugones notes that women who have experienced arrogant perception can nevertheless be arrogant perceivers. However, rather than have us remain focused on who is to blame for what, and so on confession and absolution, she moves in another direction:

> Women who are perceived arrogantly can perceive other women arrogantly in their turn. To what extent those women are responsible for their arrogant perceptions of other women is certainly open to question, but I do not have any doubt that many women have been taught to abuse women in this particular way. I am not interested in assigning responsibility. I am interested in understanding the phenomenon so as to understand a loving way out of it.[35]

Blame and complexity

Further, a primary focus on praise and blame keeps our attention exclusively on ourselves, or alternatively, on the "bad" person, and not on the interactive nature of the situation. Hence it promotes atomistic individualism. We tend to either accept or deny total responsibility in a situation, ignoring the fact that everyone involved has a part, that everyone involved is to some degree a moral agent, even though some are also victimized.

Focusing on praise and blame also keeps us justifying our behavior, and hence focused away from the full complexity of a situation. If I can determine I am not to blame for something, then I can forget about it and my part in it. For example, suppose you and I agree to meet and I don't show up because I had an accident. You still went out of your way, you still worried, there was still harm to you, whether or not I am to blame for it. Under our existing concept of 'moral accountability', if I fail to keep our date because I had a car accident, you really can't say you were hurt because I was hurt so much worse. But you *were* hurt.[36]

Or, along another line, a lesbian tells a heterosexual woman she no longer can be friends with her because the woman keeps trying to get closer to the lesbian and start something even though she just got pregnant and so is situating herself in a way that will make it much harder to leave her husband. The lesbian judges this to be a dangerous situation and goes out with the woman one more time to try to explain her concerns so the woman will understand why the lesbian is ending the friendship. Upon hearing this, the woman gets upset and has a car accident. The accident is minor, but the lesbian takes her to the hospital. The woman subsequently miscarries. The lesbian is extremely upset. In addition, she is worried, for the woman is likely to tell her husband, upon being questioned, why she was so upset that she had the accident. A counselor tells the lesbian that she is absolutely not to blame. But the lesbian is not satisfied: regardless of blame, a tragedy occurred, and a mess. Focusing on where blame lies is an inadequate consideration. In both these cases, focusing on who is to blame denies important aspects of the situations.

In addition, focusing on praise and blame can leave us thinking that if harm results in a situation and we can't blame someone else, then we must blame ourselves. For example, one lesbian makes a promise to another and then backs out. We tend to focus on blame because we want an ethics that will guarantee that anyone who promises something will stick to what she said. But sometimes we just don't. (And other times there are very good reasons why another backs out of a promise—for example, if she feels manipulated.) Now, since harm resulted from the situation, unless I can blame her, it seems I must blame myself, at the very least for trusting her. And obviously I did, on that occasion, make a mistake in trusting her or in otherwise assessing the situation. But this is not to say the harm that results is my fault because I trusted her. It just didn't work.[37]

More generally, we tend to believe that if we make "good" choices, we are morally praiseworthy such that if any "bad" comes from our choices, either our choices weren't "good," after all, or the "bad" consequences have nothing to do with us. For example, a lesbian might choose to take time to write music. Aside from economic consequences, that choice may mean spending long periods alone to unfocus and let critical mass develop, time perceived as leisure time by others. It may involve having little time to spend with lovers and friends, not proceeding according to schedule, and, even, not having a product to show in the end. Alternatively, we might instead choose to participate in, say, the women's pentagon action and find ourselves jailed for a period of time. We may regard these as good choices. But what happens if lovers are hurt as a consequence, if our companion-animals don't understand the lack of usual attention, if we spend less time with a collective or book group or co-op?

When double- or triple- or even quadruple-edged consequences ensue from our choices, we may begin to wonder if perhaps what we chose was not the right thing. Or, if our friends complain, we might get angry at them for not supporting us, for not understanding that we made a choice and why.

By making such choices, we are embarking on a path from which will emerge a variety of consequences, some perhaps exhilarating, others quite painful. Of course, we may want to reevaluate a given choice if things keep going in directions that undermine our purposes and what we value. But what I want to challenge is the notion that only "good" will come from good choices—that is, that only what we plan on and agree to will come from our choices. And rather than focus on praise and blame in these cases, I think we might work to understand that complexity emerges from our choices. After all, we do not engage in a vacuum.

Another aspect of what I'm suggesting here is that we come as package deals. We come as a collection of needs and wants and fears and abilities and dreams. We don't all fit together nicely, nor do we work in harmony all the time. While we also work to make changes and to transform ourselves over time, we aren't in any way simply "good" or "bad." For example, one lesbian can be quite inconsiderate of others' needs and interests, yet she paints portraits of lesbians. In her sessions she is extremely attentive and helps a lesbian shine for this portrayal of her spirit. Another lesbian is overbearing and egocentric, yet she also attends other lesbians in a way that encourages them to believe in themselves. Or another lesbian interacts in a way that lets lesbians heal; yet the next moment she has disappeared.

A focus on praise and blame becomes a matter of determining that particular individuals are bad or good. I don't find that this focus has been especially useful in the community, or at all accurate. We still seriously attack each other. As Florynce Kennedy wrote fifteen years ago, there is phenomenal horizontal hostility among us.[38] Too often we want to name a sinner with whom we can contrast ourselves and hence feel that, because she's wrong, we must be right. We focus on praise and blame and retreat wounded and so justified in our anger; or we try to make another say "uncle," admit she was mean and nasty, and, when she is unwilling to, affirm our judgment of her.

My concern is not with nailing so-and-so for a given act and holding her up before the community for condemnation. That is not what I have in mind in developing a concept of Lesbian Ethics. My concern is to develop a way of thinking that helps us understand the parameters of our lives, that encourages us to heal ourselves, that helps us move toward new value, and that keeps our rebellious spirit alive. My concern is with an ethics which functions, not as social control, but to help us develop our integrity, moral agency, and autokoenony and so keep alive the spirit of lesbianism.

The situations we face in our interactions are almost always far more complex than our ethical reactions now allow. (That is why I think ethical considerations are so often irrelevant to so many of us.) For example, consider one episode of "As the Queer Turns."[39] A lesbian visits a longtime friend/lover. Having been in town before, the visiting lesbian knows others as well and wants to see them. One of them invites her to a party while not inviting her friend/lover because she (the one having the party) and the friend/lover of the visiting lesbian were themselves lovers only recently and have broken up, rather badly at that. The visiting lesbian chooses to go to the party from which her friend/lover has been excluded, and the friend/lover feels hurt and left out. The friend/lover feels her ex-lover (the one having the party) has engineered the situation (and several others) to hurt her. The ex-lover, on the other hand, does not want to run into her ex-lover (the friend/lover of the visiting lesbian) and has in the past made that clear. The friend/lover does not understand why others in the community are not calling her ex-lover on these attempts to exclude her. That the visiting friend is also participating in this is too much, so the friend/lover gets angry and begins to regard the visiting lesbian as abandoning her. The visitor, on the other hand, feels this is not her home, that these are not her customs, and that this is not her battle. She had a certain connection with the ex-lover, and if it is going to expire, it will do so of its own merit (or lack thereof). She feels trapped by a situation she didn't ask for; and, had she realized what was going on, she wouldn't have come to visit. Is any one of these lesbians "blameless" or is any one "bad"? Judging the details of our lives in this way is simplistic.

I am suggesting here that developing our moral agency involves finding ways to avoid de-moralization and go on, as well as not reducing our judgments to the level of praise and blame. Our lives and our interactions are far more complex than that. Our judgments should be too.

I do not mean to suggest that we make no judgments. After all, to perceive, to notice, is to make judgments. I mean to suggest that our ways of making moral judgments are often superficial. I want to suggest that our judgments move to a deeper level. I am interested in dissolving the furor of moral righteousness as well as the moral apathy that infests our communities. Neither impulse moves us anywhere.

We demand of each other that we be accountable, and yet that demand smacks of expecting someone to stand before a judge and jury to be found guilty or innocent. This, again, invokes the perspective of one who has the power to excuse, a judge. It suggests a lesbian must justify her behavior and gain our approval. It requires the illusion of impartial observers. And it encourages us to separate her behavior from ours and so not examine our part. Accountability invites all the pitfalls of focusing on praise and blame which I've been discussing. *Intelligibility*

Marilyn Frye suggests we may not want the idea of justification – of justifying ourselves to someone else or expecting her to justify herself to us – at the center of our notion of moral agency. Rather than appeal to 'accountability' in understanding moral agency and making judgments, she suggests we develop a concept of 'intelligibility'.[40]

One aspect of intelligibility is explanation – being able to offer explanations for our choices. For intelligibility involves self-understanding and thus an ability to examine what is going on in our lives. It is part of our *Justification versus explanation* process of understanding our own changes and transformations. As Deidre McCalla sings:

Hey Mama, I'm back in town.
So many changes 'been comin' down.
I hope some day I can say to you
Why it is that I must live the way I do.[41]

However, I want to distinguish between explanation and justification. To justify something is to try to prove it just or right or valid — hence that it, or the lesbian involved, is free from blame. To justify is to try to absolve.[42] On the other hand, to explain something is to try to clarify it.

I may have done something in haste which involved making unwarranted assumptions about you. I ask you to do something in connection with a project I am working on and when you don't, I simply write and make nasty remarks. Later, perhaps years later, I write to apologize and explain what was going on in my life that led to my decision to write as I did: I had been working on the project for two years with many blocks; I had had refusals from other lesbians for the same thing, some of which stemmed from liberal guilt; and I was fed up with the shallowness of so many lesbians' judgments. Or, another example: I may go to your house, accusing, and insist on talking to you because of something I've heard about you. Years later I may apologize, explaining that owing to a number of factors in my own life, such as being harassed, I was nervous and suspicious.

To express such things to you, assuming you are willing to attend, need not be an attempt at justification, at absolving myself of what I did. Rather it can be an explanation in an attempt to reconnect or even just to clear up things hanging from the past. An apology was due; an explanation goes with it.

Further, in distinguishing between explanations and justifications, I think we can understand how intention is important and significant in our considerations.[43] For in our intimate and close connections, intentions matter. Yes, something I do can result in a harm to you regardless of my intentions. But we need to consider intentions, because we hurt each other quite a bit, and that will continue to be a dynamic among us — not because we are inherently mean and nasty — but in part because of the different wounds and scars we carry as well as our different personalities. Further, we will continue to hurt each other because, despite our most careful plans and best intentions, the effects of our choices and interactions are so intricate. Hence assessing intentions and energy is important in determining our connections, particularly when we hurt each other, because we need information about what was going on with the other during the interaction. Judging intention and energy aids us to better understand the dynamics between us.

For example, there may be serious miscommunication between you and me. If we are able to discuss the situation later, I may explain to you why I made the choices I made. Again, this need not be a matter of justifying my actions as if the idea were for you to judge me not bad. The point is that I did make a choice, and I am explaining my intentions to you, as well as perhaps clarifying for myself the factors that went into the choice. Because you are a friend and I am responding to you, I give you this information. If my choice led to confusion or pain, in the future we may determine to be more careful within a certain type of situation. Or it may be that you were surprised by my choice and such choices are not ones you want to deal with in your intimate circle. As a result you decide to distance. And I, in response, may be surprised and displeased that you got so upset at the confusion, and so may distance myself. The point is, with this information we can both better decide how we want to engage in the future and what some of the consequences of accommodating each other's needs and expectations might be.

A focus on explanation rather than justification is also important because so many problems between us are simply a matter of not fitting. In one relationship there is general harmony and support, particularly through difference; in another there is constant conflict that is destructive. I may find that one lesbian simply ignores or fails to notice my attempts at manipulation so that I begin to work out of the habit, while another gets caught up with them and so unwittingly reinforces my behavior. I may find I am threatened by, and so react to, the patterns of one lesbian who had been abused, while the patterns of survival of another lesbian don't catch me up. In one relationship I can begin to grow out of certain patterns while in another I find myself falling back into old habits I thought I'd worked out of. Thus, that two lesbians together keep thwarting each other doesn't make one or both "bad." Instead it may just be that their patterns, habits, wounds, and skills grate. Focusing on the energy of explanation rather than that of justification between us will more likely help us understand this.

Intelligibility, thus, means being able to offer explanations for our choices and being able to assess the energy between us, including our abilities, defenses, intentions, goals, and needs. These are all central factors in our engaging. The idea is not that we make no mistakes or that we never hurt another; the idea is that we understand the full dynamics of our interactions.

A second aspect of intelligibility is understanding other lesbians' choices, particularly choices we don't approve of. And this involves at-

Intelligibility and understanding choices

tending and understanding another lesbian's transformation of energy in her choices, our part in her choices, and how such choices are or could be our own.

Consider, for example, a lesbian who chooses to deny her lesbianism and go straight. There are significant political dynamics in such a choice. Nancy Todor's *Choices* clarifies some of the factors, particularly the fear, involved in such a choice for some lesbians.[44] Or a lesbian deeply engaged in building lesbian community, trying to materialize a dream, may finally burn out, no longer able to deal with lesbian energy.

Now, we might regard either one as a total victim and simply pity her, or we might judge her a coward or even a fool. However, what can get lost in these judgments is understanding the transformation of lesbian energy that led to such a choice, and her subsequent transformation of energy and integrity as a result of it. For over time, as a result of the political context and her choices in it, a lesbian changes; she becomes a different being. It may be that she is someone we want to avoid, and we may regard her as cowardly or foolish. But my point is that understanding her process and transformation is important to understanding our lives as lesbians.[h] When we focus on praise and blame and accountability, we cease to notice the energy of the whole being.[47]

We tend to focus less on the transformation of energy in part because of a development in the use of the "king's english." Over the last several centuries the english language has undergone an increase in nouns (categories, characteristics) with an accompanying decrease in verbs (actions, processes); and users of english focus more on categories and classifications which define a thing and fix its nature for all time, and are less concerned with processes, movement, and change.[48]

Within ethics we lean more toward labeling someone a liar, for example, and less toward understanding the process and interaction of lying. When we talk about 'liars', we focus more on one who has the character of a liar, who is essentially or through and through a liar. As a result, when we've been lied to, we are less tempted to ask whether we realized we were being lied to, and if not, what that means. We are less likely to ask what our part was in the lying.[49] Our concern more often is to define and fix what she is. Yet understanding another's choices includes understanding our part in them.

h As Denslow Brown has pointed out, gaining information about each other's choices and their effects, especially how they change us, is one of the functions of gossip in the lesbian community, and it is why gossip is so important among us.[45] (Lesbians in england published a journal called *Gossip*.[46])

In addition, if we are going to understand the choices we have to make, if we are going to claim greater moral agency – the ability to make choices and to perceive ourselves as making choices – I think we will benefit from understanding the choices other lesbians have made, understanding the context in which those choices made some kind of sense, and understanding how we, as lesbians, could make or have made any one of those choices and many others. After all, our choices reflect as well as contribute to the context in which they take on meaning.

What happens to our energy, for example, if we stay in the closet? What happens to it if we are out and a target? In what ways do we change, transform? What happens to a lesbian who has a male child? What of a lesbian who rests with her internalized racism or, alternatively, her racism? What happens to a lesbian who goes through the court system seeking justice because of the actions of another lesbian? What happens to a lesbian who takes a path of alcoholism? How did she get there? What transformations does her energy go through? What keeps her there? This evaluation of energy and tranformation within the context in which we live, I believe, is what will most help us in making choices.

As it is now, we are not particularly adept at learning from each other's choices, and we're not particularly adept at enacting change. More often we simply retreat, when threatened, into the security (familiarity) of old patterns. Intelligibility, as part of lesbian moral agency, involves judging, that is perceiving, the dynamics of our choices.

Thus, a third aspect of intelligibility involves being able to perceive what other lesbians perceive. For example, Selma Miriam notes a number of instances in which nonjewish lesbians miss or ignore antisemitism.[50] Instances of missing or ignoring abound in all areas. And when criticized for missing or ignoring something, we may go home seething with our own anger and defensiveness, especially when the charges romanticize and do not include the full story, as happens; or appear to or actually prioritize injury, as happens; or disguise legitimate political differences, as happens. But we can also sort through all that. Intelligibility involves attending. Irena Klepfisz, for example, notes: "I find I am preoccupied not with countering anti-Semitism, but with trying to prove that anti-Semitism exists."[51] As Selma Miriam asks, "Won't any non-Jews take notice?"[52]

In other words, intelligibility involves what María Lugones terms "an act of love." She talks about her failure to love her mother: both in abusing her, by grafting her mother's substance to her own, and in distancing from her, necessarily, to avoid becoming like her mother and accepting such abuse herself. She suggests that between u.s. white anglo women and women of color there is a similar failure of love in the "failure to iden-

Intelligibility and attending

tify with another woman, the failure to see oneself in other women who are quite different from oneself."[53] She suggests this failure is a failure to feel a need to identify with and connect:

> I am particularly interested here in those cases in which White/Anglo women do one or more of the following to women of color: they ignore us, ostracize us, render us invisible, stereotype us, leave us completely alone, interpret us as crazy. All of this *while we are in their midst.* . . . Their world and their integrity do not require me at all. There is no sense of self-loss in them for my own lack of solidity. But they rob me of my solidity through indifference.[54]

Baba Copper points out that we can be extremely sensitive and attentive in certain respects while inattentive in others:

> I feel as if I am involved in some subtle competition not of my own making. Although feminist lesbians attempt to resist participation in power/over scenarios, we still listen carefully for the subtle indicators of respect from other women. Competitiveness seems connected to the attention we pay to power differences. Sources of power such as looks, skills, sexual confidence, resources, political correctness—all play their part in the complex process of figuring out whether one is "ahead" (and feeling confident and easy because of it) or "behind" (and feeling uncomfortable). Although old lesbians often receive deference, I seldom experience a feeling of real respect from others. Almost never do I sense that I am being approached by a younger woman in the spirit of acceptance, learning or wonder.[55]

María Lugones suggests that the failure to identify and connect results from a failure to go into another's world. Going into another's world is more than just attending another in our world; it is a matter of understanding another in her own world, where we are outsiders. Of her mother María Lugones writes:

> To love my mother was not possible for me while I retained a sense that it was fine for me and others to see her arrogantly, but loving my mother also required that I go into my mother's world, that I see both of us as we are constructed in her world, that I witness her own sense of herself from within her world. Only through this dangerous travelling to her "world" could I identify with her because only then could I cease to ignore her and to be excluded and separate from her. Only then could I see her as a subject even if one subjected and only then could I see at all how meaning could arise fully between us.[56]

In other words, as Marilyn Frye suggests, intelligibility means being willing to situate ourselves in such a way that others who make choices different from ours can be intelligible to us.[57]

The problem with accountability and praise and blame, finally, is that they keep us riveted on ourselves: justifying ourselves so others will understand that we at least meant well; or demanding that others justify themselves on our own terms. They do not encourage us to attend the other and understand how it goes with her. One lesbian, feeling guilty upon learning that her cat was dying, wished she could speak with her cat so the cat would understand how much she loved the cat and that she was doing all she could. Another lesbian, upon attending her goat who was dying, wished she could speak with her goat to understand how it was with the goat.[58]

Accountability encourages a one-way process. If I am accountable to you, then the idea is that you judge me on your own terms. If you are accountable to me, then I judge you on my terms. This is where the arrogance of those who have the power to excuse, the power of judges, comes in. The problem is not with the judging; we all make judgments all the time. The problem is with the arrogance of perception—that to make a judgment, I need consider you only within my framework. For if it is only my framework that counts, then in being accountable, you are simply adjusting to my framework. And insofar as that judging carries the moralistic fervor of finding another a good person or a bad person, it sets me up to regard my framework as reality (the only framework there is) and myself as an objective judge (one who has or needs no perspective of her own).

Intelligibility, on the other hand, is a two-way process; and it enables a foundation—an axis, held in place by what surrounds it—of cooperation.[59] Within the framework of accountability, if you are to be accountable to me for something and there is a failure, the failure is yours: for example, you did not explain yourself well enough and you must come after me trying to get my attention and make me understand. Within the framework of intelligibility, on the other hand, if you are trying to explain something to me, I try to situate myself in such a way that your choices become intelligible to me. Intelligibility involves both of us trying to reach each other, to connect, at some level. Thus it involves, minimally, a presumption of cooperation, not a presumption of antagonism. Much of our work in dismantling classism, racism, and antisemitism, for example, among ourselves has taken the form of accountability rather than intelligibility.

Only when we engage in a way that allows us to really understand one another can we truly connect at various levels and maintain connection across patriarchal boundaries and meanings as well as across our own limits, pain, and anger. For in connecting this way, though we may not like everyone, we take each other seriously, we acknowledge each other as moral agents. Moral agency includes a form of cooperation involved in intelligibility. And the judgments of intelligibility involve both self-awareness and attending.

This is not to say that we'll all fit mutually compatible patterns.[60] I do *Intelligibility is not* not mean to preclude situations in which we reach an understanding of *uniformity* another's circumstances, sense that her energy conflicts with ours, and decide to stay distant and not engage.[61] Nor do I mean to preclude situations in which I notice someone stuck, for example, in racism or abusiveness or alcoholism, and decide that until she changes, I am not willing to connect at any deep level.

Further, this is not to say that putting myself in a position which allows me to fully understand another means I must therefore agree with all her choices. Intelligibility does not preclude judging (again, to perceive is to judge), and it does not mean I agree with another's choices. If I understand your choices, not only on my terms, but also on your terms, even if I can understand how I can or have made those same choices, I am still a distinct lesbian. I may make different choices while respecting yours. Or I may understand your choices but still not agree that they are the best ones for you. I may also understand your choices and find I do not respect them, especially as I get to know you over time and observe the transformations of energy you are undergoing.

I am simply suggesting that as we make judgments regarding each other, we focus, not on an antagonistic process of another justifying herself on my terms or of me justifying myself on her terms – the process of judges – but rather on a process that involves both an ability to explain and an ability to understand. That is not yet to say at what level we'll then decide to engage or continue to engage.

Moral agency, thus, involves avoiding de-moralization; it also involves *Withdrawal* the self-examination and the reaching out of intelligibility. Thirdly, I want to suggest, it involves the option of withdrawal among ourselves. For all the attempts in the world to communicate and be intelligible may not work to smooth out disagreement. Sometimes the problems go too deep, and with each subsequent attempt to interact, still more harm results. Or sometimes we are simply obnoxious, and no amount of discussion is going to unravel it all. Thus, I want to discuss the idea of withdrawal among ourselves, as part of claiming moral agency, when we can no longer accept another's choices, particularly as a means of dismantling the ideology of control between us.

For example, if a lesbian feels trapped in an interaction because the other is manipulating her, then she can try to resist the manipulation, possibly becoming cold, even abusive, in not responding to the other's agenda. Alternatively, she can try to outwit, to manipulate, the other – for example, by making the other in turn feel guilty, in order to gain control herself. If we find ourselves participating in such a trap, there can be yet another option for us as moral agents. And that option is withdrawal.

I believe the option of withdrawal is crucial to lesbian moral agency. If we have an ethics which does not include the possibility of leaving an untenable situation, then we are locked into each other's agendas. And this can lead to a battle of wills in an attempt to control both the arena and all those involved. We may want to remain within a given situation; but if we feel forced to remain, we will act to control it – through manipulation, for example, or even emotional or physical abuse.

Through withdrawal we have a greater chance of staying centered when in coercive situations in community. This is often not acknowledged in the community. Some will suggest that to distance from a lesbian in pain, for example, is abandonment. And in some situations it may well be. However, if a lesbian's pain is so intense and she is so out of touch with it that she simply hurts everyone she cares about, there may be nothing to do but walk away. And this is taking her seriously. If she is so afraid of losing what is dear to her that she turns on it to destroy it first, then withdrawal is crucial. To remain under such circumstances is only to feed the pain and fear and hence to perpetuate the situation. Further, she may only begin to heal once the immediate target of her frustration is no longer available.

Actually, this description is too one-sided. I posed it in the extreme to make a point. In most situations which involve manipulation and control, each has a part. As I've suggested, some lesbians' survival defenses and reactions touch deep wounds in us while those of others don't bother us in the least. Thus some relationships just don't work, not because one or the other is bad, but because together we keep thwarting each other's needs while rubbing raw each other's wounds. These relationships can bring out the worst behavior in both of us. In other situations, we just are obnoxious to others. I'm suggesting that withdrawal is an important ethical option in such situations, particularly when the interactions dissolve into the dominance and subordination framework of manipulation and control.

In this respect, withdrawal need not be permanent, though perhaps it will be. Its function is to avoid certain patterns in relationships and to stop further harm when it is primarily harm that results from our interactions. If at some point it becomes clear the manipulation will not continue, that the damaging patterns have been dissolved, then we might reconnect. After all, we did respond to each other once; we did connect. There was something there . . .

When more than one lesbian is involved, the situation becomes more complex. For example, within a collective, one lesbian may be dominating the decision-making. Another lesbian, finally tired of this and not perceiving any possibility of change, decides to withdraw from the collective. A third lesbian, who is close to the one who plans to withdraw, gets upset: as long as the one who plans to withdraw is there, her friend has a chance of affecting the outcome of some projects. But without the withdrawing lesbian, the remaining lesbian would become isolated and ineffective. Thus she considers the withdrawing lesbian's actions as abandoning her. In such situations there are no easy answers, and the choices we have may be difficult. However, in terms of the question of withdrawal, I will mention one thing: sometimes in trying to hold others together we are trying to maintain, not what exists, but rather what we wish would exist – often what once existed and no longer exists. It is important that the lesbians who are friends seriously discuss what they think the real possibilities are and make their decisions accordingly.

I am not offering a formula or rule here to guarantee our interactions. Withdrawing can be used in an attempt to control another. It can also be a way of hurting another when we are hurt and want to hurt back. Further, withdrawal is no guarantee that "good" will result. Rather, it simply takes us in a different direction. While I am suggesting that withdrawal be acknowledged in the community as an ethical option, this is not to state when to choose it. That is up to lesbians in particular situations.

Choice and moral agency   A concept of lesbian moral agency focuses on judgments in the realm of intelligibility, not accountability, for as I have been trying to suggest, such a focus holds in place as its foundation cooperation rather than antagonism. As a result, the question of whether we could have done otherwise is not pivotal. Nevertheless, there remains the question of constraints on our choices, for we, still, live in a context of oppression. And this brings us back to the question of moral agency in terms of the concept of 'freedom'. So I want to discuss acting within limits as an aspect of moral agency.

We tend to believe that a proper moral choice is one in which there are no constraints on us, no boundaries or limits. We tend to believe that to be moral agents we must be in charge, taking control over the forces that appear to control us. Yet, to state the obvious, it is not likely that in our lifetime we will understand what it is like to act without the constraints of oppression.

Further, whether or not we live under the coercion of oppression, we nevertheless live within boundaries and limits. And our moral choices are made within them. That is, we live in specific situations, and those situations present limits. Further, within those situations we choose from among alternatives, and that in itself would appear to involve limits. Yet this is what moral choice is all about: choice among alternatives within specific situations.

In one of my classes, I asked students to consider the concept of 'freedom'. By the end of the first day's discussion, they had decided that being in jail was not significantly different from making a promise. They argued that both situations function as restraints on our subsequent actions. Yet by this line of reasoning the very act of choosing among alternatives contributes to our loss of freedom. That is, the fact that I choose one path, rather than another, itself yields a loss of freedom. But following this line of reasoning, someone could argue that to have freedom, we must be in situations which present no alternatives from which to choose; 'freedom' would mean "action under no conditions of choice," and that is ridiculous.

Perhaps my central point about 'moral agency' is this: choice is at the very core of the concept of 'moral agency'. *It is not because we are free and moral agents that we are able to make moral choices. Rather, it is because we make choices, choose from among alternatives, act in the face of limits, that we declare ourselves to be moral beings.* [62] That is what it *means* to be a moral being. Just as choice is a matter of creation, not sacrifice, so making choices within limited situations is a matter of affirming moral agency, not undermining it.

My suggestion here goes against the grain of dominant anglo-european thought. Generally, moral good within this tradition is connected to a fear of death and reflects a desire to transcend the limits of the "human condition" to achieve "perfection." The idea is that we must transcend our animal nature, our limits, and our separateness (uniqueness) in order to gain "freedom" and achieve what is "real" (i.e., permanent, fixed and unchanging, inflexible). The priestly desire to rise above the limits of this living is connected to the characterization of choices as "good" or "bad" and the attempt to deny connection to the "bad" by finding a scapegoat. Living, of course, is far more complex than any such dualism can accommodate, and it is precisely from such living that phallic morality purports to save us.

My thesis is that moral agency simply is the ability to choose in limited situations, to pursue one possibility rather than another, to thereby create value through what we choose, and to conceive of ourselves as ones who are able to and do make choices — and thus as ones who are able to make a difference for ourselves and each other in this living. Moral agents are autokoenonous beings.

Thus, I think one step in developing our moral agency is to embrace the idea of working within limits and acknowledging boundaries. The state of having limits is not a drawback, something to be overcome — though certainly there are some limits and boundaries we want to change.

Acknowledging boundaries

But, in general, boundaries and limits need not work against us; indeed it is boundaries and limits—contexts, in other words—which help us give form to and create depth of meaning.

To approach it from another direction: To say we are each limited in certain ways is, among other things, to say we are unique. We each have our unique consciousness, our unique concatenation of conditioning, scars, concerns, agendas, things which draw us, things we avoid, things which bore or excite us, ways of responding in situations, and so on—all of which have been developed in a social context. And we each face specific situations. That combination of interests, focus, and circumstances comprises the means by which we draw together the energy, the forces of the universe, and fashion it in our own patterns within a community. It is the means by which we transform energy and create our meaning. Further, it is through understanding the boundaries and the limits of our paths, that we can, by means of our choices and interactions, seek to transform our selves in certain respects and hence to change certain boundaries and limits.

Thus, boundaries and limits are a matter both of frameworks within which we make choices and of the development of our selves. In what follows, I focus on our boundaries as individuals, both because we are not yet good at addressing them and because I believe that, once we become competent at acknowledging our own boundaries and those of others, we will function better within other, more far-reaching limits, to resist demoralization and resignation under oppression.

Identity in community   Acknowledging our boundaries as individuals and understanding our limits is especially difficult at this point in lesbian community. In *The Mirror Dance* Susan Krieger discusses dilemmas lesbians face involving identity. Living within a community of midwest lesbians for a year, she found that the dilemma of lesbian identity arises because of the double-edged nature of the lesbian community as it now exists:

> The community I had studied, it seemed to me, presented a basic identity conflict to members and potential members. On the one hand, it promised them that, within it, they would be affirmed for who they truly and fully were. Here they might find haven from the outside world, acceptance not available elsewhere, and confirmation of crucial feelings they had about themselves, feelings related to their lesbianism, their feminism, and their identification as women. On the other hand, in this community, they would often feel that their differences from others were not valued, their own unique identities given little recognition or room. The community, in other words, would often seem to threaten their sense of selfhood.[63]

Susan Krieger suggests this was true in part because the community was a community of likeness, one in which intimacy was encouraged, one which held an ideology of the oneness of women, one which was stigmatized, one which was new and relatively unformed, and one in which individuals tended to view the giving up of self to others as virtuous.[64] She goes on to note that the loss of sense of self characteristically took one of two forms: feeling overwhelmed or feeling abandoned.[65]

In her introduction, Susan Krieger notes that the community seemed to push members to define and protect their sense of personal identity, that members used experiences of loss of identity as an opportunity to clarify their sense of self.[66] This definition and clarification occurred, she suggests, through a push-pull process of joining and separating from the community in various ways:[67]

> By structuring her relationships both with the community as a whole and with its members, the individual could, it seemed, emerge from experiences of loss of a sense of self with resources for dealing with the distressing feeling of being overwhelmed or abandoned. She would have a better sense of boundaries between herself and others and, as a result, she would be more aware of herself as a complete and separate person.[68]

Yet Susan Krieger also notes that such experiences were often full of conflict and pain—and that only sometimes, and after the fact, would a lesbian realize this had been part of a process of self-clarification.[69]   *Acknowledging differences*

Our development of identity or self-consciousness—our sense of boundaries—is so difficult and painful at times within the community, I believe, because of a romantic idea we embrace that to be truly connected to another, we can't be in any way separate. Consider the following passage from Audre Lorde's biomythography *Zami:*

> When Muriel and I received stares and titters on the streets of the West Village, or in the Lower East Side market, it was a toss-up as to whether it was because we were a Black woman and a white woman together, or because we were gay. Whenever that happened, I half-agreed with Muriel. But I also knew that Felicia and I shared both a battle and a strength that was unavailable to our other friends. We acknowledged it in private, and it set us apart, in a world that was closed to our white friends. It was even closed to Muriel as much as I would have liked to include her. And because that world was closed to them, it was easy for even lovers to ignore it, dismiss it, pretend it didn't exist, believe the fallacy that there was no difference between us.
>
> But that difference was real and important, even if nobody else seemed to feel that way, sometimes not even Flee herself, tired as she was of explaining why she didn't go swimming without a bathing cap, or like to get caught in the rain.
>
> Between Muriel and me, then, there was one way in which I would always be separate, and it was going to be my own secret knowledge, if it was

going to be my own secret pain. I was Black and she was not, and that was a difference between us that had nothing to do with better or worse, or the outside world's craziness. Over time I came to realize that it colored our perceptions and made a difference in the ways I saw pieces of the world we shared, and I was going to have to deal with that difference outside our relationship.

This was the first separation, the piece outside love. But I turned away short of the meanings of it, afraid to examine the truths difference might lead me to, afraid they might carry Muriel and me away from each other. I sometimes pretended to agree with Muriel, that the difference did not in fact exist, that she and all gay-girls were just as oppressed as any Black person, certainly as any Black woman.[70]

Here we have two lovers in a relationship, separated because one had certain experiences and perceptions which the other could and did ignore. Actually, there were two key differences involved in this relationship: elsewhere Audre Lorde states that Muriel had once had a nervous breakdown and had undergone shock treatments.[71] And since this was something else she and Muriel never directly addressed, it posed, I assume, a difference Muriel had to deal with outside the relationship if she dealt with it at all. In addition, 'difference' here is equated with different degrees or amount of oppression – so that if we notice that we are different, then we are forced to start quantitative measuring of oppression. No wonder neither of them wanted to notice difference.[72]

Now, the separation here falls outside their love as a result of the risks the lovers chose not to take. (Again, safety is not a goal.) Their relationship was only able to accommodate ways they were alike, ways they fit together. And had they brought those other parts of their identities into the relationship, they would have been separate in certain ways: because one has to deal with something the other does not, there will always be a separateness. But that separateness or difference need not threaten or undermine the relationship or the love; instead it can be an integral part of them.

Nevertheless, when differences do emerge we are tempted to suppress them.[i] As a result we must separate from parts of ourselves to participate

---

i This same romantic model of connecting as merging with no boundaries, no separateness, resides in the cry that attending to our differences is divisive. One main reason women and lesbians came to feminism out of isolation in a man's world was because of the fertile ground there for female friendship. To some, feminism was primarily a matter of forming friendships with women in a society that pits women against each other in competition for male attention and isolates women within the confines of male boundaries (especially religious and national boundaries). Feminism was the chance, finally, to connect with many women and feel grounded, as if we belonged somewhere. And yet as separate

in the relationship. And when a difference can no longer be ignored, the relationship will break apart, thereby seeming to confirm the idea that boundaries undermine connecting, that any difference or separateness threatens the connection.

What the passage from *Zami* also illustrates is how the fear of differences can lead us to not attend each other. A fear of differences and separateness can lead us to those patterns of ignoring, those lapses of attending, those separations, which really do undermine relationships.

Further, when we believe connecting with another must be a merging we tend to ignore our own and each others' boundaries, believing that our agendas are identical with the agendas of those close to us. Often the closer we become, the less respect we seem to have for the other's unique self. In this way an intimate relationship can become a battle of wills. Connecting and interacting—engaging—is not, even ideally, a merging. And acknowledging differences does not in itself invite antagonism.

Perhaps one of the most influential philosophers promoting the idea that acknowledging differences and boundaries involves antagonism is Hegel. Antagonism is necessary, according to him, because it is part of how we come to self-conscious awareness. The section of Hegel's argument I am interested in runs like this: To be human and moral beings (thus distinct from inanimate objects and animals), we must develop self-conscious awareness of our own existence (our distinctness, our separateness). In order for this to happen, a person (self) must be recognized and acknowledged by another conscious being (self). To gain this recognition, the one person (self) must assert himself over the other person. The other, because he too is a person (self), will try to do the same. The assertion of self must be an assertion over others because recognition from the other must occur on one's own terms; the recognition and acknowledgment must reflect one's own value. The one cannot afford to have the other perceiving him in just any way. Thus in the process of coming to self-conscious awareness, the two engage in mortal combat.[74]

Self-conscious awareness

caucuses formed to address specific issues, or as conflicts arose because of differences of class, race, ethnicity, and nationality especially, all of that seemed suddenly taken away.[73] On the other hand, those whose differences were not accommodated, whose differences were being ignored, never really had felt connected to begin with.

Another aspect of the same phenomenon is that much of our original understanding in this wave of the feminist movement grew out of c-r groups which focused largely on how we were victims of male domination. This focus was essential, yet it did not allow for consideration of how we also participated in the system. When it could no longer be ignored, such consideration seemed to threaten our unity. But, of course, a connection based on victimization is a bond turned bind, and it does not provide ground for creating new value.

Now, while this combat is deadly, it cannot result in one actually annihilating the other since that would defeat the purpose of gaining recognition. Each person recognizes that the life of the other is crucial to his own
purpose such that rather than annihilating the other, the rational choice
is dominating the other. The one who is successful in this combat becomes the master and imposes himself and his values on the other in such
a way that the other, the slave, comes to perceive his essence through the
master's values:

> The one is independent, and its essential nature is to be for itself; the other
> is dependent, and its essence is life or existence for another. The former is
> Master, or Lord, and the latter is the [Slave].
>   The master is the consciousness that exists *for itself;* but no longer merely
> the general notion of existence for self. Rather it is a consciousness existing
> on its own accord which is mediated with itself through an other conscious-
> ness, i.e. through an other whose very nature implies that it is bound up
> with an independent being.[75]

Hegel's primary translator, J. B. Baillie, wrote of this aspect of Hegel's
work:

> The background of Hegel's thought is the remarkable human phenomenon
> of the subordination of one self to another which we have in all forms of ser-
> vitude — whether slavery, serfdom, or voluntary service. Servitude is not
> only a phase of human history, it is a principle condition of the develop-
> ment and maintenance of the consciousness of self as a fact of experience.[76]

Hegel goes on to argue that this master/slave arrangement is not fully
successful. By not recognizing an independent self in the slave, the
master deprives himself of the recognition of his own freedom: he is, in
fact, dependent on the slave. And the slave, although acting out of fear,
by carrying out the master's will and objectifying himself, nevertheless
achieves some self-realization through his labor. Hegel thus argues that
this effort at self-consciousness does not bring full freedom. To gain full
freedom, man ultimately embraces laws institutionalized through social
life, beginning with the family and culminating in religion. Through
these institutions, according to Hegel, man's spirit is embodied and can
reach its highest levels. Duty thereby becomes the concept central to an
ethical existence.[77] Nevertheless, Hegel feels that the master/slave relationship is a necessary phase in man's higher development.

Permeating anglo-european thought is the idea that individuals must
come into conflict as they discover their boundaries, that this conflict
takes the form of each trying to assert his will over the other, and that to
work together one must give in to the other such that even cooperative

efforts are perceived as one or more submitting to another who dominates.[j]

While we may have to reevaluate our limits by coming up against or even into conflict with others, the interaction need not involve each trying to assert her value over and against the other in order to gain or maintain a sense of self. Nor need it involve one giving up her own judgment to find her value as reflected in the other. Yet that is precisely the sort of romantic thinking which lies in the background of our conceptual schema, fueled by the popularization of Hegel's work. As Monique Wittig points out, when my sense of self emerges over and against you, our identities are primarily heterosexual.[78]

Our sense of self, of identity, does not need to come from asserting or attempting to assert ourselves over others. Gaining recognition need not be a matter of blotting out the other's values. The process of interacting with one another (encountering difference and so expanding our horizons, delighting in agreement and so conspiring) need not take the form of placing one self over and against another self. Further, it is not the case that when we find ourselves separate from one another in consciousness in certain ways, our relationship will therefore be antagonistic, as Hegel thought. Connecting is not a merging, it is not a matter of finding one self in another. As Marilyn Frye argues:

> What *is* the case, surely, is that unlike the slave or the master, the loving perceiver can see without the presupposition that the other poses a constant threat or that the other exists for the seer's service; nor does she see with the other's eye instead of her own. Her interest does not blend the seer and the seen, either empirically by terror or *a priori* by conceptual links forged by the arrogant eye. One who sees with a loving eye is separate from the other whom she sees. There are boundaries between them; she and the other are two; their interests are not identical; they are not blended in vital parasitic or symbiotic relations, nor does she believe they are or try to pretend they are.[79]

I agree that to claim moral agency we need self-conscious awareness as well as recognition and acknowledgment from others; but I disagree that *One among many* we need dominance and subordination to achieve them. Rather than perceive our selves as essentially related to all others antagonistically, we can perceive our selves in a form of cooperative relationship with each other. Rather than perceiving our selves as essentially isolated, as unlimited and

---

j Hegel's characterization of the emergence of self-conscious awareness permeates freudian psychoanalysis, marxian theories of labor, and existential humanism.

hence thwarted, even threatened, when we come across another, we can perceive our selves as *one self among many* and so enhanced by others.

Hegel was concerned that another's acknowledgment might not be on our own terms: while I may be earnestly engaged in some project, someone else may perceive me as a jerk. To maintain my self, on Hegel's theory, I must dominate the other and force her to perceive me through my own values. However, if I perceive my self as one among many, then I am not dependent on any one lesbian for acknowledgment (though I may depend on her). Thus, that a lesbian perceives me as a jerk may be something I want to address (or I may not), but it is not something I need to control in order to maintain my sense of self.

Among lesbians, often when we are afraid of others' perceptions of us it is because we are afraid of a phantom we've conjured. In my experience, our own phantoms are usually worse than the perceptions of us others have; and through interacting, we gain perspective on those phantoms and so can address them. Alternatively, by perceiving our selves as one among many, we can learn that another's perception of us is just that—a perception—and it tells us as much about her as it tells us about our selves. If we find a dominant stereotype in her perception, for example, it tells us how she has not questioned (some) dominant values. If we find our selves as representing dominant values, it tells us something about her experience. By perceiving our selves as one among many, we can realize no one perception defines us and each one gives us some information we can use in making choices. And we can realize that the answer to differences in these perceptions lies neither in trying to dominate others' perceptions nor in trying to subordinate our selves to their perceptions or prescriptions.

By perceiving our selves as one among many, autokoenonously, we can perceive our possibilities as enhanced by our engagement with others, engagements which create possibilities that did not exist before. We can gain greater awareness of our selves through attending and being attended by others; in a pluralistic setting, we gain a sense of self in relation to others. We also gain a sense of our uniqueness: no one will do or say or be to another quite what I will. Further, what I say or do or am is enhanced by and enhances what others say and do and are—both those who agree with me in certain ways and those who disagree with me in various respects. Their engagement contributes to my possibilities, as mine does to theirs. Thus, to return to the concern expressed in the passages from *Zami,* we do not need to try to deny difference to gain connection. Far from presupposing antagonism and undermining our connections, differences can enhance them.

Lesbians journeying have many projects – as healers, instigators, educators, archivists, and on, and on. Not all of these will fit together smoothly. For example, a lesbian educator may be acting as a catalyst to shake things up while a lesbian healer may be acting to soothe and bring resolution.[80] As activists and theoreticians and dreamers, we each create different elements to add to lesbian value. Yet no one cancels out another. If we find community among lesbians, it is not because we act as one, nor is it because we dominate another or fit someone else's program. It is because, as we make our choices, we contribute to the ground of lesbian being.

Thus, perceiving our selves as one among many, and so as autokoenonous, encourages a unique sense of self as well as an understanding and real appreciation of difference. As Audre Lorde later wrote, it is not our goal to tolerate difference but rather to embrace it:

Advocating the mere tolerance of difference between women is the grossest reformism. It is a total denial of the creative function of difference in our lives.[81]

Nevertheless, embracing difference is easier stated than accomplished, especially when dealing with the question of difference as constructed by the dominant society, for example, in dealing with racism and classism. In discussing difference, Audre Lorde goes on to state:

Difference and antagonism

Difference must be not merely tolerated, but seen as a fund of necessary polarities between which our creativity can spark like a dialectic.[82]

Audre Lorde's remarks occurred in the context of a conference in which black feminists and lesbians appeared on only one panel, a panel which dealt with the role of difference in the lives of american women. As she notes, it is academic arrogance to assume that any discussion – including all the other discussions of the conference – does not need the input of poor women, black and third world women, and lesbians.[83] It was a context which invited antagonism by virtue of omission and in which dispelling the state of ignoring was important.

However, to characterize embracing difference at a general, theoretical level in terms of polarities and dialectic is problematic. To characterize difference in terms of polarities (or opposing forces) and to characterize our interaction as a dialectic (or a process involving contradicting forces which must be synthesized and out of which will grow new contradicting forces which in turn must be synthesized, and so on) is still to invoke an hegelian conception of the self and interaction. It is simply the other side of the belief that to connect we must suppress (antagonistic) differences, only now pursuing antagonistic differences is to enhance creativity and connection.

The problem is that such a theory presupposes an inherent conflict of interests (with an accompanying focus on egoism versus altruism), and we thereby approach each other in terms of accountability rather than intelligibility. As a result, our understanding of connection resolves itself into a matter of coalitions, not friendships. And our interactions will thereby hold in place a foundation of antagonism, though amended in form. In my opinion, characterizing difference among us in terms of polarities and dialectic ultimately undermines rather than supports lesbian connection.

One among many and limits

To embrace difference, we do not need to engage antagonistically as Hegel's theory implies. Again, rather than perceive our selves as unlimited and hence as thwarted and threatened when we encounter one another, we can perceive our selves autokoenonously, as one among many.

My suggestion has several levels. By perceiving our selves as one among many, we develop a sense of our boundaries – of where they are not to be trespassed (at least for now), of where they are more flexible and hence open to expansion, of where they block us, and so on. In this way we have a better sense of when another is trespassing – and, if they have power over us, of ways to retain our moral sense of self despite the trespass. We also have a better sense of where and how and when we are able to make commitments and embark on a course – a better sense of what we can carry out and what we cannot such that our choices become more grounded.[k] In other words, perceiving our selves as one among many contributes to our self-conscious awareness, our self- understanding.

Secondly, by perceiving our selves as one among many, we come to better realize that moral agency is not a matter of controlling situations but rather of addressing our part and acting within situations; it means we perceive our selves as functioning, not in isolation, but within situations

---

k   For example, it is from understanding our boundaries that the possibility of trust emerges. I trust someone whose actions I can rely on. In some respects, I can trust even those who fight against me if I can be certain of what they will do – if I can depend on it. Those close to me may nevertheless be unreliable; and I may lose my grounding if I trust them to do what they say when they aren't aware of their own limits. That is, the first step of trust is reliability – and that involves self-awareness, each understanding herself, her limits and boundaries, what she can commit herself to. Of course, there is a deeper meaning of trust. I trust at a basic level those who may differ from me but who contribute to the context of lesbian value, to the ground of lesbian be-ing. And I trust deeply those with whom I have grown intimate. Finally, trusting someone does not mean trusting her not to change, but trusting she will be honest with us. Thus, at all levels, trust involves understanding our boundaries as well as the boundaries of those we trust.

and in relation to others. Moral agency then becomes a question of, not how we are going to stop all the injustice, but rather what our part is and what we are going to do next. In this way, acknowledging our boundaries does not detract from our interactions but rather locates us in a context wherein we act.

That is, perceiving our selves as one among many means we begin to understand how to work within limits. And with such an understanding, I believe, we can better deal with the constraints and coercion of oppression and so better resist de-moralization. In addition, we can better connect at various levels with selected others who in many ways are different so that we come to engage and form networks that are effective and do not disintegrate.

I am suggesting that while there are constraints on our choices because of oppression, what we can realize from acknowledging our boundaries is that moral agency means going on and making choices within limited situations (including the choice to challenge some of those constraints and limits). I believe it is in this way that we can begin to transform ourselves into an energy field capable of resisting oppression, into beings who are not accustomed to participating in relationships of dominance and subordination.

Playing Through Boundaries

THE QUESTION NOW remains, if we do not relate to each other antagonistically, as Hegel and many other anglo-european theorists imply, how then are we to relate? How do we address difference and embrace plurality? What does the moral agency of intelligibility really mean? *Embracing difference*

To begin with, by perceiving our selves as one among many, we gain a sense of loss when others who are different from us are not among us. In this way, acknowledging our separateness (distinctiveness, difference) is what encourages connection across differences. If we perceive our selves as autokoenonous, as selves within community, then the process of acknowledging our boundaries is a process of becoming aware of our limits and hence of our need for others who have different limits and so who have the capacity to help us expand. Lesbian community is a rich source of diversity and offers us access to a multitude and variety of differences virtually not available elsewhere, certainly not to us. As we may seek growth and comfort in commonness with those of races and classes similar to ours, so also we find growth and comfort in the enrichment resulting from the diversity around us.

In this respect, then, embracing intelligibility involves reaching out with a real desire to understand and engage with others. It becomes an awareness of our need for others, a need which is not a subordination[84] but rather a participation. That others offer what I do not have direct access to is a gift I cherish, and it is part of what makes lesbian community so very special.

Yet how do we invoke this participation, especially given that we are all *Playful world travel* affected by the dominant society's perception of difference in terms of antagonism? María Lugones offers the idea of 'playful world travel'. It is through playful world travel that we can learn to love cross-culturally and cross-racially.[85]

María Lugones argues that world travel involves two elements: flexibility and playfulness. Flexibility is something we have acquired necessarily simply by being outsiders relative to straight society. Consequently it is an ability we can adapt to other situations. What animates our flexibility among ourselves, according to María Lugones, is playfulness. This is perhaps a difficult ability for many of us to manifest whose flexibility emerged from surviving under oppression, but it is a central ability for Lesbian Ethics. For the ability to be playful is the ability to travel to the different worlds of other lesbians/women.[86]

María Lugones's idea of playfulness contrasts radically with men's ideas of play. Upon reviewing the literature, she found that men characterize 'play' in an agonistic or antagonistic sense.[87] 'Play' is developed in terms of winning and losing, in terms of competition, rules, and battles, and in terms of role playing. In this sense of 'play', competence is central. María Lugones notes that by his own admission, western man is an imperialist when he plays—that's what play means to him. And she argues that as an agonistic player, western man fails in his attempts to travel to other worlds precisely because he tries to conquer them.[m]

In contrast, lesbian playfulness can involve becoming a world traveler, journeying to other lesbians' perceptions, frameworks, worlds. Playful world travel involves being able to go into the world of another who is quite different from us without trying to destroy it. It involves being able to embrace ambiguity. It involves being open to uncertainty and surprise. This is what Gloria Anzaldúa calls "atravesando fronteras" (crossing borders). In describing la conciencia de la mestiza (the mestiza consciousness), she writes:

> She has discovered that she can't hold concepts or ideas in rigid boundaries.

---

m   As a result, María Lugones notes, playfulness in her sense is not always healthy. Being playful with imperialists, for example, is not healthy because there is, to put it mildly, no reciprocity in loving. Thus, although we travel in the dominant world, it is dangerous to try to do so with an attitude of playfulness.

The borders and walls that are supposed to keep the undesirable ideas out are entrenched habits and patterns of behavior; these habits and patterns are the enemy within. Rigidity means death. Only by remaining flexible is she able to stretch the psyche horizontally and vertically.[88]

To be able to play, we have to let go of our world/reality/sense of order. And to let go, we need self- centering and self-understanding; while we acknowledge and understand our boundaries, we also need the flexibility to cross them. To be a playful world traveler, as María Lugones notes, we need a sense of being partly at ease with our selves.[89]

And that is because playful world travel involves the ability to suspend not belief, but *disbelief*.[90] It is not our beliefs so much as our disbelief that leads us to discount others and keeps us loyal to patriarchal perception. In speaking of her mother, María Lugones writes:

> My mother was apparent to me mostly as a victim of arrogant perception. I was loyal to the arrogant perceiver's construction of her and thus disloyal to her in assuming that she was exhausted by that construction. . . . I came to realize through travelling to her "world" that she is not . . . exhausted by the mainstream argentinian patriarchal construction of her. I came to realize that there are "worlds" in which she shines as a creative being.[91]

María Lugones explains the importance of world travel to our ability to connect:

> The reason why I think that travelling to someone's "world" is a way of identifying with them is because by travelling to their "world" we can understand *what it is to be them and what it is to be ourselves in their eyes*. Only when we have travelled to each other's "worlds" are we fully subjects to each other.[92]

Thus being playful means fully attending each other.

In part, being playful also means being open to being a fool, "which is a combination of not worrying about competence, not being self-important, not taking norms as sacred and finding ambiguity with double edges as a source of delight."[93] As Anne Throop Leighton suggests, playfulness involves a willingness to be inarticulate and a willingness to hold a connection even though there are gaps, leaps, awkward moments, stumbling, mistakes, and confusion, because there are no rules.[94]

Being a fool has another dimension:

The trickster

> I can . . . be in a particular "world" and have a double image of myself as, for example, playful and as not playful. But this is a very familiar and recognizable phenomenon to the outsider to the mainstream in some central cases: when in one "world" I animate, for example, that "world's" caricature of the person I am in the other "world." I can have both images of myself and to

the extent that I can materialize or animate both images at the same time I become an ambiguous being. This is very much a part of trickery and foolery. It is worth remembering that the trickster and the fool are significant characters in many non-dominant or outsider cultures. . . . I can be stereotypically intense or be the real thing and, if you are Anglo, you do not know which one I am *because* I am Latin-American. As Latin-American I am an ambiguous being, a two-imaged self: I can see that gringos see me as stereotypically intense because I am, as a Latin-American, constructed that way but I may or may not *intentionally* animate the stereotype or the real thing knowing that you may not see it in anything other than in the stereotypical construction. This ambiguity is funny and is not just funny, it is survival-rich. We also can make the picture of those who dominate us funny precisely because we can see the double edge, we can see them doubly constructed. . . . So we know truths that only the fool can speak and only the trickster can play out without harm.[95]

That is, being playful is itself double-edged and ambiguous, and involves being a trickster as well as an explorer. And as we come across someone in lesbian community who is too serious or too fixed in herself or too fixed in dominant ideology, we can play in a way that dissolves her fixity by putting it in perspective.

Further, this is one way to dismantle the power of privilege among us, power that derives from such institutions as antisemitism or classism or racism, for example, as well as ageism, sizeism, and ablebodyism. While we have named the problem of the power of dominant privileges, we haven't yet come up with much in the way of dismantling it. (And each one of us feels the effects of that power in some way or other, and we each have that power in some way or other.) For example, affirming that we attend each other still leaves an imbalance. She who acts from dominant privilege can simply choose to not attend, to ignore. And that is one of her choices. However those who feel the effects of that choice do not, in lesbian community, have to simply live with it. We can withdraw, as happens, or confront. We can also invoke the trickster.

That is, the issues of size privilege or ablebodied privilege or age privilege, for example, are still significant. I have been suggesting that we pursue intelligibility as opposed to accountability, and this in certain respects presupposes an equality of stance which does not take these differences of privilege into account.[96] Intelligibility invokes a two-way process such that when when a gentile lesbian, for example, ignores a jewish lesbian because of ignorance, it would appear to be a two-way failure. Thus it seems that intelligibility would encourage the imbalance of dominant privileges and their ignorance/ignoring. So we need something to offset these privileges and their ignorance/ignoring.

Encouraging the trickster is one way. For example, a working-class lesbian might hoodwink or spoof or pull a middle-class lesbian's leg who, because of her class privilege, remains ignorant of (ignoring) the realities of working-class life and instead holds on to dominant values. Or a black lesbian might bamboozle or dupe or string a white lesbian along. A lesbian who plays a trickster is challenging the privilege and ignorance another lesbian uses to interact with her. And the other lesbian, because she knows the trickster lurks among us and may appear at any time in any form, finds herself needing and wanting to address the ignorance her privilege left her with and hence the privilege itself so that she avoids the tricks, avoids being a fool, . . . or enjoys the tricks: for being centered includes being able to laugh at ourselves.

More generally, a trickster or clown can challenge our attempts to control ourselves and situations, particularly through the hierarchy of the fathers. As Anne Throop Leighton notes, being playful involves our abilities of intuition, imagination, and above all, *mischief.*[97] The trickster or clown, along with witches and amazons, has been roundly suppressed by patriarchy and its seriousness. As Kate Clinton remarks: "Early on, I learned to deny my wisecracks, to say I was just kidding. I learned to apologize for insights which flew unplanned and unbidden out of me."[98] It is time the trickster reawaken in full power (ability) among us. As Granny tells it in *Daughters of Copper Woman:*

We had clowns . . . Not clowns like you see now, with round red noses and baggy costumes. Our clowns wore all different kinds of stuff. Anythin' they felt like, they wore. And they didn't just come out once in a while to act silly and make people laugh, our clowns were with us all the time, as important to the village as the chief, or the shaman, or the dancers, or the poets.

A clown . . . made comment on everythin', every day, all the time. If a clown thought that what the tribal council was gettin' ready to do was foolish, why the clown would just show up at the council and imitate every move every one of the leaders made. Only the clown would imitate it in such a way every little wart on that person would show, every hole in their idea would suddenly look real big.

It was like if you were real vain about your clothes, all of a sudden, the clown would be there walkin' right behind you all decked out in the most godawful mess of stuff, but all of it lookin' somehow like what you were wearin'. Maybe you had a necklace you always wore and showed off, well, the clown would have bits of bark and twigs, and feathers, and dog shit, and old broken clam shells, and anythin' else you can think of, and it'd all be made up in a necklace like yours. And if you walked a certain way because you were vain, the clown would walk the way you did. Where you had on your best clothes, the clown would be in rags and tatters and old bits of fern and you-name-it, and the clown's hair would look like a bird's nest, all mud and sticks and crap, and everywhere you went, the clown would go. Everythin' you did, the clown did. And nobody would ever dare blow up at the clown! If you did that, well, you were just totally shamed. A clown didn't do what a clown did to hurt you or make fun of you or be mean, it was to show you what you looked like to other people, let you see for yourself just how foolish it is to get yourself all tied in knots over some clothes and stuff instead of what counts, like bein' nice to people, and bein' lovin', and tryin' to fit in with the people you live with.[99]

A playful attitude From this we can understand that flexibility and playfulness involve not being fixed in particular constructions of the self. María Lugones distinguishes the playful world traveler from the serious human being, someone with no multidimensionality, with no fun in life, someone who has had the fun constructed out of her. She points out that the danger of role playing is that it leads to a fixed conception of self.[100] (It thus leads to not taking others seriously.)[n]

Playfulness, on the other hand, does not presuppose rules.

> Rather *the attitude that carries us through the activity, a playful attitude, turns the activity into play.* . . . We are not self-important, we are not fixed in particular constructions of ourselves, which is part of saying that we are open to *self-construction.* . . . We are there *creatively.* We are not passive.[101]

Thus acknowledging our boundaries allows us to perceive our selves as one among many and so seek out others, which in turn allows us to break through to begin our own self-construction.

In this respect, as well as being open to surprise, playfulness involves a sense of adventure, curiosity, desire—a sense of excitement.[102] Now, this is *not* a moral prescription, a rule of behavior: "You must be excited." Notice how inadequate such an idea is. Rather it is a suggestion of focus and attitude, of the energy with which we make choices and engage in the world. And it is one which can encourage new value and help us move out of the defending and the defensiveness of the old.

I am suggesting that we can develop our moral agency by developing our attending and intelligibility, by perceiving ourselves as one among many, autokoenonously, and by developing our playfulness—our ability to travel in and out of each other's worlds. This is, in my opinion, the heart of lesbian moral agency. However such a focus seems to take the power out of ethics, of being able to make each other behave; ethics itself ceases to be a tool of control. That is, we have tended to turn to ethics to decide what is the most moral thing to do—to ascertain our 'duty', or to make others behave and do right—to gain 'justice'. But as I have suggested, I think these uses of ethics are a mistake. Thus I want to consider the concepts of 'duty' and 'justice' in the next chapter.

n   This serious human being is similar to Simone de Beauvoir's serious man, who pretends value is ready-made and hides behind a role.

6
Moral Revolution: From Antagonism to Cooperation

I HAVE BEEN focusing on how the concept of 'control' permeates our lives. In chapter two I discussed control from a position of subordination, through the use of the feminine virtues. In chapter three I discussed paternalism, an attempt to control, from a position of dominance, situations for others. In chapter four I discussed the fragmentation of reasoning and emotions involved with the idea of 'self-control'. And in the last chapter I discussed the idea that we must be free of constraints to be moral agents; another way of putting this is that we must control our situation before we can make ("free") choices and be moral agents. In this chapter I want to discuss the function of patriarchal ethics as social control. According to the ideas we've inherited from the fathers, to be ethical, we must act from duty, and when others are not being ethical, we can seek justice, making sure they get their deserved punishment. In discussing the concepts of 'duty' and 'justice', I want to develop my suggestion that the function of Lesbian Ethics be, not social control, but rather the development of lesbian integrity and agency.

Fatherly Ethics

I HAVE BEEN challenging ethical concepts we appeal to, concepts emerging primarily from modern anglo-european thought. In chapter two I briefly noted shifts from classical to medieval to modern thought in order to establish a sense of how modern anglo-european ethics places

Overview

clashes of interests at center, along with the dichotomy between egoism and altruism. Here I want to explore the refinements of modern anglo-european ethical thought—'duty' and 'justice'—and suggest that they hold in place a foundation (axis) of antagonism. That is, I will argue, while they are supposed to help us deal with each other ethically, these concepts interrupt lesbian connection.

To begin with, as is true of 'altruism' and 'self-sacrifice', the concepts of 'duty', 'obligation', and 'justice'—so central to modern patriarchal ethics—played minor parts in ancient greek ethics from Homer through Aristotle. In ancient greece, 'virtue' and 'merit' were key ethical concepts. A moral man was a virtuous man. Aristotle's virtues are a matter of practical wisdom and involve character. Examples include courage, self-control, generosity, magnificence, high-mindedness, a nameless virtue between ambition and lack of ambition, gentleness (as a median between short temper and apathy), friendliness, truthfulness (as a median between boastfulness and self-depreciation), wittiness (as a median between buffoonery and boorishness), and so on.[1] A moral man was one who engaged in action and developed his character by developing these virtues.

Aristotle included justice as a virtue, and claimed that it consists of treating equals equally and unequals unequally.[2] Thus, slaves were justly treated unequally. And Plato's idea of justice involved a state in which every man did the job he was most suited for as ultimately determined by paternalistic philosopher-kings.[3] 'Justice,' however, was not central to the ancient greek system of values; ancient greek ethics focused on the aristocratic values of virtue and living the good life.

Medieval anglo-european ethics focused on certain religious beliefs, and duty began to emerge as a matter of following the will of a god. The catholic church connected virtue to self-deprivation and warned of the seven deadly sins or vices: avarice, pride, anger, lust, gluttony, envy, sloth, and deception. Virtue was no longer a matter of ability, save the ability to resist temptation. It was not a matter of what people did but what they didn't do. Still, the focus was not on duty or obligation toward others, except for one's duty toward priests and the recipients of certain charitable endeavors. And the concept of 'justice' was virtually nonexistent. The old testament, that bastion of fatherly wisdom, provided the basis: "an eye for an eye and a tooth for a tooth." This, combined with Solomon's willingness to cut a baby in half to determine its biological mother, was about the extent of the biblical concept of 'justice'.[4] Earthly justice was not the church's concern: it would all be sorted out in an afterlife by a god. Injustice, including coercive aspects of the state such as war, slavery, unequal economic and social status, and unjust rulers, was a divine "remedy and punishment for original sin."[5] The concept of 'social justice', along with the concepts of 'duty' and 'obligation', would not become refined until social domination and subordination themselves were refined.

Rather, the church focused on establishing itself as the moral authority, eroding individual moral agency by affirming that a virtuous person would accept guidance from the church on faith. Reinforcing church dogma in europe was feudalism, an economic and political system (flourishing from the ninth to about the fifteenth century) based on the relationship of lord and vassal, in which peasants as serfs held land on condition of homage and service to their master. As a result, ethical concepts that became refined during this time included loyalty, fealty, obedience, respect, and fidelity—all owed a superior—as well as honor, benevolence, charity, and noblesse oblige—virtues of the masters.

During the renaissance and the reformation, belief in original sin dominated theories of human nature, and means of categorizing people as christian or heathen and "civilized" or "savage" flourished—those designated as heathen or barbarian were not considered part of the moral community.[6] As a result, british and european rulers pursued policies involving a divine right to conquer groups they designated as "other": policies of exploitation and conversion as well as policies of extermination (as in the holy crusades against the muslims).

Along with the decline of feudalism and the rise of mercantilism and then industrial capitalism came a decline in the belief in original sin and the emergence of enlightenment ideas of equality among all men, the heart of liberal philosophy.[7] Equality among men involved the idea that all men have something in common which makes them special and distinct from nature, from plants and animals (and women)—namely, a rational capability which indicates a moral capacity.[a] In part as a result of this theory of the rationality of human nature, which is our present heritage, modern anglo-european ethics, beginning around the end of the sixteenth century with Hobbes (after Machiavelli), focused on utilitarian self-preservation and peace through social organization.

The resulting central ethical question is this: Under what circum-

---

a   This idea of equality did not include political equality. For example, during abolition in the u.s., white northern radical republicans argued against slavery on the grounds that slaves had this moral capacity; nevertheless, they still felt blacks inferior (note, for example, the lincoln/douglass debates) and thought it appropriate for whites to be guardians of blacks. Thus although "radical," they felt segregation acceptable for a transition period during which blacks would develop and learn to be full citizens (i.e., adopt white values). In their justification of slavery, on the other hand, southern conservatives argued that blacks had no moral capacity.[8]

stances would egoistic and solitary men agree to come together and co-operate?[9] As I noted in chapter two, the answer involves variations on a social-contract theory.[b] Again, as the theory goes, men are perceived as violent and aggressive as well as egoistic and solitary. However, they also have an added capacity which allows them to rise above this natural state: their rational capacity allows them to realize that they could maximize their self-interest if they were to give up some of their natural rights, such as the right to pillage and plunder their neighbors, to a central authority which could regulate pillaging and plundering, thus creating order and "cooperation."

That is, it is enlightened self-interest which allows us to understand that we can maximize our interests if we cooperate with, rather than aggress against, others around us. For example, in his nineteenth-century refinement and development of utilitarianism, John Stuart Mill argues

b   As Alison Jaggar notes, "If liberals were to stop viewing human individuals as essentially rational agents and were to take theoretical account of the facts of human biology, especially though not only the facts of reproductive biology [i.e., one person alone cannot raise a child but needs the help of others], the liberal problematic would be transformed. Instead of community and cooperation being taken as phenomena whose existence and even possibility is puzzling, and sometimes even regarded as impossible, the existence of egoism, competitiveness and conflict, phenomena which liberals take as endemic to the human condition, would themselves be puzzling and problematic."[10] In other words, because we expect humans to be aggressive, we find the idea of cooperation puzzling. If, instead of focusing on antagonistic interactions, we focused on cooperative interaction, we would find the idea of competition puzzling.

When considering how societies might function cooperatively rather than antagonistically, we can consider anthropological data such as that explored by Susan Cavin, who argues that society is dependent upon the female homosocial relationship for its very existence: "An important point here is that from the beginning, female society is equivalent to society itself. Society is always at core a gynosociety. Female homosocial relations are critical to the formation and maintenance of the family, community, and society. Due to both sexism and heterosexism, patrisociologists miss this point and falsely assume that society is sex neutral. Internal social organization at origin consists of the cooperation between adult females in defense of offspring and in food sharing."[11]

Susan Cavin investigated a number of societies to determine if there were differences between those with a greater number of females relative to males and those in which females and males exist in equal numbers. Among societies with greater numbers of females relative to males, she found some gatherer and hunter societies, some warring primitive peoples, and some polygynous peoples — societies one might not expect to find where females exist in greater numbers. However in societies with greater numbers of females she also found matrilocality, extended mother/child family and household, preurban society, and an absence of stratification or class systems. Further, in societies with near-equal numbers of males and females she found "the classic constructs of patriarchal society: patrilocality, the heterosexual monogamian family (nuclear/independent), complex stratification systems, plow agriculture subsistence, animal husbandry, and the development of cities."[12]

that our rational capacity provides for our moral capacity, namely, our ability to act impartially with regard to our interests and those of others: through reason I can realize that in the long run my interests are best secured through the greater good of the whole.

Also focusing on rationality, reformers of the german enlightenment sought to undermine the power of tradition and central religious authority, and toward the end of the eighteenth century Immanuel Kant strove to give a ground for moral decision-making centered in the individual and away from authority – based, nevertheless, on the concept of 'duty'.[13] He was concerned with the moral autonomy of individuals and developed the idea of a moral agent as one with a good will who uses pure reason to make laws and acts from duty alone.

While Kant held to the primacy of man's rationality and located moral authority in the individual, he opposed a morality focused on self-interest. He suggested that to appeal to self-interest is simply to appeal to our animal nature, and he argued that what makes man moral is what allows him to rise above his animal nature and thus achieve autonomy (freedom from the rule of his passions). Nevertheless, utilitarianism eventually won out in popular thinking over a theory based on duty and principles derived from pure reason because, among other things, it is more conducive to capitalist economics (regulated pillaging and plundering).

Thus, there is considerable difference between what was called ethics in the ancient greek system and what we now consider ethics. Ancient greek ethics concerned character, abilities, competency, and living a good life. With the transition to modern anglo-european ethics comes a focus on duty, obligation, enlightened self-interest, altruism and self-sacrifice, social utility, and justice. In my opinion this transition, rather than a major shift in value, was actually a natural development of the split between reasoning and emotions in ancient greek patriarchal values. For it was this split that fathered the idea of 'self-control', which, as patriarchy became more refined, replaced concern with integrity altogether. Nevertheless, to modern patriarchal sensibilities there is a major shift: these ancient greek values smack of something alien, even heathen – at the very least, inadequate.

How did this change occur and why do the ancient greek values seem so alien? Arthur W. H. Adkins offers a thesis based on certain military aspects of the societies involved.[14] He argues that the ancient greek values derived primarily from what he calls the 'competitive values' whereas dominant present-day values derive from what he calls the 'cooperative values'.

Competitive to "cooperative" values

When the competitive values form the center of a society's system of values (such as was the case in ancient greece), success becomes the most important gauge of an act's worth. Those who are most successful in performing acts vital to a society's well-being will be most highly valued, and their skills considered virtues. Men so honored typically exhibit warrior skills and skills in statesmanship. By possessing select virtues or abilities which contribute to the successful maintenance of society, a man will be honored by virtue of merit alone.[c]

On the other hand, when a society adheres to the "cooperative" values (as in modern europe, england, and the u.s.), duty and obligation and justice become the focal points. That is, under the "cooperative values," the concepts of 'duty' and 'obligation' and 'justice' become a means of checking the possibly selfish ambition of those who are the most highly valued (virtuous) under a competitive system of values. In a "cooperative" society sanctions exist to protect the weaker from the stronger, or so the theory goes.

One of the main differences between these two systems of value concerns the nature of 'moral error' or 'sin'. Again, under the competitive system of values, ability and success are central. As a result men's failures and inabilities become sin and vices respectively: someone who failed to prevent disaster in ancient greece was not significantly different from someone who willfully did what resulted in disaster, since the effects of each on the security and well-being of the society were the same.

Moral failure under the "cooperative" system has a different flavor. In modern thought, that a man fails to do something becomes less important than why he fails. And that a man succeeds becomes less important than the intention with which he acts. Thus, if someone does something that results in a good to society but does it for selfish gain, that matters. And if someone does something that results in harm but didn't intend harm, that matters. As a result, under the "cooperative" system of values, distinctions between voluntary and involuntary actions arise along with a fairly elaborate system of excuses, including consideration of whether an act

---

c   These are the aristocratic values. And over generations certain families have been presumed to have and will be educated to exhibit such virtues as a result of their birthright. Under the aristocratic system, one possessed of such virtue has no real obligation toward members of society not part of this birthright. In her discussion of the slander trial brought by Miss Woods and Miss Pirie against Lady Cumming Gordon, who had essentially closed their boarding school with (privately circulated) charges that Miss Woods and Miss Pirie engaged in lesbian sexual activities in view of their students, Lillian Faderman gives us a glimpse of this ethic as refined in nineteenth-century scottish society. Of Lady Cumming Gordon she writes, "So when she was outraged by the rumor of the mistresses' behavior, it would not have occurred to her that she needed to check the facts before she acted. Just as she had *made* the mistresses, virtually on a whim, she could *break* them, virtually on a whim. To whom was she accountable?"[15]

was done voluntarily, deliberately, intentionally, or on purpose.[16]
Adkins's thesis is that the competitive values are central to the external survival and security of a society, particularly a small city-state, while the "cooperative" values are concerned with the internal stability of a society, particularly a larger, more militarily secure nation.[d]

Thus it is Adkins's contention that, of political necessity, the competitive values won out over the "cooperative" values in ancient greek city-states: He notes that ancient greek society was devoted to maintaining its own autonomy, rarely imposed its will on its neighbors, and was not efficient enough to count on a stable prosperity. Under such conditions, those capable of preventing disaster were crucial to the society. Hence they would be honored for their abilities, and there would be no pressure on them to be considerate of other, "less valuable" members of society; there would be no attempt to curb the excesses of these heroes. In other words, if the talents and service of particular citizens are needed when crises arise, the society is dependent on their services and goodwill; and so it cannot afford to alienate them.[18]

Adkins argues that for the "cooperative" values to take precedence, there must be a societal dread of divine sanction against those who take

---

d Adkins argues that while in Homer's time the competitive values were central to the greek city-state, nevertheless there were certain checks on the behavior of the warrior class. Belief in the power of intervention of gods and goddesses served as a means of protecting the weak and the lower classes from the excesses of those heroes, and so had a democratizing effect. By the time of Plato and Aristotle, however, belief in such deities had waned, and both Plato's and Aristotle's systems of ethics include attempts to insert the "cooperative" virtues in the greek system of values. Thus, in their systems the aristocracy, or the virtuous class, were not simply those who possessed warrior (athletic and military) skills but those who also acted in terms of justice.

Adkins points out that, consistent with the competitive values, we find no distinction between voluntary and involuntary actions in Homer's time: that the gods decreed a certain turn of event – Orestes's murder of his father and rape of his mother, for example – in no way affected the ascription of responsibility to individual men for the outcome of their actions. That is, Orestes was responsible for what he did even though the gods determined he would do it. By Plato's time we find a distinction between voluntary and involuntary actions, and by Aristotle's time even more refined distinctions were made (e.g., acting in ignorance versus acting from ignorance) regarding failure in action.

Thus, it seemed that a distinction between 'moral error' or 'sin', on the one hand, and 'mistake', on the other, was beginning to be embraced such that 'duty', 'obligation', and 'justice', not 'virtue' and 'merit', would become central moral concepts. Nevertheless, in both Plato's and Aristotle's systems of thought, if the failure in ability backed by a good intention (an accident) had an equally devastating effect on the society as did a willful breach of the society's security (a sin), the actions were punished equally and the distinction between 'mistake' and 'moral sin' mattered little. In other words, regardless of certain refinements of thought, the competitive values still took precedence.[17]

unfair advantage of others, despite their social status. Alternatively, the "cooperative" values can emerge once the society is large and stable enough to ensure that the courts judge without fear or favor. That is, once a society is militarily secure, citizens can be treated equally before the courts. Even though some talented aristocrats may be alienated as a result of losing their special privileges, the society won't be harmed if they withhold their talents from its service.

Thus, as long as the state depends on special individuals for its survival or stability, 'virtue' (ability) and 'merit', rather than 'duty' and 'obligation', will be the central ethical concepts, and the rights of those less essential to the survival of the state will not necessarily be protected. But once a system is large enough to impose sanctions equally without fear of the loss of certain citizens' goodwill, human interactions can be based on "cooperative" values because then the society can focus on inner stability and harmony rather than external survival. Under these conditions judgment of our duty, rather than judgment of our ability, will be the key ethical consideration. And in such a system, according to Adkins, justice will prevail. Yet is this true?

Ethics and the state Is it true that in a state such as the u.s. – bigger and stronger and more militarily secure than the ancient greek city- states – justice prevails, even in our moral considerations? Certainly, 'duty' and 'obligation' are central ethical considerations – obligations or responsibilities husbands have to wives and obligations or responsibilities wives have to husbands, for example. But does this moral focus on duty or obligation toward others protect some groups of individuals from the excesses and abuses of other groups? Is the system functioning in a way that we can pretend that even ideally justice will prevail? More interestingly, why is justice a primary moral consideration at all?

While the "cooperative" values (justice and duty) are prevalent, citizens are not treated equally before the courts – the rights of some groups are simply not protected from the excesses of other groups. Rather, the state institutionalizes the interests of some groups over and against the rights of other groups and thereby imposes a certain social order. The u.s. courts continue to dismiss native american land and treaty claims. In the case of women as a group, those in power claim women are equally protected, just different. Even ideally, the system does not function to protect all equally. Certainly, it does not function that way when the competitive values of economic exploitation are considered essential to the motivation of individual citizens.

Further, even when it is supposedly protecting the rights of its citizens, the state becomes a separate entity with its own rights, and these rights are protected against the interests and just claims of some individuals and groups. For example, the supreme court recently engaged in a cost-benefits analysis, deciding in the name of "state security" that it is acceptable to abrogate the rights of citizens who are suspected of a crime but who have not been tried if this will aid the police in obtaining evidence against them – providing, of course, that police intentions are morally good. And the courts deny injustice in the u.s. internment of japanese american citizens and confiscation of their property during w.w.ii (though congress may be about to "apologize" to the 60,000 surviving victims,[19]). In these cases the interests of the state itself take precedence over the "just" claims of people.

The state does not protect the institutionally weak from the institutionally strong, either those with political hegemony (successful white male corporate executives) or those who function to ensure the continued existence of the state (the police and the armed forces). In other words, a larger, more secure state which incorporates a focus on 'duty', 'obligation', and 'justice' does not promote fairness and equity.[e] With a larger and more secure state, concepts of 'justice', 'duty', and 'obligation' emerge, but they are used in place of 'virtue' and 'merit' to maintain the existing power structure.

More significantly, I don't think a system of ethics focused on the concepts of 'duty', 'obligation', and 'justice' will in and of itself yield more equitable behavior than one focused on 'virtue' or 'ability'. If a system focused on 'virtue' and 'ability' yields problems, it is because there is a power structure which values some abilities over others, particularly under patriarchal rule. That is, while those operating under a system of merit pretend that the best and the brightest are honored, only certain abilities are acknowledged. Thus 'merit' refers, not to the possibility of each developing her own abilities and virtues, but rather to a ranking and hierarchy of abilities.

When concepts such as 'justice' and 'duty' and 'obligation' are focal points of ethical theory, their primary function is to make us believe we have a way to ensure ethical behavior in ourselves and others. They are attempts at guaranteeing humane, "cooperative," behavior among individuals who are considered egoistic, solitary, and aggressive, when other-

---

e   One might object that neither did ancient greek society protect virtue or the good life. And this is true. My point, however, is that while the term 'justice' is prevalent in u.s. society, the type of impartiality Adkins envisioned does not exist even as an ideal. And this is not simply because the system is imperfect. Rather, it is a matter of what institutional justice amounts to. The state protects itself. And whether it stresses virtue and merit or something else, those with institutional power are protected from the claims of those without institutional power unless it is in the interest of the state to do otherwise.[20]

wise there has been no basis established through personal interaction. In other words, these "cooperative" values presuppose antagonism among individuals. And it is my contention that in presupposing antagonism, these values thereby encourage it.

Within the community, lesbians turn to ideas of 'duty', 'obligation', 'responsibility', and 'community justice' in an effort to get each other to behave. We tend to appeal to the ideas of 'obligation' and 'responsibility' when deciding what is the most moral thing to do, and 'justice' when others are not behaving "appropriately." My suggestion is that such appeals presuppose antagonism, develop ethics as social control, and undermine lesbian connection. I want to explore the concepts of 'justice' and 'duty', and consider problems I find with their use in lesbian community.

Duty   "What is my duty?" or "What is my obligation?" are considered primary questions of ethics. Indeed, 'obligation' and 'duty' are so central to ethics as understood and developed in modern anglo-european thought that in certain respects they appear to embody the *meaning* of ethics. Within modern anglo-european thought and within lesbian community, we tend to think that ethics just means what we should and shouldn't do, that to be ethical means we have obligations toward each other to follow rules of right behavior.

Yet, as I've discussed above, concepts of 'duty' and 'obligation' are recent developments in anglo-european thought. Not all ethical systems focus on 'duty' and 'obligation': 'obligation' played a very minor part in ancient greek ethics; and within the hopi language, there is no phrase which corresponds to the english phrase "Your duty is . . ."[21f]

Within anglo-european ethics, the concept of 'duty' reaches a pinnacle with the work of Kant. And while Kant's program is not the focus of our ethical thinking, still we are left with the concept of 'duty' as a central ethical concept. Consequently, it is worth considering the structure of duty which we have inherited from Kant.

---

f   This observation comes from a book on hopi ethics by Richard Brandt, a classic attempt to impose modern anglo-european ethical concepts on a distinctly different culture in order to "understand" it. I am assuming, however, that the observation is accurate. It is interesting to compare Brandt's treatment of hopi ethics with Adkins's treatment of ancient greek ethics. Both are trying to find the place of 'moral responsibility' in cultures in which this concept is not central. But Adkins realizes the concept need not be central for a system to be an ethical system; Brandt does not and so tries to superimpose it. (For example, Brandt writes: "Or, more exactly (since we do not want to call a term 'ethical' unless it is equivalent to one of the English terms like 'duty', 'blameworthy,' and so on), what concepts are expressed by those Hopi terms which interpreters regard as the nearest equivalents of 'right,' 'duty,' 'blameworthy,' etc., when applied to conduct? This is an empirically decidable question."[22])

Briefly, Kant holds that laws are of two sorts: laws of nature, which are descriptions of what is, of fact, and moral laws, which are prescriptions of what ought to be. Man's desires and inclinations conform to the laws of nature. In this respect, to act from desire or inclination or self-interest is merely to conform to natural law and hence to be no different than plants and animals. To be moral, one must be an autonomous lawmaker, someone who determines his own laws and acts independently of his inclinations or desires. Reason, combined with man's will, allows him to overcome the laws of nature and so be moral: by using reason he can determine moral laws, and then by using his will, he can act from duty rather than inclination.[23]

Now, these laws a man determines can't be just any laws. They must be laws that are a matter of pure reason (otherwise, they involve emotions or inclination and hence are part of the laws of nature). And to be rational, these laws must be universal (or 'categorical'). So Kant offers a formula, what he calls the "categorical imperative": "Act only on that maxim through which you can at the same time will that it should become a universal law."[24]

The idea of this formula is that every rational being be treated as an end in itself and not merely as a means. For example, by this formula I could not will slavery, for according to the formula I would have to will slavery universally: Always enslave everyone. But if I willed it universally, then I would be included among those to be enslaved; and as a slave I would not be a being who could will laws. In other words, I would be willing myself to be a being who could not will anything – a contradiction. Thus, it is not possible for me to will such a law morally. It is logic – pure reason, not inclination – which prohibits the willing of such a principle.

More generally, we could not will a universal law that treats everyone merely as a means. Since we are one of that group, it would mean willing a law that treats us as a mere means; and if we were merely a means, we would no longer be the sort of being who could will laws. On the other hand, if we willed such a law for everyone but ourselves, the law would be no longer universal or categorical, hence moral, since it would be excepted in our own case, and thus based on inclination or desire, not reason. It is logically impossible to universally will such laws.[g]

Having determined which laws are permissible, we overcome our in-

---

g Kant holds that some laws are themselves contradictions, for example making false promises. If such a law were willed universally, the institution of promising would become meaningless (as we find it has with politicians). Other laws are contradicted only in the willing, as discussed above.

clinations by acting from duty. Duty is the only motive by which we can ensure an absolutely good will. In this way we achieve autonomy. We become ends in ourselves rather than merely means. Under Kant's theory, thus, we are morally subject to no one's laws but our own.[h]

While the theory is interesting, Kant considers 'autonomy' a matter of being able to act independently of emotion or inclination; to be moral, we must rise above the boundaries of nature. Thus, Kant regards autonomy and morality achievable only if we fragment our selves. I have already discussed in chapter four the idea of integrating rather than fragmenting reasoning and emotions. And in chapter five I have discussed the idea of 'moral agency' as a matter of functioning within boundaries rather than "rising above" them. We are, nevertheless, drawn by the idea of 'duty'.

Basically we do not use Kant's formula to determine our moral judgments, nevertheless, the concept of 'duty' is engrained in our thinking about lesbian community, particularly in terms of 'responsibility' and 'obligation'. And the *structure* of acting from 'duty' involves severing reasoning and emotions, regarding reason as controlling emotions – shutting off our feelings and doing what is "right" regardless of our inclinations – hence fragmenting our selves and thus undermining our integrity. The structure of 'justice' has related problems.

Justice   John Stuart Mill argues that the basic element of 'justice' is conformity to law: while men make bad laws such that 'justice' is not coextensive with 'legality', nevertheless conformity to law is the general force of justice.[25] He argues that moral obligation concerns things which people are bound to do and for which they deserve punishment if they don't. He goes on to suggest that the two essential ingredients in the sentiment of justice are the desire to punish someone who has done wrong and the knowledge that there is some definite individual or individuals to whom harm was done. He argues that the desire to punish comes from the impulse of self-defense, which itself has nothing to do with morality. We make such an impulse moral by subordinating it to the social sympathies so that we exercise it only in conformity to the general good – the greatest good for the greatest number.

Now Mill, who is renowned as a liberal thinker, does argue that moral rules which forbid men to harm one another are more important than rules for managing human affairs.[26] Nevertheless, in my opinion his

---

h   Kant's theory challenges centralized moral authority. While acting from duty means acting according to laws, unlike militaristic propaganda this does not mean acting according to the dictates of other beings: to act according to the dictates of other beings, including gods, is to act from inclination (for example, fear) or self-interest, not from duty.

work exhibits little real understanding of 'harm'. He thought women and others oppressed were morally harmed under the existing social structure. He thought slavery was wrong. And he felt that the history of social improvement had been a series of transitions whereby one custom or institution went from being regarded as necessary for social existence to being universally stigmatized as tyranny and injustice.[27] But in my opinion he showed no understanding of the absolute devastation and rage of those who have been violated by white, imperialist, male social structures. Further, he showed no understanding that establishing british culture through colonialism was either exploitation or a violation of individuals or social groupings. He felt colonialism and despotism to be legitimate modes of government for "barbarians."[28][i] And in the end, as all true liberals do, he upheld the social structure over and against fairness to individuals. His ultimate sense of justice was a matter of social utility:

> All persons are deemed to have a *right* to equality of treatment, except when some recognized social expediency requires the reverse.[31]

In a more contemporary liberal vein, John Rawls argues that justice is more a matter of fairness than a matter of social utility. Nevertheless, the focus of 'justice' concerns the basic structure of society (social organization). The theory is based on an idea of a hypothetical social contract,[32] and Rawls assumes that the contract begins with "an equal and self-sufficient association of persons."[33] In his view, people already part of a society would agree to cooperate and evaluate their concerns by a set of uniform principles for two reasons: because they would feel greater goods can come from such cooperation, and because they would believe they can gain advantages through a governing body distributing those greater goods "fairly." Thus Rawls's focus primarily concerns distributive justice,[j] and he claims that:

> institutions are just when no arbitrary distinctions are made between persons in the assigning of basic rights and duties and when rules determine a

---

i Significantly, Mill worked for the (british) east india company, starting as a clerk directly under his father in 1822 and eventually holding the post his father held, chief examiner, which was equivalent in power and responsibility to a secretary of state.[29] The company, while a private institution, virtually administered an empire and commanded a sizeable military and naval force.[30]

j Distributive justice concerns itself with the division and distribution—by means of certain socially defined principles—of goods, rights, and duties: taxes, welfare, kickbacks, wages, profits, equal protection for some, and so on. Criminal justice concerns itself with punishment of those who breach socially defined principles.

proper balance between competing claims to the advantage of social life.[34]

I hope I have made it clear that the distinctions involved in discrimination and oppression are never arbitrary. And those charged with enforcing the social order use perfectly rational principles, within a context of dominance and subordination, to determine a proper balance between competing claims—the interests of men and children on the one hand as against the interests of women on the other, for example, or the interests of whites ("society") against the interests of native americans.

Rawls goes on to state that the proper subject of justice is the social structure—that is, the institutions designed to distribute goods. And he lists the institutions he thinks capable of fair distribution:

> By major institutions I understand the political constitution and principal social and economic arrangements. Thus legal protection of freedom of thought, private property in the means of production, and the monogamous family are examples of major social institutions.[35]

In Rawls's system of justice, principles of efficiency and stability are central. Thus, authorities are to "fit together" the plans of individuals (i.e., define individual interests) so they are compatible, and they are to use force against "infractions" of the social order in order to restore the existing arrangement.[36] In other words, paternalism and punishment—corrective (criminal) justice—are central to the maintenance of a just society.

In a vein less euphemistic than that of liberals Rawls and Mill, Friedrich Nietzsche points out that, historically, 'justice' had nothing to do with ensuring fairness among all men. Rather, it was a matter of goodwill among parties possessing equal power such that they would come to terms with each other, combined with an ability to compel parties of lesser power to settle their differences among themselves.[37] Nietzsche argues that the relevant metaphor for just interactions is the oldest form of social alliance: the relationship of debtor and creditor. The idea that justice is a matter of a criminal deserving punishment because he could have done otherwise is a recent development. Throughout the greater part of history, according to Nietzsche, such punishment emerged simply from anger modified by the idea "that every injury has its *equivalent* and can actually be paid back, even if only through the *pain* of the culprit."[38] Should the debtor fail to repay his debt, the creditor can claim something the debtor had control over, for example his wife or his freedom. Primarily, however, the creditor could inflict any kind of indignity on the body of the debtor. Thus

> an equivalence is provided by the creditor's receiving, in place of a literal compensation for an injury . . . a recompense in the form of a kind of *pleas-*

ure—the pleasure of being able to vent his power freely upon one who is powerless . . . the enjoyment of violation. This enjoyment will be the greater the lower the creditor stands in the social order. . . . In "punishing" the debtor, the creditor participates in a *right of the masters:* at last he, too, may experience for once the exalted sensation of being allowed to despise and mistreat someone as "beneath him". . . . The compensation, then, consists in a warrant for and title to cruelty.[39]

However, in his later work, and reflecting on christian justice and revenge, Nietzsche admonishes the reader to mistrust all who clamor for punishment and justice, suggesting that when they call themselves the just and the good, they would act otherwise if only they had the power.[40] As long as 'justice' was part of what Nietzsche calls 'master morality', and was a matter of equals paying back equals, he found it an honorable if initially bloody affair. But once it becomes part of what he calls 'slave morality' (of which christianity is a paradigm), he notes it is born of resentment and becomes an excuse for man's petty and vulgar impulses. He considers 'justice' under this value mere revenge and sanctimonious retaliation.[k]

k Nietzsche distinguishes what he called 'master morality' and 'slave morality'. (The distinction covers roughly the same phenomena Adkins discusses.) Nietzsche suggests that both moralities have been mixed in all civilizations, but that they began with the ruling class and the oppressed, respectively. Master morality, historically, distinguished between good and bad. The good are the powerful who excel and distinguish themselves, who create value and are not judged, who repay good with good and evil with evil, who accept duty only toward equals, and who are hostile to selflessness. The good man honored his enemy, for his enemy was his true competitor. The bad, in contrast, were the common, the vulgar, the meek, the petty, the downtrodden, the oppressed, the herd, and they were despised by the powerful.

Slave morality, on the other hand, emerged when the highest caste turned into the priestly caste, obsessed over purity, turned from action, stopped fighting or enjoying any of the lusty elements of life, and alternated between brooding and emotional explosions. They focused on continence, abstention, asceticism, and were antilife. They became the great haters, and out of this hate grew their idea of love—self-crucifixion for salvation (jesus-types). Slave morality distinguishes between good and evil (rather than good and bad), begins with a negation and a focus on those who are evil (the masters), feeds on hatred and resentment, and requires an enemy (which it would eradicate) as well as a hostile environment in order for there to be moral action at all. Under this value, the wretched alone—the poor, the lowly, the impotent—are good, while the noble and the powerful are evil, cruel, and insatiable. As the bad is an afterthought in master morality, so the good is an afterthought in slave morality. The values of the herd include impotence (called 'goodness of heart'), anxious lowliness (called 'humility'), subjugation (called 'obedience'), and retaliation (called 'justice'). Nietzsche saw this as a morality of pity which stops life, and he snorted at the idea that the lamb would hold the bird of prey accountable. He saw slave morality as the effeminization of man.[41]

I find the play between 'master' and 'slave' morality a rather androgynous affair.

Regardless of whether we take the euphemistic description of justice as *Punishment* fairness or the blatant assessment of justice as the right to cruelty when a debt goes unpaid, justice ultimately is tied to punishment. Even the idea of justice as fairness involves the idea of an authority being able to enact sanctions against those who are unfair. The theory is that for justice to reign, there must be ways to make people be just and fair and not selfish, to make people "cooperate." 'Justice', as the concept has been refined, presupposes that people are antagonistic and seek to maximize their own interests in a context of limited resources – and that there must be some check on this.

Within dominant society, there tend to be three justifications for punishment: reform, deterrence, and retribution. The reform theory involves the idea that, through punishment, the wicked will perceive the error of their ways and repent. It is the idea that when an authority punishes someone who has offended the order of that authority, the offender will, as a result of the punishment, learn to want to not offend against that order. This is what parole boards expect prisoners to say. In fact there is a certain habit of speech one can discover in parolees, not unlike that of football players, going on about a god and wanting to be good, totally devoid of any hint of anger. These, then, become model citizens, grateful for the change in their fate which those in power grant them. (The reform theory is difficult to substantiate in the case of capital punishment except by means of logic or pure reason: those executed certainly will not commit another offense against the order – at least in this lifetime.)

Interestingly, Nietzsche claims that of the many functions of punishment – rendering harmless, recompense, isolation of a disturbance, inspiring fear, payment, compromise with revenge, or declaration of war, for example – waking a feeling of guilt is not one. Rather, punishment makes men hard and cold, since in being caught and punished, they witness authorities practicing the same things they themselves are being punished for:

> spying, deception, bribery, setting traps, the whole cunning and underhanded art of police and prosecution, plus robbery, violence, defamation, imprisonment, torture, murder, practiced as a matter of principle and without even emotion to excuse them.[42]

Reform, he thinks, is pure hypocrisy.

Under the deterrence theory, someone either cannot or will not want to commit some bad act. The theory presupposes that those who commit murder, for example, will be deterred by being put in prison. This, of course, is untrue; prison collects and isolates, it does not deter. The theory also presupposes that those who might want to commit 'bad act *x*' would be deterred by watching others who were caught and punished for 'bad act x'. There are significant arguments to the effect that those who have committed crimes were not deterred because they never thought they'd be caught. Still, I have heard it argued that fear of punishment deters the vast majority of us. Now I could be wrong, but I don't think most lesbians restrain ourselves from murdering each other because of a fear of being punished.

More significantly, under the "cooperative" values, punishment is not uniformly meted out. If one is planning murder, there are a number of ways one can reduce the risk, for example, by being a rich, white, christian preppy male who murders a female he has sex with. And evidence was recently presented to the supreme court showing that the controlling factor in whether a prosecutor asks for the death penalty for a person found guilty of murder is the race of the victim and, to a lesser extent, the race of the defendant: those most likely to receive the death penalty are blacks accused of killing whites.[43] Again, under the "cooperative" values, the state protects the hegemony of those in power. Real deterrence would focus on the conditions of crime.

Deterrence also has an exploitive element: authorities punish someone because of the effect they think it will have on others. The military is notorious for this in court-martial proceedings—particularly ones during a war, which carry a sentence of death.[44] Further, in civil courts even when a parole board determines that a prisoner is "reformed," it will deny parole if the members think the public is not yet "satisfied."[45]

The more overt justification for punishment is retribution or, in its noneuphemistic form, 'revenge'. Perhaps most familiar is "an eye for an eye and a tooth for a tooth." Under more refined arguments, the idea is that the wicked should be punished so that they don't prosper more than the virtuous. Thus, we punish others (it's always others, of course) in order to maintain a kind of cosmic distributive justice.[46] In the long run, the idea is that allowing some to inflict revenge on others helps maintain a harmonious social order.

Now, punishment and social order are certainly the focal points of our criminal-justice system. Nevertheless, for the sake of preserving the social order, many crimes go unnamed, especially the crimes of those in power. Society protects those in power by legalizing their endeavors, particularly through the very institutions Rawls lists: protection of freedom of thought, private property in the means of production, and the monogamous family. *Social order*

And as Ann Jones notes:

Americans clamor for law and order. We may overlook those criminals who rob, defraud, and kill us by the thousands—the corporate executives and their political allies who commit Three Mile Island, thalidomide, DES, Rely tampons, Agent Orange, and the Ford Pinto – but we cry out for protection from random criminals in the streets.[47]

Punishment, like altruism, accrues to those with lesser institutional power.

Finally, even for those who receive punishment, the judgments of the system have little if anything to do with the realities of their everyday lives other than to simply be a coercive force. Exploring everyday death and everyday justice in the case of Bernadette Powell,[m] Ann Jones writes:

> Our adversarial system of justice, a vestige of distant times and simpler beliefs, stages a contest between the truth and falsehood, good and evil, God and the devil. It never has been able to make allowances for the complexity we now see to be the human condition. . . . To the life of Bernadette Powell, to the life and death of Herman Smith, the courts were not so much unjust as immaterial. The process of trial and appeal and appeal again was an arduous exercise in irrelevancy.[48]

And she concludes:

> In the end it seemed to me that all our systems and our institutions for "dealing with" people are makeshift contraptions, cut to fit our prejudices and expectations, prefabricated to shelter and contain us, to save us from genuine human concern, to spare us alike the suffering we might see and the love we might achieve.[49]

I want to suggest that setting up a system of lesbian social justice will, in the long run, have the same result. What happens in the u.s. court system is not so much a matter of the miscarriage of justice as it is simply what 'justice' means.

'Justice' is a concept that exists to sort out competing claims within a system that has as its axis dominance and subordination. The function of justice is social control. And the *structure* of justice involves a paternal body which makes judgments for the purpose of enforcing a certain social order through punishment. Further, the concept presupposes a context in which people are egotistical, seek only to maximize their own self-interest, and must compete for limited resources. It presupposes and thus contributes to an essential relationship of antagonism among people. It is not clear that 'justice' would be a meaningful concept outside this framework.

---

m   In 1978, Bernadette Powell shot and killed her husband, who had beaten her and from whom she had subsequently separated. The charges began as involuntary manslaughter but developed into second degree murder.

The focus of justice is social organization and control. Our appeal to justice presupposes that institutions function for the good of their members when actually institutions function to preserve themselves and our need for them. Our appeal to justice presupposes that there is and should be such a creature as an impartial observer. It presupposes that the business of authorities is to define the interests of others and that those others, while perhaps having the right of appeal, nevertheless submit to judges. Thus, it encourages individuals to hand over their moral ability to a decision-making body. It may allow us to feel righteous at times. But it does not enable our moral agency. While a focus on duty fragments our integrity, a focus on justice undermines it.

When lesbians aspire to the ethics of the fathers, we lack imagination. As Mary Daly suggests in *Pure Lust:*

> Only by understanding [the] concept of universal gynocide can women begin to think, speak, and act beyond phallic "justice" and "injustice," and to bring forth the reign of Nemesis.[50]

She goes on:

> Unlike "justice," which is depicted as a woman blindfolded and holding a sword and scales, Nemesis has her eyes open and uncovered—especially her Third Eye. Moreover, she is concerned less with "retribution," in the sense of meting out of rewards and punishments, than with an internal judgment that sets in motion a new kind of psychic alignment of energy patterns.[51]

My desire, in writing this book, is to participate in a new kind of psychic alignment of energy patterns, a moral revolution.

Lesbians, Justice, Duty, and Caring

WITHIN LESBIAN COMMUNITY we are tempted to reach for a concept of 'social justice' when someone has done something we consider beyond the pale, particularly something one lesbian does willfully and intentionally to hurt another. For example, two lesbians are lovers and purchase a house together. They also start a business. Over time the relationship becomes a battering one. Finally one leaves and wants the community to boycott her ex-lover's business because in leaving the relationship she had to leave her home and her part of the business while the ex-lover kept it as her own.

Lesbians and social justice

Or another lesbian, not of u.s. citizenship and without a green card,[n]

---

n   A green card gives non-u.s. citizens permanent residency status in the u.s.

lives with her lover in a house with other lesbians. The two have provided the furnishings, china, and other necessities. Over time different values concerning material goods surface, the two being careful and neat, the others not. Eventually the two decide to move, and upon discovering that more of their things were lost or damaged than they realized, refuse to pay a bill. One of the other lesbians threatens to expose them to the immigration authorities.

In discussing such cases I have a number of things to say. However, none of them will be especially satisfactory, for there is no real satisfaction possible in these situations. In the first place, such actions did not come from nowhere, "out of the blue." A series of events took place, a series of actions; and finally one act or series of acts crossed a limit. When our interactions cross a limit, it is because there has been increasing and compounded failure in our relationships up to that time. And the function of the ethics I am attempting to outline concerns our interactions *before* they reach that point. More often than has been the case, we can attend individuals and individual interaction and begin changing our behavior before our frustration or misjudgments reach an explosion point.

Secondly, in stating this I am *not* advocating what Beverly Brown calls "the liberal lesbian-feminist process of endless discussion, the refusal to name any woman more culpable than another, and the mutual responsibility to struggle through a difficulty until it's resolved—even at the cost of our physical and emotional well-being."[52] In her article on lesbian battering she points out that the "elevation of non-judgmentalism in the community puts a lesbian who is beaten at a disadvantage."[53] She goes on:

> For friends and community the challenge is the acceptance of our right and obligation to voice ethical opinions without devolving into self-righteous moral pronouncements, uninformed gossip or conveniently dismissive psychologizing. If we avoid taking a stance by insisting that all actions and decisions of the batterer and the battered lesbian are equally valid, we aggravate the spread of manipulation, violence, and dismissal.[54]

What we need, she suggests, is to transform criticism from a weapon to a tool for growth.[55] And with this I agree.

It is important that lesbians attend each other, and make judgments—very specific judgments. Without this attending, we are not really engaging with each other—we're either ignoring each other or taking each other for granted. As it stands, we tend to remain aloof or ignore problem situations until they reach crisis proportions. They then catch us by surprise, and we rush in with simple judgments of right and wrong. I am suggesting we make judgments and choices, and that we do this with each other long before a crisis erupts.

So my first two points concern avoiding the need for systems of justice. My third point concerns systems of justice themselves. While we don't have a formal system of lesbian justice, we tend to be attracted by the idea of such a system. We tend to feel that without a system of justice, mean and nasty lesbians will go around intimidating others. And that may happen at times. But under full-blown legal systems intimidation still happens. What we forget is that a state can do exactly the same things as mean and nasty individuals; only when the state does them, they're called "legal." And the state has far greater capacity to do them.

We already have the ingredients we need to interact: our psychic faculty, intuition, attention, dreams, imagination, humor, emotions, playfulness, and reasoning. We need to develop these abilities. And at times things just don't work out. But if in our relationships we cannot create an environment in which integrity flourishes, even though at times harm also occurs – or at least if when things go sour, we can't keep them from progressing to the inexcusable limits – no institution and no system of justice ever will. Relying on individual lesbians and individual lesbian judgments within the community won't guarantee fairness all the time. But neither will any institution. There simply are no guarantees, though we can create illusions.

As an ideal of social order, 'justice' is irretrievably connected to punishment. We want fairness to reign, but at times it just doesn't. So when it doesn't, we call for a system of justice to punish the offenders. Someone's hurt me; I want to hurt her back. I want to feel her remorse, or I want to recapture some dignity I feel I lost. We're all familiar with the energy. And we don't have to make a mockery of it by calling it "reform" or "deterrence" or "legal" or even "ethical." The feelings are understandable, but institutionalizing them is altogether a different matter.

The punishment lesbians most often reach for is ostracizing. Ostracizing someone is pointing the finger and labeling her "sinner" while expecting others to conform to that judgment without making their own. I mean to challenge the idea of 'ostracizing'.   *Ostracizing*

In the first place, threats of ostracizing only intensify the problem. When someone suggests a lesbian has done something to another so heinous that she should be judged and collectively ostracized, the energy of the lesbians directly involved will focus on trying to "prove" their side, defending themselves against the perceptions and presumptions of the community, attempting to appear good – or at least not bad or wrong – and trying to determine the agendas of their "judges." While previously they may not have been concerned with assessing their part in the situation, threats of ostracizing will push them further from that task.

The idea of 'ostracizing' also presupposes there is a sharply defined absolute right and wrong which overrides any and all complexities of a situation. (In my experience this is not true.) Ostracizing, thus, moves our judgment to the superficial level of praise and blame. And if community members act to judge a lesbian at this level, she must either dissociate from fools or accept the authority of those "wiser" than she, thereby dissolving whatever integrity she has.

Further, in the process of ostracizing, as in any process, each lesbian involved will have her own agenda. For example, some lesbians who participate will do so because they are running from (rather than dismantling) that aspect of the "sinner" which they find in themselves.

Rather than embracing an idea of 'social justice', each lesbian can assess the particular situation for herself, decide her relationship to it and to those involved, and choose how she will act. In this respect I distinguish ostracizing from withdrawal. Withdrawing attention is a very serious matter among us. And we may do it to break certain patterns between us. Or we may do it because we understand how much withdrawal of attention hurts. But withdrawal is different from ostracizing a lesbian. Withdrawal is my own decision about my ability to respond in the situation and to the lesbian(s) in question. This is my choice based on my own reasons and feelings (which are subject to error), my own assessment, and based on my own limits. The idea of ostracizing someone suggests the idea of ganging up, enforcing certain rules of right behavior, and casting out the heathen.

Consider one approach to alcoholism. If a lesbian has a drinking problem, no one can get her to stop unless she asks for help. We can point out her problem. But if she rejects us, then we may have to withdraw from her–no matter how much we care for her. In fact that may be the only way left to us of caring for her. And we may lose her anyway. But if she won't decide to stop, staying with her only enables her alcoholism. Now if we withdraw, and others close to her also evaluate the situation for themselves and, having addressed this with her, decide they will withdraw, she may ultimately be isolated, finding no one who will tolerate her behavior. But this is not ostracizing, we don't cast her out as a sinner. There is a significant difference.[p]

---

p In other communities which exist within the dominant society–for example, jewish communities–ostracizing is sometimes used to get someone to stop something which, if they won't stop, would bring gentile (dominant) state intervention in the community.[56] Among lesbians, if the action in question is that serious, and if ostracizing is a possibility, then the same result can be accomplished as each lesbian makes her own judgment and withdraws.

I believe the processes we are going through now involve healing, and that is hardly a matter of one clear-cut path. A lesbian may even choose to remain an alcoholic because it is the only skill of survival under hetero-patriarchy she knows and trusts. That is her choice. That must be her choice. Another lesbian, however, does not have to participate in it.

Harriet Ellenberger notes that community energy involved in ostraciz-ing emerges from a therapeutic model, particularly as practiced with re-gard to alcoholism.[57] It involves a lesbian being expected to give herself over, in spirit at least, to a higher power. It involves the idea that she must give up her judgment to the judgment of others. It involves the idea that to be accepted back into the fold, a lesbian must accept the mothers' judg-ment of her.

In some programs, those trying to get a lesbian to deal with her alcohol-ism will tell the lover of a lesbian who has a drinking problem that her lover doesn't love her, that her lover cares for nothing but the bottle. And they will tell the lesbian who has a drinking problem that everything she has done and is doing is meaningless. No matter what projects she's en-gaged in—creating a business, creating a relationship—she is told they are all a matter of evasion and that she must admit she has no control. In some cases a lesbian is told that to pursue "the cure," she must leave her lover, sever herself from all projects she engaged in when drinking, and burn all her letters and journals from the past—she is to be born again, so to speak.

Now, if a lesbian can jump into a new way of being without transform-ing herself, then of course she can always jump back. Hence she must, for the rest of her life, regard herself as having submitted to a higher power which helps her find the strength to resist loss of control.

This model is one of turning ourselves over to counselors and thera-pists who will, by subtle means, tell us what to do, though often they simply wait in professional judgment for us to "discover" what it is we must do—we continue to attend the silent approval or disapproval of our "judges"; we turn over our will to a higher power. Now, it may be the case that for some lesbians who are alcoholics this is the only option besides re-maining drunk. And certainly there is some sense in which a lesbian must let go to heal herself, though by 'letting go' I do not mean 'surrender'.

My concern involves, however, the attitude the therapeutic model fosters in us toward lesbians whose actions have gone beyond the pale—the attitude that it is reasonable or useful or a good thing for a lesbian to let go of her own judgment and simply submit to the judgment of others. The problem with 'lesbian social justice' is the assumption that there is or could be a final judge.

It is important we make our own judgments rather than depend on others (a judge) to make them for us. And it is also important to realize that over time our judgments may change. Further, one judgment doesn't complete the matter. In almost any situation, we have to continue evaluating the circumstances, making new judgments as events progress. The point is that we make judgments, but we are not final judges. There are no final judges, nor should there be. The same spirit that keeps us from being dominated completely by heterosexual society will also rise up among us when social control is fostered from within the community. I do not want this spirit killed or even tamed.

We have, on a number of occasions in community, ostracized lesbians. Our ostracizing has not been formal or organized, but neither have our choices been a matter of individual judgment and withdrawal. Rather, they have been the actions of a herd, of catching a scent and shunning, neither confronting nor making our own judgments, leaving the lesbian in question utterly isolated and feeling persecuted.[58]

Further, the ostracizing has occurred, not because of the particular "crime" the lesbian committed, since others have committed the same "crimes," but because subsequently she would not prostrate herself before the community and accept judgment — because she did not declare the "error of her ways," change her judgments, and beg to be excused and accepted back into the fold.

While we may find we lose respect for a lesbian at a given time as a result of something she's done, we don't have to act to destroy her. Such desires involve a scenario of one lesbian saying "fie on thee foul dyke" and the other saying "hit me again," while the community sits in silent approval. The scenario we would enact is sadomasochism pure and simple. And while such scenarios are damaging to the lesbian, they do not destroy her. What they destroy is the ground of lesbian be-ing. By engaging in them, we make plausible the idea that a lesbian should give up her judgment to the mothers; we make plausible the idea that undermining a lesbian's moral agency is legitimate (has a social function); we make plausible the idea that within community it is appropriate for us to de-moralize a lesbian.

Now some may object, arguing that abandoning the idea of 'social justice' is unfair. Consider again the example of the two lesbians with the business. In this situation, as there is no lesbian "police force" to require the lesbian who battered her lover to give up her ex-lover's share of the house and business, then theoretically the ex-lover might at least get some satisfaction from a lesbian system of social justice in which the community collectively judges and ostracizes the lesbian who beat her.

Certainly the lesbian who was abused by her lover will reclaim dignity by fighting back. But I do not think her dignity will be restored by means of her ex-lover being collectively ostracized. Nor will ostracizing the ex-lover enable the lesbian to avoid a similar development of events in the future. I think movement out of the effects of abuse takes other forms.

Nevertheless, sometimes withdrawal won't end the interaction. It may be that one lesbian continuously harasses and begins to terrify another. For example, two lesbians are lovers. One breaks off the relation and starts a relationship with another. The ex-lover begins to harass her. She and her new lover move to a new town, but the ex-lover follows and continues the harassment. Ultimately, any words I have here are inadequate. This is a crisis, and lesbians in crisis have to use all our wit, ingenuity, skills, and resources to get through it. But there is a difference between making choices in a crisis and reaching for community social justice.

The problem with crises is that they interrupt all else that we're doing and rivet us on someone else's agenda which we didn't agree to, often one we wanted to ignore. However, a system of punishment allows us to continue to ignore the other's agenda only at a certain level; it structures our agendas too. In other words, while we want to turn to an authority to protect us from being riveted on someone else's agenda, we will nevertheless still be focused on that agenda and away from our own.

If, instead, we attend the crisis, asking for help from friends, doing whatever is necessary to take care of ourselves, and go through the time it takes to dissolve it (sometimes years, if one can't let go), as has been happening, we may begin gaining understanding of ways to keep similar situations from reaching crises in the future. For our goals include, not just terminating a crisis, but transforming ourselves and our interactions — learning from what goes on, developing different habits, and letting our experience and understanding affect the community.

The idea of 'ostracizing' encourages us to believe there is such a creature as an impartial observer. Yet it is we who make up the community, and it is we who interact with each other; and out of that interaction comes the meaning of our lives. Thus, again, I do not mean to suggest we make no judgments; the decision to withdraw, for example, involves very specific judgments. And I do not mean to suggest we not pass on information. I am simply suggesting that we dispense with the belief that it would be ideal to have a lesbian authority who enforces our "impartial" judgments and punishes "offenders"; I am suggesting that we resist any urge for lesbian social control. Should we work toward developing an authority, it will mean that we have decided we don't want to attend each other. Further, if in our communities we continue to choose to flirt with ritual violence — in the form of punishment, in the form of controlling and humiliating another with or without her consent — then dominance and subordination will become part of lesbian meaning.

Lesbian revolution will not happen by an authority *making* us behave, nor will it occur through therapeutic or herd behavior. Tyranny results, as Simone de Beauvoir tells us, when we flee choice by trying to submit ourselves to values which we pretend are not chosen but rather are unconditional.[59] My argument is that what we have done through ostracizing is just such a fleeing of choice. 'Justice' is like a drug, and it keeps us hooked on the structures of patriarchy, and dominance and subordination – the fathers' idea of "cooperation."

Clowns   It is not lesbian social justice we need, in my opinion. We need (more) clowns. Clowns are central in many non-dominant cultures.[60] And as Granny explains in *Daughters of Copper Woman*, clowns show us things about ourselves, help us to gain perspective:

> If you thought every word you spoke was gospel, the clown would just stroll along behind you babblin' away like a simple-mind or a baby. Every up and down of your voice, the clown's voice would go up and down until you finally Heard what an ass you were bein'. Or maybe you had a bad temper and yelled a lot when you got mad, or hadn't learned any self control or somethin' like that. Well, the clown would just have fits. Every time you turned around there'd be the clown bashin' away with a stick on the sand or kickin' like a fool at a big rock, or yellin' insults back at the gulls, and just generally lookin' real stupid.
>
> We needed our clowns, and we used'em to help us all learn the best ways to get along with each other. Bein' an individual is real good, but sometimes we're so busy bein' individuals we forget we gotta live with a lot of other people who all got the right to be individuals too, and the clowns could show us if we were gettin' a bit pushy, or startin' to take ourselves too serious. Wasn't nothin' sacred to a clown. Sometimes a clown would find another clown taggin' along behind, imitatin', and then the first one knew that maybe somethin' was gettin' out of hand, and maybe the clown was bein' mean or usin' her position as a clown to push people around and sharpen her own axe for her own reasons.
>
> But mostly the clowns were very serious about what they did.[61]

And as Kate Clinton writes:

> Each of us is equal to the task of making light, shedding light on our experiences, encouraging each other to change and move.[62]

If we go on to encourage clowns and develop our attending, intelligibility, and playful world travel, we will not be fleeing choice but embracing it – choice about how to understand ourselves and each other, choice about how to engage, choice about the energy we invoke.

In the long run, holding an ideal of 'lesbian social justice' in an attempt to ensure that goodness will prevail among us interrupts rather than aids us in our judgments and interactions, and as such it interrupts lesbian connection. What we as lesbians have within our power is choice – choice about how we are going to care.

Thus, I want to consider the ideas of 'duty' and 'obligation' among les- *Lesbians and duty* bians. For aside from crises, it is from the ideas of 'duty' and 'obligation', and hence the idea of the need for sanctions against those who don't fulfill their duty and accept their fair share of obligation, that the attraction to 'social justice' arises among us.

Someone might argue that, even if there are problems with institutionalized justice, at least 'duty' and 'obligation' are central ethical concepts for lesbians because they lie at the heart of moral responsibility. That is, being ethical *means* being responsible to others, and that means accepting our obligations toward others.

Yet does a focus on duty, on following rules, and on obligation enhance lesbian connection and community? I want to suggest that acting from duty and obligation interrupts lesbian connection rather than enhancing it. In fact, a focus on obligation and duty is part of the whole dominant/subordinate value of the rule of the fathers, which would have us substitute control for integrity.

Duty has always struck me as an empty and boring consideration in choice and action, equal in its lack of ethical import to utilitarian judgments of social expediency. Marilyn Frye suggests the problem is that duty lacks emotion:[63] we are supposed to ascertain our duty by means of reason alone. Yet ethical considerations involve how we interact, and how we interact involves how we respond to each other – hardly a matter of pure reason.

Nevertheless, some philosophers contrast an ethic of duty with an ethic of care, and argue that acting from duty makes a person more moral than *Duty versus caring* acting from care.[64] For example, suppose we have a friend sick in the hospital. The idea is that if we act from duty, we will do the "right" thing even when we are not so inclined: for example, we will visit our friend on a cold winter day when we'd rather stay home in bed.[65]

Now in the first place, when we are connected with someone and she's in the hospital, we just visit her. That's part of our connection. If we need duty or obligation as a motive, we haven't a connection.

Secondly, as an intimate of yours, I may nevertheless have a significant reason why going to the hospital is a horrible prospect. It may be that I've had very bad experiences under the power and attitudes of doctors – being coerced into a mastectomy, for example – and that I hesitate to attend you at the hospital because of what it calls up in me. I may also be able to attend you precisely because of my experience. But if I cannot, it may be worse for both of us if I visit rather than if I don't. Certainly, under such conditions I won't likely bring my healing energy, and I instead may contribute panic to the energy you have to handle. When we engage, we engage because of who we are individually. If we try to pursue a relationship because of who we think we ought to be, then that relationship will turn into a bind.

There tend to be two main ideas involved in the appeal to duty as a regulator of caring. On the one hand (from the kantian tradition), some philosophers appeal to obligation and duty as a means of making sure we are "perfectly moral beings."[66] The idea is that if we act from duty, we will always do the right thing for the right reason. If I simply rely on my ability to care, I might not do the right thing and, even if I did, I would be somehow less moral than if I instead acted from duty.

Alternatively (from the utilitarian tradition), philosophers appeal to duty as a matter of addressing competing interests.[67] My friend has a need—being visited at the hospital—which competes significantly with my desire to stay home in my warm bed. Thus, I need a sense of obligation to sort it out, to help me be impartial in assessing needs, to show me that in this case I ought to put aside my own needs and interests in order to accommodate hers.

I want to discuss three assumptions in these two appeals to duty: (1) that interacting is essentially a matter of sorting out competing claims, (2) that choice, therefore, is a matter of sacrifice and compromise rather than focus and creation, and (3) that caring is a matter of happenstance and at the very least needs the guidance of authority (reason) and duty to be worthwhile.

The idea that interacting is a matter of sorting out competing claims is *Interacting is not* perfected in mercantile culture.[68] And our considerations are peppered *negotiating* with such language. We talk of our investment in a relationship, of investing time and energy in each other, of negotiating differences; we want to make sure we get our fair share in return for what we give, that we get our needs met, and we often regard the relationship itself as an investment. Indeed, such mercantile considerations have replaced our caring in many instances.

Yet responding to each other need not be an exchange of debits and credits. If we regard our connections as essentially a matter of negotiating competing needs and wants and of sacrificing ourselves for the other or of maintaining our interests at her expense, then we will begin to take each other for granted or we will be trying to control each other.

For example, one lover has an exam coming up, and the other takes on extra chores in their home so the first can devote more of her time to study. As a result, the first feels she owes something to her lover and, the next time the lover has a need, does something to pay her off. If this assessment of the situation continues, each will be responding to the other primarily in terms of who owes whom what. For example, one might do something for the other just to gain a "credit" which she can call in, or to maintain the "control" of not being "in debt" to the other. The energy of their responses, particularly their desire, will get lost, and ultimately the connection will become at best tedious.

We can decide not to regard our interactions as a series of power checks and balances. On one occasion I may take on extra chores while you go into an intense period of work; on another occasion I may not, and expect you to make other arrangements. These choices concern how I focus my energy, and it is through them that I create meaning. What we get from connecting with another is not a series of bargains in return for a few compromises. What we get from connecting with another is the connection.

Now, someone might object that these suggestions come from an assumption of material security such that the duties (literally *debts)* others owe us are not that important, nor can such suggestions involve any great worry about not being able to meet our own debts. 'Obligation', someone might argue, is at its root, a bond.[69] I think this is true, and I want to suggest that focusing on duty and obligation solidifies those bonds into binds. That we have had to rely on duty and obligation to ensure our own survival does not mean we should embrace them as inherently valuable.[70] Further, in the long run, if there are problems with one lesbian meeting her "debts" to another, appealing to duty is not going to solve them.

In addition, we often use money to control each other — we invest in someone to ensure our connection as if we were investing in the relationship itself. Just as we use vulnerability to force a connection, we use economics to do the same; in fact, we can make ourselves economically vulnerable. And when we find the relationship changing or when we find it was not what we thought it would be, we focus on economics, using it to force a continued connection, to keep some level of access; or we insist on an immediate division and settlement to "punish" the other.

When we do enter into economic connections with each other, the point is not to tie the other to us but rather to make something possible that was not possible for either alone. We may buy a house or start a business with a lover or with a friend. When we start such a venture, we may make agreements with each other about what we plan. But our choice to stick with them need not come from obligation, instead it comes from our involvement in the venture.

Such ventures include risk, and just as not all economic ventures work economically, so not all economic ventures work in other ways. What we sought to create may not be possible . . . for us, here, now, under these conditions. And understanding that can help us keep from panic so that we don't use the economic connection against each other. After all, while at times an economic connection with an intimate can be a matter of financial survival, if we had never met her, we would have gone on to find other means of survival.

Regarding our interactions as a matter of sorting out competing interests presupposes a basic antagonism between us precisely because it presupposes our needs are inherently in conflict. But this model of needs is inaccurate. In the first place, it draws on the false dichotomy between egoism and altruism. Secondly, it is simply not true that our interests are inherently in conflict. And thirdly, the model ignores (is ignorant of) what goes on in sharing.[q] Sometimes I want to do something by myself. Other times I want someone else I care about to be there with me, enjoying the event too. This second situation is not a matter of one compromising some of her individual wants to accommodate another. Rather, the experience in sharing is different.

There is something magical about someone else being there with me to enjoy something special. (There is also something magical about another sharing in time of trouble.) This phenomenon of sharing, of our energies entwining and so enhancing the situation, is not a matter of the quantitative calculation of interests, needs, or desires, nor can the question of competing interests find fertile ground here. Sharing is not about compromise, it is about creating something new that emerges from the two lesbians (or three or thirteen or three hundred) combined.

Nevertheless, sometimes we do come into conflict, and an appeal to duty is supposed to help us do the "right" thing, for example, when interacting with lesbians who we dislike or with lesbians whose dearest values are in conflict with ours.[71] Now, when in a community project we come into conflict with someone, we can assess the situation: we can use intelligibility to understand the importance of her value as she perceives it, gain perspective on the situation, and decide whether there is a difference of values that undermines the project. If we decide we can and will still work on the project, we can proceed being aware that not only our values but also hers contribute to what we are creating and that this creation involves various lesbians together, for we cannot do this alone. In this case, since duty keeps us focused only on our selves and what we are supposed to do, an appeal to duty may interrupt the engagement of intelligibility. At best it is superfluous to the process. If, on the other hand, the differences are too great, then what we sought to create won't emerge from this

---

q   In discussing 'sharing', I do not invoke the psychotherapeutic use of 'sharing' which turns interactions into a unidirectional, mercantile exchange as in "Talking isn't talking, it's sharing," or "Thank you for sharing."

project, and the two lesbians (or groups of lesbians) simply have to carry on their projects separately or not at all. In this case, an appeal to duty is useless.

The same is true when the problems we face are a matter of personal dislike among lesbians. If the conflict is so bad, it may be that we decide to withdraw, since what we sought to create will not emerge. Conversely, if working together is possible, then through intelligibility we may come to understand that both embrace the same ultimate values – being deeply committed to lesbians, for example. And this can help us keep perspective on the situation. In the long run, interacting is not an antagonistic matter of sorting out competing claims, it is a matter of creating value.[r]

And this leads to the second theme involved in a focus on duty – namely, how we perceive choice. I argued in chapter two that choice is a creation, not a sacrifice. We can regard our ability to make choices as a source of power, the power to create – to focus attention and so care – rather than as a loss or sacrifice or compromise. And if we learn to approach our choices as a matter of creation, not sacrifice, then we will be less likely to be focused on an antagonistic process of who owes us what as a result of what we "sacrificed," and hence less likely to need a motive of duty to keep us doing the "right" thing.

Duty as undermining responsiveness

And this leads to the third idea behind the focus on duty, namely the nature of care. The idea, from anglo-european tradition, is that acting from duty means we have a desire to do the morally right thing *because* it is the morally right thing, not just because we happen to care. As a result of the anglo-european split between reasoning and emotions, caring is viewed as a matter of mere happenstance. On this theory, when we care, we are simply reacting to whatever is around us. We have made no judgments in caring. Thus, we need a sense of duty to help us do the "right" thing.

---

r   Some collectives have found ways of working together such that essentially the same core of lesbians comprise the collective over years to run a restaurant, for example, or publish a newspaper. In other collectives, members are more transient, often out of necessity due to the nature of the work involved such as rape crisis or shelter work. Even though the process of selection weeds out lesbians who tend to dominate, for example through the training involved in learning to work a rape crisis line, a lesbian can work on such a project only so long before she begins to diminish. Sometimes the amount of work (rather than the type of work) involved is so much that a lesbian can sustain the time commitment only for a fixed period. In such cases a collective might create something like "friends of the collective" so that those who are committed to the projects can remain involved at a less intense level.[72] Through all of this, however, duty has not been the energy through which the problems are solved.

Recall the structure of acting from duty. It involves severing reasoning and emotions, regarding reason as controlling emotions (self-control), and attempting to rise above the boundaries of nature (rather than working within them). Focusing on duty severs reasoning from emotions, and totally discounts dreaming, imagination, humor, psychic faculty, playfulness, and intuition in the development of an ethical being. In other words, acting from duty undermines our ability to care by discounting the majority of our faculties.

On the other hand, caring, and so connecting, involves our whole being; it is a matter of judging and focus, not of happenstance. When I care, I am making a choice of whom or what to focus on for a number of reasons. When I don't care, that is also a matter of choice and focus, and there are reasons for such choices. How I focus my attention is how I participate in creating meaning in this living.

Acting from duty and obligation relegates caring to the background in our interactions, or even renders it irrelevant. As Nettie observes in *The Color Purple:*

> [The Missionary Society of New York] is run by white people and they didn't say anything about caring about Africa, but only about duty.[73]

In many cases, when people do what they consider the "morally right" thing, they assume it doesn't matter if they care. In fact, acting from duty – in this case noblesse oblige – is a way to avoid attending what is going on rather than addressing it. Intelligibility and playful world travel – reaching toward others on their own terms, not just on ours – has not been a part of ethical theory owing, I would suggest, to anglo-european and u.s. imperialism named paternalism. In the name of knowing what is best for others, duty has replaced caring.

Within lesbian community, relying on duty and obligation has undermined our responsiveness to each other. Consider one way lesbians are caught up with obligation as lovers. In the movie *Tread Softly* two lesbians are breaking up – both have had expectations of the other which have not been met, and both have felt betrayed.[74] One lesbian tends to equate care and concern with commitment in the form of actual promises of time. She feels that when someone isn't where she says she'll be, it is an indication that the other doesn't care and is treating her without respect, callously. The other lesbian feels restricted by such a definition of commitment and finds it inhibits her ability to open herself and give. She feels that someone so focused on form isn't paying attention to who she is and the nature of their interactions, but only to a show of relating.

Now, both have intelligible concerns and needs. The one who regards commitment as a matter of appointments and dates, of fulfilling what was

promised, may function better when she can plan time together, antici-
pate the interaction, put down her other concerns, and "dress up her
heart."[75] The other may function better when she can devote her full attention to what she's doing at the moment without having to keep part of
her attention on whether it's time to stop now and what she's going to do
next. In this case, if each is clear about her own focus and limits, then she
can respond to the other through intelligibility—by understanding that
they are not alike in this respect—and thus not become threatened by the
difference. In so responding, both can work out ways to interact. (And it
may be that they find they just don't fit as lovers. Nevertheless, they can
work to find a way to remain connected.)

Alternatively, each can settle back, secure with obligation—the one has
an obligation to be where she says she will be; the other has an obligation
to understand her lover's idiosyncrasies. After all, to accept responsibility, according to the dictionary, is to accept "constraints on our conduct
or on our choice of course."[76] And that is what we are told commitment
means. Nevertheless, although acting from obligation may cement the
connection, at least temporarily, it will not develop the connection or the
commitment. Instead, duty will come to replace the actual basis for the
relationship. Obligation was not the reason the two got together to begin
with—that reason, whatever it was, tends to get lost.

Reliance on duty also undermines our responsiveness in more particular ways. An appeal to duty hides the issues behind whatever problems
arose which led to the appeal. To say we have a duty to do something can
be a way of bypassing the points of contention. For example, if a choice I
make hurts you, saying what I did was a matter of obligation is a way of
bypassing or discounting the fact that, while my choice may involve important things, it also has the consequence of hurting you. Thus, one way
obligation helps us ensure that we made the "right" choice is by allowing
us to ignore any "bad" consequences.

Beyond this, focusing on duty can be a way to avoid considering or explaining action.[77] For example, saying I have a duty to do something with
another can take the place of examining why I am doing it. I may, for example, hope I will change her feelings about something, I may want to
avoid her criticism or community criticism, or I may be afraid of losing
her; and so I act. But the *reason* I give is that it is my obligation. In this
way, duty undermines our intelligibility.

The sense that we have a duty often sets in when we begin to experience
ourselves as lacking resources, and we begin to feel we aren't present
enough, not engaged enough.[78] Partly because of this, the appeal to duty
and obligation surfaced through political correctness, which transformed
from an energy of caring and connection into a set of rules. And as a result

we began to lose the responsiveness of our lesbian perceptions. As Juana María Paz notes:

> I existed in a social atmosphere that did not allow for honest, direct communication of basic needs and goals and I stood helplessly by while all of our real motivations went underground, only to surface again couched in political terms.[79]

As a result of our frustration, we talked about the need for justice; we appealed to obligation as a way of guaranteeing rightness in our choices; and we watched what we had begun to create slip away. The point is, duty does not yield lesbian connection, only caring can do that.

Now in challenging the concept of 'duty', I do not mean to suggest that care can't be used as a means of control.[80] For example, most of us have heard or exclaimed, "If you *really* cared, you would . . ." And many of us have been told we must care about others when we really have no such feelings for them at all. Notice, however, such ideas don't really address the judgments of our caring but instead operate in a context of duty and obligation – only now it is caring itself which has become our duty.[s]

Caring is not a matter of duty, though it does involve effort. Baba Copper writes:

> As for how old lesbians want to be treated within the lesbian world, that is difficult to describe. There is a kind of care which we take with women we wish to know. We give them our attention. We make allowances for their peculiarities. We monitor our own behavior for impositions or assumptions which we cannot justify to ourselves, or to them. Caring treatment involves effort.[81]

When we care, we look forward to each other's company. We think about and plan things together, we seek each other out. And when we are apart from those we love – children, companion animals, friends, and lovers – they are still with us, often present in our consciousness, part of the meaning of what we do. Duty does not encompass this.

As Audre Lorde has implied, a system which reduces our work to a travesty of necessities, to duty, is one which robs our work of its lesbian desire.[82] Such a system has us resort to paternalism rather than intelligi-

---

s   Often familial "caring" operates on obligation. There may be genuine concern. The mother, the brother, the father, the sister, may be concerned about the other, or they may think of the other on significant holidays, they may miss the other. But such concern does not necessarily involve intelligibility, it does not involve the attempt to understand the other or be understood by her. Thus, they miss the daughter/sister they wanted or wish they had, but not the one they have. As a result, their concern is not real caring – emotion without understanding is not emotion.

bility, and it encourages self-control instead of integrity. When we find ourselves appealing to duty in order to act, we have lost the focus of our lesbian desire.

When we appeal to duty, we have also lost the focus of our lesbian anger. When we reach for duty or obligation, we are ignoring these energies and judgments rather than embracing them. Hence we split ourselves and lose the energy of connection, the energy of caring. In contrast, Pat Parker vows:

> I will come with my many sisters
> and decorate the streets
> with the innards of those
> brothers in womenslaughter.
> No more, can I dull my rage
> in alcohol & deference
> to *men's* courts.
> I will come to my sisters,
> not dutiful,
> I will come strong.[83]

The energy that moved women toward liberation and the energy that moved us to come out was not a matter of duty. We did not determine the morally right thing to do and then act from duty.[†] Rather, suddenly parts of our selves connected—our anger, perhaps, our perceptions, our intuition, our humor, our imagination, our desire, nuestra facultad, our sense of play, for example—and we made choices. It is reviving and continuing this movement that concerns me.

Thus I do not mean by 'care', 'care-taking'—for example, being "charged with the protection, welfare, or maintenance of something or someone,"[84]   *Care-taking* or otherwise caring for someone perceived to have lesser abilities than our own. Such an attitude still involves paternalism, in this case the idea that we must take over for another because they don't have our abilities. Behind this idea is the assumption that when we interact among peers, we treat others as equals in all regards.[85] Thus we assume we need special consideration for those we regard as not our peers.

---

†   At times there was a sense among some that women had an obligation to come out. But we also discovered that those who slept with lesbians out of political obligation exploited their lovers—not necessarily because they were inherently exploitive but because of their energy in responding to a sense of duty. I will add that if we hear an argument we find compelling and so act, it is a mistake if we regard ourselves as acting from duty. Any given argument may be wrong. If we find ourselves acting on it, it is because we are thinking the same thing, because this something has become our choice too.

The assumption that we treat peers as having equal abilities to our own is erroneous. Part of really responding to each other involves acknowledging our different abilities. You may help me to develop my psychic ability and I may help you to learn to take photographs – how to frame an image, how the angle of the shot affects the composition, and so on. But we don't treat each other as lesser for having differing abilities.

That is, when interacting with those we consider our peers, we do not treat each other as if our abilities were the same, and we do not treat each other as lesser for it. More likely we just treat each other as regular, and get on with helping each other. Thus, when we interact with someone in a way that treats them as lesser than us, it is not (simply) because we perceive them as not having abilities we have, but because we perceive them as incompetent in general. Consequently, it is crucial to examine our attitudes when we engage with someone we decide to treat as lesser than ourselves.

The mother-child relationship offers one such possible situation. Some will argue that the mother-child relationship involves a special sort of care-taking, a care-taking from which special moral values emerge because of, not in spite of, the child's dependency and the differences in power and abilities between mother and child.[86] Thus, so one argument goes, the mother responds to the child precisely because the child is vulnerable and dependent. Yet the special, vulnerable position of the child in no way guarantees responsiveness from the mother. In many cases of incest, the mother will side with the father and gaslight the daughter's perceptions. I do not find that dependency itself necessarily inspires caring or even care-taking.

Nevertheless, clearly an infant needs a lot of tending to. On the other hand, the purpose of parenting is to raise children to be able to develop their abilities and make their own choices. And that isn't going to happen if a child is treated as lesser.

My point is, how do we treat each other? Do we act to take over and control, or do we act to enable and develop our own and each others' integrity and agency? The type of caring I am invoking is the caring we show those we respect, including children, the kind of caring that invokes the other's integrity. And my concern is that when we regard ourselves as taking over for someone else, when we invoke paternalism (or maternalism) as care-taking and regard *that* as caring, we undermine her integrity and agency.

Able-bodied lesbians interacting with lesbians who are differently abled often operate from duty and so tend toward objectification. Because of the concept of normalcy promoted by educational, athletic, and medical institutions, we locate ourselves on a continuum. We tend to reify those who have "important" abilities we don't have and we tend to pity those who don't have our abilities. Thus many lesbians who can see tend to approach a lesbian who does not as if she can't perceive what is going on, as if she is less competent, can't think as well. For example, a lesbian who sees may slow down her speaking and increase her volume when talking to a lesbian who does not, leaving it to the lesbian who does not see to tell her friend to snap out of it.[87] In such situations, lesbians who see often shift gears from comfortable attention and interaction right into duty and obligation. Again, the issue is not the difference in abilities but the perception of general incompetence. That we rely on duty and obligation to interact in a world where people are differently abled is a sign of how rotten our values really are.[88]

The bottom line of the value I'm suggesting is respect—for ourselves and each other—not establishing authority and chain of command (even benevolent): enabling, not controlling, playing with, not dominating, and so on. And I include in this not just lesbians of whatever abilities, but other animals—domesticated and wild—and, indeed, the whole planet. The caring I'm concerned with is a caring among those whom we would give the respect of peers whose abilities are quite varied.

Caring is a choice we make. If we don't choose to attend each other, if we ignore or cease caring about each other and about how we interact as lesbians, if we cease trying to understand the long-range and complex consequences of our means of interacting, then appeals to duty and obligation aren't going to bring in new value, won't encourage the transformation of consciousness which began as we came out, won't result in anything but a slow and progressive referring back to the values of heterosexual society—beginning with the seductive and deceptive value of paternalism. If we come to lesbian community because we feel lesbians have a duty to treat us better than everyone else treats us, or because we feel we have a duty toward lesbians, lesbian community won't work. *Lesbian connection*

The question is: What are we going to make of lesbian connection, of those interactions between us which have been so enlivening and so creative, of that context in which lesbianism, not heterosexualism, is the value we embrace? Again, it is not obligation which will carry us through the transformation of consciousness necessary to dismantle the values among us of the fathers. Rather, it is caring, caring which results in our sparking and igniting as well as our cajoling and challenging.

As Jan Raymond writes:

Affection has a meaning which conveys more than the personal movement of one woman toward another. Affection in this sense means the state of influencing, acting upon, moving, and impressing, and of being influenced, acted upon, moved, and impressed by other women.[89]

The concepts of 'duty' and 'obligation' do not represent lesbian connection. Obligation does not measure lesbian caring and network. Duty is not the essence of our connection, nor is it the reason we are lesbians. Lesbians do not come together out of duty, nor does obligation hold us together as lovers, friends, collectives, or community. And neither duty nor obligation will hold us together over time in a way that we become an energy field capable of resisting oppression.

I am suggesting that duty and obligation are not part of Lesbian Ethics. And I am also suggesting that caring, while not the sort of energy that can be forced or guaranteed, nevertheless comprises the heart of lesbian connection.

Integrity and Agency

Moral revolution

I HAVE BEEN trying to develop an ethics relevant to lesbians under oppression, one which avoids both blaming the victim and victimism. We do not control situations, we act in them. We are here now, and what we do has made and will continue to make a difference. Whatever limits we face, our power lies in understanding that, and so in choice.

I also want an ethics which honors and embraces our lesbian spirits. I am interested in that essence, that agency, through which we began rejecting the norms of heterosexualism. As Julia Penelope notes:

If there's one thing that all lesbians have in common, it's the ability to say "no" to coercion. Tell a lesbian not to do something, and she'll turn right around and do it. That's the essence of the lesbian. (JEB calls it our "bad attitude.")[90]

We are an obnoxious, unruly bunch. And so an ethic that suits us is not going to be one which functions to keep us in line. An ethic that suits us is one which will provide fertile ground for the development of our lesbian be-ing.

By coming out, we have been able to break at some level from the dominant ideology and so, in certain respects, we have exhibited the capacity for being solitary, independent, self-reliant, and aggressive. But what we broke to was a connecting with other lesbians. Our desire has been, not to remain solitary and independent, but to connect, to pool our resources, and to build something which makes real our dreams and what we imagine.

And so I also want an ethics that embraces plurality, not uniformity, one which locates us in relationship to each other where we gain perspectives and develop interactively. As autokoenonous beings, we are individuals in a context; this in turn makes it possible for us to develop the complexity of lesbian meaning. We both create and are created by lesbian community.

So I have called for a moral revolution. In the process I have challenged the concepts of 'altruism', self-sacrifice', 'unconditional loving', 'vulnerability', 'paternalism', 'protection', 'safety', 'reason' over and against 'emotions', 'self-control', 'privacy of feelings', 'praise and blame', 'accountability', 'justice', 'duty', and 'obligation', arguing that all involve power as control and thus are not part of Lesbian Ethics. So what, then, is ethics about?

In my opinion, the heart of ethical focus, the function of ethics, and what will promote lesbian connection, is enabling and developing individual integrity and agency within community. I have always regarded morality, ideally, as a system whose aim is, not to control individuals, but to *make possible,* to encourage and enable, individual development. *[Integrity]*

Ethics need not lie with laws, avoidance of error, nor group interest or self-interest. My concern with ethics is not in bargaining or juggling or calculating interactions to secure either justice ideally or social control practically. All those considerations, together with considerations of principle and duty in traditional ethics, tend to shortchange or even bypass individual integrity and agency because, in a sense, they presuppose antagonism and so nourish it.

The modern tradition in anglo-european ethics starts with egoistic strangers and then works to devise a set of values that will get them to "cooperate." Its focus is regulation or conformity and coercion ("cooperation").

The ethics I am moving toward begins with those who have resisted, at some level, that "cooperation" and who have refocused. It starts with those who live under oppression. It starts with those who have a sense of desiring connection, who move toward each other. It starts with those who have many differences and who also have a ground on which to learn from those differences; thus it starts with those can find the richness with which to tolerate the contradictions that must necessarily (in our generations) appear.

By acknowledging a starting point different from that of modern anglo-european ethics, we find that different questions come into focus, for example: how to survive and resist patriarchy, including patriarchal privilege; how to avoid de-moralization; how we go on in situations which we do not control and among others whose agendas don't always match ours; how to address different boundaries; how we develop the ability to attend; how we gain perspective and understanding from each other; what works among us and what seems not to; how we individually and collectively create value. And all of this is connected with lesbian integrity and lesbian agency.

The concept of 'integrity' is problematic, for one meaning of 'integrity' is "a rigid adherence to a code of behavior." This is not what I invoke when I talk of integrity.[91] I invoke, rather, a concept of wholeness. Janice Raymond argues that 'integrity' means a whole "from which no part can be taken."[92]

Lesbians are a deeply wounded people as a result of oppression, and each carries in her a violence capable of devastating others when she perceives herself as being backed into a corner. In suggesting that the focus of lesbian ethics be integrity and agency, I am suggesting we can start with where each is—rather than trying to force some idea of where we should be—and concern ourselves with what enables us to develop our moral agency. The changes that have come and those that will come, come from the heart. And they come in each lesbian's own time—as she is able and ready—not on someone else's schedule.

The bloodroot collective writes:

> We want to create a context where women can make vital connections: the careful weaving and mending which must be done on a daily basis, so that we and other women can begin to heal ourselves and our sense of wholeness. To hold on to some part of the truth of our lives and to have the strength of conviction to continue: this is our challenge.[93]

Focusing on integrity means acknowledging our selves, which in no way is equivalent to regarding our selves as fixed or unchanging. It means proceeding from self-understanding and developing that understanding through attending how we are reflected in the perspectives of other lesbians. It means becoming aware of what parts of our selves we want to change, what parts go on hold for now, what parts center us, and what parts we want to develop at any given point. It means periodically assessing our selves in terms of our values and in relation to others and their values.

Concern with integrity also means acknowledging and addressing our contexts. It means acknowledging the dominant society and which of its values we reject. It means exploring our racial, ethnic, religious, and class backgrounds, and considering which values from these contexts enrich and enhance lesbian meaning.[94] And it means acknowledging our lesbian context—developing a steadfastness and persistence as lesbians.

Concern with integrity, thirdly, means having an awareness of our selves as agents acting in situations and hence an awareness of what is our part in any given situation; it means having a sense of our selves as one among many. In general, integrity means being aware of and assessing our selves among others in our many aspects. And agency, as I argued in chapter five, involves being able to go on in situations and act.

I believe an ethics which focuses on developing lesbian integrity and agency promotes lesbian connection because it can enable us to develop *Lesbian ability* lesbian ability and lesbian responsiveness outside the framework of both the competitive and the "cooperative" values of the rule of the fathers.

We can work toward interacting in such a way that we each acknowledge and value (judge, evaluate) each lesbian's abilities as the means by which she draws the energies of the universe together and fashions patterns within a context.

Someone might object to this, pointing out, for example, that some lesbians' abilities include verbal character assassination. Certainly, verbal character assassination is an ability a lesbian develops in consideration of the world she lives in. But while she may use it against lesbians, it also can be a significant survival skill. Further, we can ask what values are emerging in lesbian context that make the choice to use it plausible to her. Hers is an ability to perceive aspects of others, together with verbal facility; this combination can be a tremendous skill. My concern is with the development of our abilities outside the framework of the fathers.

Among lesbians we have been learning to let our varied abilities complement each other, for example the abilities of a street-wise hustler and the abilities of someone skilled in socially "polite" behavior. In a lesbian context, the abilities of lesbians from all backgrounds have been emerging. I want this process to be recognized and to continue, for it is here that our abilities can develop. For example, the trickster or clown can develop her abilities in a context which does not promote hierarchy and bureaucracy.

Now if we focus on ability, it is important that we realize we do not need to pursue the competitive values of the fathers such that our en- *The competitive* deavors become a matter of proving that one lesbian is better than all *values* others at something. We need not regard developing and recognizing ability itself as establishing a hierarchy (a "stack o' priests"[95]), for ability does not simply involve those activities designated as deserving award by an external authority. Each lesbian's abilities are different, and what she offers is her own concatenation of energy.

After all, to claim that one is the best in the world isn't to state very much at all. For example, to state that at some point in time one person is the fastest runner in the world must leave cheetahs laughing. On the other hand, the ability of a runner, her beauty – whether she is a cheetah, an olympic athlete, or a snail – lies in her form and flow of movement. That one has created this pattern of energy, this flow and form, here and now . . . well, that's quite impressive.

Consider, for example, the lesbian theory available or the lesbian music or the work of healers or of collectives. Is one book or one song or one remedy or one joke or one project better than all the rest? Certainly, at any given moment we may be especially drawn to one song or album, for example, since it crystallizes something deep within us. But to try to rank lesbian contributions one on top of another is to lose the way each contributes to a ground of be-ing which helps the rest of us create.

We can be curious about, appreciate, and even delight in what others offer without evaluating our own offerings against theirs. In developing our own ability, we can then realize that each writer or artist or healer or comic or community organizer offers something unique with her energy, something which is both limited and focused. We are one among many. Each has her own talents and needs and agendas which can develop in a lesbian context. Remembering this, we can realize that we also make a difference. And this ability is part of our moral agency.

Lesbian responsiveness

As for the ability of responsiveness, I am suggesting that rather than focusing on how we have responsibility to others, we focus on how each is able to respond to others. 'Responsibility', like 'accountability', encourages a one-way process—she's responsible to me; I'm responsible to her. As María Lugones notes, responsibility encourages us to act to stay in charge.[96] It is one of the ways we manage to keep (some) control over each other. Responsiveness, on the other hand, is two-way and focuses, rather, on the interactive nature of our engagements. Thus, when someone close to us is not responsive to us, does not respond to us, rather than react in outrage, feeling hurt at some injury, we might work to discover why the connection is broken.

Responsiveness is the energy and perception that brings us together, that draws us, the energy referred to by the slogan "lesbians ignite."[97] That energy keeps us moving, keeps us taking risks, finding ways to attend, to connect. When we have lost that energy, we start talking about responsibility. After that we become de-moralized and work toward resigning ourselves to authorities.

Responsiveness is the ability to acknowledge each other, to listen to, argue with, criticize, play with, get angry at, joke with, befriend, celebrate—in short, to engage. And we don't always respond well. I don't mean that we simply aren't nice often but rather that, given the best of our abilities, we sometimes nevertheless botch it. However, if we regard responsiveness as an ability, then we can realize it does not come full-blown in lesbians. We can develop it by developing our abilities of attending, intelligibility, and playful world travel, learning from our mistakes and our successes.

Responsiveness also involves the ability to appreciate what we have accomplished. I think too often we take for granted what we have done. Do we count having created connections, having woven patterns of gynocentric[98] or womanist[99] friendships among our accomplishments? When we do engage with others, whether as friends, lovers, daughters and amazons, collective members, or part of the community, we have woven an intricate pattern of energy. And even if individual relationships end on painful terms, a connection remains. In weaving connections among ourselves, we are creating new patterns of energy, tapestries. As Deidre McCalla muses:

> I've been thinking lately
> how different life would be
> if I had never met you
> and you had not met me.[100]

When responsiveness becomes the ability—not the obligation—to respond, intimacy becomes compatible with autokoenony.

Responsiveness involves our ability to take each other seriously and make judgments. And as we increase our responsiveness with each other, we contribute to the context in which our lesbian values gain sense, and so we develop the means to be really able to respond to the needs—emotional, economic, psychic, and creative—of those with whom we're intimate, and we are able to move from there to widen our web of response. As such, responsiveness is the ability to participate in the creation of lesbian community.

Yet in suggesting that responsiveness is the ability to participate in the creation of community, I want to caution against pursuing the "cooperative" values of the fathers which lead to community being regarded as an entity, an institution, even a state, which can or must be protected and preserved over and against the integrity and agency of individual lesbians. These "cooperative" values exist to coerce the association of antagonistic individuals, and lesbian connection is an altogether different fabric.

The "cooperative" values

In the first place, there will always be lesbian communities, or at least subcultures, as long as there are lesbians. As Paula Gunn Allen writes:

> so dykes
> are like indians
> because everybody is related
> to everybody
> in pain
> in terror
> in guilt
> in blood

in shame
in disappearance
that never quite manages
to be disappeared [101]

Secondly, neither subculture nor community has ever protected lesbians. Lesbian community does not exist to protect us either from an outside threat or from ourselves. Nor do we need to focus on community as an entity or an institution whose boundaries must be protected; for then it becomes defined by virtue of the outside force, and our interactions are directed toward its preservation rather than toward creation.

As I suggested in the introduction, lesbian community is a context. It makes possible and is created by lesbians engaging and networking. It has been a context in which to grow, a context in which to assuage wounds and heal, to create and develop possibility, to focus anger, to let loose imagination, to develop analyses, to engage in playful world travel, to issue challenges, to learn, to laugh, to enact ideals.

In this respect the community is a whole; for without it no individual lesbian could make any of the changes that are taking place here, at least not with any degree of depth. However, it is a whole, not as an entity, but, as I have suggested, as a ground of our lesbian be-ing. If there is an entity, it is not a state, an institution; it is our energy and the contextual reality that emerges from it. And as long as we value our own and each other's integrity and moral agency, as long as we encourage the ability to create, to grow, to learn, and to respond to each other—rather than shutting ourselves off by means ranging from rules of obligation all the way to ethnic and national boundaries—there will exist a context for lesbian be-ing.[u] It can be created over and over in different forms by different lesbians. As Lee Lanning and Nett Hart note:

> Living in community requires that none of us be self-sacrificing because the needs of the community are precisely to have each one be herself, offer her uniqueness in a self-loving way. In a community in which each wommon is fiercely herself, the community is valued for itself, as a place of strong self-loving wimmin, strong in their differences as well as their com-

---

u　While purporting to deal with man's development, fascist doctrine has a radically different concept of the individual. Mussolini argues that "Man is man only by virtue of the spiritual process to which he contributes as a member of the family, the social group, the nation, and in function of history to which all nations bring their contribution. . . . Outside history man is a nonentity. . . . Anti-individualistic, the fascist conception of life stresses the importance of the State and accepts the individual only in so far as his interests coincide with those of the State, which stands for the conscience and that universal will of man as a historical entity."[102]

mon commitments. The community does not become a place in which the individual is lost; the diversity of persons promotes creative interchange. Self-loving wimmin form community to expand the possibilities for self-loving wimmin.[103]

Lesbian community will remain solid as long as lesbian responsiveness revolves around it. It disintegrates where lesbians cease responding to concerns and events as lesbians. *For it is not because the ground of lesbian be-ing exists that we move on it. Rather, it is because we move on it, choose to move on it and find each other here, that it exists.*[104]

The value which has emerged from this burst of lesbian be-ing, concomitant with the feminist movement and the gay liberation movement, and based on the value in the lives of lesbians who went before us, lies in all we have created, particularly the reality of lesbian context, problematic though it also is. And focusing on lesbian integrity, moral agency, and lesbian existence is key, I believe, to that value continuing to evolve from our choices.

Lesbian transformation depends on us and our choices, not on some utopic social structure with strict rules we might set up. It may be that we don't succeed in continuing to create lesbian value. That is always a possibility. I simply don't want to hide from that reality by resting in the false security of an ethics of control which itself not only can't guarantee ethical behavior but actually works against it. What we have, what we have had and will continue to have, is choice.   *Choice*

I still hear the cry, "But what about lesbian batterers or racists or lesbians who try to hurt others? What about all the other mean and nasty things lesbians do to each other? What about all those who just won't change?" To this I answer, "What about them/us?" "But," comes the cry, "I'm involved," to which I answer, "Then you have a judgment to make, and a choice." Or the cry might be, "But my friend is involved," to which I reply, "Then she has some choices to make." Or the cry might come, "But she's asked me to help," to which I answer, "Then you have some choices to make."

In the long run, if we regard Lesbian Ethics as rules of right behavior and obligation, we are not seeking help in making choices – we are seeking to avoid choice. We imagine that if only everyone would behave (indeed, in some cases, disappear), we wouldn't have to think about problems and face a choice. We appeal to rules and obligation so we *don't* have to understand the complexities out of which problems arise. Moral revolution will not emerge from such ignoring and ignorance.

I want to suggest that lesbian value and revolution emerge from lesbian creation, not lesbian regulation. The energy of this creation involves not preservation and security, but risk and change. And an ethics appropriate to creativity, I believe, focuses on enabling our integrity and agency.

When we are centrally lesbian, our actions spin around, and so hold in place, a foundation, not of antagonism, but of a form of cooperation. This is not a cooperation that we can directly choose or pursue or force. It is a cooperation which flowers through the choices we make, as we engage, acting one among many, autokoenonously. My suggestion is that this co-operation emerges as a foundation (axis) of our actions when we focus on our own and each other's integrity and agency. This foundation is not really nameable, in fact if we try to name it, and thus focus on it, we will distort it. But it is there, just as the antagonism of the fathers' values is present in patriarchal interactions.

I think the strength of lesbian community lies in many strong, auto-koenonous, limited (i.e., unique) lesbians making choices and operating in a lesbian context — at times angry, at times tacky, at times comforting, at times pushy, often irreverent, always with something to offer which the rest of us can grow from. (And often with something the rest of us may wish to avoid.) The breaks we have made from patriarchal thinking come from lesbians daring to create something new. Such focus, away from control, on integrity and agency, and toward the courage to take risks and try changes, yields the energy of Lesbian Ethics.

Conclusion

WHAT WE BEGAN with this wave of lesbian moving, at least in the u.s., has gone through significant changes. As we dis-covered and began Lesbian space to explore ourselves, we wanted to create something new and we set about doing just that. We were (and still are) boundary dwellers.[1] Atravesamos fronteras.[2] And the first task at hand was developing lesbian space. To create something new, we needed relief from heterosexualism and the presumption that the business of women is men. We needed to have sufficient time and room to create without the constant threat of being dissolved by dominant perceptions, which, even in the best of all possible dominant worlds, hold lesbianism to be marginal.

We focused on ourselves.[3] We told our coming-out stories.[4] We celebrated lesbianism.[5] We began many different lesbian projects. We created space in which we could develop a new context and build collectivity.

This was an exuberant time but also an extremely painful one because we were having to make the idea of ourselves and our spaces credible, because creating lesbian space was not a clear-cut matter, and because those of us who became openly political held ideals with an iron grip — everything had to be exactly right.

In her history of *Lavender Woman*, Michal Brody discusses the bitter fights that occurred in the lavender woman collective, in the larger chicago lesbian community, and in many other lesbian communities:

Many communities experienced a euphoric coming together followed by a period of intense activity. When conflicts arose, as they inevitably would, over priorities, or strategies, or even just what to name the baby, bitter struggles often occurred. These wars, as they were called in some places, caused many women to withdraw, while the energy of those who remained was severely depleted. Once this fatigue set in, the momentum could not be sustained, and unless a new inspiration burst forth to start the cycle all over again, the endeavor would disperse.

This is a universal process, shared by any co-identified group in motion. The steps of the process are conjoining, inspiration, activity, conflict, exhaustion, and dispersion.[6]

Michal Brody goes on to suggest that while the process she describes is inevitable, the "particular alienation and ugliness that resulted from the conflicts in many lesbian communities in the mid-1970s was not inevitable."[7] She argues that the lavender woman collective had focused so strongly on each other as lesbians that members had not developed a language to address difference:

> The lesbians who originally formed the web of activity that included CLL and Lavender Woman were a vastly diverse population from many different backgrounds, with different educations, different jobs, different needs, and different ideas about where to go from here. The things we had in common were that we were all lesbians, and we all believed strongly that being lesbians had a deep and profound effect on our worldviews. Plus, we loved each other. Other components of our lives, such as race, religion, cultural and social background, all those and more were suppressed by our identity as lesbians. The strength of that identity was so fragile in those early days that we put enormous pressure on ourselves to forge a unity in lesbianism that discarded anything else.
>
> When the time for conflict arrived, as it inevitably does in any group, we had become so intensely involved in one another that the pain of discord was almost unbearable; and we had ignored the major differences for so long that we had no skills or common language to work with.[8]

During this period we thought being lesbian was enough; we did not acknowledge differences. We focused on definitions and rules: A lesbian does *x*, a lesbian does not do *y*. We focused on what counts as being a lesbian or a lesbian project, and who belongs in our spaces. As a result, we developed no ability to address differences, including differences of opinion—that had to be fought for. And the fight took place, Michal Brody suggests, over the issue of separatism because separatism was an abstract issue—abstract since the actual and daily lives of those most heatedly involved in the debates/wars were not significantly different:

> It is important to understand that the ones on the front lines of these

battles, on both sides, were women who already had minimal contact with men. The lifestyles of separatist and non-separatist combatants were largely indistinguishable.[9]

While I agree that our inability to acknowledge difference has led to devastating splits, denial, and burnout, I'm not convinced that the wars were not inevitable. As I've stressed throughout this book, while we challenged patriarchal politics, we relied on many other patriarchal values, in particular, patriarchal ethics. And that ethics promotes antagonism and control rather than integrity and connection.

Secondly, the idea that there could be a lesbian *anything* was not initially credible, even to us; as Michal Brody suggests, lesbian identity was fragile at best. That there might be a lesbian-centered context, that lesbians might create it—this was something we had to prove and defend to ourselves. In a way, an iron grip was necessary if lesbians were going to forge something within a void.

Thirdly, much of our lesbian energy focused on limits and definition rather than complexity and difference because of the very real threat of cooptation—of once having sparked a possibility, sliding back or being undermined before we'd had a chance to create what we'd imagined and dreamed. So I think the process was inevitable; nevertheless, I don't find it cause for despair.

Through all we did, we managed to create time and space away from those dominant perceptions which, when empowered by our own acceptance of them, could render lesbian existence, lesbian focus, and especially lesbian imagination, meaningless. We have made lesbian space credible to ourselves. We no longer feel the need, for example, to justify the idea of "womyn's" music festivals to ourselves or even feel defensive about them. They are a reality. They happen. And their existence is part of lesbian existence. We can choose to go; we can choose to cast a wary glance at those "politicos"; or we can refuse to go in anger over some aspect. But they are a part of our lives about which we can make those choices, and they are part of the context within which we explore, challenge, change, and develop our values.

In addition, we have been growing, healing, learning, and changing despite the dominant society all around us and the wars between us. We have been exploring our differences. And while rarely smooth or graceful, this process has occurred as a result of lesbian responsiveness.

We have suffered many internal defeats, but I think our work to date has also been successful. While this is a time for deep reevaluation, I want to suggest it is also a time of lesbian celebration. We have accomplished as much as we have because we have believed in ourselves—we have believed in our selves and each other even though we have also hurt, attacked, withdrawn, and burned out.

Nevertheless, lesbian space is still extremely problematic. We are barely beginning to develop ways to explore and handle difference; at the same time lesbian space is fragile and cooptation still threatening. The problem we face is to reconcile plurality with a lesbian focus. I think we can accomplish this through perceiving lesbian space as a context rather than a fortress, and by working control out of our interactions.

So the question now is, are we going to go on? Having been devastated, can we take time out, heal, recover, learn to play, and come back? Or are we going to crawl into whatever niche we can find to fit and live the rest of our lives licking our wounds? Are we going to continue to work with this monster we have created? We have made lesbian space credible, and we have learned in our guts that simply being lesbian is not enough. What are we going to do now?

Summation

IN "THE MIND-DRIFTING Island," Micheline Grimard-Leduc describes the process of lesbians emerging from exile to find each other and create community. As lesbians within heteropatriarchy, we have no social selves; we are without a collective system of values. We are deprived of "collective points of reference by which to 'plug' into a collective reality."[10] However, she goes on:

> As soon as I share my dream with another lesbian, I start breaking through the alien circle. This single act of communication materializes the dream. By this exchange we build reality.[11]

By engaging, lesbians have the possibility of making magic, of making a moral revolution. So what is the moral revolution of Lesbian Ethics? What values are being challenged, and what value can emerge from lesbianism?

I have been trying to articulate the extent of the antagonism inherent in the values of the fathers, particularly how dominance and subordination have permeated our lives in ways we haven't thought to question or even suspect. I have tried to show that there is a very close relationship — philosophically, an 'internal relationship' — between ideas and ways of thinking that normalize oppression, and ideas and ways of thinking central to traditional anglo-european ethics. And I have been making suggestions about moving away from these values, ways we can be radically serious about loving lesbians,[12] serious beyond the romantic haze of lesbian utopia as well as beyond the bitter disappointments in lesbian community. I have tried to suggest other ways of approaching situations, a different focus which involves creating and functioning in a different conceptual framework—one which is not without serious problems but one which rejects the values of dominance and subordination, no matter how palatable they may appear on the surface.

I am proposing an ethics which recognizes separation or withdrawal at any level as a moral option; one which has as its prerequisite, not altruism, but self-understanding, which regards choice, not as sacrifice, but as creation, and which encourages, not vulnerability, but intimacy; one which recognizes power, not as controlling, but as enabling, which enables neither merging nor estranging but interacting, and so which encourages, not binding, but engaging; one which integrates or politicizes reasoning and emotions as well as dreaming, psychic faculty, intuition, humor, and imagination; one which treats moral agency, not as rising above our boundaries nor as controlling situations, but as acting one among many and as making choices within situations; one which has as its central focus, not enforcing rules and social control, but enabling integrity and agency—one which has as its axis, not the antagonism of dominance and subordination, but a form of cooperation held in place by autokoenony. Through such an ethics, we can continue to develop self-awareness, intimacy (deep understanding with a few), our ability to attend, our ability to withdraw, the cooperation of intelligibility, our ability to make choices and go on in situations, our playful world travel, our ability to make judgments, our responsiveness, and our caring—in short, our lesbian integrity and moral agency.

Now, in posing lesbian value in lieu of heterosexualism, I am not invoking a new dualism. The two frameworks are not opposites—one the denial of the other—like good and evil. If we embrace a conceptual framework which has dominance and subordination as its axis, we will simply be focused differently than if we withdraw from that framework and create lesbian value. The one set of values is meaningless within the context of the other set.

Further, Lesbian Ethics, as is true of heterosexual ethics, functions only for those who choose its values. It functions only for those of us who create its values by virtue of the choices we make—the elements in ourselves we work with, those we work to transform, the risks we take, and the dreams we pursue.

In addition, it may well be that I am wrong about all this. It may be that social groupings can only function under antagonistic principles of social control. It may be that the only order we can embrace in groups is heterosexualism, that we can only function under principles of dominance and subordination if we are to have any social interaction at all. Certainly, principles holding dominance and subordination in place have a tremendous draw when we seek meaning in our lives. But what we have inherited from patriarchy is an ethics of fear, of control, of resentment, of strutting, of coercion, of obligation, of oppression, and of destruction — of antagonism . . . all well-justified and, within a patriarchal context, all necessary. I think we remain engrossed with heterosexualism, beyond the acknowledgment we must give it to survive — at times we *believe* it — because of a desire to give a certain sort of meaning to our lives. And it is possible that dominance and subordination provide the only framework in which we *can* create certain meaning in our lives.

Meaning

CONSIDER THE CERTAINTY and security, or rather the alleged certainty and security, we're used to. For example, when in the dominant society evil forces are delineated, we know where we belong. If we are threatened by an outside force, we have a reason for working together; we can put aside our "petty" differences. When there is a crisis, we know what to do. Our efforts can be heroic. Or we can be revolutionary — misunderstood, martyred perhaps, but stoically righteous nevertheless, doing what must be done. Or we can be the "evil" force, gleefully thwarting the presumptions of naive fools or measuring our abilities against a formidable opponent. And if we are wronged, we can summon all the energy of moral righteousness to channel our frustration and pain.

Within this type of framework we can find a mission, a purpose. Our duty is clearly delineated, and we know who owes us what. What we should do is sharply defined, not confusing, ambiguous, multidimensional. And what happens is not partly accidental, at times of no consequence, or in any way absurd, ambiguous, or unnecessary. We can go about our business in a framework of dominance and subordination with a feeling of belonging to a higher order, of fitting in, of being needed beyond the mundane, ordinary events of our daily lives. We have a purpose in life, our lives are meaningful.

The search for meaning lies behind the choices, for example, of the right-wing, white, christian women Andrea Dworkin interviewed.[13] She argues that right-wing, white, christian women embrace femininity, partly as a result of the aversion therapy that passes for growing up female, but also in a desperate attempt to find safety and to give some meaning to their apparently otherwise meaningless existence as women. They find meaning through binding with and adopting the agendas of their protectors/predators, in the face of a chosen and created common enemy.

A search for meaning also lies behind the structure of heterosexualism as Monique Wittig describes it: the dualism of self and 'other' and the creation of meaning by finding oneself in the other. It is the fear of being outside the perception of the arrogant eye.[14]

This same search for meaning lies behind the ideology of romanticism and conquest – needing evil so that we can vanquish it, finding purpose in the effort to restore order. As Barbara Myerhoff suggests, "meaningless accidents, chaos, and inexplicability are more insupportable than suffering and cruelty."[15] In other words, better to perceive a world in which evil reigns than one which has no apparent meaning or order.

This search for meaning comes in part, I would suggest, from being caught up in dynamics such as war – and from happenings not among our daily choices, such as birth and death. It comes from our wanting to have a framework in which we can understand and hence try to gain some control over these things, at least the control of predictability. So our attempts at control involve the simplicity of dualistic categories – light and dark, good and evil. As with stereotypes, they help us to make choices but in such a way that we don't have to understand or attend or respond to each other. And so we repeat the same mistakes over and over.

Further, when at times these categories start to appear less sharply defined, we have to regain sharpness by creating crises. We can appeal to the melodrama of soap operas, where every event involves an intense encounter, wherein we don't distinguish between a heart attack and a sneeze, and where there is no humor. Alternatively, as men do, we may create a war to generate the possibility of heroics. Our meaning comes thus from conquest and control, and we may triumph or fail. Either way we can perceive our endeavor as meaningful: as having a purpose defined by some external order, and as being part of a system in which everyone eventually gets their just rewards – that is, a system which always makes some kind of sense.

We can create categories with sharp edges and so we can fit in the order of things and know who we are. But we will need crises again and again, like a fix, as reaffirmation of sense and order in an apparently senseless world – at least it would appear senseless if any of these crises should turn out to be unnecessary. Better there be a form we can fit, even if it is harmful, misfires, or turns out false – better this than no objective form at all.

Or is that so? It is a fear of change, I think, a fear of things being in flux, that fuels the struggle to create meaning in this way: we seek an objective standard for all time against which we can be judged, against which we can – with certainty – measure ourselves and our actions, within which we can find ourselves, and by means of which we can feel secure about making judgments of others. Yet this objectivity is nothing but a collection of perceptions which agree. Should we begin to disagree . . .

Now, should we reject the idea of such a standard, we lose a certain type of security in an already uncertain world. So instead we shun the idea of creating our own value, affirming what we perceive to be value outside ourselves, value on which we can depend rather than value which depends on us. We can depend on the idea of an external authority and use scapegoats to explain away failure. We can feel more secure if we have someone else judging us. Even if we rebel against the judgment, it is an apparently permanent fixture which grounds us. And our purpose, what gives us meaning, comes in finding our place in that framework. We are acknowledged, and we can live knowing that we are part of a larger purpose, that we have a destiny.

But what if there is no larger purpose? Perhaps our living is open-ended and in flux with no higher being and no higher purpose to hold it. Perhaps it is all simply a matter of energy, the energy that comes from each one of us as we make choices as moral agents, energy that mingles with the energy of all things around us and in the universe. Perhaps it is a matter of energies interacting with no overall plan, only the variety of plans which emerge from the context in which we make our choices. Perhaps purpose emerges from our interacting; perhaps we create it by engaging in this living.

Again, what I am suggesting is not an individual endeavor, for meaning emerges from a context. But the context is one we create by means of our interactions, from the patterns we respond to, participate in, and create by our living. The kind of choices we make both reflect and create the community we live in. Lesbian meaning arises out of lesbian context as a result of lesbians interacting as lesbians. Without that, there is no lesbian meaning.

Weaving

IN OTHER WORDS, I am suggesting that we create meaning as we go, by what we focus on, by what we are drawn to, by what we attend, by what we find important, and by what we deem insignificant as we move within lesbian community. The values of lesbian existence emerge, not through regulation or preservation, but rather through imagination and creation. And we create as we make choices in this living. The ideology of dominance and subordination pretends to provide us with the means of avoiding this.

The breaks we have made as lesbians come from acting, from daring to create something new, and from being willing to risk making mistakes. Further, what we create, including change in our reactions and perceptions, is not valuable because of its permanence but because it contributes to a lesbian ground of be-ing, because it sparks and stimulates and helps create a context in which lesbians can continue to engage, to create, to make choices. As Alix Dobkin sings:

You and me
We're goin' deep and dark
We're goin' oh so far not even close
To yesterday
Seek adventures
Brave, wild, sweet darlin'
Bear down, breathe easy
We're on
Some new ground[16]

Lesbian value emerges through creation. And yet we have been fairly limited in our imagining of creativity; for one ideal has emerged as the paradigm for all creativity – namely, the patriarchal ideal of 'mothering', in particular the feminine ideal of being all-nurturing and the maternal ideal of care-taking. I am not suggesting that actual mothering is not creative; certainly amazoning is creative. I am suggesting, however, that it is but one of the many forms of lesbian creativity, and that as an ideal for all creativity, it is distorting. Under the mothering metaphor, creating is giving birth – giving birth to ourselves, our products, our children. Seeds are planted in us (by whom?); they gestate; we give birth to ideas and songs as we might babies, and we nurture them.

Now, the energy lesbians bring to this living – whether as amazons or healers or musicians or teachers or writers or legal interpreters or photographers or potters or dog and cat tenders or house painters or hairdressers or athletes or lesbianspace providers or computer programmers or editors or trip makers or re-searchers or organizers or jewelry makers or all the many, many other things lesbians are doing – may be birthing or nurturing energy; but quite likely it is not. Lesbian energy includes not just birthing and nurturing – but sparking, igniting, cajoling, sweating, developing, unearthing, interpreting, seeking, holding, imagining, puzzling, refreshing, harassing, cleaning up, figuring out, making over, slowing down, piecing together, and on, and on.

I find the power in this living closely connected with limits and choice and finite boundaries and energy. We can draw what flies around us and put it together, making a stew from leftovers, brewing an herbal remedy, engaging musical notes to define a desire, entangling a net of demonstrators around the pentagon, extracting a visual configuration, plotting a revolution at the hairdresser's, piecing together the energy of a tarot reading, unraveling deep pain, taking back the night, conversing across the kitchen table, forming a secret warrior society, determining a course of action – picking and choosing from among a myriad of sparks, and imagining others . . . not all of which fit together or match or even complement each other, but all of which are intricate and complex, and all of which create and are created by lesbian context – weaving a moral revolution.

I find 'weaving' a metaphor for lesbian creativity because of the centrality of the concept of 'choice'. Weaving involves understanding and creating patterns, and it includes, among other things, the choice of which threads to select, which to leave behind, which colors and thicknesses to use, what to unravel and discard, what to do over again, where to repeat, and when to end.

What I think important about lesbian creation, lesbian weaving, is that we change the energy, the patterns, around us by refocusing our attention. The moral revolution of Lesbian Ethics, what I am after in talking about Lesbian Ethics, is a revolution in female agency – away from dominance and subordination and toward autokoenony. That is the *possibility* of lesbian be-ing, the possibility of lesbianism.

Endnotes

Introduction
pages 1–23

1. Adrienne Rich, *Women and Honor: Some Notes on Lying* (Pittsburgh: Motheroot Publications, 1977); reprinted in *On Lies, Secrets, and Silence: Selected Prose 1966–1978* (New York: W.W. Norton & Co., 1979), pp. 185–94.

2. This phrase comes, of course, from *Lesbian Connection*, Helen Diner Memorial Women's Center, Ambitious Amazons, P.O. Box 811, East Lansing, MI 48823.

3. Note, for example, Pamela Kearon, "Man-Hating," in *Radical Feminism*, ed. Anne Koedt, Ellen Levine, and Anita Rapone (New York: Quadrangle, New York Times Book Co., 1973), pp. 78–80; Joanna Russ, "The New Misandry," in *Amazon Expedition: A Lesbian Feminist Anthology*, ed. Phyllis Birkby, Bertha Harris, Jill Johnston, Esther Newton, and Jayne O'Wyatt (Albion, Calif.: Times Change Press, 1973), pp. 27–32; and Jeffner Allen, "Remembering: A Time I Will Be My Own Beginning," in *Lesbian Philosophy: Explorations* (Palo Alto, Calif.: Institute of Lesbian Studies, 1986), pp. 13–26. There is also an argument to the effect that to be free of a colonial mindset, the colonized must call the world into question by an act of absolute violence: note Frantz Fanon, *Wretched of the Earth* (New York: Grove Press, 1963).

4. Note, for example, Helen Andelin, *Fascinating Womanhood* (New York: Bantam Books, 1975) or Marabel Morgan, *The Total Woman* (Old Tappan, N.J.: Fleming H. Revell Company, 1973).

5. Bev Jo, personal correspondence.

6. Sue Fink and Joelyn Grippo, "Leaping Lesbians," recorded by Meg Christian, on *Face the Music* (Los Angeles, Calif.: Olivia Records, 1977, now at 4400 Market Street, Oakland, CA 94608).

7. Lillian Faderman, *Surpassing the Love of Men: Romantic Friendship and Love Between Women from the Renaissance to the Present* (New York: William Morrow & Co., 1981), p. 20.

8. Marilyn Frye, "Some Thoughts on Separatism and Power," *Sinister Wisdom* 6 (Summer 1978): 35. This paper is reprinted under the title "Some Reflections On Separatism and Power" in *The Politics of Reality: Essays in Feminist Theory* (Trumansburg, N.Y.: The Crossing Press, 1983, now Freedom, Calif.); reference is to p. 103 in the book.

9. Note, for example, Peggy Allegro, "The Strange and the Familiar: The Evolutionary Potential of Lesbianism," in *The Lesbian Reader: An Amazon Quarterly Anthology*, ed. Gina Covina and Laurel Galana (Oakland, Calif.: Amazon Press, 1975), pp. 167–84.

10. Alix Dobkin, "Gywn's Tune," on *XX Alix*, distributed by Ladyslipper Music, P.O. Box 3124, Durham, N.C. 27705, 1980.

11. Billie Potts, *Witches Heal: Lesbian Herbal Self-Sufficiency* (Bearsville, N.Y.: Hecuba's Daughters, to be reissued by Du Rêve, P.O. Box 7772, Ann Arbor, MI 48108, 1981), p. 3.

12. Actually, according to Cheris Kramarae and Paula A. Treichler, in 1970 Ti-Grace Atkinson wrote, "Feminism is a theory, but lesbianism is a practice," in dissociating feminists and lesbians; note Sidney Abbott and Barbara Love, *Sappho Was a Right-on Woman: A Liberated View of Lesbianism* (New York: Stein and Day, 1972), p. 117. In 1975 Jill John-

ston said, "Feminism is the complaint and lesbianism is the solution," as cited by Sara Scott in *A Feminist Dictionary*, ed. Cheris Kramarae and Paula A. Treichler (Boston: Pandora Press, 1985), p. 229.

13. T. Z. Lavine, *From Socrates to Sartre: The Philosophic Quest* (New York: Bantam Books, 1984), p. 373.

14. Note, for example, Susan Krieger, *Mirror Dance: Identity in a Women's Community* (Philadelphia: Temple University Press, 1983), chapter 5, especially p. 46.

15. Adrienne Rich, *Women and Honor*.

16. Note, for example, Donna Hawxhurst and Sue Morrow, *Living Our Visions: Building Feminist Community* (Fourth World, 110 W. Geneva Drive, Tempe, AZ 85282, 1984); Tia Cross, Freada Klein, Barbara Smith, and Beverly Smith, "Face-to-Face, Day-to-Day — Racism CR," in *All the Women Are White, All the Blacks Are Men, But Some of Us Are Brave: Black Women's Studies*, ed. Gloria T. Hull, Patricia Bell Scott and Barbara Smith (Old Westbury, N.Y.: Feminist Press, 1982); also Phyllis Jean kinheart Athey and Mary Jo kinheart Osterman, *The Lesbian Relationship Handbook* (Kinheart, 2214 Ridge Ave., Evanston, IL 60201).

17. Denslow Brown, workshop on conflict resolution, Michigan Womyn's Music Festival, August 1982.

18. For further discussion of the problem of appealing to principles, note Nel Noddings, *Caring: A Feminine Approach to Ethics & Moral Education* (Berkeley, Calif.: University of California Press, 1984).

19. Conversation, Jeffner Allen.

20. Note Susan Leigh Star, "The Politics of Wholeness II: Lesbian Feminism as an Altered State of Consciousness," *Sinister Wisdom* 5 (Winter 1978): 82–102; note also Barbara Starrett, "I Dream in Female: The Metaphors of Evolution," in *The Lesbian Reader*, pp. 105–21.

21. Ludwig Wittgenstein, *Philosophical Investigations*, 3d ed., trans. G.E.M. Anscombe (New York: Macmillan Co., 1968), remark 24, for example.

22. For a critique of the empiricist/positivist tradition in science, note Sandra Harding, *The Science Question in Feminism* (Ithaca, N.Y.: Cornell University Press, 1986).

23. Ludwig Wittgenstein, *On Certainty*, ed. G.E.M. Anscombe and B.H. von Wright, trans. Denis Paul and G.E.M. Anscombe (Oxford: Basil Blackwell, 1969), remark 152.

24. For a fuller development of these ideas, note Sarah Lucia Hoagland, "The Status of Common Sense, G.E. Moore and L. Wittgenstein: A Comparative Study," (Ph.D. diss., University of Cincinnati, 1975).

25. Julia P. Stanley, "Generics, Gender, and Common Nouns in English: Usage and Reference," published as "Gender-marking in American English," in *Sexism and Language*, ed. Alleen Pace Nilsen, et. al. (Urbana, Ill.: National Council of Teachers of English, 1977), pp. 43–7; note also Julia Penelope [Stanley] and Susan W. Robbins "Sex-Marked Predicates in English," in *Papers in Linguistics* 11, 3–4 (Fall–Winter 1978): 487–516 and Julia P. Stanley, "Sexist Grammar," in *College English* (March 1978): 800–11.

26. Mary Daly, *Beyond God the Father: Toward a Philosophy of Women's Liberation* (Boston: Beacon Press, 1973), p. 8. This is an example of how men have stolen from us the power of naming through (christian) religion.

27. Muriel R. Schulz, "The Semantic Derogation of Women," in *Language and Sex: Difference and Dominance*, ed. Barrie Thorne and Nancy Henley (Rowley, Mass.: Newbury House Publishers, 1975), pp. 64–75.

28. Julia P. Stanley [Julia Penelope], "Paradigmatic Woman: The Prostitute," in *Papers in Language Variation*, ed. David L. Shores and Carole P. Hines (Birmingham: University of Alabama Press, 1977), pp. 303–21.

29. Dale Spender, *Man Made Language* (London: Routledge & Kegan Paul, 1980), p. 19.

30. Ibid., p. 23.

31. This was brought to my attention by Kathy Hagen and Mardi Steinau.

32. Example from Julia Penelope.

33. Conversation, Julia Penelope.

34. Julia Penelope, "Patriarchal False Descriptions of Language: Through a Glass Darkly," paper read at the National Women's Studies Conference, Bloomington, Indiana, May 16–20, 1980; note also Julia Penelope [Stanley] and Susan J. Wolfe, "Style as Meaning," in *Proceedings of the 6th LACAS Forum* ed. W.C. McCormack & H. J. Izzo (Columbia, S.C.: Hornbeam Press, 1980), pp. 45–52 and Julia P. Stanley, "Prescribed Passivity: The Language of Sexism," in *Views on Language*, ed. Reza Ordoubadian (Murfreesboro, Tenn.: Inter-University Publishing, 1975), pp. 96–108.

35. This question is raised by Ann Jones in *Women Who Kill* (New York: Holt, Rinehart, and Winston, 1980), p. 299.

36. This question is raised by Marilyn Frye in "In and Out of Harm's Way: Arrogance And Love," *The Politics of Reality*, p. 72.

37. This question is raised by Kathleen Barry in *Female Sexual Slavery* (Englewood Cliffs, N.J.: Prentice-Hall, 1979), chapter 5.

38. Conversation, Anne Throop Leighton.

39. Thomas Kuhn, *The Structure of Scientific Revolution*, 2d ed. (Chicago: University of Chicago Press, 1970), p. 5; note also Gloria Anzaldúa, *Borderlands/La Frontera: The New Mestiza* (San Francisco: Spinsters/Aunt Lute, 1987), p. 80.

40. Vivian F. Mayer, "The Questions People Ask," in *Shadow on a Tightrope: Writings by Women on Fat Oppression*, ed. Lisa Schoenfielder and Barb Wieser (Iowa City: Aunt Lute Book Co., 1983, now Spinsters/Aunt Lute, San Francisco), pp. 23–36.

41. Sonia Johnson, *Going Out of Our Minds: The Metaphysics of Liberation* (Freedom, Calif.: The Crossing Press, 1987), chapter 7, pp. 143–75.

42. Tremor, "The Hundredth Lezzie: Evolution by Design," *Trivia* 6 (Winter 1986): 33–7.

43. Mary Daly, *Beyond God the Father*, p. 19.

44. Susan Leigh Star, "Politics of Wholeness II," p. 96.

Chapter 1
Separating from Heterosexualism
pages 25–68

1. Kathryn Pyne Parsons [Addelson], "Nietzsche and Moral Change," in *Woman in Western Thought*, ed. Martha Lee Osborne (New York: Random House, 1979), p. 235.

2. Ibid.

3. Ibid.

4. Note David K. Shipler, *Arab and Jew: Wounded Spirits in a Promised Land* (New York: Random House/Times Books, 1986). Bette S. Tallen brought this to my attention.

5. Simone de Beauvoir, *The Second Sex*, trans. H.M. Parshley (New York: Bantam Books, 1970), p. xvii.

6. Ibid., pp. xvii–xviii.

7. Ibid., pp. 58–9.

8. Nancy C.M. Hartsock, *Money, Sex, and Power* (Boston: Northeastern University Press, 1985), p. 288.

9. Simone de Beauvoir, *Second Sex*, p. xix.

10. Ibid.

11. Ibid., p. xx.

12. Ibid., p. xxi.

13. Ibid., p. 249.

14. Janice G. Raymond, *A Passion for Friends: Toward a Philosophy of Female Affection* (Boston: Beacon Press, 1986), chapters 2 and 3, pp. 71–147; note also Marjorie Topley, "Marriage Resistance in Rural Kwangtung," in *Women in Chinese Society*, ed. Margery Wolf and Roxane Witke (Stanford, Calif.: Stanford University Press, 1975), pp. 67–88.

15. Celia Kitzinger, "Heteropatriarchal Language: the Case Against 'Homophobia'," *Gossip* 5, pp. 15–20.

16. Conversation, Marilyn Frye. Note Andrea Dworkin, *Pornography: Men Possessing Women* (New York: G.P. Putnam's Sons, 1979), p. 61.

17. Adrienne Rich, "Compulsory Heterosexuality and Lesbian Existence," *Signs* 5, no. 4 (Summer 1980): 647; reprinted in *Women-Identified-Women*, ed. Trudy Darty and Sandee Potter (Palo Alto, Calif.: Mayfield Publishing Co., 1984), p. 133.

18. Janice G. Raymond, *A Passion for Friends*, p. 11.

19. Conversation, Ariane Brunet.

20. Note, e.g., Andrea Dworkin, *Pornography*, p. 61–2.

21. Julien S. Murphy, "Silence and Speech in Lesbian Space," paper presented at Mountain Moving Coffeehouse, Chicago, Ill., 1984.

22. For further development of this point, note Marilyn Frye, "Oppression," in *The Politics of Reality: Essays in Feminist Theory* (Trumansburg, N.Y.: The Crossing Press, 1983, now in Freedom, Calif.), pp. 5–6.

23. Note Susan Griffin, "Rape: The All-American Crime," in *Feminism and Philosophy*, ed. Mary Vetterling-Braggin, Frederick A. Elliston, & Jane English (Totowa, N.J.: Littlefield, Adams & Co., 1977), especially p. 320.

24. Andrea Dworkin, *Woman Hating* (New York: E.P. Dutton & Co., 1974), pp. 29–49.

25. Sonia Johnson, presidential campaign speech, Chicago, Ill., 1984; conversation, Pauline Bart. The figure on wife-beating comes from the "Uniform Crime Reports of 1982," federal reports on incidences of domestic crime. According to a fact sheet from the Illinois Coalition on Domestic Violence, "National Domestic Violence Statistics, 1/84," ten to twenty percent of American children are abused. Another fact sheet, "Verified Domestic Statistics," researched and compiled by the Western Center on Domestic Violence (San Francisco, Calif.), cites estimates of Maria Roy, *The Abusive Partner* (New York: Van Nostrand Rernhold, 1982) as indicating that violence against wives will occur at least once in two-thirds of all marriages. Another fact sheet, "Wife Abuse: The Facts" (Center for Woman Policy Studies, 2000 P. Street N.W., Washington, D.C. 20036), cites Murray Straus, Richard Gelles and Suzanne Steinmetz, *Beyond Closed Doors: Violence in the American Family* (Garden City, N.Y.: Doubleday, 1980) as saying that twenty-five percent of wives are severely beaten during their marriage. There are many more statistics . . . you get the idea. Bette S. Tallen was extremely helpful in obtaining some of this information. Note also Del Martin, *Battered Wives*, revised and updated (Volcano Press, Inc., 330 Ellis St., #518, Dept. B, San Francisco, CA 94102, 1976, 1981); Leonore Walker, *The Battered Woman* (New York: Harper & Row, 1979); Florence Rush, *The Best Kept Secret: The Sexual Abuse of Children* (Englewood Cliffs, N.J.: Prentice-Hall, Inc., 1980); Diana E. H. Russell, *Sexual Exploitation: Rape, Child Sexual Abuse, and Workplace Harassment* (Beverly Hills, Calif.: Sage Publications, 1984); and Elizabeth A. Stanko *Intimate Intrusions:*

Women's Experience of Male Violence (Boston, Mass.: Routledge & Kegan Paul, 1985) among others.

26. Marilyn Frye, "In and Out of Harm's Way: Arrogance and Love," *Politics of Reality*, p. 72.

27. Sonia Johnson, "Excerpts from the last chapter of *Going Out Of Our Minds and Other Revolutionary Acts of the Spirit,*" *Mama Bears News & Notes* 3, no. 2 (April/May 1986): 15; also in *Going Out of Our Minds: The Metaphysics of Liberation* (Freedom, Calif.: The Crossing Press, 1987), p. 336.

28. Note, for example, Barbara Burris, "The Fourth World Manifesto," *Notes from the Third Year*, 1971, revised and reprinted in *Radical Feminism*, ed. Anne Koedt, Ellen Levine, and Anita Rapone (New York: New York Times Book Co., 1973), pp. 322–57; Margaret Small, "Lesbians and the Class Position of Women," in *Lesbianism and the Women's Movement*, ed. Nancy Myron and Charlotte Bunch (Baltimore: Diana Press, 1975), pp. 49–61; Robin Morgan, "On Women as a Colonized People," in *Going Too Far: The Personal Chronicle of a Feminist* (New York: Random House, 1977); Anne Summers, *Damned Whores and God's Police: The Colonization of Women in Australia* (Ringwood, Victoria, Australia: Penguin, 1975); and Kathleen Barry, "Sex Colonization," in *Female Sexual Slavery* (Englewood Cliffs, N.J.: Prentice-Hall, 1979), pp. 163–204.

29. Walter Rodney, *How Europe Underdeveloped Africa* (Washington, D.C.: Howard University Press, 1982).

30. Conversation, Bette S. Tallen.

31. Sonia Johnson, "Telling the Truth," *Trivia* 9 (Fall 1986): 21; also in *Going Out of Our Minds*, p. 249.

32. Ann Oakley, *Women's Work: The Housewife, Past and Present* (New York: Vintage Books/Random House, 1974), p. 19.

33. Gena Corea, *The Mother Machine: Reproductive Technologies from Artificial Insemination to Artificial Wombs* (New York: Harper & Row, 1985), p. 303.

34. Alice Molloy, *In Other Words: Notes on the Politics and Morale of Survival* (Oakland, Calif.: Women's Press Collective, n.d., write Alice Molloy, Mama Bears, 6536 Telegraph Ave., Oakland, CA 94609).

35. Pat Robinson and Group, "A Historical and Critical Essay for Black Women in the Cities," in *The Black Woman*, ed. Toni Cade [Bambara] (New York: New American Library, 1970), p. 202.

36. Merlin Stone, *Ancient Mirrors of Womanhood: Our Goddess and Heroine Heritage*, 2 vols. (New York: New Sibylline Books, 1979).

37. Carol Moorefield, talk presented at Women and Children First Bookstore, Chicago, Ill., October 1982.

38. Pat Robinson et al., "Essay for Black Women in the Cities," p. 202.

39. Mary Daly, "The Second Passage," in *Gyn/Ecology: The Metaethics of Radical Feminism* (Boston: Beacon Press, 1978).

40. Sonia Johnson, presidential campaign speech, Chicago, Ill., 1984; also *Going Out of Our Minds*, p. 244.

41. *Sunday Sun-Times* (Chicago, Ill.), 9 September 1979.

42. Helen Diner, *Mothers and Amazons* (New York: Doubleday, 1973), pp. 95–105.

43. Maxine Feldman, "Amazon," recorded on the album *Closet Sale* (Galaxia, P.O. Box 212, Woburn, MA 01801). Some exceptions include Susan Cavin, *Lesbian Origins* (San Francisco: Jism Press, 1985); Mary Daly, *Gyn/Ecology;* Audre Lorde, *The Black Unicorn* (New York: W.W. Norton & Co., 1978); Merlin Stone, *When God Was a Woman* (New York: Harcourt, Brace, Jovanovich/Harvest, 1976); Monique Wittig, *Les Guérillères* (New York: Avon, 1969), and Monique Wittig and Sande Zeig, *Lesbian Peoples: Material for a Dictionary* (New York: Avon, 1979); Carol Moorefield and Kathleen Valentine, "Matri-

archy: A Guide to the Future?," in *For Lesbians Only: A Separatist Anthology*, ed. Sarah Lucia Hoagland and Julia Penelope, forthcoming, Onlywomen Press, London; "Amazons," in *The Woman's Encyclopedia of Myths and Secrets*, Barbara G. Walker (New York: Harper & Row, 1983), p. 24–7; Judy Grahn, *Another Mother Tongue: Gay Words, Gay Worlds* (Boston: Beacon Press, 1984); Anne Cameron, *Daughters of Copper Woman* (Vancouver, B.C.: Press Gang Publishers, 1981); Micheline Grimard-Leduc, "The Mind-Drifting Islands," *Trivia* 8 (Winter 1986): 28–36, published in *l'île des amantes: essai/ poèmes*, Micheline Grimard-Leduc, C.P. 461, Station N, Montréal, Québec, H2X 3N3, Canada, 1982; and Jeffner Allen, *Lesbian Philosophy: Explorations* (Palo Alto, Calif.: Institute of Lesbian Studies, 1986).

44. For reference to the Dahomey, note Audre Lorde, *The Black Unicorn*, p. 119; also Carol Moorefield and Kathleen Valentine, "Matriarchy: A Guide to the Future?;" for reference to the Nootka, note Anne Cameron, *Daughters of Copper Woman*.

45. Adrienne Rich, "Compulsory Heterosexuality and Lesbian Existence," p. 632 or pp. 119–20.

46. Harriet Desmoines [Ellenberger] "There Goes the Revolution . . . ," *Sinister Wisdom* 9 (Spring 1979): 22.

47. Radicalesbians, "The Woman Identified Woman," in *Notes From the Third Year*, 1971, reprinted in *Radical Feminism*, p. 244. Note also Anita Cornwell, "Some Notes on the Black Lesbian and the Womin-Identified Womin Concept," in *Black Lesbian in America* (Tallahassee, Fla.: The Naiad Press, 1983), pp. 26–30.

48. Kathleen Barry, *Female Sexual Slavery*.

49. Julia P. Stanley [Julia Penelope] "Paradigmatic Woman: The Prostitute," in *Papers in Language Variation*, ed. David L. Shores and Carole P. Hines (Birmingham: University of Alabama Press, 1977), pp 303–21.

50. This point was made in a talk by Marilyn Frye.

51. Claudia Dreifus, "Sterilizing the Poor," in *Seizing Our Bodies: The Politics of Women's Health*, ed. Claudia Dreifus (New York: Vintage Books/Random House, 1978), pp. 105–20.

52. E.O. Wilson, *Sociobiology: The New Synthesis* (Cambridge, Mass.: Harvard University Press, 1975), p. 531, also pp. 291, 552, 568. For a fuller development of the arguments in this section, note Sarah Lucia Hoagland, "Androcentric Rhetoric in Sociobiology," *Women's Studies International Quarterly* Vol. 3, 2/3 (1980): 285–93, now *Women's Studies International Forum*, reprinted in *The Voices and Words of Women and Men*, ed. Cheris Kramarae (London: Pergamon Press, 1980), pp 285–93, forthcoming in *Of Voice and Vision: A Collection of Articles from the First 10 Years of WSIF*, ed. Renate Klein and Deborah Lynn, Pergamon Press, London.

53. E.O. Wilson, *Sociobiology*, p. 36.

54. Ibid.

55. Ibid., p. 169.

56. Ibid., p. 438.

57. Ibid., p. 242.

58. Ibid., p. 514.

59. Note ibid., pp. 283, 153; my emphasis.

60. For an analysis of this same point about male judgment in the context of the prison system, note Susan Brownmiller, *Against Our Will: Men, Women, and Rape* (New York: Simon and Schuster, 1975), pp. 257–68.

61. Alix Kates Shulman, *Memoirs of an Ex-Prom Queen* (New York: Bantam Books, 1973).

62. Information on this film can be obtained from the American Film & Video Network, 1723 Howard, Evanston, Ill.

63. This monologue is based on my memory and possibly inaccurate in detail. I believe,

however, that I have invoked the general idea the woman was expressing.

64. Sheila Jeffries, *The Spinster and Her Enemies: Feminism and Sexuality, 1880–1930* (Boston: Pandora Press, 1985); Andrea Dworkin, *Pornography.*

65. This is one of the themes in *Lesbian Nuns: Breaking the Silence* (Tallahassee, Fla: The Naiad Press, 1985).

66. Kate Millett, *Sexual Politics* (New York: Doubleday, 1969), p. 26.

67. Naomi Weisstein, *Psychology Constructs the Female, or: The Fantasy Life of the Male Psychologist,* reprint (Boston: New England Free Press, 1968); reprinted in *Sisterhood Is Powerful: An Anthology of Writings from the Women's Liberation Movement,* ed. Robin Morgan (New York: Random House, 1970), pp. 205–20; and in *Women in Sexist Society,* ed. Vivian Gornick and Barbara K. Moran (New York: Signet, 1971), pp. 207–24; also in *Radical Feminism,* ed. Anne Koedt, Ellen Levine, and Anita Rapone, pp. 178–97.

68. Research of Betty Carpenter, personal communication.

69. Mary Daly, *Pure Lust: Elemental Feminist Philosophy* (Boston: Beacon Press, 1984), p. 38.

70. Kate Millett, *Sexual Politics,* p. 347.

71. Angela Davis, *Women, Race and Class* (New York: Vintage Books/Random House, 1983), chapter 1, pp. 3–29.

72. Bell Hooks, *Ain't I a Woman: Black Women and Feminism* (Boston: South End Press, 1981), chapters 2 and 3, pp. 51–117.

73. Angela Davis, "Reflections on the Black Woman's Role in the Community of Slaves," in *Contemporary Black Thought: Best From The Black Scholar,* ed. Robert Chrisman and Nathan Hare (Indianapolis: Bobbs-Merrill, 1973), p. 148; note also Herbert Aptheker, *American Negro Slave Revolts* (New York: International Publishers, 1970) (1st. ed., 1943), as cited by Angela Davis.

74. Note, for example, Earl Conrad, *Harriet Tubman* (New York: Paul S. Eriksson, Inc., 1969).

75. Ruthe Winegarten, "I Am Annie Mae: The Personal Story of a Black Texas Woman," *Chrysalis* 10 (Spring 1980): 15; later published: *I Am Annie Mae: An Extraordinary Woman in Her Own Words: The Personal Story of a Black Texas Woman,* ed. Ruthe Winegarten (Austin, Tex.: Rosegarden Press, 1983).

76. After formulating this thesis, I came across documented evidence of it. Note Gilbert Osofsky, ed., *Puttin' On Ole Massa* (New York: Harper & Row, 1969); Aran Bontemps, ed., *Great Slave Narratives* (Boston: Beacon Press, 1969); and Willie Lee Rose, ed., *A Documentary History of Slavery in North America* (New York: Oxford University Press, 1976). Unfortunately, these collections almost exclusively address the lives of men. For a ground-breaking work on women slaves, note Erlene Stetson, "Studying Slavery: Some Literary and Pedagogical Considerations on the Black Female Slave," in *All the Women Are White, All the Blacks Are Men, But Some of Us Are Brave: Black Women's Studies,* ed. Gloria T. Hull, Patricia Bell Scott, and Barbara Smith (Old Westbury, N.Y.: Feminist Press, 1982), pp. 61–84; note also, Angela Davis, "Reflections on the Black Woman's Role in the Community of Slaves."

77. Simone Wallace, Ellen Ledley, Paula Tobin, letter to *off our backs,* December 1979, p. 28.

78. Note, for example, Barbara Harford and Sarah Hopkins, eds., *Greenham Common: Women at the Wire* (London: Women's Press, 1984); also Alice Cook & Gwyn Kirk, *Greenham Women Everywhere: Dreams, Ideas and Actions From the Women's Peace Movement* (Boston: South End Press, 1984).

79. Charlotte Perkins Gilman, *The Yellow Wallpaper* (Old Westbury, N.Y.: Feminist Press, 1973).

80. For information on S. Weir Mitchell, note G. J. Barker- Benfield, *The Horrors of the*

Half-Known Life: Male Attitudes Toward Women and Sexuality in Nineteenth Century America (New York: Harper & Row, 1976).

81. Elaine R. Hedges, "Afterword," in *The Yellow Wallpaper,* Charlotte Perkins Gilman.

82. Eugene O'Neill, *Long Day's Journey into Night* (New Haven, Conn.: Yale University Press, 1955).

83. Phyllis Chesler, *Women and Madness* (Garden City, N.Y.: Doubleday, 1972).

84. *The Compact Edition of the Oxford English Dictionary,* 1971.

85. Susan Glaspell, "Trifles: A Play in One Act," in *Plays* (Boston: Small Maynard & Co., 1920, an authorized facimile of the original book was produced by Xerox University Microfilms, Ann Arbor, Michigan, 1976). Blanche Hersh brought this play to my attention.

86. Ann Jones, *Women Who Kill* (New York: Holt, Rinehart, and Winston, 1980), p. 291.

87. Kathleen Barry, *Female Sexual Slavery,* pp. 142–4.

88. For some discussion of this, note Jean Carey Bond and Pat Peery, "Is the Black Male Castrated?" in *Black Woman,* ed. Toni Cade, pp. 113–9; Patricia Bell Scott, "Debunking Sapphire: Toward a Non-Racist and Non-Sexist Social Science," in *But Some of Us Are Brave,* pp. 85–92; Bonnie Thornton Dill, "The Dialectics of Black Womanhood," in *Feminism & Methodology,* ed. Sandra Harding (Bloomington: Indiana University Press, 1987), pp. 98–9; and Angela Davis, "Reflections on the Black Woman's Role in the Community of Slaves"; note also Erlene Stetson, "Studying Slavery."

89. Note Marilyn Frye, "Oppression," in *The Politics of Reality,* pp. 1–16.

90. Note, for example, *Breaching the Peace: A Collection of Radical Feminist Papers* (London: Onlywomen Press, 1983).

91. Kathleen Barry, *Female Sexual Slavery,* pp. 43–6.

92. William Ryan, *Blaming the Victim* (New York: Vintage Books, 1976).

93. Kathleen Barry, *Female Sexual Slavery,* p. 45.

94. Andrea Dworkin, *Right-Wing Women* (New York: G. P. Putnam's Sons/Perigee, 1983), p. 14.

95. Ibid., p. 15.

96. Ibid., pp. 17, 21.

97. Brunetta R. Wolfman, "Black First, Female Second," in *Black Separatism and Social Reality: Rhetoric and Reason,* ed. Raymond L. Hall (New York: Pergamon Press, 1977), p. 228.

98. Ibid., p. 229.

99. Jacquelyn Grant, "Black Women and the Black Church," in *But Some of Us Are Brave,* p. 141.

100. Brunetta R. Wolfman, "Black First, Female Second," p. 230.

101. Ibid., p. 231.

102. I've adapted this from Franz Kafka, "Couriers," in *Parables,* trans. Willa and Edwin Muir (New York: Schocken Books, 1946), pp. 268–78; however, Kafka's point is not about change and his parable contains no king to begin with.

103. Reported to me by Juana María Paz and Bette S. Tallen.

104. For example, this statement was made by Barbara Smith at a panel on racism, "Racism and the Lesbian Community," at the National Women's Studies Association Conference, Storrs, Conn., June, 1981.

105. Sarah Lucia Hoagland, "Introduction," in *For Lesbians Only,* forthcoming, Onlywomen Press, London; a shortened version was published as "Lesbian Separatism: An Empowering Reality," in *Gossip* 6, pp. 24–36 and in *Sinister Wisdom* 34 (Spring 1988): 23–33.

106. Kate Millett, *Sexual Politics,* p. 157.

107. Communication, Marilyn Frye.

108. Kathleen Barry, "Josephine Butler: The First Wave of Protest," *Female Sexual Slavery*, pp 12–32.

109. Conversation, Ariane Brunet.

110. Susan Griffin, "Sacred Images," in *Pornography and Silence* (New York: Harper & Row, 1981), pp. 8–81; Mary Daly, *Gyn/Ecology;* Catharine A. MacKinnon, *Feminism Unmodified: Discourse on Life and Law* (Cambridge, Mass.: Harvard University Press, 1987); Andrea Dworkin, *Pornography*.

111. For an earlier development of this argument note Sarah Lucia Hoagland, "Sadism, Masochism, and Lesbian-Feminism," in *Against Sadomasochism: A Radical Feminist Analysis*, ed. Robin Ruth Linden, Darlene R. Pagano, Diana E. H. Russell, and Susan Leigh Star (East Palo Alto, Calif.: Frog in the Well, 1982), pp. 153–63.

112. Michal Brody, *Are We There Yet? A Continuing History of 'Lavender Woman': A Chicago Lesbian Newspaper, 1971–1976* (Iowa City: Aunt Lute Book Co., 1985, now Spinsters/Aunt Lute, San Francisco), p. 184.

113. Communication, Claudia Card.

114. Marilyn Frye, "Some Reflections on Separatism and Power," in *Politics of Reality*, pp. 96, 98–9.

115. Ibid., pp. 103–5.

116. Mary Daly, *Gyn/Ecology*, p. 381.

117. Resignation is one of the plastic passions Mary Daly names in *Pure Lust*, pp. 200–26.

118. Monique Wittig, "The Straight Mind," *Feminist Issues* 1, no. 1 (Summer 1980): 110.

119. Monique Wittig, "One Is Not Born a Woman," *Feminist Issues* 1, no. 2 (Winter 1981): 49.

120. Christiane Rochefort, *Les Stances à Sophie* (Paris: Grasset, 1963) as cited by Monique Wittig, "One Is Not Born a Woman."

121. Monique Wittig, "One Is Not Born a Woman," p. 53.

122. Ibid., p. 50.

123. Ibid.; note also Monique Wittig, "The Category of Sex," *Feminist Issues* 2, no. 2 (Fall 1982): 64.

124. Monique Wittig, "Category of Sex," p. 64.

125. Marilyn Frye, "In and Out of Harm's Way," p. 80.

126. Conversation, Harriet Ellenberger.

127. Alice Molloy, *In Other Words*, p. 39.

128. Judy Grahn, *Another Mother Tongue: Gay Words, Gay Worlds* (Boston: Beacon Press, 1984), pp. 29–30.

129. Audre Lorde, *Zami: A New Spelling of My Name* (Watertown, Mass.: Persephone Press, 1982, now published by The Crossing Press, Freedom, Calif.), p. 176.

130. Elana Nachman [Dykewomon], *Riverfinger Women* (Plainfield, Vt.: Daughters, Inc., 1974), p. 174.

131. Caryl B. Bentley, "My Third Coming Out At Last Has My Own Name," in *The Coming Out Stories*, ed. Julia Penelope Stanley and Susan J. Wolfe (Watertown, Mass.: Persephone Press, 1980), pp. 79–88.

132. Beth Brant, *Mohawk Trail* (Ithaca, N.Y.: Firebrand Books, 1985), p. 85.

133. Cheryl Clarke, "Lesbianism: An Act of Resistance," in *This Bridge Called My Back: Writings by Radical Women of Color*, ed. Cherríe Moraga and Gloria Anzaldúa (Watertown, Mass.: Persephone Press, 1981, now published by Kitchen Table: Women of Color Press, P.O. Box 908, Latham, NY 12210), p. 128.

134. Joan Nestle, "Butch-Fem Relationships: Sexual Courage in the 1950's," *Heresies* 3, no. 4, issue 12 (1981): p. 21; reprinted in *A Restricted Country* (Ithaca, N.Y.: Firebrand Books, 1987), pp. 100–9.

135. Ibid., p. 22.

136. Lillian Faderman, *Surpassing the Love of Men: Romantic Friendship and Love Between Women from the Renaissance to the Present* (New York: William Morrow & Co., 1981), p. 17.

137. Judy Grahn, *Another Mother Tongue*, p. 31.

138. Joan Nestle, "Butch-Fem Relationships," p. 22.

139. Audre Lorde, *Zami*, p. 205.

140. Julia Penelope, "Whose Past Are We Reclaiming?" *Common Lives/Lesbian Lives* 13 (Autumn, 1984): 27.

141. This point has been made many times before; for example note Shulamith Firestone, *The Dialectic of Sex: The Case For Feminist Revolution* (New York: Bantam/William Morrow & Co., 1972), chapter 6; Ti-Grace Atkinson, *Amazon Odyssey* (New York: Links Books, 1974), p. 43; and more recently, noting the reverse – namely, that in "no other form of slavery are those in power called upon to love those whom they have found to be inferior and despicable" – Kathleen Barry, *Female Sexual Slavery*, p. 136.

Chapter 2
The Feminine Virtues and Female Agency
pages 70–113

1. Note, for example, Donald M. Borchert and David Stewart, *Exploring Ethics* (New York: Macmillan Co., 1986), p. 2; Robert E. Dewey and Robert H. Hurlbutt III, *An Introduction to Ethics* (New York: Macmillan Co., 1977), pp. 1–2; and Norman E. Bowie, *Making Ethical Decisions* (New York: McGraw-Hill Book Co., 1985), pp. 2ff.

2. Robert E. Dewey and Robert H. Hurlbutt III, *An Introduction to Ethics*, pp. 1–2.

3. Ayn Rand, *The Virtue of Selfishness* (New York: New American Library, 1964).

4. Note for example, Andrew G. Oldenquist, *Moral Philosophy: Text and Readings*, 2nd ed. (Prospect Heights, Ill., Waveland Press, Inc., 1978), pp. 38–46; William K. Frankena, *Ethics* (Englewood Cliffs, N.J.: Prentice-Hall, Inc., 1963), pp. 16–21.

5. Parts of the summation that follows come from Alasdair MacIntyre, "Egoism vs. Altruism," in *The Encyclopedia of Philosophy*, vol. 2 (New York: Macmillan Publishing Co., Free Press, 1967), pp. 462–6.

6. Conversation, Jeffner Allen.

7. Alasdair MacIntyre, "Egoism vs. Altruism," p. 463; Alison Jaggar, *Feminist Politics and Human Nature* (Totowa, N.J.: Rowman & Allanheld, 1983), p. 40.

8. Thomas Hobbes, *Leviathan* (Indianapolis: Bobbs-Merrill, 1958). Some of these ideas come from Bette S. Tallen's work on Hobbes; note Bette S. Tallen, "Liberal Equality and Feminism: The Implications of the Thought of John Stuart Mill," (Ph.D. diss., University of Michigan, Ann Arbor, 1980).

9. Communication, Bett Farber.

10. Correspondence, Marilyn Frye.

11. Virginia Held, "Non-Contractual Society," in *Science, Morality & Feminist Theory*,

ed. Marsha Hanen and Kai Nielsen (Calgary, Alberta, Canada: The University of Calgary Press, 1987), p. 113.

12. Alasdair MacIntyre, "Egoism vs. Altruism," p. 466.

13. Several of these ideas come from Anne Throop Leighton's work on capitalism and socialism.

14. Conversation, Anne Throop Leighton.

15. For an indication of some problems of f.e.n., a feminist economic venture of the 1970s, note Martha Shelley, "What Is FEN?" (underground publication).

16. Conversation, Anne Throop Leighton.

17. For a beginning, note Jeffner Allen, "Lesbian Economics," *Trivia* 8 (Winter 1986): 37–53; Nett Hart, "Lesbians Feed Lesbians: A Lesbian Food Coop," *The Lesbian Insider/Insighter/Inciter* 11 (July 1983): 10; Nett Hart, "Appropriate Distribution: Toward a Lesbian Economy," *Maize: A Lesbian Country Magazine* 3 (Winter 9984/85): 4–7; Lee Lanning, "A Vision of Interdependence," *Maize* 3, p. 13.

18. Myrna Margulies Breitbart, "Anarchist Decentralism in Rural Spain, 1936–1939: The Integration of Community and Environment," *Antipode* 10:3 and 11:1 (1978–79); reprinted in *Antipode: A Radical Journal of Geography* 17, nos. 2 & 3, ("The Best of *Antipode*, 1969–1985," 1985): 105.

19. Ibid., p. 115.

20. Note *Beyond God the Father: Toward a Philosophy of Women's Liberation* (Boston: Beacon Press, 1973) and *Gyn/Ecology: The Metaethics of Radical Feminism* (Boston: Beacon Press, 1978).

21. Claudia Card, conversation.

22. For a discussion of the "helping professions," including education, note Marilyn French, *Beyond Power: On Women, Men, and Morals* (New York: Summit Books, 1985), pp. 356–7.

23. John Kenneth Galbraith, *Economics and the Public Purpose* (Boston: Houghton Mifflin Co., 1973), p. 33.

24. Jeffner Allen, "Looking at Our Blood: A Lesbian Response to Men's Terrorization of Women," *Lesbian Philosophy: Explorations* (Palo Alto, Calif.: Institute of Lesbian Studies, 1986), p. 36.

25. Ibid.

26. Nel Noddings, *Caring: A Feminine Approach to Ethics & Moral Education* (Berkeley, Calif.: University of California Press, 1984), pp. 16, 33.

27. Ibid., pp. 52, 14, 99.

28. Sarah Lucia Hoagland, "Some Thoughts on Caring," paper presented to a joint session of the Radical Philosophy Association and the Society for Women in Philosophy at the Central Division meeting of the American Philosophical Association, Cincinnati, Ohio, April 28, 1988.

29. Note, for example, Carol Gilligan, *In a Different Voice: Psychological Theory and Women's Development* (Cambridge, Mass.: Harvard University Press, 1982).

30. Claudia Card, *Virtues and Moral Luck*, Series 1, Institute for Legal Studies, Working Papers, University of Wisconsin-Madison, Law School, November 1985, pp. 14–15.

31. Gene Damon [Barbara Grier] "The Least of These: The Minority Whose Screams Haven't Yet Been Heard," in *Sisterhood Is Powerful: An Anthology of Writings from the Women's Movement*, ed. Robin Morgan (New York: Random House, 1970), p. 297.

32. Claudia Card, *Virtues and Moral Luck*, pp. 16, 17.

33. Ibid., p. 23.

34. Conversations, Deidre D. McCalla, Anne Throop Leighton.

35. Conversation, Marilyn Frye.

36. [Susan] Leigh Star, "The Politics of Wholeness: Feminism and the New Spiritual-

ity," *Sinister Wisdom* 3 (Spring 1977): 39.

37. Mary Daly, *Gyn/Ecology*, pp. 374–5.

38. Marilyn Frye, "In and Out of Harm's Way: Arrogance and Love," in *The Politics of Reality: Essays in Feminist Theory* (Trumansburg, N.Y.: The Crossing Press, 1983, now in Freedom, Calif.), p. 73.

39. Ibid., pp. 66–72.

40. For further discussion, note Judith Tourmey, "Exploitation, Oppression, and Self-Sacrifice," in *Women and Philosophy*, ed. Carol C. Gould and Marx W. Wartofsky (New York: G. P. Putnam's Sons, 1976), pp. 206–21; and Larry Blum, Marcia Homiak, Judy Housman, and Naomi Scheman, "Altruism and Women's Oppression," in *Women and Philosophy*, pp. 222–47.

41. For further discussion, note James Rachels, "Morality and Self-Interest," in *Philosophical Issues: A Contemporary Introduction*, ed. James Rachels and Frank A. Tillman (New York: Harper & Row, 1972), pp. 120–1.

42. Marilyn Frye, "In and Out of Harm's Way."

43. This function argument comes from the work of Jim Kimble, University of Colorado.

44. Rid Brown, "The Monkeys Who Kill Their Young," *Mother Jones* 2, no. 1, (1977): 322–39.

45. Richard Dawkins, *The Selfish Gene* (New York: Oxford University Press, 1976).

46. Marilyn Frye, "On Being White: Toward a Feminist Understanding of Race and Race Supremacy," in *The Politics of Reality*, p. 124.

47. Sally Gearhart, "The Future – If There Is One – Is Female," in *Reweaving the Web of Life: Feminism and Nonviolence*, ed. Pam McAllister (Philadelphia: New Society Publishers, 1982), pp. 266–84.

48. For a more in-depth discussion of the nature/nurture dichotomy, note Nancy Tuana, "Re-fusing Nature/Nurture," *Women's Studies International Forum* 6, no. 6 (special issue featuring *Hypatia*, 1983): 621–32.

49. Elsa Gidlow, *Ask No Man Pardon: The Philosophical Significance of Being a Lesbian* (Druid Heights Books, 685 Camino del Canyon, Mill Valley, CA 94941).

50. Note, for example, Z. Budapest, *The Feminist Book of Lights and Shadows;* and Billie Potts and River Lightwomoon, *Amazon Tarot* and *New Amazon Tarot* (Bearsville, N.Y.: Hecuba's Daughters, n.d.); for information, write Billie Potts, 18 Elm Street, Albany, NY 12202. Jean and Ruth Mountaingrove edited *Womanspirit* from 1974 to 1984.

51. Marilyn Frye, "A Note on Anger," in *The Politics of Reality*, p. 92.

52. Diane Mariechild, "Interview on 'Womanpower,'" *Woman of Power: A Magazine of Feminism, Spirituality, and Politics* (Spring 1984): 18–21.

53. Conversation, Florencia Carolina.

54. Note for example, Adrienne Rich, *Of Woman Born: Motherhood as Experience and Institution* (New York: W. W. Norton & Co., Inc., 1976).

55. Jeffner Allen, "Motherhood: The Annihilation of Women," in *Mothering: Essays in Feminist Theory*, ed. Joyce Trebilcot (New Jersey: Rowman & Allanheld, 1984), pp. 315–30; republished in *Lesbian Philosophy: Explorations*, Jeffner Allen (Palo Alto, Calif.: Institute of Lesbian Studies, 1986), pp. 61–86.

56. Monique Wittig and Sande Zeig, *Lesbian Peoples: Material for a Dictionary* (New York: Avon, 1979), pp. 108–9.

57. Baba Copper, correspondence.

58. Ibid.

59. Bell Hooks, *Ain't I a Woman: Black Women and Feminism* (Boston: South End Press, 1981), pp. 84–85.

60. The point about perception comes from the work of Jim Kimble, Philosophy De-

partment, University of Colorado.

61. Baba Copper, "The View from Over the Hill: Notes on Ageism Between Lesbians," *Trivia* 7 (Summer 1985): 57; revised and reprinted in *Over the Hill: Reflections on Ageism Between Women* (Freedom, Calif., The Crossing Press, 1988).

62. Barbara Macdonald with Cynthia Rich, *Look Me in the Eye: On Women, Aging and Ageism* (San Francisco: Spinsters Ink, 1983, now Spinsters/Aunt Lute).

63. Baba Copper, "View from Over the Hill," p. 57.

64. Adrienne Rich, "Introduction," in *The Coming Out Stories*, ed. Julia Penelope Stanley and Susan J. Wolfe (Watertown, Mass.: Persephone Press, 1980), pp. xi–xiii.

65. Adrienne Rich, *Women and Honor: Some Notes on Lying* (Pittsburgh: Motheroot Publications, 1977); reprinted in *On Lies, Secrets, and Silence* (New York: W.W. Norton & Co., 1979), pp. 185–94.

66. Note for example, *The Emile of J.J. Rousseau*, trans. and ed. William Boyd (New York: Teachers College Press, 1971), book 5: "Marriage," pp. 129–69; also, Sarah Lucia Hoagland, "On the Reeducation of Sophie," *Women's Studies: An Interdisciplinary Collection* (Westport, Conn.: Greenwood Press, 1978), pp. 13–4.

67. For a portrait of this, note Lee Lynch, *Toothpick House* (Tallahassee, Fla.: The Naiad Press, 1983), especially pp. 122, 124.

68. Conversation, Deidre D. McCalla and Sally Yeo.

69. Conversation, Anne Throop Leighton.

70. Audre Lorde, "The Transformation of Silence into Language and Action," *Sinister Wisdom* 6 (Summer 1978): 11–5; reprinted in *The Cancer Journals* (Argyle, N.Y.: Spinsters Ink, 1980, now Spinsters/Aunt Lute), pp. 18–23; and in *Sister Outsider* (Trumansburg, N.Y.: The Crossing Press, 1984, now in Freedom, Calif.), pp. 40–4.

71. Conversation, Deborah Snow.

72. Jeffner Allen, "Looking at Our Blood," p. 35.

73. Melanie Kaye [/Kantrowitz], "Scrambled Eggs 3: Women and Violence," *Sinister Wisdom* 9 (Spring 1979): 75–9; reprinted in *Fight Back! Feminist Resistance to Male Violence*, ed. Frédérique Delacoste and Felice Newmann (Minneapolis, Minn.: Cleis Press, 1981, now in San Francisco), pp. 160–3; note also Melanie Kaye/Kantrowitz, "War Stories, 197–:," *Sinister Wisdom* 33 (Fall 1987): 20–31.

74. Jeffner Allen, "Looking at Our Blood," p. 39.

75. Conversation, Jeffner Allen.

76. Jeffner Allen, "Looking at Our Blood," p. 43.

77. Sally Gearhart, *The Wanderground: Stories of the Hill Women* (Watertown, Mass.: Persephone Press, 1978, now published by Alyson Publications, Inc., Boston), p. 5.

78. Ibid., pp. 4–6.

79. Communication, Marilyn Frye.

80. This phrase comes from Adrienne Rich, *Women and Honor*.

81. Janice G. Raymond, *A Passion for Friends: Toward a Philosophy of Female Affection* (Boston: Beacon Press, 1986), p. 112.

Chapter 3
Power, Paternalism, and Attending
pages 115–156

1. Julie A. Murphy, "A Philosophical Analysis of Social Types: Schutz and Sartre," (Ph.D. diss., De Paul University, June 1982).

2. This point comes from the work of Jim Kimble, Philosophy Department, University of Colorado.

3. Juli Loesch, "Testeria and Penisolence – A Scourge to Humankind," *Aphra: The Feminist Literary Magazine* 4, no. 1 (Winter 1972–73): 44.

4. To the best of my knowledge, Carol Hanisch introduced the phrase in her paper "The Personal Is Political," in *Notes from the Second Year: Women's Liberation, Major Writings of the Radical Feminists,* ed. Shulamith Firestone and Anne Koedt, 1970; reprinted in *Radical Therapist,* ed. The Radical Therapist Collective, produced by Jerome Agel (New York: Ballantine Books, 1971), pp. 152–7. Of course, nineteenth-century feminists were making connections between the personal and the political, particularly in believing that becoming enfranchised would change women's lives and in arguing that marriage is a political institution.

5. Simone de Beauvoir, *The Second Sex,* trans. H.M. Parshley (New York: Bantam Books, 1970).

6. Betty Friedan, *The Feminine Mystique* (New York: W.W. Norton & Co., 1963).

7. Kate Millett, *Sexual Politics* (New York: Doubleday, 1969), p. 23.

8. Mary Daly, *Beyond God the Father: Toward a Philosophy of Women's Liberation* (Boston: Beacon Press, 1973).

9. Robin Morgan, ed., *Sisterhood Is Powerful: An Anthology of Writings from the Women's Movement* (New York: Random House, 1970); note also *Notes From the First Year,* June, 1968, *Notes From the Second Year,* 1970, and *Notes From the Third Year,* 1971; Leslie B. Tanner, ed., *Voices From Women's Liberation* (New York: New American Library, 1970); Deborah Babcox and Madeline Belkin, comps., *Liberation Now! Writings From the Women's Liberation Movement* (New York: Dell Publishing Co., Inc., 1971); Vivian Gornick and Barbara K. Moran, eds., *Woman in Sexist Society: Studies in Power and Powerlessness* (New York: New American Library, 1971); Anne Koedt, Ellen Levine, Anita Rapone, eds., *Radical Feminism* (New York: Quadrangle, 1973); Redstockings, *Feminist Revolution* (P.O. Box 413, New Paltz, NY, 1975, republished by Random House, New York, 1975); and Cheris Kramarae and Paula A. Treichler, *A Feminist Dictionary* (Boston, Mass., Pandora Press, 1985).

10. Note, for example, Juliet Mitchell, *Women's Estate* (New York: Vintage Books/Random House, 1971); Sheila Rowbotham, *Woman's Consciousness, Man's World* (Baltimore, Md: Penguin Books, 1973); Sheila Rowbotham, *Women, Resistance and Revolution: A History of Women and Revolution in the Modern World* (New York: Vintage Books/Random House, 1974); and Evelyn Reed, *Women's Evolution: From Matriarchal Clan to Patriarchal Family* (New York: Pathfinder Press, 1975).

11. Conversation, Daniel Bennett; note, for example, Peggy Kornegger, "Anarchism – The Feminist Connection," *The Second Wave* 4, no. 1 (Spring 1975): 26–37.

12. Note Julia Penelope and Susan J. Wolfe, "Style as Meaning," in *Proceedings of the Sixth LACUS Forum,* ed. W. C. McCormack and H. J. Izzo (Columbia, S.C.: Hornbeam

Press, 1980), pp. 45–52; Julia P. Stanley, [Julia Penelope], "Prescribed Passivity: The Language of Sexism," in *Views on Language*, ed. Reza Ordoubadian (Murfreesboro, Tenn. Inter-University Publishing, 1975), pp. 96–108; Julia P. Stanley, "Paradigmatic Woman: The Prostitute," in *Papers in Language Variation*, ed. David L. Shores and Carole P. Hines (Birmingham: University of Alabama Press, 1977), pp. 303–21; Julia P. Stanley, "Sexist Grammar," *College English* (March 1978): 800–811; Julia Penelope and Susan W. Robbins, "Sex-marked Predicates in English," *Papers in Linguistics* 11, 3–4 (Fall–Winter 1978): 487–516; and Julia Penelope, "Gender-marking in American English," *Sexism and Language*, eds. Alleen Pace Nilsen, et. al. (Urbana, Ill.: National Council of Teachers of English, 1977), pp. 43–74, for example.

13. Pat Robinson et. al., "A Historical and Critical Essay for Black Women in the Cities," in *The Black Woman*, ed. Toni Cade [Bambara] (New York: New American Library, 1970), pp. 198–210.

14. Naomi Weisstein, "Psychology Constructs the Female" in *Women in Sexist Society*, ed. Vivian Gornick and Barbara K. Moran, pp. 207–24.

15. Marilyn Frye, "Some Reflections on Separatism and Power," in *The Politics of Reality: Essays in Feminist Theory* (Trumansburg, N.Y.: The Crossing Press, 1983, now in Freedom, Calif.), pp. 95–109.

16. Note Kathie Sarachild, "Feminist Consciousness Raising and 'Organizing'" (Outline Prepared for a Lake Villa Conference Workshop, November, 1968), in *Voices From Women's Liberation* and "Consciousness Raising," in *Radical Feminism*.

17. the carpenter, *The Cook and the Carpenter* (Plainfield, Vt.: Daughters, Inc., 1973), p. 50.

18. Note, for example, Tony Cade [Bambara], ed., *The Black Woman;* Robin Morgan, ed., *Sisterhood Is Powerful;* Leslie B. Tanner, ed., *Voices From Women's Liberation;* Deborah Babcox and Madeline Belkin, comps., *Liberation Now!;* Joan Gibbs and Sara Bennett, eds., *Top Ranking: A Collection of Articles on Racism and Classism in the Lesbian Community* (February 3rd Press, c/o Joan Gibbs and Sara Bennett, 306 Lafayette Ave., Brooklyn, NY 12238, 1980); Lorraine Bethel and Barbara Smith, eds., *Conditions: Five: The Black Women's Issue;* much of this was reprinted in *Home Girls: A Black Feminist Anthology*, ed. Barbara Smith (Brooklyn, N.Y.: Kitchen Table: Women of Color Press, 1983, now P.O. Box 908, Latham, NY 12110); and Cherríe Moraga and Gloria Anzaldúa, eds., *This Bridge Called My Back: Writings by Radical Women of Color* (Watertown, Mass.: Persephone Press, 1981, now published by Kitchen Table: Women of Color Press, P.O. Box 908, Latham, NY 12110).

19. Note, for example, Evelyn Torton Beck, *Nice Jewish Girls: A Lesbian Anthology* (Watertown, Mass., Persephone Press, 1982, now published by The Crossing Press, Freedom, Calif.); and Melanie Kay/Kantrowitz & Irena Klepfisz, *The Tribe of Dina: A Jewish Women's Anthology* (Sinister Wisdom Books, P.O. Box 1308, Montpelier, VT 05602, 1986 and 5746).

20. Note, for example, Robin Morgan, ed., *Sisterhood Is Powerful;* Leslie B. Tanner, ed., *Voices From Women's Liberation;* Deborah Babcox and Madeline Belkin, comps., *Liberation Now!;* and Charlotte Bunch and Nancy Myron, eds., *Class and Feminism: A Collection of Essays From THE FURIES* (Baltimore, Md.: Diana Press, 1974).

21. Note, for example, Carol Costa, Janet Costa, Joan Costa, Paula Gomez, and Sally Wigginton, eds., *Holding Her Own: An Anthology of Young Women's Works* (Women Words Publishing Co., 1757 W. Wilson, Chicago, IL 60640, 1982); Barbara Macdonald with Cynthia Rich, *Look Me in the Eye: Old Women, Aging and Ageism* (San Francisco, Spinsters Ink, 1983, now Spinsters/Aunt Lute); and Baba Copper, *Over the Hill: Reflections on Ageism Between Women* (Freedom, Calif.: The Crossing Press, 1988).

22. Note, for example, Susan E. Browne, Debra Connors, and Nancy Stern, *With the*

Power of Each Breath: A Disabled Women's Anthology (San Francisco: Cleis Press, 1985).

23. Note, for example, Marsha Millman, *Such a Pretty Face: Being Fat in America* (New York: W.W. Norton & Co., 1980); and Lisa Schoenfielder and Barb Wieser, *Shadow on a Tightrope: Writings By Women on Fat Oppression* (Iowa City: Aunt Lute Book Co., 1983, now Spinsters/Aunt Lute, San Francisco).

24. Note, for example, Starhawk, *Dreaming the Dark: Magic, Sex, and Politics* (Boston: Beacon Press, 1982).

25. Conversation, Anne Throop Leighton.

26. Conversation, Claudia Card.

27. *The American Heritage Dictionary of the English Language, New College Edition,* 1969.

28. James R. Hamilton, Charles Regan & B.R. Tilghman, *An Introduction to Philosophy* (New York: Macmillan Publishing Co. 1976), pp. 359–60.

29. Lynn Mabel-Lois, " 'We'll Worry About That When You're Thin,' " in *Shadow on a Tightrope*, pp. 62–6.

30. Vivian F. Mayer, "The Fat Illusion," in *Shadow on a Tightrope*, p. 9.

31. This interpretation of responsibility was first offered to me by Ellen Meredith. Note, for example, Alice Molloy, *In Other Words: Notes on the Politics and Morale of Survival* (Oakland, Calif: Women's Press Collective, n.d., write Alice Molloy, Mama Bears, 6536 Telegraph Ave., Oakland, CA 94609), p. 61.

32. Celinda Cantu, interview, "In Sobriety, You Get Life," in *Out From Under: Sober Dykes and Our Friends,* ed. Jean Swallow (San Francisco: Spinsters Ink, 1983, now Spinsters/Aunt Lute), p. 85.

33. Conversation, diane hugs.

34. Conversations, Lola Lai Jong and Sarah Valentine.

35. Conversation, Anne Throop Leighton.

36. Note, for example, [Lola] Lai Jong, "When the Lesbians Came," *Common Lives, Lesbian Lives: A Lesbian Quarterly* 10 (Winter 1983): pp. 81–3.

37. Communication, Anna Lee.

38. Alice Molloy, *In Other Words,* especially p. 43.

39. Communication, Dayo.

40. Juana María Paz, *The 'La Luz' Journal* (Fayetteville, Ark.: Paz Press, 1980, now at P.O. Box 820, New Port Richey, FL 34656-0820), p. 38.

41. Conversation, Jane Kennedy.

42. Sally Gearhart, "The Remember Rooms," in *The Wanderground: Stories of the Hill Women* (Watertown, Mass.: Persephone Press, 1978, now published by Alyson Publications, Inc., Boston.), pp. 138–66.

43. diane hugs, "Look If You Like," unpublished essay.

44. Claudia Card, personal communication.

45. Nancy Wainer Cohen and Lois J. Ester *Silent Knife: Cesarean Prevention and Vaginal Birth After Cesarean* (South Hadley, Mass.: Bergin and Garvey, 1983).

46. Communication, Dayo.

47. Conversation, Harriet Ellenberger.

48. Note, for example, Mary Daly, *Gyn/Ecology: The Metaethics of Radical Feminism* (Boston: Beacon Press, 1978), pp. 274f.

49. Anna Lee, "Therapy: The Evil Within," *Trivia* 9 (Fall 1986): 35.

50. Joanna Russ, "Power and Helplessness in the Women's Movement," *Sinister Wisdom* 18 (Fall 1981): p. 56; reprinted in *Magic Mommas, Trembling Sisters, Puritans and Perverts: Feminist Essays* (Trumansburg, N.Y.: The Crossing Press, 1985, now in Freedom, Calif.), p. 54.

51. Naomi Weisstein, "Woman as Nigger," in *The American Sisterhood,* ed. Wendy

Martin (New York: Harper & Row, 1972), p. 296.

52. Anna Lee, "Therapy," p. 44.

53. Ibid., pp. 42, 43; note also Judi Chamberlin, "Consciousness-Raising," *Madness Network News* 3, #4 (December 1975): 1–6.

54. Ibid., p. 42; note also Janice G. Raymond, *A Passion for Friends: Toward a Philosophy of Female Affection* (Boston: Beacon Press, 1986), pp. 155–60.

55. Janice G. Raymond, *Passion for Friends*, pp. 156–58; Caryatis Cardea, "The Lesbian Revolution and the 50 Minute Hour: A Working-Class Look at Therapy and the Movement," *Lesbian Ethics* 1, no. 3 (Fall 1985): 59.

56. Juana María Paz, *The 'La Luz' Journal*, p. 85.

57. Harriet Ellenberger, transcript of a talk presented to The Eastern Division meeting of the Society for Women in Philosophy, Mt. Holyoke College, North Hadley, Mass., April 14, 1985.

58. Mary Daly, *Pure Lust: Elemental Feminist Philosophy* (Boston: Beacon Press, 1984), p. 373.

59. Sheila Mullett, "Only Connect: The Place of Self-Knowledge in Ethics," in *Science, Morality & Feminist Theory*, ed. Marsha Hanen and Kai Nielsen (Calgary, Alberta, Canada: The University of Calgary Press, 1987), p. 309–38.

60. Conversation, Adrienne Rich.

61. Communication, Bett Farber.

62. Ellen Pence, "Racism–A White Issue," in *All the Women Are White, All the Blacks Are Men, But Some of Us Are Brave: Black Women's Studies*, ed. Gloria T. Hull, Patricia Bell Scott, and Barbara Smith (Old Westbury, N.Y.: Feminist Press, 1982), p. 46.

63. Barbara Smith, "Racism and Women's Studies," *But Some of Us Are Brave*, pp. 49–50.

64. Judit Moschkovich, "–But I Know You, American Woman," in *This Bridge Called My Back*, p. 79; note also Audre Lorde, *Sister Outsider* (Trumansburg, N.Y.: The Crossing Press, 1984, now in Freedom, Calif.).

65. Conversation, Anne Throop Leighton.

66. Lorraine Bethel, "What Chou Mean *We*, White Girl? Or, the Cullud Lesbian Feminist Declaration of Independence," *Conditions: Five*, pp. 86–92.

67. María Lugones, "On the Logic of Pluralist Feminism," paper presented to the Midwest Division meeting of the Society for Women in Philosophy, Michigan State University, East Lansing, March 4–6, 1988.

68. Marilyn Frye, "The Problem That Has No Name," in *The Politics of Reality*, p. 43.

69. Ibid., p. 44.

70. Ellen Pence, "Racism–A White Issue," p. 46.

71. Mitsuye Yamada, "Asian Pacific American Women and Feminism," in *This Bridge Called My Back*, p. 71.

72. María Lugones, "On the Logic of Pluralist Feminism."

73. Ibid.

74. Simone de Beauvoir, *The Ethics of Ambiguity*, trans. Bernard Frechtman (Secaucus, N.J.: The Citadel Press, 1972), p. 83; Mary Daly, *Gyn/Ecology*, p. 260.

75. Conversation, Sandra Stanley.

76. Micheline Grimard-Leduc helped me with the word and the change in spelling from ancient to modern greek.

77. Julia Stanley [Julia Penelope], "Lesbian Relationships and the Vision of Community," *Feminary* 9, no. 1 (Spring 1978): 5.

78. Ibid., pp. 5–6.

79. Ibid., p. 6.

80. Ibid., p. 57.

81. Juana María Paz, *'La Luz' Journal*, p. 49.

82. Conversation, Betty Carpenter.

83. dolores bargowski and coletta reid, "Garbage Among the Trash," in *Class and Feminism*, p. 89.

84. Conversation, Jane Vanderbosch.

85. Marilyn Frye, "In and Out of Harm's Way: Arrogance and Love," in *The Politics of Reality*, pp. 52–83.

86. Joanna Russ, "Listen, There's a Story For You..." *Sinister Wisdom* 12 (Winter 1980): 90.

87. Nel Noddings, *Caring: A Feminine Approach to Ethics & Moral Education* (Berkeley, Calif.: University of California Press, 1984), p. 30.

88. María Lugones, "On the Logic of Pluralist Feminism."

89. For a different type of situation in which to pity someone and hence have no expectations of them is to treat them as expendable, note Anne Cameron, *The Journey* (New York: Avon, 1982).

90. The term comes from Sally Gearhart, *The Wanderground*.

91. Barbara Myerhoff, *Number Our Days* (New York: Simon and Schuster, 1978), pp. 27, 131. Alix Dobkin brought this book to my attention.

92. Billie Luisi Potts, "Owning Jewish Separatism and Lesbian Separatism 9982," *The Lesbian Insider/Insighter/Inciter* 9 (December 1982): 3. Bette S. Tallen notes the tradition of jewish separatism has been a central factor in holding the center old people together and a factor Barbara Myerhoff hints at but does not directly address.

93. Barbara Myerhoff, *Number Our Days*, pp. 3, 29, 30.

94. Ibid., pp. 27, 84, 171, 172, 187.

95. Ibid., p. 191.

96. Ibid., p. 180.

97. Ibid., p. 182.

98. Mary Daly, *Gyn/Ecology*, p. 16.

Chapter 4
Integrating Reasoning and Emotions
pages 158–197

1. Mary Daly, *Beyond God the Father: Toward a Philosophy of Women's Liberation* (Boston: Beacon Press, 1973), p. 103.

2. Conversation, Deidre McCalla.

3. Note, for example, Susan Griffin, *Women and Nature: The Roaring Inside Her* (San Francisco: Harper & Row: 1980).

4. Friedrich Nietzsche, *Beyond Good and Evil*, trans. Marianne Cowan (Chicago: Henry Regnery Co., 1955), #239, p. 168.

5. Walter Kaufmann, *Nietzsche: Philosopher, Psychologist, Antichrist*, 4th ed. (Princeton, N.J.: Princeton University Press, 1974), pp. 211, 214.

6. Mary Daly, *Pure Lust: Elemental Feminist Philosophy* (Boston: Beacon Press, 1984), p. 198.

7. Ibid., pp. 200–1.

8. Ibid., pp. 200–6.

9. Ibid., pp. 206–7.

10. Note, for example, Ludwig Wittgenstein, *Philosophical Investigations,* 3d ed., trans. G. E. M. Anscombe (New York: Macmillan Co., 1968), remark 476.

11. *The American Heritage Dictionary of the English Language: New College Edition,* 1969.

12. *The Random House Dictionary of the English Language: The Unabridged Edition,* 1966.

13. Gertrude Stein, *Fernhurst, Q.E.D., and Other Early Writings* (New York: Liveright, 1971), pp. 54–5. Alice Molloy brought this to my attention.

14. Jeffner Allen offered discussion on this point.

15. Nett Hart, "Radical Lesbian Spirit," presentation at Mountain Moving Coffeehouse, Chicago, Ill., January 23, 1988.

16. Naomi Scheman, "Individualism and the Objects of Psychology," in *Discovering Reality: Feminist Perspectives on Epistemology, Metaphysics, Methodology, and Philosophy of Science,* ed. Sandra Harding and Merrill Hintikka (Boston: D. Reidel Publishing Co., 1983), p. 226.

17. Ibid., p. 229.

18. Ibid., p. 232.

19. Ibid.

20. Ibid., p. 233.

21. Note, for example, Susan Griffin, *Rape: The Power of Consciousness* (San Francisco: Harper & Row, 1979), part 1, pp. 3–22; Susan Brownmiller, *Against Our Will: Men, Women, and Rape* (New York: Simon and Schuster, 1975), pp. 257–68; and Sheila Jeffreys, *The Spinster and Her Enemies: Feminism and Sexuality, 1880–1930* (Boston: Pandora Press, 1985).

22. Audre Lorde, *Uses of the Erotic: The Erotic as Power* (Brooklyn, N.Y.: Out and Out Books, 1978), p. 2; reprinted in *Sister Outsider* (Trumansburg, N.Y.: The Crossing Press, 1984, now in Freedom, Calif.), p. 54.

23. Mary Daly, *Gyn/Ecology: The Metaethics of Radical Feminism* (Boston: Beacon Press, 1978).

24. The thesis of the four kinds of love from the greek tradition was first proposed to me in a class by Dr. Walter Weir, University of Colorado.

25. Conversation, Mariel Rae.

26. Claudia Card, "The Symbolic Significance of Sex and the Institution of Sexuality," paper presented to the Society of Sex and Love at the Eastern Division meeting of the American Philosophical Association, New York City, December 28, 1984. A revised version of this paper was published as *Intimacy and Responsibility: What Lesbians Do,* Series 2, Institute for Legal Studies, Working Papers, University of Wisconsin-Madison, Law School, October 1987.

27. Ibid.

28. Marilyn Frye, "To See and Be Seen: The Politics of Reality," in *The Politics of Reality: Essays in Feminist Theory* (Trumansburg, N.Y.: The Crossing Press, 1983, now in Freedom, Calif.), p. 157.

29. Philip Blumstein and Pepper Schwartz, *American Couples* (New York: William Morrow and Company, 1983).

30. Marilyn Frye cites Dotty Calabrese who presented this information in a workshop on long-term lesbian relationships at the Michigan Womyn's Music Festival, 1987.

31. Marilyn Frye, "Lesbian 'Sex,'" *Sinister Wisdom* 35 (Summer/Fall 1988):46–54.

32. Ibid.

33. Conversation, Harriet Ellenberger.

34. JoAnn Loulan, *Lesbian Sex* (San Francisco: Spinsters Ink, 1984, now Spinsters/ Aunt Lute), p. 71; note also Sidney Spinster, "Orgasms and the Lesbian Touch," *Lesbian Inciter* 13 (July, 1984): 17, 18, 19.

35. JoAnn Loulan, *Lesbian Sex,* p. 73.

36. Claudia Card, "Symbolic Significance of Sex," pp. 10–11.

37. Ibid., p. 11.

38. For fun, note Tee Corinne, *Cunt Coloring Book* (San Francisco: Pearlchild Productions, 1975, subsequently published as *Labia Flowers* (Tallahassee, Fla.: The Naiad Press), and forthcoming as *Cunt Coloring Book* (Last Gasp, 2180 Bryant St., San Francisco, CA 94107).

39. Note Debbie Alicen's analysis of the language we often use to begin our sexual and love relationships, in particular 'crush' and 'infatuation': "Intertextuality: The Language of Lesbian Relationships," *Trivia* 3 (Fall 1983): 6–26. Note also Kathryn Pauly Morgan, "Romantic Love, Altruism, and Self-Respect," *Hypatia* 1, no. 1 (Spring 1986): 117–48.

40. Note, Debbie Alicen, "Intertextuality," pp. 6–26.

41. Kate Clinton, "Making Light: Another Dimension: Some Notes on Feminist Humor," *Trivia* 1 (Fall 1982): 42.

42. Ibid., pp. 39–40.

43. Marilyn Frye, "To See and Be Seen," p. 172.

44. Anna Lee, "Lust," unpublished paper.

45. Harriet Ellenberger, transcript of talk presented to the the Eastern Division meeting of the Society for Women in Philosophy, Mt. Holyoke College, North Hadley, Mass., April 14, 1985.

46. Julia Penelope, "The Mystery of Lesbians: II," *Lesbian Ethics* 1, no. 2 (Spring 1985): 36.

47. Conversation, Deborah Snow.

48. Conversation, Deidre McCalla.

49. Kate Moran, "When They Pick Sides, No One Asks Me To Play," *Lesbian Ethics* 1, no. 2 (Spring 1985): p. 95.

50. Ibid., p. 96.

51. Baba Copper, "The View from Over the Hill: Notes on Ageism Between Lesbians," *Trivia* 7 (Summer 1985): 50–1; revised and reprinted in *Over the Hill: Reflections on Ageism Between Women* (Freedom, Calif., The Crossing Press, 1988).

52. Communication, diane hugs.

53. diane hugs, "Pleasures," in *With the Power of Each Breath: A Disabled Women's Anthology,* ed. Susan E. Browne, Debra Connors, and Nancy Stern (San Francisco: Cleis Press, 1985), p. 342; also in *My Story's On! Ordinary Women Extraordinary Lives,* ed. Paula Ross (Berkeley, Calif.: Common Differences Press, 1985), p. 32.

54. Audre Lorde, "Uses of the Erotic," p. 54.

55. Ibid., p. 55.

56. Ibid.

57. Adrienne Rich, "(*The Floating Poem, Unnumbered*)," in *The Dream of a Common Language: Poems 1974–1977* (New York: W.W. Norton & Co., 1978), p. 32.

58. Mary Daly, *Pure Lust,* p. 3.

59. Vicki Spelman, paper presented at the Midwest Division meeting of the Society for Women in Philosophy, University of Wisconsin-Madison, March 7, 1982.

60. Audre Lorde, "The Uses of Anger," *Women's Studies Quarterly* 9, no. 3 (Fall 1981): 9; reprinted in *Sister Outsider,* p. 129.

61. Marilyn Frye, "A Note on Anger," in *The Politics of Reality,* pp. 86–93.

62. Ibid., p. 92.

63. Conversation, Julien S. Murphy.

64. Julia Penelope, "Whose Past Are We Reclaiming?" *Common Lives, Lesbian Lives* 13

(August 1984): 34.

65. Conversation, Anna Lee.

66. Susan Griffin, *Women and Nature: The Roaring Inside Her* (San Francisco: Harper & Row, 1978), p. 62.

67. Elana Dykewomon, "Traveling Fat," in *Shadow on a Tightrope: Writings by Women on Fat Oppression,* ed. Lisa Schoenfielder and Barb Wieser (Iowa City: Aunt Lute Book Co., 1983, now Spinsters/Aunt Lute, San Francisco).

68. *The American Heritage Dictionary.*

69. Thomas Kuhn, *The Structure of Scientific Revolution,* 2d ed., enlarged (Chicago: University of Chicago Press, 1970), p. 5.

70. Mary Daly, *Pure Lust,* p. 370.

71. Conversation, Florencia Carolina.

72. Mary Daly, *Pure Lust,* p. 187.

73. Micheline Grimard-Leduc, as stated in the lesbian video *Amazones d'Hier, Lesbiennes d'Aujourd'hui.* For information, contact Amazones d'hier, lesbiennes d'aujourd'hui, P.O. Box 1721, Succ. Place du Parc, Montréal, Québec H2W 2R7 Canada.

74. Conversation, Jeffner Allen.

75. Mary Daly, *Pure Lust,* p. 111.

76. Conversation, Candace Margulies.

77. Mary Daly, *Pure Lust.*

78. Conversation, Anna Lee.

79. Conversation, Julien S. Murphy.

80. Anne Cameron, *Daughters of Copper Woman* (Vancouver, B.C.: Press Gang Publishers, 1981), p. 134.

81. Conversation, Julia Penelope.

82. Conversation, Anna Lee.

83. Billie Potts, *Witches Heal: Lesbian Herbal Self-Sufficiency* (Bearsville, N.Y.: Hecuba's Daughters, 1981, to be reissued by Du Rêve, P.O. Box 7772, Ann Arbor, MI 48108), p. 3.

84. Toni Cade Bambara, writing workshop, Northeastern Illinois University, Chicago, Spring 1985.

85. Note, for example, *The Kin of Ata Are Waiting For You* (New York: Random House, 1971).

86. Conversation, Ellen Meredith.

87. Gloria Anzaldúa, *Borderlands/La Frontera: The New Mestiza* (San Francisco: Spinsters/Aunt Lute, 1987), pp. 38–9.

88. Note, for example, Edwina Lee Tyler and A Piece of the World, "Fanga," recorded on *Michigan, Live '85,* August Night Records, a product of WWTMC, Box 22, Walhalla, MI 49458.

89. Kate Clinton, "Making Light," p. 39.

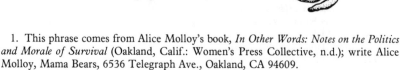

Chapter 5
Moral Agency and Interaction
pages 199–246

1. This phrase comes from Alice Molloy's book, *In Other Words: Notes on the Politics and Morale of Survival* (Oakland, Calif.: Women's Press Collective, n.d.); write Alice Molloy, Mama Bears, 6536 Telegraph Ave., Oakland, CA 94609.

2. Jean-Paul Sartre, *Being and Nothingness*, trans. Hazel E. Barnes (New York: Philosophical Library, 1956), p. 554.

3. Jean-Paul Sartre, *Existentialism and Human Emotions* (New York: Philosophical Library, 1957), p. 23.

4. Jean-Paul Sartre, *Being and Nothingness*, p. 55.

5. Marilyn Frye, "In and Out of Harm's Way: Arrogance and Love," in *The Politics of Reality: Essays in Feminist Theory* (Trumansburg, N.Y.: The Crossing Press, 1983, now in Freedom, Calif.), p. 55; Jean-Paul Sartre, *Being and Nothingness*, p. 54.

6. Jean-Paul Sartre, *Anti-Semite and Jew*, trans. George J. Becker (New York: Schocken Books, 1965).

7. Jean-Paul Sartre, *Nausea*, trans. Lloyd Alexander (New York: New Directions Publishing, 1964).

8. Marion Weinstein, *Positive Magic: Occult Self-Help*, rev. ed. (Phoenix Publishing Co., P.O. Box 10, Custer, WA 98420, 1981), chapter 5, pp. 94–125.

9. J.L. Austin, "A Plea for Excuses," *Philosophical Papers* (Oxford: Oxford University Press, 1970), p. 180.

10. Ibid.

11. J.L. Austin, *Sense and Sensibilia* (Oxford: Oxford University Press, 1962), p. 70.

12. J.L. Austin, "Three Ways of Spilling Ink," *Philosophical Papers*, p. 273.

13. Aristotle, *Nicomachean Ethics*, trans. Martin Ostwald (New York: Bobbs-Merrill Co., 1962) book 3, pp. 52–82.

14. Simone de Beauvoir, *The Ethics of Ambiguity*, trans. Bernard Frechtman (Secaucus, N.J.: The Citadel Press, 1972).

15. Ibid., part II, pp. 35–73.

16. Cherríe Moraga, as cited by Mitsuye Yamada, "Asian Pacific American Women and Feminism," in *This Bridge Called My Back: Writings by Radical Women of Color*, ed. Cherríe Moraga and Gloria Anzaldúa (Watertown, Mass: Persephone Press, 1981, now published by Kitchen Table: Women of Color Press, P.O. Box 908, Latham, NY 12210), p. 72.

17. Conversation, Anne Waters; note Barbara Cameron, "Gee You Don't Seem Like an Indian from the Reservation," in *This Bridge Called My Back*, pp. 46–52.

18. Conversation, Lola Lai Jong; note also "Coming Together and Coming Out," a slideshow on Asian/Pacific Lesbians presented by Trinity Ordoña and Kitty Tsui, for information write Trinity Ordoña, P.O. Box 2594, Daly City, CA 94017.

19. Baba Copper, "The View from Over the Hill: Notes on Ageism Between Lesbians," *Trivia* 7 (Summer 1985): 48; revised and reprinted in *Over the Hill: Reflections on Ageism Between Women* (Freedom, Calif., The Crossing Press, 1988).

20. doris davenport, "The Pathology of Racism: A Conversation with Third World

Wimmin," in *This Bridge Called My Back,* p. 89.

21. Marilyn Frye, "On Being White: Toward a Feminist Understanding of Race and Race Supremacy," in *The Politics of Reality,* p. 119.

22. Baba Copper, "The View from Over the Hill," p. 61.

23. Aristotle, *Nicomachean Ethics,* p. 54.

24. William Styron, *Sophie's Choice* (N.Y.: Random House, 1976), a movie by the same name was subsequently produced.

25. Conversation, Glennon Graham. For more information, note his Ph.D. dissertation, *From Slavery to Serfdom: Rural Black Agriculturalists in South Carolina, 1865–1900,* available from University Microfilms, University of Michigan, Ann Arbor.

26. Marilyn Frye, "In and Out of Harm's Way," p. 54.

27. Ibid., pp. 56–7.

28. Ibid., p. 60.

29. *The Random House Dictionary of the English Language, The Unabridged Edition,* 1966.

30. George M. Fredrickson, *White Supremacy: A Comparative Study in American and South African History* (New York: Oxford University Press, 1981), pp. 25–7.

31. Starhawk, *Dreaming the Dark: Magic, Sex, and Politics* (Boston: Beacon Press, 1982), p. 113.

32. Conversation, Claudia Card.

33. Joanna Russ, "Power and Helplessness in the Women's Movement," *Sinister Wisdom* 18 (Fall 1981): 49–56.

34. Conversation, Anne Throop Leighton.

35. María Lugones, "Playfulness, 'World'-Travelling, and Loving Perception," *Hypatia* 2, 2 (Summer 1987): 5–6.

36. Conversation, Anne Throop Leighton.

37. Communication, Jeffner Allen.

38. Florynce Kennedy, "Institutionalized Oppression Vs. the Female," in *Sisterhood Is Powerful: An Anthology of Writings from the Women's Liberation Movement,* ed. Robin Morgan (New York: Random House, 1970), p. 438–46.

39. Title of lesbian soap opera, compliments Deidre McCalla.

40. Marilyn Frye, "Notes for comments on presentations by S. Hoagland, C. Card and M. Lugones in honor of *The Politics of Reality*– S.W.I.P. meeting at the A.P.A. in St. Louis, Spring, 1986," unpublished notes.

41. Deidre D. McCalla, "Long Lonely Road," copyright, Chetwood Arts Music, 1986.

42. *The American Heritage Dictionary of the English Language: New College Edition,* 1969.

43. Conversation, Anne Throop Leighton.

44. Nancy Todor, *Choices* (Watertown, Mass.: Persephone Press, 1980, now published by Alyson Publications, Inc., Boston).

45. Conversation, Denslow Brown.

46. *Gossip,* Onlywomen Press Ltd., 38 Mount Pleasant, London WC1 XOAP, England. The journal ceased publication with issue 6.

47. Conversation, Anne Throop Leighton.

48. Conversation, Julia Penelope [Stanley].

49. Conversation, Anne Throop Leighton.

50. Selma Miriam, "Anti-Semitism in the Lesbian Community: A Collage of Mostly Bad News by One Jewish Dyke," *Sinister Wisdom* 19 (Winter 1982): 50–60.

51. Irena Klepfisz, "Anti-Semitism in the Lesbian/Feminist Movement," in *Nice Jewish Girls: A Lesbian Anthology,* ed. Evelyn Torton Beck (Watertown, Mass.: Persephone Press, 1982, now published by The Crossing Press, Freedom, Calif.), p. 46.

52. Selma Miriam, "Anti-Semitism in the Lesbian Community," p. 59.

53. María Lugones, "Playfulness, 'World'-travelling, and Loving Perception," p. 7.

54. Ibid.
55. Baba Copper, "View from Over the Hill," p. 53.
56. María Lugones, "Playfulness, 'World'-travelling, and Loving Perception," p. 8.
57. Marilyn Frye, "Notes."
58. Conversation, Billie Potts.
59. Conversations, Marilyn Frye, Anne Throop Leighton.
60. Marilyn Frye, "Notes."
61. Conversation, Anne Throop Leighton.
62. This type of 'because' point comes from the work of G.E.M. Anscombe, Cambridge University, England; however, she is not responsible for this application.
63. Susan Krieger, *The Mirror Dance: Identity in a Women's Community* (Philadelphia: Temple University Press, 1983), p. xii.
64. Ibid.
65. Ibid., p. xiii.
66. Ibid., p. xiv.
67. Ibid., p. xvii.
68. Ibid., p. xiv.
69. Ibid.
70. Audre Lorde, *Zami: A New Spelling of My Name* (Watertown, Mass: Persephone Press, 1982, now published by The Crossing Press, Freedom, Calif.), pp. 203–4.
71. Ibid., p. 184.
72. Communication, Marilyn Frye.
73. Conversation, Mary Jo Lakeland.
74. G. W. F. Hegel, *The Phenomenology of Mind,* trans. J. B. Baillie (New York: Harper & Row), pp. 228–40.
75. Ibid., pp. 234–5.
76. J. B. Baillie, commentary, in *The Phenomenology of Mind,* G. W. F. Hegel (New York: Harper & Row, 1967), p. 228.
77. G. W. F. Hegel, *Phenomenology of Mind,* p. 484.
78. Monique Wittig, "The Straight Mind," *Feminist Issues* 1, no. 1 (Summer 1980): 103–11.
79. Marilyn Frye, "In and Out of Harm's Way," pp. 74–5.
80. Conversations, Ellen Meredith, Elaine Stocker.
81. Audre Lorde, "The Master's Tools Will Never Dismantle The Master's House," in *Sister Outsider* (Trumansburg, N.Y.: The Crossing Press, 1984, now in Freedom, Calif.), p. 111.
82. Ibid.
83. Ibid., p. 110.
84. María Lugones, "Playfulness, 'World'-travelling, and Loving Perception," p. 8.
85. Ibid., pp. 3–4.
86. Ibid., passim.
87. Hans-Georg Gadamer, *Truth and Method* (New York: Seabury Press, 1984), pp. 91–119; J[ohan] Huizinga, *Homo Ludens: A Study of the Play-Element in Culture* (Boston: Beacon Press, 1950).
88. Gloria Anzaldúa, *Borderlands/La Frontera: The New Mestiza* (San Francisco: Spinsters/Aunt Lute, 1987), p. 79.
89. María Lugones, "Playfulness, 'World'-travelling, and Loving Perception," pp. 12–4.
90. Conversation, Anne Throop Leighton.
91. María Lugones, "Playfulness, 'World'-travelling, and Loving Perception," p. 18.
92. Ibid., p. 17.
93. Ibid.

94. Conversation, Anne Throop Leighton.
95. María Lugones, "Playfulness, 'World'-travelling, and Loving Perception," pp. 13–4.
96. Conversation, Elaine Stocker.
97. Conversation, Anne Throop Leighton.
98. Kate Clinton, "Making Light: Another Dimension: Some Notes on Feminist Humor," *Trivia* 1 (Fall 1982): 38. Note Kate Clinton, *Making Light, Live At the Great American Music Hall,* and *Making Waves* (Whyscrack Records, Making Light Productions, P.O. Box 493, Cazenovia, N.Y. 13035); and Alison Bechdel, *Dykes to Watch Out For* (Ithaca, New York: Firebrand Books, 1986).
99. Anne Cameron, *Daughters of Copper Woman* (Vancouver, B.C.: Press Gang Publishers, 1981), pp. 109-10.
100. María Lugones, "Playfulness, 'World'-travelling, and Loving Perception," p. 15.
101. Ibid.
102. Conversation, Anne Throop Leighton.

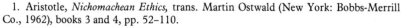

Chapter 6
Moral Revolution: From Antagonism to Cooperation
pages 248–292

1. Aristotle, *Nichomachean Ethics,* trans. Martin Ostwald (New York: Bobbs-Merrill Co., 1962), books 3 and 4, pp. 52–110.
2. Ibid., book 5, pp. 111–45.
3. Plato, *The Republic,* in *The Collected Dialogues of Plato,* ed. Edith Hamilton and Huntington Cairns (New York: Pantheon Books, 1961).
4. Conversation, Kate Burke.
5. Gordon Leff, *Medieval Thought: St. Augustine to Ockham* (Middlesex, England: Penguin Books, 1958), p. 73.
6. George M. Fredrickson, *White Supremacy: A Comparative Study in American and South African History* (New York: Oxford University Press, 1981), pp. 7–12.
7. I draw much of my discussion from the work of Alison Jaggar, *Feminist Politics and Human Nature* (Totowa, N.J.: Rowman & Allanheld, 1983); and George M. Fredrickson, *White Supremacy.*
8. George M. Fredrickson, *White Supremacy,* chapter 4.
9. Alison Jaggar, *Feminist Politics and Human Nature,* p. 40.
10. Ibid., p. 41.
11. Susan Cavin, *Lesbian Origins* (San Francisco, Jism Press, 1985), p. 41.
12. Ibid., pp. 116–8; note also Janice G. Raymond, *A Passion for Friends: Toward a Philosophy of Female Affection* (Boston: Beacon Press, 1986), for example, pp. 124–5.
13. Note Raziel Abelson, "History of Ethics," in *The Encyclopedia of Philosophy* vol. 3, ed. Paul Edwards (New York: Macmillan Co., 1967), p. 95.
14. Arthur W. H. Adkins, *Merit and Responsibility: A Study in Greek Values* (Oxford: Clarendon Press, 1960).
15. Lillian Faderman, *Scotch Verdict* (New York: Quill, 1983), p. 209.
16. J. L. Austin, "Three Ways of Spilling Ink," in *Philosophical Papers* (Oxford: Oxford University Press, 1970), pp. 273–87.

17. Arthur W. H. Adkins, *Merit and Responsibility.*

18. Ibid., pp. 348-9.

19. *Time* 131, no. 18 (May 2, 1988), p. 70; note also Kitty Tsui, *The Words of a Woman Who Breathes Fire: Poetry and Prose* (San Francisco: Spinsters Ink, 1983, now Spinsters/Aunt Lute), pp. 62-3.

20. Conversation, Claudia Card.

21. Richard A. Brandt, *Hopi Ethics: A Theoretical Analysis* (Chicago: University of Chicago Press, Midway Reprints, 1974), p. 91.

22. Ibid., pp. 82-83. For more fruitful work on Hopi culture, note Frank Waters, *Book of the Hopi* (New York: Penguin Books, 1979). Note also Dennis Tedlock and Barbara Tedlock, eds., *Teachings from the American Earth: Indian Religion and Philosophy,* (New York: Liveright, 1975).

23. Immanuel Kant, *Groundwork of the Metaphysic of Morals,* trans. H. J. Paton (New York: Harper & Row, a Harper Torchbook, 1964).

24. Ibid., p. 88.

25. John Stuart Mill, *Utilitarianism* (Indianapolis: Bobbs-Merrill, 1983), chapter 5.

26. Ibid., p. 73.

27. Ibid., p. 78.

28. John Stuart Mill, *On Liberty* (Indianapolis: Bobbs-Merrill, 1956), p. 14. Bette S. Tallen brought this to my attention; note also Bette S. Tallen, "Liberal Equality and Feminism: The Implications of the Thought of John Stuart Mill," (Ph.D. diss., University of Michigan, Ann Arbor, 1980).

29. Michael St. John Packe, *The Life of John Stuart Mill* (New York: The Macmillan Co., 1954), p. 387. Bette S. Tallen brought this to my attention.

30. Bruce Mazlish, *James and John Stuart Mill: Father and Son in the Nineteenth Century* (New York: Basic Books, 1975), pp. 143-5. Bette S. Tallen brought this to my attention.

31. John Stuart Mill, *Utilitarianism,* pp. 77-8.

32. John Rawls, *A Theory of Justice* (Cambridge: Belknap Press of Harvard University Press, 1971), p. 3.

33. Ibid., p. 4.

34. Ibid., p. 5.

35. Ibid., p. 7.

36. Ibid., p. 6.

37. Friedrich Nietzsche, *On the Genealogy of Morals & Ecce Homo,* trans. Walter Kaufmann and R.J. Hollingdale (New York: Vintage Books/Random House, 1969), *Genealogy,* II, 8, pp. 70-1.

38. Ibid., II, 4, p. 63.

39. Ibid., II, 5, pp. 64-5.

40. Friedrich Nietzsche, *Thus Spoke Zarathustra,* in *The Portable Nietzsche,* trans. and ed. Walter Kaufmann (New York: Viking Press, 1964), II, 7, p. 212.

41. Friedrich Nietzsche, *Genealogy,* first essay, and *Human, All-Too Human,* #45, in *On the Genealogy of Morals & Ecce Homo,* pp. 25-56 and pp. 167-8.; *Beyond Good and Evil,* trans., Marianne Cowan (Chicago: Henry Regnery Co., 1955), #260, pp. 202-6.

42. Friedrich Nietzsche, *Genealogy,* II, 13-4, pp. 80-2.

43. Conversation, Anna Lee. *McCleskey Vs. Kemp,* 107 S.Ct., 1756 (1987). The study, entitled "The Baldus Study," was conducted by David Baldus, George Woodworth, and Charles Pulanski. Shelley Bannister helped me obtain this information.

44. Conversations, Anne Throop Leighton and Claudia Card.

45. Note, for example, Ninette Beaver, B.K. Ripley and Patrick Trese, *Caril* (New York: Bantam Books, 1976). Caril Ann Fugate was finally paroled in 1976.

46. Stanley I. Benn, "Punishment," in *The Encyclopedia of Philosophy* vol. 7, ed. Paul

Edwards (New York: Macmillan, Co., 1967), pp. 29–36.

47. Ann Jones, *Everyday Death: The Case of Bernadette Powell* (New York: Holt, Rinehart, and Winston, 1985), p. 7.

48. Ibid., p. 199.

49. Ibid., p. 11.

50. Mary Daly, *Pure Lust: Elemental Feminist Philosophy* (Boston: Beacon Press, 1978), p. 240.

51. Ibid., p. 275.

52. Beverly Brown, "Lesbian Battery," *The Lesbian Insider/Insighter/Inciter* 8 (July 1982): 3.

53. Ibid., p. 23.

54. Ibid., p. 25.

55. Ibid., p. 24.

56. Conversation, Bette S. Tallen.

57. Conversation, Harriet Ellenberger.

58. Harriet Ellenberger offered valuable discussion of this material.

59. Simone de Beauvoir, *The Ethics of Ambiguity*, trans. Bernard Frechtman (Secaucus, N.J.: Citadel Press, 1972), chapter 2, especially pp. 45–50.

60. María Lugones, "Playfulness, 'World'-travelling, and Loving Perception," *Hypatia* 2, 2 (Summer, 1987): 13.

61. Anne Cameron, *Daughters of Copper Woman* (Vancouver, B.C.: Press Gang Publishers, 1981), p. 110.

62. Kate Clinton, "Making Light: Another Dimension: Some Notes on Feminist Humor," *Trivia* 1 (Fall 1982): 42.

63. Conversation, Marilyn Frye.

64. Note, for example, Marcia Baron, following a kantian thesis: "The Alleged Moral Repugnance of Acting from Duty," *The Journal of Philosophy* 81, no. 4 (April 1984): 197–220. Claudia Card brought this material to my attention. For a treatment of care, note Nell Noddings, *Caring: A Feminine Approach to Ethics and Moral Education* (Berkeley: University of California Press, 1984).

65. This example comes from Michael Stocker, "The Schizophrenia of Modern Ethical Theories," *Journal of Philosophy* LXXIII:14 (August 12, 1976): 453–66.

66. Marcia Baron, "Alleged Moral Repugnance of Acting From Duty."

67. Ibid., footnote 23, p. 221.

68. Conversation, Anne Throop Leighton.

69. Communication, Claudia Card.

70. Conversation, Anne Throop Leighton.

71. Conversation, Claudia Card.

72. Conversation, Kathy Munzer.

73. Alice Walker, *The Color Purple* (New York: Washington Square Press, 1982), p. 127. p. 127.

74. "Tread Softly," directed by Di Drew (Australia, 1979), available from Women Make Movies, Inc., 225 Lafayette Street, Suite 213, New York, NY 10012.

75. Antoine de Saint-Exupéry, *The Little Prince*, trans., Katherine Woods (New York: Harcourt, Brace & World, 1943), p. 68. (This rendering is my own translation.)

76. *The American Heritage Dictionary of the English Language: New College Edition*, 1969.

77. Conversation, Anne Throop Leighton.

78. Conversation, Jeffner Allen.

79. Juana María Paz, *The 'La Luz' Journal* (Fayetteville, Ark.: Paz Press, 1980, now at P.O. Box 820, New Port Richey, FL 34656-0820).

80. Communication, Claudia Card.

81. Baba Copper, "The View from Over the Hill: Notes on Ageism Between Lesbians," *Trivia* 7 (Summer 1985): 63; revised and reprinted in *Over the Hill: Reflections on Ageism Between Women* (Freedom, Calif.: The Crossing Press, 1988).

82. Audre Lorde, *Uses of the Erotic: The Erotic As Power* (Brooklyn, N.Y.: Out and Out Books, 1978), p. 3; reprinted in *Sister Outsider* (Trumansburg, N.Y.: The Crossing Press, 1984, now in Freedom, Calif.), p. 55.

83. Pat Parker, "Womanslaughter," *Womanslaughter* (Oakland, Calif.: Diana Press, 1978), p. 62; reprinted in *Movement in Black* (Oakland, Calif.: Diana Press, 1978, later published by The Crossing Press, now out of print), p. 150.

84. Nel Noddings, *Caring,* p. 9.

85. Conversation, Anne Throop Leighton.

86. Note, for example, Virginia Held, "Non-Contractual Society," in *Science, Morality & Feminist Theory* (Calgary, Alberta, Canada: The University of Calgary Press, 1987).

87. Conversation, Pat Washburn.

88. Conversation, Anne Throop Leighton.

89. Janice G. Raymond, *A Passion for Friends,* p. 8.

90. Julia Penelope, "Whose Past Are We Reclaiming?" *Common Lives, Lesbian Lives: A Lesbian Quarterly* 13 (Autumn 1984): 21.

91. Conversation, B.J. Miller.

92. Janice G. Raymond, *The Transsexual Empire: The Making of a She-Male* (Boston: Beacon Press, 1979), p. 154.

93. Bloodroot Collective (Betsey Beaven, Noel Furie, and Selma Miriam), *The Second Seasonal Political Palate: A Feminist Vegetarian Cookbook* (Sanguinaria Publishing, 85 Ferris St., Bridgeport, CT 06605, 1984), p. xxv.

94. Conversation, Anna Lee; note also Anna Lee, letter, *Womanews* 8, 5 (October 1987): 15.

95. Conversation, Nett Hart.

96. María Lugones, "On the Logic of Pluralist Feminism," paper presented to the Midwest Division meeting of the Society for Women in Philosophy, Michigan State University, East Lansing, March 4–6, 1988.

97. Maricla Moyano, as cited by Susan Cavin, *Lesbian Origins,* p. 2.

98. Janice G. Raymond, *A Passion for Friends.*

99. Alice Walker, *In Search of Our Mother's Gardens: Womanist Prose* (New York: Harcourt Brace Jovanovich/Harvest, 1983).

100. Deidre D. McCalla, "Celebration," copyright Chetwood Arts Music, 1986.

101. Paula Gunn Allen, "some like indians endure," *Common Lives, Lesbian Lives* 3 (Spring 1982): 77.

102. Benito Mussolini, "The Doctrine of Fascism," in *Social and Political Philosophy: Readings From Plato to Gandhi,* ed. John Somerville and Ronald E. Santoni (Garden City, N.Y.: Anchor Books, Doubleday, 1963), pp. 424–40.

103. Lee Lanning and Vernette [Nett] Hart, *Ripening: An Almanac of Lesbian Lore and Vision* (Word Weavers, Box 8742, Minneapolis, MN 55408-0742, 1981), p. 90.

104. Note Adrienne Rich, "XXI" in *Dream of a Common Language: Poems 1974–1977* (New York: W.W. Norton & Co., 1978), pp. 35–6.

Conclusion
pages 294–302

1. Mary Daly, *Beyond God the Father: Toward a Philosophy of Women's Liberation* (Boston: Beacon Press, 1973).

2. Gloria Anzaldúa, *Borderlands/La Frontera: The New Mestiza* (San Francisco: Spinsters/Aunt Lute, 1987).

3. Note, for example, Nancy Myron and Charlotte Bunch, eds., *Lesbianism and the Women's Movement* (Baltimore, Md.: Diana Press, 1975); Phyllis Birkby, Bertha Harris, Jill Johnston, Esther Newton, and Jane O'Wyatt, eds., *Amazon Expedition: A Lesbian Feminist Anthology* (New York: Times Change Press, 1973); Marie J. Kuda, *Women Loving Women: A Select and Annotated Bibliography of Women Loving Women in Literature* (Chicago: Womanpress, 1975); Elly Bulkin and Joan Larkin, eds., *Amazon Poetry* (Baltimore, Md.: Diana Press, Out and Out Books, 1975); Barbara Grier and Coletta Reid, eds., *Lesbian Lives: Biographies of Women From The Ladder* (Oakland, Calif.: Diana Press, 1976); Jane Rule, *Lesbian Images* (London: Peter Davies, 1976); Kay Van Deurs [Kady], *The Notebooks That Emma Gave Me: The Autobiography of a Lesbian* (Published by Kady van Deurs, Box 199, Youngsville, New York: 12791, 1978); Monique Wittig and Sande Zeig, *Lesbian Peoples: Material For a Dictionary* (New York: Avon Books, 1979); and J. R. Roberts, *Black Lesbians: An Annotated Bibliography* (Tallahassee, Fla.: The Naiad Press, 1981).

4. Note, for example, Julia Penelope Stanley and Susan J. Wolfe, eds., *The Coming Out Stories* (Watertown, Mass.: Persephone Press, 1980); Margaret Cruikshank, ed., *The Lesbian Path* (Monterey, Calif.: Angel Press, 1980); and Ruth Baetz, ed., *Lesbian Crossroads: Personal Stories of Lesbian Struggles and Triumphs* (New York: William Morrow, 1980).

5. Note, for example, Sidney Abbott and Barbara Love, *Sappho Was a Right-on Woman: A Liberated View of Lesbianism* (New York: Stein and Day, 1973); Rita Mae Brown, *Rubyfruit Jungle* (Plainfield, Vt: Daughters, 1973); Jill Johnston, *Lesbian Nation: The Feminist Solution* (New York: Simon and Schuster, 1973); the carpenter [June Arnold], *The Cook and the Carpenter* (Plainfield, Vt.: Daughters, 1972); Elana Nachman [Dykewomon], *Riverfinger Women* (Plainfield, Vt.: Daughters, 1974); Ann Allen Shockley, *Loving Her* (New York: Bobbs-Merrill, 1974); Gina Covina and Laurel Galana, eds., *The Lesbian Reader: An Amazon Quarterly Anthology* (Oakland, Calif.: Amazon Press, 1975); The Nomadic Sisters, *Loving Women* (Sonora, Calif.: The Nomadic Sisters, 1976); Emily L. Sisley and Bertha Harris, *The Joy of Lesbian Sex* (New York: Simon and Schuster, 1977); and Ginny Vida, ed., *Our Right to Love: A Lesbian Resource Book* (Englewood Cliffs, N.J.: Prentice-Hall, Inc., 1978).

6. Michal Brody, *Are We There Yet? A Continuing History of 'Lavender Woman': A Chicago Lesbian Newspaper, 1971–1976* (Iowa City: Aunt Lute Book Co., 1985, now Spinsters/ Aunt Lute, San Francisco), p. 183.

7. Ibid.

8. Ibid., p. 185.

9. Ibid.

10. Micheline Grimard-Leduc, "The Mind-Drifting Islands," *Trivia* 8 (Winter 1986): 29, 31; published in the original French in *l'île des amantes: essai/poèmes,* write Micheline Grimard-Leduc, C.P. 461, Station N, Montréal, Québec, H2X 3N3, Canada, 1982).

11. Ibid., p. 31.

12. Alix Dobkin makes reference to a "lesbian" as "a woman who is radically serious about loving women," a definition coined by Mary E. Hunt: Alix Dobkin, "Boy-Girl Rap," on *Never Been Better,* distributed by Ladyslipper Music, Box 3130, Durham, NC 27705, 1987.

13. Andrea Dworkin, *Right-Wing Women* (New York: G.P. Putnam's Sons/Perigee, 1983), chapter 1, pp. 13–35.

14. Marilyn Frye, "In and Out of Harm's Way: Arrogance and Love," *The Politics of Reality: Essays in Feminist Theory* (Trumansburg, N.Y.: The Crossing Press, 1983, now in Freedom, Calif.), p. 80.

15. Barbara Myerhoff, *Number Our Days* (New York: Simon and Schuster, 1978), p. 25.

16. Alix Dobkin, "New Ground," copyright 1988, Alix Dobkin.

Index

PHOTOGRAPH BY IRENE YOUNG

Sarah Lucia Hoagland is a chicago dyke and a philosopher. She came out in 1975, a year after being labeled p.d.o.f. (potential dyke on faculty) by her lesbian students, and she named herself 'separatist' in 1976. She has been teaching philosophy and women's studies at northeastern illinois university in chicago since 1977, and has given talks in lesbian communities around the u.s. for 13 years. Along with Julia Penelope she has co-edited *For Lesbians Only: A Separatist Anthology* published by Onlywomen Press of London. Her three cats strongly resent the amount of time she spends petting her computer keyboard.